IRA: THE BOMBS AND THE BULLETS

To the memory of my father,
a Belfast child

IRA

THE BOMBS AND THE BULLETS

A History of Deadly Ingenuity

A.R. OPPENHEIMER

Foreword by
RICHARD ENGLISH

IRISH ACADEMIC PRESS

DUBLIN • PORTLAND, OR

First published in 2009 by Irish Academic Press

10 George's Street
Newbridge
County Kildare

© 2009 by A. R. Oppenheimer, 2016

www.iap.ie

British Library Cataloguing in Publication Data
An entry can be found on request

978 0 7165 2895 1 (paper)

Library of Congress Cataloging-in-Publication Data
An entry can be found on request

Contents

Acknowledgements

I want to thank all the kind individuals and institutions who gave me invaluable help and advice in the preparation of this my first published book. The idea for the book had long been in my head and I had longed to write it for many years – but the time was not right until the Good Friday Agreement had been signed. So, above all, I must thank my publisher Lisa Hyde for taking my suggestion on board and for all her kind help, support, encouragement and patience during the entire duration of this project. Her boundless enthusiasm for my efforts to put together what could be quite controversial material, and at a time when I was under significant pressure at work, has been invaluable. And, as someone who has edited, proofed and managed books in a 'past life', I thank Lisa's colleagues at Irish Academic Press for all their hard work.

I must thank Professor Richard English of Queen's University Belfast for his advice, guidance and input, and for helping me keep the theme of the book within its historical context. I am grateful for the time he took out of his schedule during my visits to Belfast to ensure the book was heading in the right direction. Special thanks also go to Dr Gary McGladdery of Queen's University Belfast, who provided invaluable feedback in reviewing the book and whose comments greatly helped me to take the book forward, and Professor Keith Jeffery for encouragement and advice earlier on in the project.

I would also like to give special thanks to the many former Explosives Ordnance Disposal officers who cannot be named here, who talked to me at great length about the technical aspects of the IRA's bombs, the countermeasures to deal with them, and the effects of the attacks. These conversations not only revealed a level of detail and insight into the many ways in which the IRA built, concealed, deployed the devices, but also stark reality of what it was like to spend much of their careers trying to prevent these weapons from taking life and limb. On more than one occasion were the words 'ingenuity' and 'genius' used to describe the making of these devices. Some of the events related to me were very harrowing to describe and I am deeply grateful to these brave people for their revelations.

Special thanks also to Tom Carey at Garda HQ in Dublin for giving me a privileged view of the vast IRA inventory of weapons, providing a vital opportunity for me to see for myself in detail how some of the bombs and mortars were built and to view the vast range of guns that had been amassed. Not only did the tour reveal some surprises but also reinforced what I had already believed about the level of ingenious and deadly improvisation the IRA had achieved.

I want to thank Tommy McKearney and other individuals who agreed to talk to me about the mission, aims and methods of the Irish Republican Army, how the bombing campaigns enhanced or prevented the development of these aims, and how they have had to come to terms with the effects of their actions. Their accounts enabled me to see beyond what I had learned and discovered about the republican movement over the years.

I am also immensely grateful to the many close friends and work colleagues who supported me with words of encouragement and their many acts of kindness through the two years it has taken to write this book. At times they would have had to endure countless descriptions of bombs and the many twists and turns of the book's progress, and I thank them for their forbearance.

Finally, I have dedicated my book to the memory of my beloved father, whose vivid descriptions of growing up in Belfast before and after the Civil War inspired every moment of every day I spent writing it.

A.R. Oppenheimer
2008

Glossary

AKM	Automat Kalashnikova Modernized – Russian assault rifle similar to the AK-47
ANFO	Ammonium nitrate–fuel oil – IRA home-made explosive mix
ANNIE	Ammonium nitrate, nitrobenzene and diesel oil – IRA home-made explosive mix
AP/RN	*An Phoblacht/Republican News*
Árd Fheis	Sinn Féin annual conference
Arm Poblaigh na hÉireann	Irish National Liberation Army
ATO	British Army Ammunition Technical Officer
ASU	Active Service Unit of the IRA
BRY	Bogside Republican Youth
C3I	Control, Command, Communication and Intelligence
Co-op mix	IRA explosive – combination of sodium chlorate and nitrobenzene
Comm	IRA slang for 'communication' – usually a written message
CRA	Civil Rights Association
DERA	UK Defence and Evaluation Research Agency
DShK	Russian Dushka heavy machine-gun
Éire Nua	Concept of a federal four-province Ireland
EO	IRA Explosives Officers
EOD	Explosives Ordnance Disposal

Eta	Euskadi ta Askatasuna – 'Basque Fatherland and Liberty' – Basque insurgency group
FARC	*Fuerzas Armadas Revolucionarias de Colombia – Ejército del Pueblo* – Revolutionary Armed Forces of Colombia
FN-MAG	*Mitrailleuse d'Appui General* – Belgian general-purpose machine-gun (GPMG)
FOSF	Friends of Sinn Fein (US support group to the republican movement)
Garda Síochána	Police force of the Republic of Ireland
GFA	Good Friday Agreement
GPMG	General-purpose machine-gun
HE	High-Explosive
HEAT	High-Explosive Anti-Tank – principle of equipping a mortar or rocket with a steel cone coupled with the explosive charge and impact fuse for greater penetration
HME	Home-Made Explosive
IAAG	Improvised Anti-Armour Grenade
IICD	Independent International Commission on Decommissioning
IED	Improvised Explosive Device
IND	Improvised Nuclear Device
INLA	Irish National Liberation Army
IRA	Irish Republican Army – used mostly throughout to designate the original IRA and further, the Provisional IRA
IPG	Improvised Projected Grenade
LED	Light-Emitting Diode (semi-conductor chip used for small indicator lights on electronic devices)
MoD	UK Ministry of Defence
NI	Northern Ireland
NORAID	Northern Aid Committee – US (Irish-

	American) supplier of funds and weapons to the republican movement
Óglaigh na hÉireann	Irish name for the IRA, although this translates literally as 'soldiers of Ireland' (Irish army) and was later used by the Real IRA
QMG	Quartermaster General (weapons procurer for the IRA)
PAC	Provisional Army Council
PBS	US Public Broadcasting Service
PETN	Pentaerythritol tetranitrate – military high-explosive (ingredient of Semtex)
PLO	Palestinian Liberation Organisation
PIRA, Provos	Provisional IRA
PRIG	Projected Recoilless Improvised Grenade
PTA	UK Prevention of Terrorism Act
OIRA	'Official' IRA (the IRA split into the PIRA and the old OIRA)
RCIED	Radio-Controlled Improvised Explosive Device
RDX	Cyclotrimethylenetrinitramine – military nitroamine-based explosive, mixed with PETN to make Semtex
RIC	Royal Irish Constabulary
RIRA	Real IRA
RUC	Royal Ulster Constabulary
RPG	Rocket-Propelled Grenade
SAM	Surface-to-Air Missile
SDLP	Social Democratic Labour Party of Northern Ireland
S-Plan	Sabotage Plan – IRA 1930s and 1940s campaign in England
Six Counties	Northern Ireland (usually the republican designation)
TATP	Triacetone triperoxide – homemade

	explosive based on hydrogen peroxide, sulphuric acid, and acetone
TD	Teachta Dála (Member of the Irish Parliament)
TNT	Trinitrotoluene – military high-explosive
TPU	Timing and Power Unit
UDA	Ulster Defence Association
UVBT	Under-Vehicle Booby Trap
UVIED	Under-Vehicle Improvised Explosive Device
UVF	Ulster Volunteer Force
UWC	Ulster Workers' Council
UXO	Unexploded Ordnance
VBIED	Vehicle-Borne Improvised Explosive Device
VOIED	Victim-Operated Improvised Explosive Device
WPU	Weapons Intelligence Unit
WMD	Weapon of Mass Destruction
WME	Weapon of Mass Effect

List of Tables

Foreword

The Irish Republican Army has been well studied by scholars for many years, and so we now possess many of what might be termed the 'known knowns' regarding the organization. Its revolutionary origins and local dynamics during the early-twentieth century have been chronicled; its re-emergence at the end of the 1960s has been analysed; its durable campaign of political violence during ensuing decades, in various factions, has been explored; and many of its main figures have been the subject of powerful biographies. In all of this the *politics* of the IRA have – in my view, quite rightly' – been prominent in our explanation.

What Andy Oppenheimer does so originally in *IRA: The Bombs and the Bullets is* to focus less on what the IRA aimed to do, or what their political effect might have been, than on the more technical details of the organisation's campaigns of violence. He aims to 'complement the many books already published on the organisation's history, motivation and strategy' and so we have here a story of bombs, detonators, timing devices, arms dumps, mortars, Semtex, booby traps, improvised explosive devices (IEDs) and rocket-propelled grenades, as well as the state's counter-measures to try to deal with the threat posed by such an arsenal. We also learn something about the people who acquired or made, who stored and used and developed IRA weapons. The organisation emerges from this tale as innovative, ingenious and brutal. And, as a weapons consultant, Andy Oppenheimer possesses the expertise which allows him to speak with authority on the technical details of the IRA's campaigns.

Despite the extraordinary public and official attention paid in recent years to terrorism, the years since 9/11 have been regrettably amnesiac regarding the actual history of that phenomenon. So much of the value of Oppenheimer's book lies in its detailed act of memory. He rightly wants us to remember the violent intensity of what the IRA did: 'It seems that the media and other observers have become so caught up in the current terrorist threat that they have forgotten, or underestimate, the relentlessness of the IRA's campaign'. He points out, for example, that the Provisional IRA carried out 1300 bombings in 1972 alone. This book is therefore a valuable antidote to those analyses of the IRA which glide too quickly over the suffering involved in the violence practised by this group (as by other agents in the Northern Ireland conflict): 'This account, while relating the ingenuity and resourcefulness of the IRA's engineers, does not spare any detail in describing the effects of its weapons on those who died or suffered horrendous injuries, or those devastated by the loss of loved ones'.

Remembering and respecting the effects of terrorist violence have become crucial again amid the recurring use of IEDs (a frequent feature again in news bulletins as I write, but this time in Iraq rather than Ireland). And Oppenheimer, in passing, highlights also the telling fact of how little the eventual reality of post-conflict Northern Ireland turned out to resemble IRA demands. In February 1991 (after their mortar attack on Downing Street) the Provos declared that `while nationalist people in the Six Counties are forced to live under British rule, the British Cabinet will be forced to live in bunkers'. Within a decade, IRA Army Council members were frequently talking peace with British politicians in Downing Street, while their political party came to administer reformed British rule in the North of Ireland.

Oppenheimer's book contains an admirable eye to the long-rootedness of Irish republican campaigns and ingenuity, and his book is packed with fascinating detail and is based on extensive research. It is a very valuable, and readable, study.

Richard English
Belfast, July 2008

Preface

On a bright, chilly Dublin morning in February 2008, I waited at my hotel to be driven to the headquarters of the Irish police, the Garda Síochána. Not to help them with their enquiries, I must add, but to be given a privileged view of the largest and most comprehensive collection of insurgent weaponry ever assembled: the Reference Collection of weapons of the Irish Republican Army. I was about to see the living evidence of what has been called the Longest War, which began in earnest on 24 April 1916, when the Irish Uprising took place in Dublin, and when the IRA, having evolved out of several incarnations, was officially born.

The incongruity of what I was about to see and do was almost palpable. Here, in the middle of a modern, prosperous capital of a nation that is approaching the sixtieth anniversary of its long-fought-for independence – but with its northern portion still in British hands, the constitutional right to which it has abandoned – I was about to handle the bombs, mortars and guns that were assembled, procured, created and deployed by the most experienced and skilled insurgency group the world has ever seen.

Once through the checkpoints in the vast Garda building – formerly the Royal Irish Constabulary HQ when under British rule – I wondered, after all the work I had done over the years on the IRA arsenal, how the gardai could fit into a handful of rooms the main examples of bomb types and guns the republicans had assembled over more than a century. But quality rather than quantity (although the plethora of weapons was still truly staggering) is the order of the day here. From the classic under-vehicle booby trap bomb – complete with its tiny mercury tilt switch – to an incomplete torpedo, no less, the array of carefully crafted devices spoke again and again of deadly ingenuity – a term you are going to read many times in this book, and one which my Irish ex-bomb disposal escorts confirmed with each improvised explosive device they presented me with from the many arms seizures they made in the Irish Republic.

Many were from the Clonaslee, Co. Laois 'bomb factory': in this instance, that oft-used media term is in no way an exaggeration.

The first, and largest, item in the collection was a Mark 15 mortar – called the 'barrackbuster', as this particular mortar was used to blast into British army bases in Northern Ireland. Mark *15*: the very designation indicates how many models were built – and the 15 was not the last – the IRA made at least seventeen models. A vast tube at least 3 metres across, it was fashioned out of a chopped – up bright orange gas cylinder with a scaffolding tube – which would have been in plentiful supply from the building trade – down its centre for the explosive charge. A photoflash bulb was used for the trigger, one of many IRA inventions from commonplace objects they adapted for initiating their explosive devices. This exhibit was a 'fire and forget' mortar – one-time use only. A slightly smaller example would have been used to train Volunteers on how to arm and fire them: a re-usable mortar. As the industrial pipe used to make it was in common use in the plumbing trade, it could have been moved around without arousing suspicion.

Among the weapons the IRA imported from Libya was the Russian DShK heavy machine-gun, which would be used to bring down British Lynx helicopters once the British were forced to move troops around by air to avoid being ambushed on the ground. And although ground attacks were still more likely to happen – the DShK was used only rarely – the very fact the IRA had purloined such an advanced military item was enough to keep helicopter pilots and troops feeling vulnerable. All part of the great trick of the insurgent: create a situation that your enemy has to adapt to and overcome – often at great expense, not only to the lives of soldiers and police, but also in having to enhance resources. And the possession of such a weapon – along with others, such as rocket launchers – also sent a message to the Catholic community of the North that the IRA had the muscle to defend it. Many such weapons, even if rarely deployed in combat, were used in publicity photos released by the Provisionals to display their military capability to the world and boost the morale of their own members.

Next was something I had no idea the IRA had tried to build: a partially completed torpedo, captured in one of the main areas where IRA weapons were developed and secreted, Co. Donegal. It was fashioned from, of all things, a sewage pipe and intended for attack against British boat patrols off the northern coast.

Then I was shown the guns. (In my career as a weapons consultant I have been more involved with bombs than guns.) Again, improvisation was key: the IRA favourite, the US-origin Armalite 15 (which I found was light enough to hold and aim) had been silenced so that it could be used on farms and in other remote training locations without drawing attention. Other weapons had been 'trimmed' so that they could easily be concealed under an ordinary jacket. Others were purpose built, such as the sniper rifle that had had its tracing removed. All were working weapons. They had been stored in barrels that were not waterproof, so some had gone rusty from underground storage in one of the world's dampest climates – an ongoing problem that would necessitate over-supply of guns so as not to hamper the IRA's firepower.

At this point I was presented with my own 'pet' area of expertise – the actual explosives that went into the bombs, and the bombs themselves – although handling the explosives was, for obvious reasons, not allowed. Jars of explosive samples were lined up on shelves and clearly labelled; I was struck by the irony of a notice, also seen elsewhere in the building, warning of letter-bombs – which in this Aladdin's Cave of death and destruction sat next to a handwritten note for safe explosives handling that had been seized from an IRA training camp. That several words in the notice were misspelled did not detract from its effectiveness as a training tool.

Among the jars of deep orange Semtex high-explosive, ground ammonium nitrate and black powder was a contraption for making detonators out of Semtex – the ultimate in home-made explosive. The Semtex (which is a cocktail of military explosives like PETN – pentaerythritol tetranitrate) would be broken down by petrol and the PETN extracted: a length of cord attached to a kind of cranking gadget was erected with the mechanism precisely honed to pump in the Semtex ingredient down into the detonating cord at exactly the right speed and density. All the components were fashioned from readily available items like water bottles, and had been made in a kitchen. Below the rows of explosives was laid out the biggest collection of bomb timers ever used by any group: everything from the vintage – but often effective – analogue alarm clocks that were used in the 1930s and 1950s campaigns, to Memopark timers, marketed to help people track the time left on their parking meter.

Therefore, details of the many IEDs – improvised explosive devices – that the IRA developed over sixty years, starting as far back as the late nineteenth century, will be laid out throughout this book. Among the most ingenious I saw that day in Dublin was a box-compartment device, one of a number constructed for deployment in eighteen London electricity substations but seized before they could be used. Had they gone off and knocked out even two of the three transformers at each station, most of London would have been without electricity for many days. If all three were knocked out, the level of chaos would be almost unimaginable. The device was expertly made; it remained dormant until a detonator housed in a metal tube was moved to connect with the explosive charge before deployment. The boxes had been mass-produced to precise specification; the circuit board was made from a reproduced homecrafted blueprint. Simple, efficient, and 'technically sweet'. And, according to my escorts, who had seized and dismantled much of these devices, state of the art.

As the gardai kept reminding me, nothing was left to chance; the devices were the result of twenty-five years of research. One does not think of a 'research and development' programme being developed by an organisation engaged in what the British called terrorism and what the Irish police regarded as subversion. But the workmanship involved in welding and assembling the devices I saw was testimony to labour-intensive manufacture resulting from R & D, and the frames for some of the models had clearly come off a kind of conveyor belt in a factory-style operation, from an original blueprint. An innocuous-looking device that sat amid the bombs was even used to rig electricity meters – not only to reduce the amount of precious electricity being used (remember the power crises of the 1970s) in bomb-making activities, but also to prevent the frequent surges that would give the game away: an early example of being green, in more ways than one. Above all, necessity – and the constant need to improvise, usually in covert and haphazard conditions – was the mother of IRA invention.

Do not think for one moment, however, that I am about to take you on an 'anorak' journey of bomb technologies and operational tactics only. I will also attempt to show you how – and why – the IRA built, amassed, stole, imported, adapted and used this vast panoply of explosive devices and guns; how, and how many, this arsenal of weaponry killed, maimed, destroyed, traumatised and terrified; how and when they were seized, dismantled, and disrupted by the British and Irish authorities who had to deal with them and their makers in order to save lives or prevent further lives being taken; how the catch-up game of Mutually Assured Disruption was played out over thirty years; and how it all came to what we think, and – many IRA members included – hope, is now the end.

A.R. Oppenheimer
April 2008

Introduction

The purpose of the terrorist is to terrorise.
Michael Collins

Throwing a bomb is bad,
Dropping a bomb is good;
Terror, no need to add,
Depends on who's wearing the hood.
R. Woddis[1]

MacDonagh and MacBride
And Connolly and Pearse
Now and in time to be,
Wherever green is worn,
Are changed, changed utterly:
A terrible beauty is born.
W.B. Yeats[2]

On 23 October 2001, only weeks after the world's most catastrophic terrorist attack in the United States, the world's oldest guerrilla group, the Irish Republican Army (IRA), completed the first act of decommissioning its vast arsenal of guns, explosives, bomb components and other weapons.

Following further tranches, the final cache of weapons was decommissioned in September 2005, although there was suspicion of remaining hidden caches; only the IRA knows the true extent of its arsenal. Nevertheless, the head of the Independent International Commission on Decommissioning (IICD), General John de Chastelain, said that the amounts that they had handled and witnessed being 'put beyond use' were consistent with the range of estimates that the security services had provided to them first in 1998 and then updated in 2004.[3]

The armoury decommissioned so far includes 1,000 rifles; 2 tonnes of Semtex; twenty to thirty heavy machine-guns, seven surface-to-air missiles (unused), seven flame throwers, 1,200 detonators, eleven rocket-propelled grenade launchers, ninety hand guns, over a hundred grenades, and bombs large enough to destroy several multi-storey buildings.[4] Only months earlier, in February 2001, an arms cache was uncovered in Co. Donegal – long the IRA's 'Nevada Test Site' – which included a PRIG (propelled rocket improvised grenade) armed with a 2.2-kg (1-lb) Semtex warhead. The PRIG represented the nexus of IRA audacity and improvisation of a new generation of launchable bombs, which will be described in Chapter 7.

How had such a vast arsenal been built? In the century-long history of the IRA, which is now seen as entering its own twilight, how did it amass enough improvised and imported weaponry to equip at least two battalions? How, when and why did it use this arsenal and the expertise needed to deploy it?

The IRA said it would follow a democratic path ending more than thirty years of violence. Why did it finally agree to decommission, having said it would declare 'not a bullet, not an ounce' of Semtex? It is believed that it was forced to decommission following 9/11 – because over a century of American financial and moral support was in danger of being withdrawn. One month before the 9/11 attacks, three alleged IRA operatives in Colombia were arrested and accused of training Revolutionary Armed Forces of Colombia (FARC) guerrillas in bomb technology. With the US-backed Colombian government fighting a war against FARC, the IRA had little choice but to give in to Bush administration pressure.[5]

As the accumulation of victims and attacks brought increased negative publicity on the republican movement, culminating in the biggest atrocity of the Troubles – the breakaway Real IRA's 1998 bombing of Omagh which killed twenty-nine and injured more than 200[6] – meant the time had come to end the armed struggle. The IRA may have been dragged kicking and screaming to the disarmament table, but for many years prior to decommissioning Sinn Féin president Gerry Adams and other leaders had gradually evolved a new strategy, bringing the IRA to finally discard the Armalite and the bomb – while still having access to them – in favour of the ballot box: electoral participation and an armed campaign was becoming incompatible.[7] Once the third tranche of decommissioning took place, the die had been cast for an entirely different future for the republican cause – one of compromise, political negotiation, public relations, bridge-building, and involvement in the social welfare of their own community.

However, the idea that neither side had lost after many generations of conflict had to be sold to each – in order for peace to be ushered in during the twenty-first century. Opposing views were reflected in front-page headlines of two Northern Ireland newspapers in July 2007, when the findings from a leaked internal report on the British army's operations in Northern Ireland – Operation Banner – were published.[8] The staunchly pro-unionist *Belfast News Letter* proclaimed: 'IRA has been defeated',[9] with the republican *An Phoblacht* claiming: 'British army could not defeat IRA.'[10] In the former, the hardline unionist William McCrea suggested that unionists should 'celebrate victory over the IRA' and that 'Republicans are locked into the British State'. He went on to say:

> After 35 years of murder and mayhem, we are still part of the United Kingdom and the designs of our enemy have failed ... The Provos did not carry out 35 years of slaughter against the unionist people of Northern Ireland to sit in a British Assembly at Stormont and a partitionist Assembly under the Crown and the Union flag. Every time republican representatives pass through the gates of Stormont, they acknowledge their united Ireland ideas have gone up in smoke ... Their Marxist, all-Ireland policies have been consigned to the dustbin of history ...
>
> *The reality is that Adams and McGuinness have sold their so-called 'foot-soldiers' out to be part of a functioning administration in the United Kingdom* [emphasis added].[11]

An Phoblacht's headline is taken from the statement in the Operation Banner report by Gen. Sir Mike Jackson, chief of the general staff: 'IRA – 'Professional, dedicated, highly skilled and resilient'.

'The British Army concludes that the IRA developed one of the most effective "terrorist" organisations in history ... Predictably, British officers are not concerned with the suffering inflicted by the British army, but the throwaway comment "Thousands of houses were destroyed and over 10,000 terrorist suspects were arrested" is a modest acknowledgement of the way in which the British army dealt with an insurgent civilian population. *Small wonder that within the Northern nationalist community and further afield British soliders were viewed as the real terrorists*' (emphasis added).

An Phoblacht concludes that 'The British Army did not and could not defeat the IRA. The shooting war stopped because of political progress gained through negotiation with republicans. The British officers acknowledge as much.' [12] From the report itself, Gen. Jackson concludes that the army's campaign against the IRA – the longest campaign in its history – was brought to a 'successful conclusion'. However, his opinion is in sharp contrast to the view of historian Martin Van Creveld, who said the British army 'did not win in any recognisable way'.[13]

Nevertheless, the IRA has effectively gone out of business – it is no longer an armed insurrectionist movement. It exists as a coherent pressure group within the Sinn Féin political party not unlike Trotskyites within the old Labour movement.[14] As such it is the historical underpinning of Sinn Féin in a new era of constitutional republicanism. Many believe that it would be impossible that some weapons could not be put aside and not decommissioned – at least for basic defence – or that weapons could not be re-acquired in the future. But decommissioning was a major political move of immense proportions.

So, neither headline is true: the Provisional IRA may not have won the war, but it won significant battles to gain attention from the British government, establishment and public, and for over thirty years waged a war of attrition against far better equipped forces; during this time it was able to catch up with its enemy and overtake its capability for response, mainly through deadly ingenuity. In terms of achievement, the discrimination that existed by the late 1960s, when the IRA arose like its emblematic phoenix as a rapidly growing insurgency group, has largely gone and many of the immediate aims of the community it set out to defend have been attained, or at least conditions have improved.[15]

The goal of a united Ireland has not been achieved; however, it is argued that the IRA's rationale for aspiring to this was that a united Ireland would best safeguard the Northern nationalist community.[16] Therefore, if such safeguards could be achieved, the community could adapt to being part of the UK – with a united Ireland as a long-term goal for a future generation. But keeping this aim, along with its claims to victory, are a vital part of IRA culture – or else the armed struggle, with all its victims, would have been for nothing.

On the other side, many unionists claim that they have won; the province is well and truly part of the UK and there is no sign of a united Ireland, despite the fact that Catholics now outnumber Protestants in Northern Ireland (but an estimated one-third are happy to remain part of Britain). But other unionists feel they have been sold out; there is disagreement about the Good Friday Agreement and consequent arrangements, and a bitter internecine battle over territory and control of various criminal activities is ongoing.[17]

Nevertheless, a new era had dawned in the troubled province. To the outside world at least, the Rev. Ian Paisley side by side in government with Martin McGuinness, a former IRA commander, was unthinkable only a few years ago. Changes in the North are palpable: a bustling, lively economy at least until early 2008, a boost in tourism and a changed atmosphere – not that Ulster people have been anything less than friendly and hospitable in the past, but in times gone by English visitors or workers settling in the province would have to avoid certain areas. Even the famous (and infamous) murals (and new ones portraying NI in a peaceful light) which adorn many buildings in Belfast and Derry are now official tourist attractions, with official guided tours available for visitors.[18] The murals are arguably the world's most striking example of Romantic political art in the twentieth century; their inspiration is so familiar to local people that even the provenance of a weapon being wielded by an IRA man may be a source of local debate.[19] There are regular bus and train services to Dublin; there are no troop checkpoints at the border, although surveillance towers still abound.[20] Troop levels are down to 5,000, having reached a maximum of 18,460 in 1992.[21] Gun attacks, punishment beatings and other paramilitary activity are almost non-existent.[22] The Sinn Féin office sells t-shirts, books and other republican paraphernalia like any museum or tourist shop.

Belfast in mid-2007 appears, on the surface, like any other northern European city. Massive reconstruction has taken place; new houses abound in the Falls and other run-down areas, although one learns that houses built for Catholics were smaller than those built in Protestant areas. Beneath the surface resentment still lurks; decades of conflict cannot be consigned to history in such a short time. The idea prevails among many that the Good Friday Agreement (GFA) and subsequent arrangements for power sharing and North–South initiatives have been phrased and formulated to sell the notion to each side that it had come out of years of conflict without defeat. This will allow both traditions to bang their own drum for a time, which will keep everyone happy[23] until a possible future when old alignments might wither and die.

Nevertheless, a healing process is under way and a peaceful atmosphere appears to prevail in Belfast and other towns, where people go about their business in a normal way. Other parts of the North are more partisan, however, most notably the border areas, where the paramilitaries are said to still hold dominance over local people, street by street, farm by farm. But the fear of being bombed or shot in the days of what has come to be known as the Troubles[24] cannot compare with the current situation. There are EU projects and other 'rehab' programmes for ex-prisoners.[25] Former IRA people and others directly involved in the conflict want a normal life, often after long prison terms; but even during the height of the conflict people carried on their lives in stoic fashion.[26] As for the Republic, a decade or more of massive economic and social change has altered the political landscape of the entire island, arguably forever. The so-called 'Celtic Tiger' – made possible by a well educated, enterprising and forward-looking population and substantial EU funding and collaboration – has resulted in the people being more concerned with economics and property booms than the reunification of the island, which is very much lower down the list of priorities, save for a handful of hardline republicans. That is not to say that the Irish people do not want to see their island as one: it is simply that the likely backlash and attendant problems of absorbing the sizeable (but shrinking in terms of proportion to the Catholic minority population) unionist Protestant contingent is, in the minds of many, not worth the bother. The GFA, and specifically   the success of former NI secretary Mo Mowlam and other members of the UK New Labour government in facilitating political change, means that a natural progression towards unity is not ruled out – but that this is sufficiently in the future to be an organic, rather than an enforced, development.

That said, there are still problems in the North. One is the rise in crime, no longer tempered or forcibly prevented by the IRA and the other paramilitary groups. There is also evidence that young people and others are missing the long traditions of paramilitary life, with its ready-made ideology and guarantee of some form of authority and dominance over local communities invested in members of such groups.[27] Paramilitary life is ingrained in Northern Irish life and culture, and it will take a generation or two for it to be left behind. There are still extremist groups in existence, particularly on the hardline unionist side, and many who did not accept the Good Friday Agreement who smoulder with resentment in the background. The tight-knit nature of small communities in a small area of only a million and a half people has made it hard to abandon entrenched positions. The very length and height[28] of the 'peace line' – of which there are fifty-two sections – reminds any visitor of this. Everyone knows someone who was killed, injured, or was a member of a paramilitary group or involved with one in some capacity. Delineations are strongly maintained: small streets are still divided between Ulster Defence Association (UDA) and Ulster Volunteer Force (UVF)[29] Protestant paramilitary factions. The harassment of communities has not ended – and sectarian problems with victims on both sides prevail – but the Northern Ireland of 2007 is barely comparable to that of the early 1970s and 1980s, at least in terms of basic freedoms: the endless searches have ceased and people are not in daily fear of being blown up.

A little republican history museum off the Falls Road – run by ex-prisoners and other IRA people – shows artefacts made in Long Kesh and other items from the 'struggle for Irish freedom'; Thompson, AK-47 and other IRA rifles are also on display, but not improvised explosive devices. Whatever you do, don't mention the bomb. The bombs are all the more noticeable for their absence in modern republican literature, political propaganda and folklore, the IRA having been responsible for the biggest array of bomb types ever used by an irregular force, and the largest number of explosions in peacetime.

How and when were such instruments of death used – which had in the past comprised far greater inventories secreted in arms dumps and safe houses throughout the Irish Republic and Northern Ireland – and what was the extent of misery and destruction they caused? Why did the IRA not use certain weapons, such as the store of surface-to-air missiles, and which types of weapon were more successful than others? Why, for example, did it not use up more of its Semtex store (of which there was 2–3 tonnes, from a previous store of up to six tonnes, enough to enable the IRA to detonate a Manchester (1996)-type bomb every day for almost six years) – before the Real IRA made off with much of it, rather than go to the trouble of primarily using homemade explosives?[30]

This book sets out to answer these questions. Many others have dealt with the history of the IRA – both the political issues and its protracted military campaign. However, I believe that in documenting the details of the IRA's machinery of death – without breaking the new anti-terrorist laws in the UK and beyond – I will show the extent of its power to create mayhem and destruction using the ultimate weapon of the terrorist (or freedom fighter, whichever you choose to call it) – the bomb.

Even when its weapons did not achieve their maximum effect, the IRA created fear and rendered necessary a massive counter-campaign by the British and Northern Irish authorities and military. Michael Collins, the IRA's first major leader and intelligence chief from the 1916 Easter rising until his assassination by anti-Treaty forces in August 1922, is reputed to have said that the purpose of the terrorist is to terrorise.[31] The group he did most to create certainly achieved this, during his lifetime and after its mutation into arguably the deadliest terrorist group until the formation of Al Qaeda. It not only terrorised the citizens of Northern Ireland on both sides of the political divide and from time to time the population of London, but also its own members and those in its supporting community suspected of being informers.

It seems that the media and other observers have become so caught up in the current terrorist threat that they have forgotten, or underestimate, the relentlessness of the IRA's campaign. In a television news bulletin in July 2006 on the ongoing and increasingly bloody insurgency in Iraq, the term 'IED' – Improvised Explosive Device – was said to be a new one that we would all have to get used to. The term IED is hardly new, having been introduced in the Second World War to describe devices used by anti-Nazi resistance groups, and then gaining regular coinage in the late 1960s and early 1970s when the Provisional IRA bombing campaign took off in earnest. Indeed, so closely connected with the IRA campaign were IEDs that you could be forgiven for calling them Irish Explosive Devices. Up to 1992 over 10,000 explosions had occurred – mostly instigated by the IRA.[32] It was the first national insurrectionist group to use IEDs – it had been using bombs since the first major attack in Clerkenwell, London, in 1867,[33] by its forebear, the Irish Republican Brotherhood (IRB), which killed twelve civilians and which was the first in the so-called 'dynamite war' of 1883–85.[34]

The news bulletin gaff showed how accustomed to the peacetime culture we have become. Even the horrific bombing attacks that took place in London on 7 July 2005 – while causing the most fatalities and injuries of any terrorist attack on mainland Britain – represented in the early years of the twenty-first century the exception rather than the norm. The constant warnings about Islamicist terrorist attacks, both conventional and non-conventional, may serve to numb the population. The Provisional IRA had discovered this by the early 1990s.[35] The relentless nature of its attacks has been replaced by a more insidious, less predictable threat. But when I arrived in London in the early 1970s, bombings were certainly the norm. Hardly a week went by without an IRA bomb attack or warning. Buildings were constantly evacuated, hoaxes abounded, and over a thirty-year period the London public grew ever more resilient and stoic.

Nevertheless, the intensity and number of attacks was off the scale in those days. On 21 July 1972 within a one-mile radius of Belfast city centre, twenty-two bombs exploded in the space of seventy-five minutes.[36] PIRA carried out a total of 1,300 bombings in 1972.[37] Terrorism abroad also hit a peak; hundreds of groups abounded, from Marxist and Maoist extremists to others, like the IRA, fighting over nationalist issues. Planes were hijacked and kidnappings, sieges and assassinations became commonplace.

The IRA's 'engineers' achieved the highest level of ingenuity and inventiveness with their IEDs. Many pioneering bomb technologies were produced, tested, and used to deadly effect. To this day, the IRA remains the world's most advanced builders of IEDs and its talent in making bombs has sadly influenced other terrorist groups. One of the largest bombs the organisation ever detonated, the 24 April 1993 Bishopsgate bomb, contained one tonne of ANFO – an ammonium nitrate and fuel-oil mixture – and had the explosive power of a 1,200 kg TNT equivalent – that is, as powerful as a small tactical (around 1-kiloton) nuclear weapon.[38] The Hiroshima bomb had a yield of 12–15 kilotons. The North Koreans, in their first underground nuclear test in 2006, did not manage to produce a kiloton yield with a nuclear device.[39]

Many have wondered whether the IRA ever tried to acquire nuclear, radiological, biological or chemical weapons. The relentless succession of explosions appearing during the 1970s led to a rumour, which also appeared in local newspapers, that the IRA was trying to acquire a nuclear device. The explosion of a bomb at Belfast gasworks, producing a large mushroom cloud and shaking the ground so hard that people in nearby streets were thrown off their feet, only served to increase such rumours.[40]

It has always been assumed, and this is well documented in interviews with former IRA operatives, that the Provisional IRA avoided the procurement and use of non-conventional weapons for both logistical – the materials are not easy to acquire and put together in viable, deliverable devices – and moral reasons. To my knowledge of the movement and the ex-IRA people I had met, non-conventional warfare was never on the agenda. As former IRA man Tommy McKearney put it: 'We were not nuclear physicists, but we were good electricians.'[41] This assessment is supported by members of the countermeasures community.

But I am sure that, had they wanted to, and given the right opportunities and materials, IRA engineers would have been capable of constructing an improvised nuclear device, known in the pantheon of military acronyms as an IND. Had the IRA been at Los Alamos (the US nuclear laboratory), the atomic bombs could have been built in less than two and a half years, but possibly at the expense of some of the facilities. But a note of caution is required, and members of the IRA have claimed that British intelligence chose to exaggerate its prowess far beyond its real capabilities in order to justify reactions and countermeasures by the security services 'for the greater good'.[42] However, while the IRA did not try to develop weapons of mass destruction (WMD), there have been claims that it did attempt to create WME, weapons of mass effect – fuel-air bombs.[43] Along with chemical weapons, such devices are termed the 'poor man's atom bomb'. This evidence emerged in the public arena following the arrest of three Irish citizens in Colombia, who were charged with assisting and training Colombian terrorists in bomb-making techniques. It was taken as tangible evidence of IRA attempts to re-arm, develop their technology and raise money by providing training to foreign terrorists.

In these days of jihadi terrorism people say, somewhat glibly, that 'you knew where you were with the IRA; at least they gave warnings.' They often didn't, or they were inadequately given, causing people to be evacuated either too late or into a target area – but this perception of the past is understandable given the current unquantifiable, unpredictable, and in some ways more terrifying threat. Today's suicide bombers do not give any kind of warnings, and try to kill as many people as possible. Although religion was seen by many as the root of Ireland's 'Troubles', the religious fundamentalism and desire for globally inspired action that pervades the new terrorism did not exist, despite the ugly religious sectarianism and tit-for-tat killings that occurred in Northern Ireland.

The IRA killed many people, either deliberately or unintentionally, when bomb warnings failed or were deliberately ambiguous, or when innocent civilians simply got in the way. Bombs, the IRA's chosen means of attack, have long been the most indiscriminate of weapons, whether used by terrorist groups or dropped from planes on cities. But on the whole the organisation avoided civilian casualties as far as possible within the frenetic mayhem of urban and rural insurgency warfare, a situation in which civilians will always get caught up in the conflict. This does not excuse the misery and injury caused, as this strategy often went wrong, but may begin to explain it. The IRA did not target non-combatants, but there were civilian targets – individuals in or connected to the British government, royal family, judiciary and other establishment figures. Otherwise, chief targets were members or associates of the British forces and security services.

My own background inspired me to write a history of the IRA's bombing campaigns, having written about the IRA long before specialising in weapons technology. My job increasingly involves analysing terrorist attacks and the types of explosives used, and although these are now emanating from groups with a more far-reaching and deadly agenda, much of the modus operandi of these organisations' acquisition and use of weapons comes from the history of the IRA.

My father was an Irish Jew from Belfast and my nanny, our housekeeper, Cissie, came from Balbriggan. From my nanny, who had family members in the old IRA, I knew enough about the so-called 'traditional' IRA long before Northern Ireland exploded in the late 1960s.[44]

But once the Provos emerged, and I had visited my father's birthplace just at the start of the renewed conflict, any romantic notions were tempered with maturity and my growing experience, knowledge and horror of the tragedy of terrorism and its many victims. The scars and pain endured by everyone involved and on the receiving end of the 'world's longest war' will persist possibly for generations.

This account, while relating the ingenuity and resourcefulness of the IRA's engineers, does not spare any detail in describing the effects of its weapons on those who died or suffered horrendous injuries, or those devastated by the loss of loved ones. The economic effects of the campaign – often the IRA's main aim – will also be taken into account. That so much of Ulster's infrastructure was destroyed or damaged, and so many lives lost, made British observers howl in despair as to how the IRA, supported by a substantial home community, could wreck so much of the beautiful land it claimed as its own. The only answer to this is that sustained action from any armed insurrectionist group is bound to claim casualties. Any suggestion that the Northern Ireland conflict was not a war is denying the basic truth of the situation. And as in any war, both sides commit atrocities.

Much of the IRA's military strategy went through several very complex phases throughout the twentieth century, due mainly to the politicisation of the republican movement – the 'Armalite and the ballot box'. But this set up an irredeemable paradox: continued bombing campaigns not only alienated the British public, but also PIRA's own community, and threatened the aspirations of Sinn Féin to become a genuinely serious political entity. Also, the Provisionals realised that continued targeting of the British army and NI security services, or civilian deaths resulting from misguided or misdirected actions (such as the Warrington shopping centre bombing in 1993[45]), was not going to alter the mindset of the Protestant majority in the North or coerce or cajole them into accepting a united Ireland.

This paradox – of having to remain committed to a military campaign according to IRA tradition while knowing it could never defeat a far stronger adversary, the British – could be seen at the time of the first ceasefire, called in 1994. PIRA had enough weapons and recruits to keep it in business for the foreseeable future, but its overall military position was in decline. Previous ceasefires in the 1970s had enabled it to regroup and rearm at the height of its campaign. But by the mid-1990s the political situation had changed beyond recognition – the Anglo-Irish Agreement of 15 November 1985, the secret talks held during the early 1990s,[46] the need to present Sinn Féin in a good and peaceful light, and an element of war-weariness had landed PIRA in a stalemate out of which it needed a face-saving release.

This book will not deal in any great detail with the political developments concerning the IRA and the Northern Ireland conflict, as this is a path that has been well trodden. I will be focusing on the bloodiest aspects of the republican movement, and some evidence will be hard to stomach, although much of it is known and has to be borne by the surviving victims and all those who have suffered as a result of the use of those weapons. Presenting a detailed account of how the IRA waged war will, I hope, complement the many books already published on the organisation's history, motivation and strategy. I will show what they used, how and when they used it, where they got it from and how it affected those on the receiving end.

A manageable solution for Northern Ireland's future is closer than it has ever been. There remain for some, however, lingering fears of a return to the bloody mayhem of previous decades, and indeed some of the loyalist paramilitaries have yet to disarm. But ten years have elapsed with no bombs exploding in Northern Ireland or mainland Britain, although sectarian attacks and gangsterism occasionally rear their ugly heads – old habits die hard. But the economy and everyday life of the North of Ireland is being transformed. It will be increasingly difficult to reverse this wonderfully positive and hopeful trend, and we can only hope that the military campaigns of the IRA and all other paramilitary groups – and the weapons used in them – will be consigned to history and remain solely a subject of academic interest, bitter memories, and perhaps nostalgia for all those involved.

NOTES

1. R. Woddis, 'Ethics for Everyman', quoted in C.A.J. Coady, 'The Morality of Terrorism', *Philosophy*, vol. 60 (1985), p.52.
2. From 'Easter 1916', in R. Finneran (ed.), *The Collected Works of W.B. Yeats*, vol. 1 (New York: Macmillan Publishing Company).
3. *Report of the International Independent Commission on Decommissioning*, 26 September 2005. The process of decommissioning will be dealt with in detail in the final chapter.
4. Oppenheimer, A.R. 'Northern Ireland: The Countdown Begins', *Bulletin of the Atomic Scientists* (May/June 2002), p.13.
5. 'The inside story: IRA blunder in the jungle sparks US rage', *The Observer*, 19 August 2001.
6. 'The Omagh bomb: main events surrounding the bomb in Omagh', 15 August 1998, CAIN Events, CAIN Web Service.
7. M.L.R. Smith, *Fighting for Ireland? The Military Strategy of the Irish Republican Movement* (London: Routledge, 1997). 'You cannot ride two horses at the same time'. Ruairi Ó Brádaigh quoted from 'In the shadow of the gunmen', *Guardian*, 28 January 1989.
8. Operation Banner: An Analysis of Military Operations in Northern Ireland, Army Code 71842, prepared under the direction of the Chief of the General Staff, 6 July 2007.
9. S. Dempster, 'IRA has been defeated', *Belfast News Letter*, 18 July 2007.
10. 'British army could not defeat IRA', *An Phoblacht*, 12 July 2007.
11. W. McCrea, 'The united Ireland bubble has well and truly burst', Opinion, *Belfast News Letter*, 18 July 2007.
12. L. Friel, 'IRA – Professional, dedicated, highly skilled and resilient', *An Phoblacht*, 12 July 2007.

13. 'Army hails its Ulster success', *Belfast News Letter*, 7 July 2007.
14. Tommy McKearney, interview with the author, 18 July 2007.
15. Ibid.
16. Ibid.
17. This section fighting between rival loyalists resulted in a Police Service of Northern Ireland officer being shot in Carrickfergus, Co. Antrim and three subsequent arrests. 'PSNI gun attack "murder attempt"', BBC News, 22 July 2007.
18. M. Taggart, 'Painting a new image of NI', BBC News, 22 June 2007. http://news.bbc.co.uk/2/hi/uk_news/northern_ireland/6231216.stm
19. I was told during a trip to Belfast, which included the customary 'murals tour', that the gun IRA Volunteer Billy Reid is carrying in one particular mural on the Falls Road is disputed.
20. The UK in general is said to have more surveillance cameras than any other Western democracy.
21. 'The Army can be proud of its legacy', editorial on Operation Banner British Army report, *Belfast Telegraph*, 17 July 2007.
22. G. Murray, 'Loyalist gun attacks "have dropped to zero"', *Belfast News Letter*, 18 July 2007.
23. Tommy McKearney, interview with the author, 18 July 2007.
24. Most republicans resent the term 'the Troubles' as a trivialisation of what happened. The IRA man who accompanied me to republican clubs and haunts on the Falls Road in November 2007 summed it up thus: 'Everyday problems, misfortunes and worries are "troubles". We were fighting a war. The events of the time were much more than just "troubles".'
25. But the scars remain. The cab driver I befriended during my first trip to Belfast since the Good Friday Agreement still jumps out of his skin when he hears a loud bang; he still sits in the pub facing the door, and if he sits with his back to the door, always looks around when someone walks in.
26. According to another driver who took me around Belfast, there were so many bombs on so many days that individual attacks went unnoticed and unreported: the reply 'what bomb?' would often be made in response to news that some device had gone off in a street in Belfast or elsewhere in Northern Ireland.
27. 'File on Four', BBC Radio 4, May 2007.
28. The 'peace line' is many metres higher than the Berlin Wall, and said to be a model for Israel's wall of separation on the occupied West Bank.
29. Ulster Defence Association and the more extreme Ulster Volunteer Force.
30. S. Boyne, *Jane's Intelligence Review*, October 1998 and October 2001. Only 1 kg is needed as a booster for an ammonium nitrate (fertiliser) bomb, which was the prime homemade explosive mixture used by the IRA.
31. Michael Collins is reputed to have said this, but it is also credited to Vladimir Lenin, and I think the statement by Prof. Richard E. Rubinstein, Director, Center for Conflict Analysis and Resolution, George Mason University, Fairfax, VA (May 1990) is also apt: 'Really, a definition of terrorism is hopeless … terrorism is just violence that you don't like.' LCDR Steven Mack Presley, MSC, USN, 'Rise of Domestic Terrorism and its Relation to United States Armed Forces', Federation of American Scientists, 19 April 1996. http://www.fas.org/irp/eprint/presley.htm
32. T. Geraghty, *The Irish War* (London: HarperCollins, 1998), p.207.
33. M.L.R. Smith, *Fighting for Ireland? The Military Strategy of the Irish Republican Movement* (London: Routledge, 1997), p.15.
34. Geraghty, *The Irish War*, p.313.
35. See Smith, *Fighting for Ireland?*, p. 214.
36. Geraghty, *The Irish War*, p.41.
37. CAIN Web Service: A Chronology of the Conflict, 1972 http://cain.ulst.ac.uk/othelem/chron/ch72.htm
38. Various personal sources, including Home Office pamphlet, 'Business as Usual: Maximising Business Resilience to Terrorist Bombings, case study Bishopsgate'.
39. A.R. Oppenheimer, 'North Korea joins the nuclear club – but only just', *Asian Military Review* (winter 2006).
40. Various personal communication, Belfast, July 2007. An improvised nuclear device (IND) that would have worked on the simplest fission design, the gun method, in which one 'slug' of highly enriched uranium (HEU) is fired within a cylindrical device at a larger explosive charge of HEU, resulting in a chain reaction. The IRA IND was rumoured to have been intended as a cone-shaped device, with HEU in the main charge and Semtex in the cone, to be shot at the

main charge. To be further investigated. I suspect this is gossip.
41. Tommy McKearney, interview with the author, July 2007.
42. P. Magee, *Gangsters or Guerrillas? Representations of Irish Republicans in 'Troubles Fiction'* (Belfast: Beyond the Pale, 2001), p. 84.
43. Personal communication, former Irish army EOD operative, November 2007.
44. The first Jewish Lord Mayor of Dublin, Robert Briscoe, was in the Irish Republican Brotherhood, and later the IRA.
45. See Geraghty, *The Irish War*, p.214.
46. See Smith, *Fighting for Ireland?*, p.200.

One

Armed Struggle: Evolving Strategies

*Everyone, Republican or otherwise, has their own particular part
to play. No part is too great or too small, no one is too old or too
young to do something.*

Bobby Sands MP,
IRA hunger striker and republican icon

*God has been pleased to save us during the years of war that have
already passed. We pray that He may be pleased to save us to the
end. But we must do our part.*

Éamon de Valera

*Two wee girls
Were playing tig near a car
How many counties would you say
Are worth their scattered fingers?*

Desmond Egan, 'The Northern Ireland Question'
http://mek.oszk.hu/00200/00271/html/poems.htm#23

On 13 December 1867, a group of Fenian rebels exploded a bomb at
Clerkenwell prison, London, killing twelve civilians and injuring 126.[1] It
was a massive blast causing immense damage to the surrounding area. The
bombers were attempting to free two Fenian prisoners from the gaol, having earlier attempted to attack Chester castle to gain weapons and ammunition. From March 1883 to February 1885 some thirteen Fenian devices
exploded in London, killing 100; two bombs on the London underground
injured sixty; one inside the Tower of London, injured sixteen; and there
were sundry attacks on railway stations. From 1867 to 1887 sixty bombs
were exploded. The authorities were so scared the queen's train would be
bombed that they ran a 'pilot' train ahead of it in case explosives were
planted.[2] Military barracks and public offices were also targeted.

The campaign was run by an Irish-American Fenian group, Clan na Gael, to distract the British from a possible uprising in Ireland. This heralded the start of long-held financial and moral support – as well as weapons – by Irish Americans for the republican cause. There were over one and a half million people of Irish birth in America towards the end of the nineteenth century and outside assistance had been sought for the 1798 Rebellion.[3]

The bombs contained dynamite, although the Clerkenwell bomb contained good old-fashioned gunpowder.[4] Therefore, the campaign was called the 'dynamite wars'.[5] Dynamite had only just been invented by Alfred Nobel, in 1866, and was the first explosive – a combination of unstable nitroglycerin and diatomaceous earth, called kieselguhr, that could be safely handled.[6] This made it popular with insurrectionists.

Not until over fifty years later and in the full-scale bombing campaigns in the 1980s and 1990s would the Fenians' progeny, the Irish Republican Army (IRA), once again 'bring the struggle to the enemy's backyard'[7] by attacking the mainland of Britain with bombs. The 7 July 2005 London bombings by Islamic extremists were redolent of early Fenian activities.

The dynamiting campaign led the then British prime minister, William Gladstone, to seriously consider what was to become known (sinisterly, to twentieth-century ears[8]) as 'the Irish question' – and the start of the movement for home rule for Ireland. This was not lost on the Fenian movement; they saw their bombing actions as arousing attention to their cause – to free Ireland from British rule. Militarised Irish republicans would continue to consider such actions – known as terrorism even then – as their main tool to achieve the goal of independence, and later, but with little or no success, to end the partition of Ireland. The military campaigns would always cause hate, resentment and alienation: after the Clerkenwell bombing, Karl Marx wrote to Friedrich Engels:

> The last exploit of the Fenians in Clerkenwell was a very stupid thing. The London masses which have shown great sympathy for Ireland will be made wild by it and driven into the arms of the government party. One cannot expect the London proletarians to allow themselves to be blown up in honour of the Fenian emissaries.[9]

The Irish Republican Brotherhood (IRB) became the best known of the Fenians – the umbrella term used to cover all the groups associated with fighting for Irish independence. Formed in 1858, the IRB was a secret organisation and may have had no more than 2,000 members, organised in military groups called 'circles'. They formed oath-bound secret societies of loyal patriots. At the time of the 1867 uprising the membership of the

IRB was estimated at over 80,000. Ireland had long had sporadic revolts, which had been put down by successive British rulers. Secret societies and teams of bandits were the forerunners of the modern IRA: the Irish were 'criminalized, leaderless but energetic and nocturnal' – making them natural terrorists.[10]

But it was the rebellion of the United Irishmen inspired by the father of Irish republicanism, Wolfe Tone, in 1798 that set the scene for future insurgencies. The British had been responsible for the oppression of Ireland for centuries – and for its poverty, underdevelopment, emigration and, ultimately, a famine that killed at least one million and led to the departure of at least a further million.[11] Military opposition to British rule became ingrained in republican thought, and by the end of the nineteenth century a discernible movement with a distinctive set of military goals to achieve Ireland's freedom from the British had evolved.[12]

THE BELIEF IN VIOLENCE

Violence was also assumed to be a unifying factor among the people of Ireland, an idea that was often doomed to failure – such as the May 1798 United Irishmen uprising, which failed to ignite any other than small groups of insurgents, and later, the 1916 Easter Uprising. It also became a long-term means of achieving a far-off goal – the 'long view' of the republican ideal if liberation from Britain that would in future be passed on through the generations.[13]

This ideal would also involve martyrdom: 'From the blood ... of the martyrs of the liberty of Ireland will spring ... thousands to avenge their fall.'[14] The call for Christ-like sacrifice and martyrdom persisted and reached a climax in the 1916 Easter Rising, but continued through to the 1970s, giving the impetus for the IRA to carry on fighting regardless of whether victory was in sight.

This may resemble present-day rallying calls from the Al Qaeda leadership, which also takes the 'long view' in setting out to achieve its aims, inviting its operatives to martyr themselves for their cause. But modern Irish republicans, while having been prepared to fight and die for Ireland, as their forebears throughout Irish history did in their thousands, did not become suicide bombers or attempt to willingly give their own lives in the course of deliberately committing mass murder of innocent civilians. If this happened, as it did either when devices did not go off at the appointed time or if coded warnings were confused and confusing and areas could not be evacuated in time, it caused major internal angst in the IRA.[15] It was counterproductive to its entire campaign, particularly in further recruiting and funding efforts in its own community at home and abroad, and also provided propaganda coups for the British.

However, the cult of force was an all-important belief system in early Irish insurrectionism and the later movement for independence. The idea that getting rid of the British could only be achieved by violence was accompanied by a disdain for political solutions – which were in any case usually deemed impossible against an all-powerful colonial power determined to hold on to its interests. Much republican writing upheld armed struggle as 'nothing to the shame of slavery';[16] that is, it was preferable to continued occupation. This meant an ingrained disdain was built up for political compromise and concession, which was seen as weakening the overall struggle – or accepting anything short of full attainment of revolutionary goals.

It also partly explained why the actions of Michael Collins in negotiating the Anglo-Irish Treaty in 1921, which led to the partition of Ireland, were so opposed and led to his assassination by anti-Treaty forces. Collins was sadly regarded as a traitor by the anti-Free Staters – the activist rump of the IRA – who were determined to carry on the fight to reclaim the North and free themselves of all vestiges of British control. In negotiating the Treaty, which Collins had little option to do – it was a choice between initial partial independence for the Irish people or nothing at all – he was regarded as having sold out to the British whom he and his comrades had fought to expel totally from the island of Ireland. Michael Collins accomplished the impossible by creating an Irish Free State.

He is remembered as the first urban guerrilla chief, having spent his entire adult life fighting for Irish independence. As well as being chairman of its Provisional Government, laying the foundations of a new, partially independent state, he then became commander in chief of its armed forces when Ireland was plunged into civil war. Collins' resilience and resourcefulness as an insurrectionist leader became such legend that he won the admiration of his enemies: Cabinet secretary Tom Jones, said: 'The tenacity of the IRA is extraordinary. Where was Michael Collins during the Great War? He would have been worth a dozen brasshats.'[17]

Collins did not want a divided country; his dream was one Ireland that was united. He wanted the fighting to stop and tried to bring about the two warring factions that were splitting the country apart. When only thirty-one, Michael Collins was assassinated in an ambush at Béal na mBláth (the mouth of flowers); questions remain about who killed him.[18] However, he is arguably the man who did more than any other in the cause of Irish freedom. His death demonstrated only too vividly how split the Irish people were and continued to be later in the century.

LOW-INTENSITY WARFARE

The 'dynamite wars' was the first major example of early Irish republican strategy and tactics: attack the occupier's territory by using shock tactics, without considering whether – even when police, military, security or establishment figures and facilities are the prime targets – civilians may be the victims.

The dynamite campaign was also one of the first examples of low-intensity warfare,[19] a term later associated with the Vietnam War and similar conflicts, where opponents of big armies wielding state-of-the-art weapons systems used whatever capabilities they had at their disposal.[20] For the IRA, and terrorist groups that followed, assassinations, ambushes, bombing campaigns and sporadic and unexpected attacks on military personnel and police were already a vital part of its doctrine before the dawn of the twentieth century. Maintaining the ability to carry on a protracted struggle punctuated by, in general, small-scale attacks was seen as the best way to exhaust, exasperate and gain advantage over a much more powerful opponent.

While successive leaderships went off in different directions regarding political aims (with splits in the movement the result – most notably when the Provisionals split from the Official IRA in 1969), military action often became an end in itself, so ingrained had it become in the republican psyche. While political goals – independence, or the ending of partition – were the ultimate aims, these were often overwhelmed by a compulsion to go on waging a guerrilla war.

Another specifically terrorist tactic of the IRA was to provoke retaliation. Coercion by the British or Northern Ireland security services of those engaged in the armed struggle in response to IRA outrages was intended to win further support for the republican cause. This policy often backfired; bomb attacks in particular showed that the IRA was capable of causing death, injury, disruption, economic damage, chaos and disgust, but subsequent clampdowns by the authorities did not always lead to increased support.

THE EASTER UPRISING – THE FIRST REAL REBELLION

When a small group of insurrectionists – the Irish Volunteers, which succeeded the IRB and was the forerunner of the IRA – seized the Dublin post office building and declared the creation of an Irish Republic on 24 April,[21] 1916, they intended to rouse the Irish people to a mass uprising. Guns from Roger Casement's German shipments were to have helped achieve this, but this operation failed (see Chapter 4).

The rebellion could possibly have passed without fanfare into the pantheon of failed Irish revolts, had it not been for the draconian response of the British in putting down the rebellion after only six days and executing its ringleaders, who became, and remain, republican legends and the founders of the Irish Republic. A small, courageous group had tried to take on the military might of one of the world's major powers, and as the most significant challenge to Britain since the 1798 Wolfe Tone revolt, the event became the most important in the republican calendar. Irish nationalism thereafter was dominated by the militant republican politics espoused by the Easter 1916 insurgents. It produced its own death cult – according to the Rising leader, Patrick Pearse, who was influenced by a mystical belief in the assumed benefit to mankind of blood spilt in violent conflict: 'Bloodshed is a cleansing and sanctifying thing.'[22]

The executions marked the beginning of a change in Irish public opinion, which had been largely passive – adding credibility to the republicans' strategy of making rebellion bring about coercion, which in turn becomes a recruiting sergeant for the rebels. It stirred Irish support for independence and created an atmosphere in which it was possible for Éamon de Valera and Michael Collins to organise the Irish War of Independence which began in 1919.

The IRB lacked weapons, whereas the British army in Ireland had as many as it needed: armed personnel carriers, tanks and artillery guns. The Ulster Volunteers – the first paramilitary group on the island of Ireland formed to stave off the rising republican influence in the South – had 35,000 rifles by August 1914 whereas the Irish Volunteers had just 1,000. The attempt by the former British civil servant and Irish republican sympathiser, Sir Roger Casement, to land German guns failed. Casement was arrested and hanged as a traitor, thereby joining the roll call of Irish martyrs. Raids on police stations to seize badly needed weapons broke out in subsequent years, and included the killing of two policemen carrying gelignite (which became a favourite IRA explosive in the 1930s mainland campaign) in Co. Tipperary in January 1919. Royal Irish Constabulary (RIC) barracks were raided for guns and some destroyed, with over 400 RIC killed. [23]

There were many military lessons to be learned from the failed uprising. It became even less relevant to continue having conventional military formations, which on the Irish side could never match the forces of the British. So future military operations would have to depend even further on low-intensity warfare. The IRA – the inheritors of that 'terrible beauty'[24] – was born.

Enter Michael Collins, the IRA's first director of intelligence and, in most other ways, leader. His highly effective disabling of British intelligence through ruthless flying column attacks the length and breadth of Ireland disabled Britain's orderly administration of the country. It led to the basic tenet of terrorist doctrine being applied by the ruling forces: coercion. This came in the form of the dreaded and often completely undisciplined Black and Tans, Britain's ragbag force of ex-First World War recruits that terrorised Irish villages and whose atrocities – sometimes in response to IRA ambushes and assassinations, but most often totally unprovoked – would have constituted indictable war crimes today. On one occasion, a party of 'Tans' captured a handful of the enemy at Kerry Pike near Cork, cut off the tongue of one, the nose of another, cut out the heart of a third and smashed the skull of a fourth. To intimidate local populations who gave support to the IRA, they set fire to villages and torched Cork city centre in reprisal for an ambush in which seventeen auxiliaries had been killed.[25] Their punitive actions sparked widespread publicity, and despite Collins' forces being vastly inferior numerically, it was becoming clear that Britain had underestimated the IRA[26] and was losing administrative control of its oldest colony.

The IRA campaign had also pushed it into protracted low-intensity warfare. Its guerrilla tactics achieved the hallmark of terrorist success – making it difficult for the British to root out IRA operatives without a wholesale subjugation of Ireland, and consequently influencing public opinion in Britain to question its Irish policy.[27] Therefore, the British began to initiate moves for at least partial disengagement and the end of the Anglo-Irish War. It would stand as the IRA's main military victory.

THE IRA IN THE NORTH – CIVIL WAR AND BEYOND

But apart from successfully disrupting British forces – to as many as fifty-five attacks per week[28] – the IRA had little real power to consolidate their advantage. Irish people and the IRA itself were increasingly war-weary – and, of great importance, it was running short of weapons, particularly in the vital Cork area – to the extent that Michael Collins privately admitted that the IRA would not have lasted another three weeks. They therefore won the Anglo-Irish War as much on threatening a war of attrition and mass disruption as actual military action.[29]

The hard bargaining that followed resulted in a truce that the IRA intended to use to re-arm, but this actually weakened the impetus behind their attacks. They had no military bases or barracks to return to, and relied – as they would in the future – on the local population. The ensuing Anglo-Irish Treaty of January 1922 that was offered to Michael Collins partitioned the island of Ireland into a 'Free State' and the province of Northern Ireland – the northern six counties – which remained in British hands. His reluctant acceptance of the Treaty was very much because the IRA had reached the limits of its power – it had not achieved military victory as such and had to be prepared for a prolonged and bitter struggle – and that a modicum of independence for the south of Ireland, leading to possible further negotiation, was preferable to continued occupation. To have forced the British hand in giving up anything in Ireland was a great achievement. It would lead to Collins being branded a traitor – as happens with so many who wage war and then sue for peace – and to the division of Ireland between pro- and anti-Treaty factions; and further, between northern Protestants and northern Catholics. That worst kind of war, civil war, was the result, along with the continuation of espousing the gun and the bomb as the answers to Ireland's problems.[30]

But in advancing forms of guerrilla warfare, the anti-Treaty IRA forces in the Civil War fought on a proving ground for republican small-scale military operations that would be the IRA standard for the future – attacks on economic and government targets and murder of soldiers and police. Many attacks were locally, rather than centrally, planned. The lack of political direction other than to rid Ireland of the British and traitors to the cause meant that tactics overcame overall strategy and long-term goals.[31] Fighting their own people – the Free Staters, backed by the old enemy the British, and enjoying majority support in Ireland – would be schismatically devastating. Although it claimed to represent the majority, the IRA would – like many terrorist groups – be seen throughout much of its ensuing history as a movement representing a minority and effecting coercion on non-supporters and any within its ranks under suspicion of spying and informing.

Opposition to the Treaty was seen as a necessary action for men who had 'surrendered their personal liberty and offered their lives'.[32] But there was a general lack of direction in fighting for full independence – just an ongoing notion of martyrdom and reliance on violence to achieve it. Militarily, IRA fighters were not under any firm command and control structure but relied on local units – a move that was to be echoed, but with a far greater level of organisation, in the 1980s when the IRA adopted the active service unit (ASU) cell structure (see below).

But at this stage, the factions that had been most involved in the War of Independence were the most difficult to control – rebellion was ingrained.[33] The victories attained in that struggle were nullified by the IRA's subsequent lack of military direction in the Civil War. This in turn diminished its ability to negotiate terms.[34] The need to go on fighting was self-perpetuating and served to maintain the ideology of the movement and keep the foot-soldiers on board and occupied. This would be the driving force behind many future campaigns.

The IRA also assumed that, having enjoyed – until the Treaty – support from its own heartland communities, fighting in the North would be a wholly different affair. The small-scale level of operations existed in most areas of Ireland, but in the North the IRA faced an especially strong anti-republican Protestant majority that wanted to remain part of Great Britain in perpetuity – whereas in the South people were seen as having been cowed into supporting the Volunteers.[35] By 1921 unionist opposition had the support of a new hardline Northern Ireland government – with the British equipping the loyalists to counter the IRA. The subsequent repression of the Catholics meant that the conflict became increasingly sectarian, marked by IRA attacks on Protestants – which went against the United Irishmen's core beliefs of embracing 'Catholic, Protestant and Dissenter' within an independent Ireland.

ATTACKING MAINLAND BRITAIN: THE 1930s

Defeat in the Civil War did not result in the end of the IRA – on the contrary, in the aftermath its members entered a period of renewed commitment and reform of its disorganised military structure in order to end the remaining British hold on Ireland, both in the Free State and, representing the ultimate and insurmountable challenge to the republicans – in the North.

Although Sinn Féin, as the movement's political arm, won forty-four seats in the 1923 Irish general election, the IRA persisted with armed struggle as the main instrument of republican advance. The growing socialist, anti-imperialist influence in IRA thinking led to it actually cutting links with Sinn Féin in 1925. But it felt increasingly marginalised by the rise of the Irish party Fianna Fail, which highlighted the dilemma of a military organisation fighting for political ends – its relevance will diminish when other means of attaining the republican dream are available to the Irish electorate.

By the 1930s internal quarrelling over political doctrine intensified. Many left-wing members went to fight in the Spanish Civil War, leaving the hardline militarist wing behind, most notably Seán Russell, who in becoming IRA chief of staff in 1938 was to lead the organisation into a politically devastating bombing campaign in England – the precursor of the relentless attacks that would be the climax of the Provisional IRA (PIRA) campaign in the 1970s.

The IRA's aim – as it would be in the 1970s – was to shake British complacency, and was based on the republican tenet that 'England's enemy is Ireland's ally'.[36] Far from influencing British public opinion, the IRA's launch of some 291 attacks resulting in seven deaths and ninety-six injured in London, Manchester, Birmingham, Liverpool and Coventry[37] caused widespread fear and intensified anti-Irish sentiment in Britain, particularly at a time when the country was facing the threat of war and invasion. Once again, there was no real direction to the campaign, nor was there sufficient political guidance. One of the biggest mistakes of the 1939 campaign was the failure to harness popular support. Political naiveté was the result of the IRA being apolitical.[38] As Gary McGladdery points out in *The Provisional IRA in England, The Bombing Campaign 1973–1997*, the campaign did not equal the success of the first bombing campaign by the Dynamiters in the 1880s, which targeted important buildings such as the Palace of Westminster rather than mailboxes, and also as the 1930s campaign expended hundreds of members, many of whom were imprisoned or deported.[39]

THE 'BORDER CAMPAIGN', 1956–62 – FAILED REVIVAL

While the Irish Republic was enduring teething troubles following full independence, the North was still under British control. This spurred the IRA, now languishing in obscurity, to begin a sporadic border campaign, accompanied by a programme of training in weapons and explosives and beginning with an attempt to raid a military college for weapons, to renew its strategy of winning back the six counties. Sinn Féin simultaneously enjoyed revived support in the North. The IRA reinforced its belief in stepping up guerrilla warfare to attain Irish unity: according to its members' Maoist-inspired handbook, 'The enemy's superiority in manpower, resources, materials … can only be overcome by guerrilla methods.'[40] The IRA was also avoiding attacks in urban areas so as not to provoke reprisals against northern Catholics.

The British were aware that the North was the focus for IRA activity despite the ineffectiveness of the border campaign, which had been due partly to the Irish government's reintroduction of internment[41] – a policy that the British would repeat, providing a boost to the IRA's recruitment drive, in the 1970s. But it was also due to the IRA's lack of political direction and the unwavering doctrine of continuing violence. Ironically, when the IRA began an introspective period of political re-evaluation in the 1960s, moving further towards a communist ideology – inherited mainly from the tradition of one of the main leaders of the 1916 Uprising, James Connolly – this was to render it severely ineffective in fulfilling any defensive role in the North during the late 1960s, when the Catholics increasingly came under siege.

FISSION OF THE IRA

The great internal conflict that was to split the IRA into two organisations in 1969 centred on the fear that politicisation of the movement would remove its military impetus – that this, in the words of the Army Council hardliner Seán Mac Stíofáin, who later became a PIRA leader, would turn the IRA into a 'paper army'.[42] In an interview with PBS/WGBH television, he summed up its predicament in the late 1960s as: 'Very bad. Very bad. No arms, very little. No training. A few hundred people and for years no contact for weapons. Bad leadership, bad policies.'[43]

Nevertheless, in 1966 plans for a renewed military campaign in the North, which were uncovered by Irish police, set out a full training programme and proposed large-scale actions to 'inflict as many casualties on the British as possible'.[44]

The attempts by the then IRA chief of staff, Cathal Goulding, and other theoretical reformists to offset the military hardliners by formulating policy objectives while maintaining the physical-force role, were to be of no avail. The leadership's change in doctrine – that military action, which had only achieved varying degrees of success in the past, could only be backed by political support achieved through campaigning towards the fulfilment of unattainable socialist ideals – proved to make the IRA of the time even less relevant and politically without teeth. Mac Stíofáin summed it up thus:

> Q: What did the people in Belfast feel about the IRA when the IRA had not been able to defend them?
> A: Well, a slogan on the walls – IRA, we run away – very unfair to volunteers. They fight sometimes [with] their hands. But they fought with the leadership in Dublin.
> Q: Because the leadership had let down …
> A: Yes.
> Q: … The people in Belfast.
> A: Yes.[45]

Indeed, the failure of the IRA to respond to the evolving crisis facing the Catholic community in the North was to sound the death knell of the new policy of left-leaning politicisation. There was a degree of involvement in the northern civil rights movement, which began campaigning in the 1960s against appalling levels of discrimination being endured by Catholics in most areas of life – housing, employment and political representation being prime examples. Behind IRA involvement in the Civil Rights Association (CRA), seen by the unionists as opportunistic bandwagon-jumping,[46] was partly the notion that Irish unity would come about once the Protestants recognised the socialist-republican aims of uniting the working classes, both Protestant and Catholic, against the British imperialist oppressor – casting the British as agitators of loyalism. This misguided notion revealed the inability of the IRA at that time to grasp the inherent reactionary nature of unionism.

The descent into anti-CRA rioting, attacks on Catholics and general chaos that ensued in 1969 in Northern Ireland exposed the failure of the IRA and others to initiate moves towards non-sectarian political development there. Many within the IRA also felt that the 1960s period of introspection and revisionism had led to inaction in defending the Catholic community, and meant the abandonment of the true republican role. This disillusionment by the rank and file was compounded by the welcome given initially by beleaguered Catholic residents to the British troops sent in to restore order – the very anathema of all they stood for in the armed struggle against the British.

Therefore, following an extraordinary army convention of December 1969, which set out a socialistic 'national liberation front' policy, Mac Stíofáin and his hardline supporters split from the main movement and set up the Provisional Army Council (PAC), splitting the republican movement into the old 'Official' IRA (OIRA) and the new 'Provisional' IRA (PIRA), which was actually an alliance of factions formed from old border campaign fighters who were against moderating the armed struggle through political philosophising. The split was long in coming rather than immediately sparked by the start of the Troubles. It was not so clear-cut: most notably, the northern radical, Gerry Adams – who was to inspire future politicisation of the movement in the 1980s – was in favour of political consciousness and agitation but criticised the shortcomings of the IRA's actions in the North.[47]

The presence of the troops gave the PIRA the impetus it needed to oppose the British through military action, and to reinstate fully the IRA's true *raison d'être*. Even the OIRA re-declared affinity to its militaristic past – as well as totally destroying its non-sectarian, socialistic credentials – with a bomb attack on Aldershot barracks in February 1972, killing five canteen workers and a Catholic priest. OIRA continued military actions until and after it declared a ceasefire on 29 May 1972, finally winding down due to a lack of resources and a reassertion by Goulding of its reformist objectives. The fission did not stop there; along with further haemorrhaging of militants in OIRA opposed to the cease-fire to PIRA, others broke away to form the implacably violent Irish National Liberation Army (INLA).

The IRA had, unlike many other terrorist groups, a high level of organisation and structure. Its supreme body, the General Army Convention, consisted of brigade delegates and met only for major policy changes. The seven-member Army Council was elected by a conven-tion-elected body, the Army Executive. The chief of staff was appointed by the Army Council, which was in charge of the IRA's eight depart-ments: Quartermaster (all weapons), Engineering (bomb-making), Publicity, Operations, Finance, Intelligence, Publicity, Security and Training. The army itself was formed of two commands: Northern (eleven counties) and Southern (twenty-one counties).[48] Southern Command did not conduct operations in the Republic but rather acted as weapons supplier for Northern Command, which was in charge of the five best-known brigades of the IRA, and controlling their operations in the war zone of the North became increasingly important.

The selection of the leadership was often from the ground up. This was said to have changed further in the 1980s, when the cell structure was well established, and when individual units may not have known who their commander was. 'They withdrew into cells, withdrawing from the people, losing the trust of the people.'[49] The IRA of street bat-tles and camaraderie had been replaced by a highly covert and anony-mous – but increasingly deadly – collection of urban war-fighters.

THE PIRA ONSLAUGHT: FROM DEFENSIVE TO OFFENSIVE

The British army's increasingly draconian responses to rioting and sec-tarian violence, exemplified by the 30 January 1972 (Bloody Sunday) shooting by paratroopers of thirteen civil rights protestors, provided a new role for the PIRA (which from now on may also be referred to as the IRA). Curfews, house raids, use of rubber bullet rounds and CS gas, and failure to defend Catholic areas from loyalist abuse, led to barricaded neighbourhoods – the so-called 'no-go' areas – and quickly removed Catholic support for the troops, thereby playing into the IRA's hands.

From taking on the role of defenders of the Catholic community, and in the process gaining a valuable heartland of support in the North, the Provisionals were able to progress to formulating military action against the occupying British forces as a means of attaining its ultimate goal – the reunification of Ireland. But the assumption that, once the British had gone, the Protestants would embrace Irish unity was well and truly rejected by the PIRA leadership, now intent on prioritising military victory over the British before politicising the population.[50] But there were indicators that the IRA would not accept opposition from the Protestant unionist population if a united Ireland was in the offing. In 1987 the Provisionals issued a pamphlet, *A Scenario for Peace*, which stated that 'anyone willing to accept a united Ireland and wishing to leave would be offered resettlement grants'.[51]

The programme of bombings and shootings waged by the PIRA in Northern Ireland and in England in the 1970s was to dwarf previous bombing campaigns in its ferociousness and intensity, reaching a height in 1972 when an average of four bombs went off daily; that bloody year saw a total of 1,300 PIRA bombings.[52] This and the subsequent bombing campaigns will be dealt with in detail in ensuing chapters.

Beginning in October 1970, the IRA focused on bombing economic targets, a policy that was to increasingly kill or maim civilians – proving the indiscriminate nature of all bombings. The economic effects were disastrous; trade in Belfast decreased by 30 per cent.[53] This period saw the first car bombs of the Troubles – the most devastating weapon in all the campaigns and in widespread use by terrorist groups ever since. Other tactics had less impact; while PIRA attacks on the army intensified, they were little more than momentary nuisance value to a vastly superior force.

It is important to point out that the IRA always saw their campaign as consisting of political, not military, actions.[54] The justification for the bombings, killings and maimings were also based on the doctrine that the IRA was the legitimate authority for the whole island of Ireland, carried out in the name of the original Provisional Government.[55]

'WORTH TEN BOMBS IN BELFAST'

While wrecking the Northern Ireland economy was seen by the IRA as a means of turning the province into an ungovernable and endless burden to the British – costing £1 billion a year[56] – the campaign was also intended to persuade the British public that withdrawal was the only outcome. Having adopted the car bomb,[57] the IRA used it to devastating effect in town centres throughout the province, reaching a climax on 21

July – Bloody Friday.[58] How the bombers went about their business and how they felt about it will be dealt with in subsequent chapters. But for now, just one quote sums up the feeling: according to a Belfast volunteer, 'Maybe you can't bomb a million Protestants into a united Ireland but you could have good fun trying.'[59]

However, this and subsequent days of carnage received far less media coverage than the outbreak of the London bombings. Some six bombs in Belfast and five in Derry were exploded on the same day as the Old Bailey and Whitehall bombs, but coverage for the Northern Ireland attacks was minimal in comparison.[60] This highlighted the 'oxygen of publicity'[61] issue – the IRA was guaranteed media coverage with their attacks in England, which steered the organisation, despite previous mainland failures, further towards intensifying the campaign there (while still continuing to bomb Northern Ireland).

A relentless barrage of small bombs such as incendiaries, book bombs and postal devices in London (some of which did not ignite) disrupted the normal running of the capital and posed an enormous challenge for the authorities, whose intelligence was less effective than in Northern Ireland. Even the smaller bombs had an effect on the economy; tourist numbers declined, particularly (and in some ways ironically) from America. Terror was achieved not, at first, by numbers of casualties but by its unpredictability and capacity to intimidate.[62] Shops, pubs, railway stations, government buildings, tourist attractions and unremarkable locations were targeted. The IRA had become the world's most danger-ous terrorist organisation and, after an initial series of volunteer losses from 'own goals', its most innovative bomb-makers.

McGladdery and others have debated the value of the IRA's cam-paign in England. What is indisputable is that the feeling among repub-licans was that '1,500 people have died in Ireland and nobody seems to care'.[63] The only way to arouse attention to the IRA's cause was to bomb the English. This would serve to, in the words of Gerry Adams, 'knock the English out of their complacency'.[64] Successive polls showed a nar-row British majority in favour of the troops returning home, which gave the IRA the mistaken impression that the UK was happy to discontinue British control of Northern Ireland.

However, if the IRA thought that the British would be ground into sub-mission, it was wrong. As is now seen during the current threat from Islamicist terrorists – either home-grown or controlled from elsewhere – what M.L.R. Smith calls the 'inexact instrument of war'[65] actually served to numb the public over the years while the intermittent campaign took place – from the initial shock of the 1970s onslaught, through to the massive bombing attacks of the 1990s. Any psychologist could have informed them that the effect of the campaign – particularly on the stoic British – would be, in general, desensitisation. However, this did not diminish the sense of terror wherever attacks took place. In an increasingly civilianised society, sudden destruction, bloodshed and mayhem did not sit easily and did not, in the end, persuade people going about their everyday lives to sympathise with this or any other violence-driven cause. The indiscriminate nature of the bomb as a guerrilla weapon – with 'economic' and 'military' targets increasingly involving the death and injury of ordinary civilians – guaranteed further alienation of the British public.

In fact, public disgust was usually the result; the Birmingham bombings of November 1974, which killed twenty-one people, and many other attacks – some without warning – horrified the public and, being outside London, intensified fear of attacks. But this was not the IRA's main concern.

The temporary truce in 1975 – as with subsequent ceasefires – was seen by the movement as a victory achieved through the intense pressure of its bombings and shootings. It also helped the IRA regroup and replenish reserves as well as test the British preparedness to negotiate.[66] As M.L.R. Smith has pointed out, this was an example of the IRA having an overconfident view of its military achievements. The achievement of the IRA in the War of Independence had carved out this hard and fast attitude to 'victory' over the British. So, when small concessions were gained, the IRA misinterpreted them as a greater victory than was actually the case. Negotiations were often not the result of the campaign. When they did take place, the IRA made extreme demands bolstered by its perception of victory – and the British usually gave nothing. So the violence, which had never gone away, intensified.[67] The paradox of guerrilla warfare – that continuing to fight was in itself tantamount to winning – led the IRA to believe it was ahead when it was either in decline or just keeping going. A grossly simplistic interpretation of the public's response, as well as the loyalists' position – which was not actually dependent on British policy – led the movement down blind alleys in its military and political campaigns.

There was also a tangible change of public attitude to 'freedom fighter' groups in the 1980s – for the UK, the period of Thatcherism, high unemployment, recession, intensification of the Cold War, and a general move to the Right in many people's personal political outlook. Whereas in the 1970s it was not uncommon to see students going to pro-IRA meetings – it was almost 'chic' to be pro-IRA, pro-PLO, and all the rest – the 1980s were somewhat different. Radicalism obviously was still in evidence, but much of its thrust was concerned with the miners' strike,

CND and other issues that had nothing to do with Northern Ireland. Hence, there was less tolerance for Irish republicans and their aims.

SMALL IS BEAUTIFUL: RESTRUCTURING

However, reform of the organisation in the late 1970s in the face of the security forces' infiltration of the movement, bombing 'own goals' and lack of discipline led to a slimming down to around 300 activists and the establishment of 'cells' (active service units – ASUs) which would become increasingly self-motivated and independent and would get their support and information secretly and anonymously. The IRA training manual, the Green Book, set out strategy, tactics and ideology: 'Volunteers must firmly believe without doubt and without reservation that, as members of the IRA, all orders issued by the Army Authority, and all actions directed by the Army Authority are the legal orders and the lawful actions of the Government of the Irish Republic.'[68] The cell structure has continued in terrorist groups since, and is currently employed by Al Qaeda and its affiliates.

First adopted for the Provisionals by Gerry Adams, along with the Northern Command, the cell structure was designed by a fellow Belfast republican, Ivor Bell. It reduced IRA active service units to small groups of five or six individuals, intended as an effective method of resisting infiltration by military intelligence and RUC special branch.[69] In reality this system failed because the Northern Command then centralised its control of all IRA operations in a vertical command structure. Operations had to be vetted before they were sanctioned. This inevitably left the IRA prone to well-placed, higher-ranking informers, who had access to the vetting process.[70]

The cell structure also radically changed the culture of the IRA. The slimmer, leaner form of the new Provisionals was no longer the 'people's army' of the old days. 'You were never parted from your weapon. You slept with your weapon.'[71] The old familiarity between volunteers lessened. Unquestioning support was not automatic from the communities: 'In the old days, all houses were 100%. Now you'd get kicked out of some.'[72]

The reorganisation was accompanied by an increase in technological skills in the bombing campaign (which will be described in detail later), which to a certain extent put paid to the prejudiced notion of 'stupid Paddy'[73] Irishness – an echo of equally long-held attitudes towards 'cowardly' Jews, many of whom were to make up the state of Israel, arguably the world's most militarised nation.

The steady enhancement of bomb-making skills also coincided with

an increased sophistication in strategic and political thinking, particularly as British countermeasures began to catch up and the organisation was
increasingly compromised through intelligence, infiltration and informers. It got to the stage that most IRA operatives were known to the
authorities; those arrested were already on file and operatives were being
shot as part of the shoot-to-kill policy, one of the policies that turned the
conflict into all-out war.[74]

THE 'LONG WAR' AND CHANGE IN TARGETING

In the following decade, attempts at politicising the movement – spear-
headed by Gerry Adams – gave the IRA the purpose and direction it had
long lacked. This move would also ensure renewed support from its heartland communities in Northern Ireland and the Republic. The 1980s
hunger strikes, whose most famous protagonist, Bobby Sands, was elected
as MP for Fermanagh and South Tyrone shortly before his tragic and agonising death in Long Kesh, put Sinn Féin back on the political map. The
movement had also realised that the armed struggle alone would not
achieve its long-term aims.

However, this did not in any way dilute its military efforts. The IRA
was, and would remain, the supreme authority.[75] Political support would
be given in the context of the military campaign: the Armalite and the
ballot box,[76] and although these elements often clashed with one another,
the armed struggle always remained uppermost. The IRA's overall
doctrine centred on the notion of the 'long war',[77] implying that after several hundred years of British occupation of Ireland, a few more decades
more of fighting would not make much difference in the attainment of its
goals. The reorganisation of the IRA also ensured it was better equipped
for a long-term campaign. This would be marked by sporadic attacks
punctuating periods of inactivity, rather than the relentlessness of the
1970s – mainly to enable it to regroup and replenish supplies of weapons
and re-train operatives, but equally to wear down British resistance
while being able to go to ground repeatedly to avoid detection.[78] The
longer the war, the more likely it would, according to IRA strategy, win
over an exhausted British public and security forces while, as in the
1970s strategy, make Northern Ireland ungovernable.

The IRA began at the end of the 1970s and into the 1980s to focus on
high-prestige targets. The list is long and bloody and these examples are
only the most well known: the double attack comprising the assassination of Lord Mountbatten and the Warrenpoint bombing (August 1979);
Chelsea barracks (October 1981); Hyde Park and Regents Park (July

1982); Harrods (December 1983); Brighton Grand hotel (October 1984); Enniskillen (November 1987); Royal Marines canteen in Deal, Kent (September 1989). However, it was the 1990s that saw the biggest and most economically devastating attacks, focused on the City of London – some attacks surpassing damage wrought during the Blitz in the Second World War – and the astonishing mortar attacks on 10 Downing Street, the closest the IRA came to assassinating the entire cabinet. The period also saw atrocities like the Warrington bombing (March 1993).

Despite the increasing magnitude and sophistication of the attacks over a thirty-year period, the IRA was no nearer its desired goal of forcing the British out of the six counties and bringing about a united Ireland. This illustrated the eternal paradox of terrorism: the nature of the ultimate military victory is not clearly defined, is virtually impossible against such a powerful adversary, and therefore the goals of the movement remain as far from being reached as before. The great unmentionable – compromise – then has to be considered in whatever negotiations are offered.

Indeed, while the Provisionals carried on their programme of action, the Northern Ireland peace process had already begun. The bombing campaign in England was a prime factor in developments – both in terms of financial damage and in giving the IRA leverage in negotiations.[79] But the attacks were also – despite the size of its arsenal of weapons and explosives – not bound to be unlimited and were draining the IRA's resources. The major attacks took enormous operational planning and execution, requiring maintenance of links with operatives on the mainland and undetected fabrication and movement of large amounts of explosives, vehicles, and so on. Many operations were cancelled often due to bombs malfunctioning or being discovered.[80] It is clear that, had the IRA been able to carry out all its intended missions throughout the 1980s and 1990s, the ensuing death and destruction would have been truly immense.

EXTREME REPUBLICANISM: THE INLA

In the shadow of the Provisional IRA, but often every bit as deadly, the Irish National Liberation Army (INLA) – a hardline Marxist offshoot from the Officials in the mid-1970s – was responsible for 125 deaths since 1975. Some of their attacks were the worst of the entire conflict and several were high-profile. But despite its persistence, the INLA remained – in republican terms – a thorn in the Provisional IRA's side and posed only a limited military challenge, growing more isolated towards the ceasefires of the 1990s. Their main coup was the May 1979 assassination of Airey Neave, MP with an under-vehicle booby trap bomb, demonstrating a similar level of expertise as the Provisionals.[81] But in the 1980s the INLA was ridden by factionalism, intra-republican rivalries, criminality and arrests. It declared a ceasefire on 22 August 1998, days after the Real IRA bombing of Omagh, although it remains opposed to the Good Friday Agreement.[82] For details of the INLA's weapons, see Chapter 4.

COUNTERING THE IRA

Details of countermeasures are described in Chapter 9. The IRA was up against not just one formidable, experienced and militarily superior opponent, but several: not just the British army but also Army Intelligence; MI5; the RUC; the Irish police and army; and the SAS, which was to be highly instrumental in the actions seen during the 1980s shoot-to-kill policy – the so-called 'dirty war'. The RUC was highly organised, with mobile support units that could be deployed rapidly into areas in the North where the IRA was active. The RUC later had its own version of the SAS and also had a highly covert unit, Echo 4 Alpha, which was involved in the 1980s 'dirty war'.[83]

The RUC and Army Intelligence had such familiarity with the IRA that it knew just about every member and could recognise them.[84] They knew where they hung out, where they lived, their families, contacts, and daily movements and habits. House searches would be conducted not just from tip-offs from informers but by regular intelligence and familiarity[85]

But despite this overwhelming superiority – both numerically and in terms of military and intelligence experience – the IRA could often remain a step ahead by being less visible – and once the cell structure had been brought in, virtually invisible – whereas the RUC and the British army were in uniform and ubiquitous. The IRA would dodge detection by blending in with the local communities, by staying on the run, and through clever deception techniques and also sheer guts. But this constant evasion and need to stay covert – and still wage a war – wore heavily on the IRA's members, and the capacity of the British state apparatus to move in on IRA units, infiltrate them, and harass the nationalist (and also non-affiliated) population meant a war weariness had set in by the late 1980s. The IRA also knew that they could not negotiate an end to the armed struggle without demanding changes to the RUC. According to an IRA veteran in September 1993, 'I don't think you'll see an end to the IRA campaign until you see the RUC disbanded.'[86]

CONCESSIONS AND AGREEMENTS

The first attempt to stop the fighting came in the mid-1970s, and failed miserably, although hopes were high among republicans that the British would withdraw, and on the British side that a ceasefire and moves to end the conflict, after six years of relentless bombings and shootings, were possible. But although the British may have negotiated a phased-in army withdrawal, they would not abandon control of Northern Ireland. At one stage it looked as though progress was being achieved – but the temporary ceasefire was becoming harder to maintain due to the clamour from the rank and file of the IRA active on the streets of the province[87] – the frontline 'troops' who had to counter growing threats from loyalist paramilitaries.

When the negotiations broke down, the IRA became seriously split and would be very reluctant to engage in talks for a long time to come. And the British vowed not to talk to the IRA while the violence continued, although they would break this rule by the 1980s. Meantime, British policy on the North switched to harsher methods against the IRA – including hunt and search, and shoot to kill – along with 'Ulsterisation': primacy for the RUC and the ending of political prisoner-of-war status for republican prisoners.[88] The IRA was in disarray and lost members while the RUC and the loyalists gained the upper hand for a while. It was this decline that ushered in the restructuring of the IRA and the cell system.

The first real attempt at concessions was the Anglo-Irish Agreement of November 1985. While bringing the IRA no nearer to its objectives – as it put the future of the Northern Irish province firmly in the hands of the Protestant majority – the agreement was interpreted by that majority as resulting from Sinn Féin's electoral successes and other republican pressure.[89] The IRA always regarded talks as both a means of reducing its strength and a sop to nationalist desires.

But as the attacks wore on, with the resultant deaths of civilians and growing doubts about the movement's reliance on violence to gain attention, the IRA was caught on the horns of the insurgent's dilemma: whether to continue the use of force – seen as the only means to bring governments to the negotiation table, and unify the movement – or end the violence, as it further alienated or numbed the target population, and therefore would not lead to broad calls from that population for the government to withdraw. The 1985 agreement highlighted another paradox – more links with the Irish Republic indicated a movement towards the middle ground, and the gradual diminishing of the Provos' influence among their own heartland supporters. Such agreement also meant the group could not escalate its violence too harshly for fear of alienating its own community.[90]

Also, any agreement would have to indicate a British commitment to withdraw from the six counties, together with a commitment – and this is the hard bit – to encourage the unionist population to plan for an eventual united Ireland, and for the IRA to emerge with a semblance of victory under its Sam Browne belt. The growing need for Sinn Féin to attain political credibility also put pressure on the IRA to enter talks.

It became increasingly evident that Sinn Féin believed an unarmed alternative was necessary to achieve its political aims: that the armed campaign was becoming 'an option of last resort'. In 1992, the party's annual conference, the árd fheis, passed a motion saying that Sinn Féin recognised the need for a 'broad front' – all the combined forces of Irish nationalism – to bring about an end to partition. Beneath the basic level of the statement was unease, most notably from the South, about the IRA campaign. The motion, which won a majority vote and was witnessed by Martin McGuinness and Gerry Adams on the platform, put the 'broad front' of opinion in the republican movement, North and South, as having primacy over the military approach. This certainly did not mean an end to bombings and shootings, but it was a distinct shift in emphasis.[91]

And the military campaign was far from over. Whatever had been going on behind the scenes, to observers on the outside, and the broader public, the campaign was gaining in its capacity for devastation. Attacks continued through much of the early 1990s; the long-practised IRA strategy of unremitting attrition continued, ensuring army and police were on constant alert and being forced to maintain heavy fortification, while also keeping the pressure on their own communities which would be targeted for arms raids.[92] Had the peace process broken down, and no Good Friday Agreement achieved, the armed campaign would have entered a more ruthless and brutal phase, and it is interesting to speculate whether the attacks would have mutated into something non-conventional.[93]

By the time the Downing Street Declaration was launched, in December 1993, the biggest IRA bomb had been detonated at Bishopsgate in the City of London (the previous April), while secret talks between the IRA and the British government had been in progress for some weeks. Sinn Féin had begun to affect the peace process. With ceasefire a condition for concessions, and a growing image of moderation in the shape of the Adams–Hume peace initiative, the talks were nevertheless backed by the threat of future IRA actions, although this would never be admitted.

The Declaration was indeed regarded by republicans as the result of IRA pressure – 'the vibrations of IRA bombs exploding in the City of London'[94] as well as mortar attacks on Heathrow airport in March. But its terms – the future of Northern Ireland still being predicated on the wishes of the unionist majority – still did not meet the very essence of republican aims, that of Irish unity. This had always been the prime demand of republicans from day one of the renewed campaign. But it had evolved. The notion of Irish 'self-determination' took over from the more extreme ambition of a British-free united Ireland under Sinn Féin. The idea of an 'Éire Nua' took root, a federal four-province Ireland. Whatever form the eventual united Ireland would take, the IRA wanted a definite decision on Irish unity. 'Too many people have died, we're too long on the road to accept something less than we've set out to get.'[95]

Of great significance also was the fact that IRA pressure was still seen as the main bargaining tool for the republicans – as, without it, their position would be reduced to having a voice through electoral strength only. This fear held some degree of foresight – as Sinn Féin's electoral support was to become far greater in the North than in the South. In the early 1990s, even in the North the party had just 10 to 12 per cent of the vote.[96] But the leadership's strategy rested on an idea that was sold from the 1980s Adams reforming period: that if the IRA gave up the military campaign, its political arm would achieve an unstoppable pace of political progress that would see it gain power – not just in the North but in the South as well, giving the republicans an all-Ireland mandate for reunification.[97]

However, its share of the vote south of the border has been in decline for many years. This made the eventual relinquishing of arms in the latter half of the 1990s all the more telling for republicans in the North of Ireland.

'THE CONFLICT IS OVER'

The City attacks and other 'spectaculars' (see Chapter 3) intensified the need for a settlement. While the IRA made noises about peace, it constantly threatened to up the ante should the talks collapse. In not arming the Heathrow mortars with ignitable warheads[98] the IRA was sending a message that worse was to come. Some have indeed questioned why the IRA called a ceasefire and subsequently wound down its military campaign. After all, British withdrawal was not forthcoming. The IRA had masses of weapons and explosives left and, as on previous occasions, continued to increase its arsenal during the ceasefire.[99] It was also using homemade explosives (HMEs) for the huge City bombs, the materials, components and expertise for which could be reconstituted.[100] However, the IRA was increasingly dependent on its fertiliser bomb factories in remote, rural south Armagh – the IRA's Los Alamos – for supply of, and expertise for, the bigger bombs.[101]

When the first, endstage ceasefire came on 31 August, there was no conclusion to the talks, and it was merely seen as breathing space for the IRA to regain the upper hand. There was also a resistance to re-entering talks due to the re-introduction of decommissioning of weapons into the process. This was anathema to the IRA, which poured scorn on 'a surrender of IRA weapons either through the front or the back door'.[102] Nevertheless, a decommissioning body under US senator George Mitchell was set up in 1996, with the intention that, while no actual decommissioning would be demanded for talks to ensue, the issue would be considered while they resumed.

The ceasefire broke down in February 1996 following a huge bomb at Canary Wharf in London's Docklands. It was believed to have been detonated to prevent further fission within the IRA, which throws up the other terrorist paradox: how to reassure the hardline rank and file that the military option is still in progress while convincing the world that 'the conflict is over'?[103]

The Docklands bomb – although the British government denied it – did contribute towards bringing the parties back to the negotiating table. Also, by then a new Labour government had been voted into power with an overwhelming majority (unlike that of its predecessor, which depended on unionist support for Commons votes), and the security forces had somewhat weakened the IRA. By sidelining Sinn Féin in future talks unless a permanent ceasefire was called, the British forced the IRA's hand to act in order that Sinn Féin be included. Again, it chose violence. When the IRA broke the ceasefire, it once again did so in England, but because of heightened security in London this time the location was the centre of Manchester, which was devastated in June 1996 by the largest IRA bomb ever detonated on the mainland. The IRA believed that, instead of pursuing talks, the British had been pursuing IRA defeat and its surrender. The Manchester bomb proved that the IRA could still destroy the heart of a British city.[104]

The military campaign, which was conducted right up until the May 1997 general election and included a series of hoax devices,[105] managed to cause as much chaos in England as possible, proving again that mainland operations spoke louder than attacks in Ulster. What has always been hard for most people to understand is that the IRA was still interested in the peace process, despite its ability to pull off explosive attacks of 'mini-nuke' proportions and having enough weapons and explosives to keep going for many years to come.[106] The organisation was, nevertheless, having less impact on the public and could no longer evade the political imperative. Sinn Féin's participation in talks and the overall political process was impossible without cessation of military operations. In effect, its biggest bomb was, therefore, its swan song.[107]

The political momentum behind further politicisation, through Sinn Féin's vital involvement in the talks, meant the pressure was on to end the armed struggle.[108] On 19 July 1997 the final ceasefire – 'complete cessation' – came and has held ever since, reflecting the IRA's 'entering a new phase of struggle with the same resourcefulness and determination that they have shown in all previous phases'.[109]

Above all, the 1990s spectaculars damaged the image of Gerry Adams and Sinn Féin in the Republicans' most important country of support – America – which brings us almost full circle in the history of the Fenians and their IRA descendants. Probably the most damaging attack in republican military history, albeit by the breakaway Real IRA, was the Omagh bomb in August 1998, which killed twenty-nine people and constituted the worst Northern Ireland atrocity, as well as showing that disparate elements – particularly in the border counties[110] – were not prepared to abandon the armed struggle until Ireland became one. Their activities persist beyond Omagh; in August 2006, the Real IRA claimed responsibility for the firebombing of local businesses in Newry, Co. Down.

TWENTY-FIRST CENTURY ENDGAME

The end product of the talks, the landmark Belfast (Good Friday) Agreement of 10 April 1998, was cleverly constructed to be all things to all men. In setting up a connective Irish element in the form of North–South bodies, scaling down of British troop levels and army installations, release of republican prisoners, and human rights and policing reforms among other measures, many republicans saw it as a transition to an eventual united Ireland – again taking the long view of the struggle. But for many it did not fulfil the aims they had fought for so many years to attain.[111] Many unionists likewise – and predictably – felt they had been sold out, despite the firm clause in the Agreement that guaranteed the union so long as a majority desired it. The Agreement was, as expected, far from perfect, and disagreements between the two communities were reflected by the deadlock in 2005 and 2006 over reinstating the Northern Ireland assembly, and will probably continue indefinitely.

Nevertheless, in May 1998 the North voted overwhelmingly (71 per cent) in favour of the Agreement, while the Irish Republic vote was even higher – 94 per cent. In relinquishing its claim to the North, the southern Irish showed that they and the world had moved on and that the Troubles had become increasingly irrelevant for them, having become a fully-fledged member of the EU and benefiting greatly from *that* particular union. That said, a 1999 survey found 86 per cent of Irish voters still wanted to unite their island.[112] Many Irish people would like to see a united Ireland, but by peaceful means and with no fear of loyalist reprisals. This must have been a most disconcerting aspect for many northern republicans who actually opposed the EU.

Despite this, they had themselves been forced to embrace, in the words of the Brighton bomber, Patrick Magee,[113] 'a savage dose of *Realpolitik*' partly as a result of the fall of Soviet communism. Even more important, however, was the unprecedented involvement by a US administration, under President Bill Clinton, in the peace process. Both the ideological and financial underpinning of the IRA was under threat. But the main reason for the IRA's apparent abandonment of the military option came from the realisation that it and the British had reached a stalemate. Much had been achieved by British intelligence services in infiltrating the IRA, and a parallel 'dirty war' had been waged, particularly during the 1980s once the IRA had introduced the cell system.[114] Although the 'long war' was accepted as part of IRA strategy and doctrine, it had – despite the maintenance of its vast covert arsenal – become weaker militarily.[115] But many historians agree that the increasing politicisation of the movement was incompatible with exploding bombs. And political power was seductive; Sinn Féin overtook the moderate nationalist party, the Social Democratic and Labour Party (SDLP), to become the fastest-growing party in the Republic (although winning Sinn Féin candidates still do not take their seats in the UK parliament). Exclusion from the corridors of power – including those in Washington, DC – was no longer a valid option for republicans.

On the social and demographic level, the idea that Irish unity was inevitable was underlined by improved cultural exchange (Gerry Adams: Belfast had become the 'most republican city in Ireland')[116] and the fact that Catholics are expected to outnumber Protestants in Northern Ireland in thirty years' time: according to the 2001 census, Catholics make up nearly 44 per cent with Protestants, just over 53 per cent.[117] Despite this, republicans – from the Adams-inspired rethinking period of the 1980s onwards – were realising that unionists could not be shot and bombed into Irish unity.

Although the North will remain British until the majority decide otherwise, the province has become an economic drain. Apart from the cost of stationing forces, it had been subsidised for decades. Successive polls among the British electorate reveal a desire for withdrawal from the six counties. Among the most recent was a *Guardian*/ICM poll in 2001, which found that 41 per cent of Britons believed Northern Ireland should be joined with the Irish republic while only 26 per cent said it should continue as part of the UK. This constituted a distinct rejection from those whom unionists regard as their fellow citizens.[118]

The big sticking point remained decommissioning. The ceasefire may have been declared and the endgame begun, but the IRA resisted giving up its insurance policy for possible future military action – its weapons, about which this book will focus from now on. To do so would have spelt humiliating defeat and the very antithesis of the movement, which had still not succeeded in attaining its goals.[119] But decommissioning was held up as the way for republicans to show they were genuine about peace – even though loyalist paramilitaries did not follow suit, and did not seem to be required to do so.

It was in the beginning of this lengthy phase of negotiations, which would last until the estimated final act of decommissioning in September 2005, that the Americans were to play a crucial role. An IRA plot to buy arms in the US was uncovered in 1999, but worse was to come. In August 2001 IRA operatives were accused of transferring bomb-making skills to members of the Revolutionary Armed Forces of Colombia (FARC), which was at war with the US-backed government and heavily involved in the drugs trade. But it was the events of 11 September 2001 that turned the Atlantic tide. The push towards the first tranche of decommissioning in October 2001 came from the Bush administration, accompanied by the subsequent revulsion against terrorism throughout the US and beyond – including among those Americans who had supported the IRA to the tune of some $11 million a year.[120] But it can be equally said that the time had come, even if 'our day' had not come, to abandon the gun and the bomb as the means of political expression.

NATURE OF THE IRA

In order to assess the IRA's role in the history of Irish resistance, how it waged its war, and how it acquired and used its weapons, one must understand that as an irregular force it operated under completely different conditions to that of a regular army – even if its earlier incarnation had a traditional army structure consisting of brigades, battalions and so on. An important factor in its development was the very speed of turnover of personnel; the pace of change – hastened with the arrests of volunteers, seizure of weapons, and the constant need to hide and move operatives, weapons and materials around a small and increasingly watched area.[121]

This continuing change also meant that the organisation could be highly flexible, unlike many regular militaries where positions, ranks and doctrine remain fixed for long periods of time, and hence their adaptability – particularly in dealing with low-intensity warfare operations – is often difficult. Provisional IRA members could be rapidly promoted: within weeks or months an ordinary volunteer could become, for example, an engineer (explosives officer), rapidly learning and honing his skills. A raw recruit could become a veteran within months. Many were very young; veterans could be still teenagers, and many members came from long-established republican families with several members having served or currently serving.[122]

The movement, in a state of constant insurrection (even during cease-fires, as these would provide the opportunity to regroup and re-arm), would evolve and continue to change. Following events such as Bloody Sunday and the British policy of internment, for example, the numbers joining the Provisionals rocketed to many thousands in a matter of weeks.

The acquisition of technology and expertise was greatly influenced by this pace of change. The constant need to improvise with materials and avoid detection meant learning had to be rapid; it also meant that the ingenuity of constructing and deploying bombs or using firearms effectively was quickly acquired but within certain parameters. Many of the technicians were 'skilled electricians' rather than rocket scientists who turned their abilities to best use. As such, IRA engineers showed genius in knowing, realistically, what their abilities and strengths were, and pursuing them with great zeal.[123]

The IRA campaign of modern times was essentially a northern phenomenon. As such, support was drawn mostly from the North, rather than the South. Republicans and nationalists in the North despaired at the lack of military or other official intervention or support from the South, particularly as matters came to a head in the 1960s. The guerrilla machine received active and benevolent support from the northern nationalist community – in all, a sizeable section of a population of only 400,000.[124] However, the Republic showed little active support for the Provisionals once the Troubles were under way – for example, although there was a constitutional claim to the six counties, it was never followed through. It has always seemed an unhappy fact that the Irish appeared to wash their hands of the North, especially when the Republic, up to the time of the Anglo-Irish Agreement, through the controversial articles 2 and 3 of its 1937 constitution laid claim to it. Politically, northern nationalists were 'unwelcome guests at the feast' in Dublin.[125]

However, for many in the South, who may have had family members or forebears who had fought in the bitter struggle against the British in the years leading to independence there was a sneaking regard for the IRA.[126] The hurt wrought by partition led to an ambivalent attitude towards the activities of the organisation.[127] The people were used to not showing overt support for guerrillas; the whole secret of their success in the Anglo-Irish war was often due to the ingenious ways local people could hide people and weapons – and their feelings. The Irish police – the gardaí – on the whole co-operated with their British mainland and Northern Irish equivalents, but there were pro-IRA members who provided valuable intelligence. To know the IRA was to defeat them. Making them understandable made them defeatable. The 'long war' was as much an intelligence war as anything fought with guns, bombs, and tanks.

THE IRA EQUATION

The IRA knew its weaknesses and was subsequently able to emphasise its strengths – something that would become the hallmark of insurgent and terrorist group doctrine. For example, in identifying that detonators and explosives were vital to its campaign, when it could not acquire them it pioneered and made its own. Therefore, in pursuing the armed struggle, the three most important components were improvisation, ingenuity and intent.

It could also be said that the IRA – despite it being at an overall disadvantage in the face of a far superior military force – could get away with more than, for example, Iraqi insurgents in present-day Basra, in the sense that some restrictions were in place, at least for a time in Northern Ireland, for the accepted level of army response. During the 1970s Provisional IRA volunteers could walk freely through housing estates and rural areas without hindrance. The vengeance of the army was, nevertheless, often visited on the nationalist civilian community of Northern Ireland, thereby fuelling further support for the Provisionals.

Nevertheless, the British army and security forces managed to infiltrate the IRA, as had occurred many times in the past; informers – 'touts' – have been a perennial problem for the republican movement over generations. There was consequently the penetration of the IRA's operational technologies, so that devices and weapons were interdicted and made to fail. This had the effect, as did the harassment of civilians, of undermining the movement, thereby damaging morale. Thus did the equation remain in balance: the cat and mouse game that both sides played was seemingly endless.

VICTIMS OF INSURRECTION

The stark reality of the IRA's campaign was such that many who made and laid the bombs were well away from the scene of the attacks when they occurred – they were often not there when the police and emergency services were picking up the dead and bits of the dead. As with many inventors and instigators of weapons and weapons systems, there is a rationale that justifies one's actions for the sake of the cause, whatever it may be. That is not to say that members of the IRA have not felt and expressed regret for their actions, particularly when civilians were caught up in their actions. But the cause would often outweigh conscience.

UNDERSTANDING THE IRA

The IRA is 'utterly comprehensible'.[128] The continuance of Northern Ireland as a denial of Irish self-determination was the main motive and thrust of the movement and will continue to be, in peace as it was in war. While this book is not an analysis of the IRA's political significance, its role in Ireland's troubled history can be summed up here as an inevitable response to Britain's occupation, and later partition, of Ireland. While its notion of Ireland as 'historically, culturally and geographically one single unit'[129] may be somewhat simplistic in view of the enduring separateness of the unionist population, the organisation was nevertheless often the only means of resistance to the British and the only expression of the fight for Irish nationhood.

It was only when conventional political representation appeared to gain in importance for the community the IRA represented that the military imperative decline and, with it, the IRA's very existence as a fighting force. The Provisional IRA itself set this process in motion as the first of the paramilitary movements to radically change its position and accede to political compromises and inevitabilities. But the support it commanded through the long years of conflict was not clear-cut, and many nationalists, both North and South, did not support the armed struggle.[130]

It is easy to conclude that the IRA lost the war – it has decommissioned much of its arsenal without achieving its aims – but the organisation will claim that whatever reforms have been achieved for Northern Ireland was because of the pressure and intensity of its programme of attacks. Its critics maintain that IRA actions could never force either the unionist majority to accept even the most minimal levels of Irish unity or the British to abandon the North. Although much of daily life in the North has been transformed in recent years, even Tony Blair admitted in 2002 that Northern Ireland is ' … part of the UK but governed unlike any other part of the UK, its communities divided, its daily life scarred in innumerable ways by sectarian bitterness'.[131] But regardless of the terrible suffering caused by the IRA, it cannot be solely blamed for prevailing sectarianism. The IRA has always been a non-religious organisation, although many of its followers may have had sectarian tendencies. And it can be said that its actions, particularly in blowing up large parts of Belfast and Derry, have – instead of managing to 'embrace' the Protestants in the North – actually increased their continuing intransigence.[132]

Whether it is still premature to conclude that the war is over – this would be foolhardy in any case of guerrilla war, or in what is arguably the longest low-intensity war in history – it is possible to ascertain the effect of the IRA's series of military campaigns and the methods used, including the motivation for specific weapons, tactics and techniques. I will attempt to describe and explain the main bombing campaigns (Chapters 2, 3); and how these changed greatly depending on the availability of weapons (Chapters 4, 5), expertise and personnel (Chapters 6, 7 and 8). The intensity of those campaigns, their terrible effects on their 1,822 victims,[133] and how IRA participants exhilarated and agonised over their part in those campaigns requires more than cold military analysis. Whatever the result of the thousands of bombs that were detonated, and millions of shots that were fired, the ingenuity, skill and persistence of the Irish Republican Army remains unmatched in the history of guerrilla warfare.

NOTES

1. M.L.R. Smith, *Fighting for Ireland? The Military Strategy of the Irish Republican Movement* (London: Routledge, 1997), p.15.
2. Interview with J. Lock, author of *Dead Fall* (Sutton, Surrey: Severn House, 2005), in *Camden New Journal*. She is chairwoman of the influential Crime Writers' Association (CWA) Gold Dagger for Non-Fiction award.
3. See Smith, *Fighting for Ireland?*, p.16, and J. Holland, *The American Connection: US Guns, Money and Influence in Northern Ireland* (New York: Viking Penguin, 1987) as an excellent source of information about US supply of arms to the IRA.
4. L. Ó Broin, *Fenian Fever: An Anglo-American Dilemma* (London: Chatto and Windus, 1971), p.213, cited in G. McGladdery, *The Provisional IRA in England: The Bombing Campaign 1973–1997* (Dublin: Irish Academic Press, 2006), p.17.
5. T. Geraghty, *The Irish War* (London: HarperCollins, 1998), p.313.
6. I. Asimov, *Asimov's Chronology of Science & Discovery* (New York: Harper and Row Publishers Inc. 1989).
7. *An Phoblacht*, 5 February 1977.

8. And to the ears of the author – as a half-Irish Jewish youngster subjected to, and vocally object-
    ing to, that unpleasant phrase in school history lessons.
9. Karl Marx quoted in K. Haddick Flynn, 'Michael Barrett: a Fenian remembered', *Irish
    Democrat*, 7 October 2004.
10. See Geraghty. *The Irish War*, p.258.
11. C. Woodham-Smith, *The Great Hunger* (London: Hamish Hamilton, 1962), p.409. In 1841 the
    population was estimated at 8,175,124. By 1851 it was 6,552,385. By then the total was estimat-
    ed at 9,018,799, meaning a loss of two-and-a-half million people. But many more could have
    died as bodies were buried in ditches. The Great Hunger has been called the Irish Holocaust.
12. See Smith, *Fighting for Ireland?*, p.7.
13. P. Pearse, *Ghosts* (Dublin: Whelan & Son, 1916), Parts I–III.
14. T. Dunne, *Wolfe Tone: An Analysis of his Political Philosophy* (Cork: Tower, 1982), p.60.
15. Personal communication, former Irish army EOD (explosives ordnance disposal) operative,
    November 2007.
16. R. Dudley Edwards, *Patrick Pearse* (London: Victor Gollancz, 1977), p.179.
17. T. Jones, *Whitehall Diaries*, vol. III, edited by K. Middlemass (Oxford: Oxford University Press,
    1971), p.60, quoted in T.P. Coogan, *Michael Collins: The Man Who Made Ireland* (Niwot, CO:
    Roberts Rinehart Publishers, 1996), p.168. The film about his life, *Michael Collins* (dir. Neil
    Jordan, 1996), features one of the most moving pieces of documentary footage I have seen, of
    Collins' funeral, attended by many British dignitaries.
18. T. P. Coogan, *Michael Collins: The Man Who Made Ireland* (Niwot, CO: Roberts Rinehart
    Publishers, 1996).
19. See Smith, *Fighting for Ireland?*, p.16.
20. D. Marston, 'Force structure for high- and low-intensity warfare: The Anglo-American expe-
    rience and lessons for the future', discussion paper, Royal Military Academy, Sandhurst, May
    2004.
21. 24 April 1916 was also when, in effect, the Irish Republican Army was born. B. O'Brien, *Pocket
    History of the IRA* (Dublin: O'Brien Press, 2005), p.8.
22. BBC History (online): Wars & Conflict: 1916 Easter Rising, 'Blood sacrifice'. The rebel lead-
    ers also hoped to 'prove', through their willingness to die, Ireland's right to freedom. The
    Proclamation stated: 'In this supreme hour, the Irish people must ... by the readiness of its chil-
    dren to sacrifice themselves ... prove itself worthy of the august destiny to which it is called.'
    http://www.bbc.co.uk/history/british/easterrising/insurrection/in05.shtml
23. See Smith, *Fighting for Ireland?*, p.34.
24. 'Now and in time to be,
    Wherever green is worn,
    Are changed, changed utterly:
    A terrible beauty is born.' From 'Easter 1916', in R. Finneran (ed.), *The Collected Works of W.B.
    Yeats*, vol. 1 (New York: Macmillan Publishing Company). This beautiful poem has also been
    used to describe the explosion of the first atomic bomb in July 1945.
25. P. Taylor, *Behind the Mask: The IRA and Sinn Féin* (New York: TV Books, 1997), review in *New
    York Times*, 21 February 1996. As a child I heard how my Irish nanny's home town, Balbriggan,
    was the centre of Black and Tan atrocities.
26. See Y. Alexander and A. O'Day (eds), *Terrorism in Ireland* (London: Croom Helm, 1984), p.153.
27. See Smith, *Fighting for Ireland?*, pp. 39, 54.
28. See C. Townshend, *The British Campaign in Ireland 1919–21* (Oxford: Oxford University Press,
    1975), pp. 113–14.
29. See F.S.L. Lyons, *Ireland Since the Famine* (London: Weidenfeld & Nicolson, 1971), p.425.
30. See Geraghty, *The Irish War*, pp.328-9.
31. See M. Hopkinson, *Green Against Green* (Dublin: Gill & Macmillan, 1988), p.41.
32. Statement of the Executive of the IRA, 28 March 1922, in F. O'Donoghue, *No Other Law*
    (Dublin: Irish Press, 1954), p.330. Cited in Smith, *Fighting for Ireland?*, p.58.
33. M. Hopkinson, *Green Against Green* (Dublin: Gill & Macmillan, 1980), p.68.
34. See Smith, *Fighting for Ireland?*, p.58.
35. R. Lynch, *The Northern IRA and the Early Years of Partition* (Dublin: Irish Academic Press, 2006),
    p.16.
36. R. English, *Armed Struggle: The History of the IRA* (London: Macmillan, 2003), p.63.
37. See McGladdery, *The Provisional IRA in England*, p.40.
38. Máirtín Pilib de Longbhuel, 'IRA Border Campaign (1956–1962)', *Ireland's Own*, 14 February

2004, http://irelandsown.net
39. McGladdery, *The Provisional IRA in England*, p.45.
40. *Handbook for Volunteers of the Irish Republican Army: Notes on Guerrilla Warfare* (Boulder, CO: Paladin, 1985, reprinted from IRA HQ 1956), p.5.
41. See Smith, *Fighting for Ireland?*, p.71.
42. S. Mac Stíofáin, *Memoirs of a Revolutionary* (Edinburgh: Gordon Cremonesi, 1975), p.104, cited in Smith, *Fighting for Ireland?*, p.76.
43. S. Mac Stíofáin, interview on 'Behind the Mask: The IRA and Sinn Fein' (Peter Taylor, PBS (Public Broadcasting Service) Frontline, 21 October 1997)., http://www.pbs.org/wgbh/pages/frontline/shows/ira/
44. The IRA's military plan was printed in 'Violence and Civil Disturbance in Northern Ireland, Report of Tribunal of Inquiry', cmd. 566, vol. 2 (Belfast: HMSO, April 1972), p.48. Cited in Smith, *Fighting for Ireland?*, p.77.
45. See S. Mac Stíofáin, interview on PBS/WGBH, published on 'Frontline: Behind the Mask, The IRA and Sinn Féin', 1998, http://www.pbs.org/wgbh/pages/frontline/shows/ira/
46. Ian Paisley said in a Belfast News Letter report on 12 October 1968 that 'two recently released criminals participated in the last Belfast demonstration', and that he felt 'CRA equals IRA'. CAIN web service, A. Scott, calendar of newspaper articles dealing with civil rights issues, 1 Jun 1968–9 Dec 1968.
47. See Smith, *Fighting for Ireland?*, pp.83–4.
48. B. O'Brien, *The Long War: IRA and Sinn Féin*, (Dublin: O'Brien Press, 1999), p.158.
49. IRA volunteer quoted in O'Brien, *The Long War*, p.161.
50. S. Mac Stíofáin, *Memoirs of a Revolutionary*, p.146.
51. L. Clarke and K. Johnston, *Martin McGuinness: From Guns to Government* (Edinburgh: Mainstream Publishing, 2006), p.183.
52. CAIN Archive.
53. M. Turner, 'Living with Bombs', *Fortnight*, 1 October 1971, cited in Smith, *Fighting for Ireland?*
54. O'Brien, *The Long War*, p.22. I noted this in conversation (in November 2007) with an ex-IRA man in Belfast who is now involved in ex-prisoners' welfare, who blanched visibly at my use of the term 'military campaign'.
55. IRA Green Book, p.5.
56. T.P. Coogan, *The IRA* (London: HarperCollins, 1970), p.471.
57. The first having been used in the late 1940s. M. Davis, *Buda's Wagon: A Brief History of the Car Bomb* (London: Verso, 2007). Although the 1970s IRA leader Daithi Ó Conaill used to claim he was a 'father of the car bomb'.
58. See Smith, *Fighting for Ireland?*, p.115.
59. See F. Burton, *The Politics of Legitimacy* (London: Routledge & Kegan Paul, 1978), p.101, cited in Smith, *Fighting for Ireland?*, p.119.
60. See R. Knox, 'Shifting if not changing', *The Spectator*, 17 March 1973, cited in McGladdery, *The Provisional IRA in England*, p.67.
61. Prime Minister Margaret Thatcher's famous quote in the 1980s: 'Democratic nations must try to find ways to starve the terrorist and the hijacker of the oxygen of publicity on which they depend.' She tried to 'suffocate' the IRA by prohibiting British broadcasters from transmitting the voice of Sinn Féin leaders such as Gerry Adams. The ban, of course, merely prompted the broadcasters to seize on a loophole and guaranteed the Sinn Féin president even more airtime, albeit with a voice-over enunciating his words.
62. See M. Taylor, *The Terrorist* (London: Brassey's, 1988), p.26.
63. Steve Jones, interview with IRA leader Ruairi Ó Brádaigh, cited in McGladdery, *The Provisional IRA in England*, p.75.
64. G. Adams, *Peace in Ireland: A Broad Analysis of the Present Situation* (Long Kesh: Provisional Sinn Féin, 1976), p.14.
65. See Smith, *Fighting for Ireland?*, p.126.
66. 'IRA split by struggle for power', *Sunday Telegraph*, 22 December 1974.
67. See Smith, *Fighting for Ireland?*, p.131.
68. IRA Green Book, p.5.
69. E. Moloney, *A Secret History of the IRA* (London: W.W. Norton & Co, 2002), p.156.
70. D. Ó Donghaile, 'Review of Moloney,' *A Secret History of the IRA*, *Sunday Times*, 27 October 2002.
71. IRA man quoted in O'Brien, *The Long War*, p.162.
72. IRA man quoted in O'Brien, *The Long War*, p.161.

73. Although the 'Paddy factor' was a term used by the security forces to describe IRA 'own goals' – their bombs going off in the process of being constructed or deployed.
74. Personal communication, former Irish army EOD operative, November 2007.
75. IRA staff report (seized by gardaí on arrest of Séamus Twomey, IRA chief of staff, in Dublin, December 1977).
76. From Danny Morrison's speech at the 1981 Sinn Féin ard fheis (annual conference): '... will anyone here object, if with a ballot paper in this hand and an Armalite in this hand, we take power in Ireland?' Quoted in 'By Bomb and Bullet', AP/RN, 5 November 1981, cited in Smith, *Fighting for Ireland?*, p.155.
77. 'IRA geared to a Long War', *An Phoblacht*, 9 December 1978.
78. See McGladdery, *The Provisional IRA in England*, p.115.
79. Ibid., p.143.
80. 'A constant level of resistance', *Iris* (July 1983).
81. J. Holland and H. McDonald, *INLA Deadly Divisions* (Dublin: Poolbeg, 1996), pp. 125–6.
82. MIPT (Memorial Institute for the Prevention of Terrorism) Terrorism Knowledge Base, the INLA group profile.
83. O'Brien, *The Long War*, p.162.
84. Former commander of 321 Squadron, Roger Davies, told me that he and his team would recognise IRA operatives in the street and rude gestures would be exchanged, in a deceptively good-humoured spirit. On the other side, Tommy McKearney told me that the brakes on the British forces coming down totally on the IRA (Gibraltar and other operations excepted) enabled continuation of military operations.
85. O'Brien, *The Long War*, p.163.
86. IRA senior campaigner quoted in O'Brien, *The Long War*, p.277.
87. O'Brien, *The Long War*, p.172.
88. Ibid.
89. Sinn Féin policy document (Dublin: Provisional Sinn Féin, 1987), p.14, cited in Smith, *Fighting for Ireland?*, p.174.
90. Smith, *Fighting for Ireland?*, p.190.
91. O'Brien, *The Long War*, p.226.
92. Ibid., p.263.
93. Using explosives, for example, other than conventional explosives, or weapons of mass effect.
94. See Geraghty, *The Irish War*, p.237.
95. IRA campaigner quoted in O'Brien, *The Long War*, p.277.
96. O'Brien, *The Long War*, p.268.
97. J. McCartney, 'Murder and scandal may stop the "Brothers" chuckling', *Sunday Telegraph*, 28 October 2007.
98. 'Mortars "not primed to go off"', *Guardian*, 14 March 1994.
99. See Moloney, *A Secret History of the IRA*, p.430.
100. See McGladdery, *The Provisional IRA in England*, p.198.
101. See T. Harnden, *Bandit Country: The IRA & South Armagh* (London: Hodder & Stoughton, 1999), pp.5–10, 13–14.
102. *Belfast Telegraph*, IRA statement, 8 December 1995, cited in McGladdery, *The Provisional IRA in England*, p.189.
103. This term, it is now believed, was never actually used in the IRA's approaches to the British to begin talks. Another misquote becoming an urban media myth.
104. Interview by Prof. R. English on the BBC's 'Inside Out in the North West' on Monday 27 February 2006.
105. 'IRA bomb threats paralyse M-ways', *Guardian*, 4 April 1997.
106. 'Semtex in terrorist armoury is key to growing threat', *Independent*, 31 December 1988, cited in Smith, *Fighting for Ireland?*, p.215.
107. S. Boyne, 'Uncovering the Irish Republican Army', *Jane's Intelligence Review*, 1 August 1996.
108. See R. English, *Armed Struggle: The History of the IRA* (London: Macmillan, 2003), p.295.
109. *An Phoblacht*, 24 July 1997.
110. For the definitive account of activities in this diehard republican area, see Harnden, *Bandit Country*.
111. See English, *Armed Struggle*, p.299.
112. J. Freedland, 'Surge in Support for Irish Unity', *Guardian*, 21 August 2001.
113. Correspondence to Richard English from Patrick Magee, 9 October 2000, cited in English, *Armed Struggle*, p.303.

114. For the definitive account of the intelligence war, see M. Urban, *Big Boys' Rules* (London: Faber & Faber, 1993).
115. See English, *Armed Struggle*, p.308.
116. G. Adams, *Who Fears to Speak...?: The Story of Belfast and the 1916 Rising* (Belfast: Beyond the Pale, 2001 (1st edn 1991)), p.viii.
117. Northern Ireland Annual Abstract of Statistics, 2002.
118. Freedland, 'Surge in Support for Irish Unity', *Guardian*, 21 August 2001.
119. See Smith, *Fighting for Ireland?*, p.335.
120. A.R. Oppenheimer, 'The Countdown Begins', *Bulletin of the Atomic Scientists* (May/June 2002).
121. Tommy McKearney, former IRA commander and Long Kesh hunger striker, interview with the author, July 2007.
122. Ibid.
123. Ibid.
124. Ibid.
125. From online review of D. McKittrick, *Making Sense of the Troubles* (Penguin Books Ltd, 2001), http://cain.ulst.ac.uk/events/directrule/mckittrick00.htm
126. Personal communication, former Irish army EOD operative, November 2007.
127. Including from so-called 'prawn-cocktail Provos' - who provided moral and financial, but not active fighting, support. See C. Ryder, *A Special Kind of Courage: 321 Squadron - Battling the Bombers* (London: Methuen, 2006), p.111.
128. See English, *Armed Struggle*, p.338.
129. G. Adams, *The Politics of Irish Freedom* (Dingle: Brandon, 1986), p.88.
130. See English, *Armed Struggle*, p.355.
131. Prime minister's speech on Northern Ireland, 18 October 2002, 10 Downing Street website, http://www.number-10.gov.uk/output/Page1732.asp
132. See P. Taylor, *Loyalists* (London: Bloomsbury, 1999), p.123.
133. M. Sutton, *An Index of Deaths from the Conflict in Ireland 1969–1993* (Belfast: Beyond the Pale Publications, 1994).

Two

Dynamiters to City Destroyers

The car bomb is the nuclear weapon of guerrilla warfare.
Washington Post columnist, Charles Krauthammer

In the lexicon of deadly instruments of destruction, the bomb was *the* weapon of the twentieth century and continues to be so. From the most primitive homemade device to the most advanced fission and fusion weapons, bombs have blasted millions off the face of the planet and constitute the most impersonal of weapons. Their victims include, apart from the vaporised and the mutilated, those bereaved by, close to, and responding to the attacks. They also include the perpetrators themselves – either through blowing themselves up (known, in the case of the IRA, rather predictably, by British forces as 'own goals') or being punished for their actions, or simply having to live with remorse over what they have done. Bombs may be the most indiscriminate of weapons, but they have been increasingly used for specific targeting, by militaries and by terrorists. The IRA's love affair with the bomb was to last for well over a century.

While the threat we now face in some ways dwarfs the IRA campaigns – on 11 September 2001, Al Qaeda took more lives in one day than the Provisional IRA in its entire history,[1] and they plan even more devastating 'spectaculars' – the relentlessness of the bombings and shootings, particularly in Northern Ireland during the height of the Troubles during the 1970s, meant the threat was constant and everyday. But the IRA, beginning with the Irish rebellion, instituted the concept of 'selective terrorism, acts of terror against representatives of a target class, to achieve political objectives. The use of terror was limited to members of the selected class: representatives of the British government operating in Ireland.'[2]

If all terrorists share the common belief that terror is a tool of change, then the bomb was the IRA's main tool of the armed struggle against British occupation. The IRA's first operational manual, issued to Volunteers in 1956, stresses the importance of bombs for sabotage, which became a common means of resistance during the Second World

War. 'For many guerrilla operations explosives can be used to make up arms deficiencies ... Breaking down enemy resistance is easier once explosives are employed.'[3]

But the IRA began bombing long before then – it in fact executed the first planned insurgent bombing campaign in history, in the 1880s – when terrorism, often waged by anarchists, typically took the form of assassination attempts on heads of state and bomb attacks on public buildings.

This chapter documents the most significant campaigns up to and including the 1970s in the north of Ireland, focusing on the types of bombs used: grenades, petrol bombs, incendiaries, dynamite and gelignite devices, letter bombs, and that most destructive of IRA adapted inventions, the car and truck bomb, with time delay, booby trap and other added sophistications. The 'spectaculars' of the 1980s and 1990s, details of weapons acquisition and training, and the explosives, expertise and IED technologies used in the campaigns will be dealt with in subsequent chapters. As stated in the Terrorist Explosives Handbook, and a British Intelligence Report on Northern Ireland,[4] 'the pikes and Thompson machine guns of bygone eras are mostly a memory now. It has become the era of the bomber.'

The IRA pioneered the homemade device. Household, agricultural, industrial and military items were all created or purloined to make thousands of devices. Targets were wide-ranging: apart from military targets – barracks, police stations, troop convoys, and individual members of the security forces and the hated Royal Ulster Constabulary (RUC). Economic targets included shops (sometimes rows of shops at a time), restaurants, pubs, hotels, public buildings, railway stations, subway trains – and whole city centres. Through thirty years of active service the bombs grew from small and basic to huge and sophisticated. Whereas it took dozens of bombs to lay waste Belfast and Derry in the 1970s, just one bomb did the job in Manchester in June 1996.

THE FENIAN DYNAMITERS

Armed uprisings against British rule took place in 1798, 1803, 1848 and 1867. But the American-led Fenian dynamiting campaign of 1881 to 1887 was the forerunner of the IRA's specific targeting of the British mainland in the 1930s, and later by the Provisionals in the 1970s, 1980s and 1990s. Between March 1883 and February 1885 thirteen dynamite devices were detonated without warning in London. Large Irish communities in Britain enabled Fenian operators to rise up in rebellion and attack the English as 'the Irishman within his gate'.[5] Two bombs exploded on the

London underground, injuring sixty, substantially increasing fears that the bombers could strike anywhere in London.[6] This was an action that the IRA did not repeat in the twentieth century, although railway stations were often targeted. And it was to be the twenty-first century before Londoners were similarly attacked, but by an entirely different type of terrorist.

The first Irish bomb to go off in England was the placing of a stock of gunpowder outside the walls of Clerkenwell prison, which blew out its walls on 13 December 1867 in order to free a Fenian prisoner, killing twelve and injuring 120.[7]

Some thirty-nine incidents were to follow. The 'Skirmishers', as they were appropriately called, aimed for targets very much according to modern terrorist strategy: stations, military barracks, gasworks, public buildings and tourist centres such as the Tower of London, on which one attack injured sixteen visitors on what became known as 'Dynamite Sunday'.[8] The Fenians' main coups, however, were to attack new government offices in Parliament Street on 15 March 1883 and to dynamite a lavatory below Scotland Yard in March 1883 destroying much of the building – actions that were eerily echoed in March 1973 when a car bomb was exploded outside the Old Bailey.[9] But the most daring attack, on 24 January 1885, involved detonating a bomb inside the House of Commons – the first and only time since Guy Fawkes (although the British do not choose to commemorate this event by burning Irish Roman Catholic effigies or setting off fireworks every 24 January, choosing instead to burn symbolically the earlier Catholic insurgent).

While the dynamite bombings did not – as with many future incidences – have the desired effect of inspiring insurrection out of resultant coercion, they set the precedent of bringing the Irish republican fight for freedom to the shores of Britain. Of prime importance was that they also forced Gladstone to consider Irish home rule – while managing to cause injury, mayhem and an anti-Irish backlash. Apart from dynamite, the Fenians used crude pipe-bombs, most notably outside London's Duke Street police station in May 1881.[10] From 1867, another forty-nine years were to pass before Irish nationalists attempted armed resistance.

THE 1916 EASTER UPRISING

The influx of weapons from Germany in July 1914 included 1,500 rifles and 45,000 round of ammunition – landed by yacht at Howth, Co. Dublin. The Ulster Volunteer Force in the North had already landed 35,000 rifles at Larne, Co. Antrim. Many of the guns the Irish Volunteers obtained from Germany were already obsolete. A further shipment of Mauser rifles and 1 million rounds of ammunition which came in on the *Aud* in April 1916 were lost to the rebels when the German captain scuttled the vessel to prevent the weapons falling into British hands. But this great loss did not deter the instigators of the uprising, in which the preferred weapon was the Webley revolver and the Mauser C96 9-mm Parabellum, which offered more firepower as a semi-automatic pistol could fire one to twenty rounds.[11] Although many home-made bombs were cobbled together for combat use, the gun and not the bomb was the weapon of the rebellion: black-market revolvers and pistols from Britain and Europe were used mainly in assassinations.[12]

BOMBING BETWEEN THE WARS: THE 1920S AND 1930S

Following the Uprising, the newly evolved and increasingly tenacious IRA in 1920 once again extended its fight to British cities. Whereas the IRA campaign in Ireland mainly comprised gunfight-and-grenade ambushes by flying columns and the shooting of targeted individuals, in Britain it involved some 427 incendiary attacks and acts of sabotage in major cities.[13] Co-ordinated arson attacks in Liverpool resulted in millions of pounds' worth of damage.[14] Railway stations were targeted once again, and the precedent for disrupting infrastructure – cutting down telegraph poles – resulted in massive disruption of communications.[15]

Grenades, also stolen from the British, formed the basis of homemade versions modelled on the No. 5 Mills grenade. They were tested by Volunteers as there was no guarantee the weapons would explode. An underground munitions factory in Dublin was churning out these homemade grenades in 1917. Some were made of a segmented iron cylinder, roughly cast with a wooden plug and equipped with a match fuse. Another early IED was a 'mud bomb' used to attack police barracks; these were made of yellow clay, which was like putty, wrapped around gelignite, which had a fuse and detonator attached. The clay would enable the bombs to adhere to roofs and walls of barrack buildings against which they were thrown, causing incendiary effects from the paraffin-soaked turf that would cave in on the occupants.[16]

In May 1923 the Civil War ended with the IRA order to its Volunteers to dump arms. By the 1930s the anti-Treaty IRA had been defeated by a combination of Irish Free State and British forces in Ireland, the island had been partitioned according to the 1922 Treaty, and the rump of the IRA, although greatly weakened, was still determined to 'assert the sovereignty and unity of the republic proclaimed in

Easter Week 1916' and 'destroy the power of British imperialism in Ireland'.[17] The IRA called upon Britain to 'withdraw her armed forces, her civilian officials and institutions, and representatives of all kind from *every part* of Ireland'.[18] With England as the 'enemy of Ireland's freedom',[19] its cities would once again, in early 1939, be the target of IRA bombs – this time made from gelignite and a variety of other substances brought onto the mainland by boat: potassium chlorate, ferrous oxide, sulphuric acid and aluminium powder, along with electrical detonators and the original timing device, the alarm clock.[20] The campaign came at a most vulnerable time for a country still recovering from the Depression and about to enter another world war.

Known as the S-plan, the campaign was arguably the most controversial ever waged by the IRA due to the growing associations of some factions with the Nazis, while most merely followed the maxim 'my enemy's enemy is my friend'. The campaign – to take the fight away from Civil War-ravaged Ireland to disrupt the economy of Britain – never bore fruit, although 291 incidents in 1939 caused mayhem and injury in London, Manchester (one fatality) and Birmingham.[21] The most deadly attack was in Coventry – soon to be the most devastated city by German bombs – on 25 August 1939, when a bomb planted in the city centre killed five people, after the IRA operative panicked and left it in a crowded area.[22] The IRA also tried, but failed, to blow up Nelson's Column in Dublin – an enduring symbol of British power. Despite having been ordered to avoid civilian casualties, the operatives made their way through crowds carrying sticks of easily ignited gelignite. An IRA splinter group succeeded in blowing up the statue on the fiftieth anniversary of the Easter Rising.

The 1930s campaign also, above all, held alarming implications for, and went against the main tenets of, a movement committed to freedom for its people. The S-plan's mastermind, Seán Russell, IRA chief of staff, former quartermaster general in the Irish Civil War and seeker of Nazi support, was backed by Irish Americans and targeted military installations, bridges, aerodromes and communications infrastructure such as the BBC's transmitters.[23] Such targets comprise an enduring contemporary threat that has still not been fulfilled, but is highly prized, by today's terrorists. Other IRA leaders opposed the plan on account that it would kill and injure ordinary English working people and so they wanted the bombings to be aimed at military targets only.[24]

This period saw the IRA succeed in bringing weapons over to England successfully, but attacks were haphazard, reckless and ill conceived, with letterboxes, telephone kiosks, cinema cloakrooms and businesses as targets

– all of which would risk or involve civilian casualties. (The IRA man who carried the Coventry bomb in the carrier of his bicycle was diagnosed as mentally disturbed.[25]) Packed cinemas were attacked with teargas. Incendiary devices were used to attack post offices and hotels. Balloon bombs (in which the explosive is detonated by acid eating through the rubber of the balloon and igniting iron oxide)[26] were detonated at Madame Tussaud's in London. On 2 July 1939 at left-luggage offices at King's Cross and Victoria stations, IRA bombs took a doctor's life and injured twenty-two. On 22 February 1940, seven people were injured by a bomb left in a bin in Oxford Street (many of which would be removed throughout London in subsequent bombing campaigns, never to be restored). But by then the campaign had petered out due to security measures, raids and arrests – and the increasing disfavour the campaign was receiving within the IRA.[27]

At such a sensitive time it achieved nuisance value only[28] and was, militarily, actually less successful than the 1880s 'dynamite war' if only because targets of far higher prestige value than in 1939–40 were attacked. It was also poorly organised and co-ordinated and had little or no political underpinning or propaganda value, but was chiefly a means of perpetuating violence as the core value of the republican tradition.[29]Nevertheless, the fear tactics of attacking British cities at a time of national crisis was not conducive to eliciting support for the Irish cause. There were also great risks taken: one Volunteer, Joe Deighan, would take his bombs in lunch boxes onto the bus; public transport was preferred as bus conductors and drivers were unlikely to remember the operative. But conveying explosives on jolting vehicles ran the risk of premature detonation.[30]

IN REMISSION: FROM THE 'BORDER CAMPAIGN' TO THE PROVOS

Once Ireland became a fully independent state in 1948, its government cracked down on the remnants of the IRA. The movement's activities in the North after partition, with sectarian violence on the increase, were sporadic, directionless and ineffective and consisted mainly of the odd bomb attack on military barracks, gunfights with the police and robberies. The IRA had been decimated by harsh security measures in both the north and south of Ireland since the Civil War. The next military campaign following several successful IRA arms raids, and acquisition of weapons from the US[31] was to focus on the northern border, its main aims being to wreak havoc among the British forces and disrupt the northern economy. When the southern government showed little interest in the problem of partition, and the growing discrimination against the north-ern Catholic minority (and RUC killings of republicans), the IRA re-assembled old elements of itself and stepped into the vacuum. There was also a re-hardening of attitudes: according to IRA leader and icon Thomas MacCurtain, 'Violence is not the best way, violence is not the most comforting way ... but it is the only way.'[32] But the IRA pledged not to attack southern targets, police or others; the authorities to a degree turned a blind eye to the revived border campaign. The US was also unwilling to help the IRA's cause, despite its vast and republican-sympa-thetic Irish-American community, because of its close alliance with Britain within NATO.[33]

Beginning on 12 December 1956, with attacks on ten separate targets, including bomb and fire attacks on communications (a BBC relay trans-mitter), a courthouse, bridges, and a failed attack in 1954 on Gough bar-racks, Co. Armagh,[34] the campaign was once again on the whole poorly organised and merely served to annoy the British and further harden the unionists (as if they needed to be), and led to the re-introduction of internment (which turned out to be the IRA's main recruiting sergeant in the early 1970s). Nevertheless, the Gough barracks attack showed signs of the old daredevil ingenuity and bravado in the IRA's campaign in the War of Independence. The barracks was infiltrated by an IRA man, Seán Garland, who had successfully signed up as a British soldier. The IRA unit that attacked the poorly guarded building was kitted out in polyglot British army gear following a raid on a Dublin army surplus store. The raid yielded a haul of guns – the unit took every weapon in the armoury. Two further raids – on Omagh barracks in October 1954 and Aborfield barracks in Berkshire in 1955 – failed, with the first pro-ducing the first gun battle between the IRA and the British since 1921.[35]

A further attack on Gough barracks on 5 September 1957 involved a 2-kg gelignite-guncotton device on an alarm-clock timer; hidden inside a zipped bag abandoned near an explosives store, it was discovered by a sentry, removed and, after one of its three electric detonators failed to ignite the explosive, was safely dismantled by an EOD operative.[36]

Bomb attacks on RUC stations followed, with the first use of booby trap bombs, one of which killed an RUC officer in August 1957. One attack, in which a landmine exploded prematurely, took the lives of five IRA men. The RUC and the British offset the border raids and ambushes by blowing up roads and bridges and drafting more men into their ranks. British troops had to keep armed guards at explosives stores and commercial dis-tributors and use escorts for transported explosives. This forced the IRA to acquire further explosives from the Republic and British mainland, where they took advantage of lax regulations. Many of the explosives thus acquired would be sent by post or freight service; police in both Belfast and Dublin made regular intercepts of these packages.[37]

The height of the border campaign was Operation Harvest, which was a series – over twenty – of multiple attacks in December 1956 by four rejuvenated flying columns of twenty volunteers per column, which had been drilled and assembled for the kind of attack seen in the 1920s. The aim was to make the North ungovernable through a 'war of liberation' – resulting in the departure of the British. Beginning on 11 December, explosions rang out for days on end in the blowing up of bridges, the local television station, police stations and other strategic targets. The Magherafelt courthouse was burned down; the barracks at Enniskillen was damaged by a bomb, as was the BBC transmitter at Derry. However, as the IRA avoided any form of sectarian conflict, it underestimated the 'inside' enemy – the viciously sectarian RUC – which alongside the British army provided an insurmountable opposition. It is also hard to imagine that in the midst of the mayhem the IRA followed strict UN rules of engagement, including always showing arms and the wearing of an Irish tricolour flash on their uniform sleeves.[38]

The Irish government, under pressure from the British, also deployed extra troops along the border. These troops turned out to be as much a thorn in the IRA's side as the British and the RUC forces.[39] This resulted in the IRA becoming weary of the campaign – particularly as many of the weapons the flying columns had seized were recaptured – along with the feeling that IRA volunteers had given their lives for nothing[40] and that the ranks had been depleted by long prison sentences[41] and further punitive measures by the Irish Republic: the Offences Against the State Act of 1958.[42] The weapons procured by the IRA for the border campaign were more sophisticated than those used by the state army in the South at the time. The landmine was a common weapon, one of which killed five republicans when it detonated prematurely in November 1957 at Edentubber, Co. Down.[43] Bombs were usually gelignite devices after the IRA stole over 110 kg of the commercial explosive from military stores at the start of the campaign. The bombs would be ignited by the bombers before they fled, and could be also made from fireworks – pillaging the gunpowder – which could also cause serious burns.[44] Most of these improvised explosive devices (IEDs) were relatively basic and resembled the 'cartoon' notion of a bomb: stick(s) of gelignite, a detonator, power unit (small battery) and alarm clock. But the cartoon resemblance ended there, as many devices were booby trapped and concealed – a foretaste of what was to come in infinitely greater measure after 1969. One such device killed a police sergeant investigating suspicious activity at an empty house near Coalisland, Co. Tyrone on 17 August 1957; when he kicked in the kitchen door to force entry, the bomb inside exploded.[45]

But these weapons were not always reliable, most notably in the attack on the RUC Brookeborough barracks on 1 January 1957 – when two planted at the door of the barracks failed to go off.[46] But after some 500 violent incidents, including the deaths of many republicans,[47] the IRA called off the campaign in 1962 after the Irish government set up Special Criminal courts to deal with border violence.[48] The organisation then sank in what appeared to be terminal decline and entered an introspective period in which the 'arms struggle was not the way forward on its own'.[49] But the 1950s and all previous campaigns would pale into insignificance compared to the mayhem that was to come.

RIOTING WEAPONS

The range of devices used by the Provisional IRA (PIRA) from the late 1960s onwards beggars belief. The early phases of the bombing campaigns in Northern Ireland and 'mainland' Britain involved frequent attacks with smaller devices, growing to include the larger command-wire mines and car and truck bombs.

However, early PIRA bombs were often crude. Batteries led to bombs being modified but most devices were small-scale, typical device containers being cigarette packets, padded envelopes and shopping bags, which featured on police posters.[50] Time bombs were constructed from a few sticks of dynamite and commercial detonators stolen from construction sites or rock quarries and attached to ordinary battery-powered alarm clocks. Neither device was very reliable and often put the bomber at considerable risk. The process of placing and actually lighting the first type of device carried with it the inherent potential to attract undesired attention while affording the bomber little time to effect the attack and make good his or her escape. Although the second type of device was designed to mitigate precisely this danger, its timing and detonation mechanism was often so crude that accidental or premature explosions were not infrequent, thus causing some terrorists inadvertently to kill themselves.[51]

The rioting that characterised the early days of the Troubles, when civil rights marchers were constantly harassed and threatened by loyalist mobs, saw the widespread and constant use of petrol bombs. The police and British army became the target of these crude incendiaries, having been moved in to restore law and order and, officially, protect the nationalist community. But it had become increasingly repressive in its treatment of members of that community; beatings, house raids, and the use of rubber bullets on rioters became commonplace.

INCENDIARIES

Before and just after the IRA split into the Official IRA and the Provisionals, weapons were few and far between and rioters and newly signed-up volunteers used anything against the troops and police, or to set fire to buildings, that they could lay their hands on. The petrol bombs were the most basic of weapons, used by rioters on both sides, consisting of milk bottles and cloth wick. A more advanced, chemical-ignition type of Molotov cocktail was also thrown. These incendiaries caused horrendous burns, injuring some 10 per cent of 3,000 serving police during the opening phase, which bordered on, and could at times be classified, as a civil war.[52]

Petrol-bombing would be orchestrated with young republicans such as Bogside Republican Youth (BRY), which would create street disorder to push the troops into vulnerable target positions. The youths would pelt Rovers with petrol bombs made from big sweets jars. These simple and deadly devices would engulf the vehicles in flames, forcing them to stall as the air supply to the engine was cut off.[53]

In 1970 came a more advanced type of incendiary, which was placed in homemade cardboard boxes held together by tape. A finger ring was attached to a protruding wooden rod, the interior end of which sat in between a spring-loaded clothes peg. The rod separated electrical contacts attached to the open jaws of the clothes peg, each of which had a small wire leading to two 1.5-V batteries that were connected in a series and which terminated in a small heating element buried in a plastic envelope filled with sugar and a glue of chloral hydrate. Withdrawing the rod closed the circuit and ignited the incendiary, resulting in an intense fireball.[54]

In 1973 these devices were further advanced, when two unexploded incendiaries in cassette boxes revealed their innards as a watch timer, battery, and torch bulb as an igniter which was embedded in the explosive. The exposed filament of the torch bulb set off the charge once the timer ran out and activated the battery. The damage wrought by these devices throughout 1974 was, according to one EOD operative, as damaging as the car bomb.[55] Both incendiaries and car bombs were in equal measure the chief tools of destruction, with 1972 the main year for car bomb attacks and 1977 the year that fire bombs were widely used to destroy shops, garages and offices. They were often deployed in conjunction, as in April 1982, when three blast incendiaries blew up an auto supplies shop in Armagh, to be followed during the same day by a welter of car bomb attacks in several towns in the province.

Soon the barrage of incendiaries and other devices became reported in the world's press on an almost daily basis. Northern Ireland became synonymous with bombing and terrorism. Posters appeared throughout the province showing a classic planted IED of the time: a cigarette packet, a padded envelope, and a shopping bag: 'They may look harmless but they could be firebombs. Report anything suspicious.' A huge effort was under way to search business premises for bombs as they would be abandoned by bombers (often female) to explode after shop staff had left for home.[56]

Much of the havoc caused was by false alarms and hoaxes, which increased along with the number of actual bombings. False alarms went up from 276 to 939 in 1971; hoaxes went from 51 in 1970–71 to 658 in 1971–72.[57] The hoaxes led to evacuation of buildings and traffic diversion and other disruption – as well as the deployment of increased numbers of police and troops. Parcels left outside buildings; bags left on buses; deliveries that weren't ordered; all of these commonplace events had the potential to interrupt normal life, if you could call it that.

No-warning devices also increased. A typical example was the Abercorn restaurant bomb in March 1972 (see below): Ann Owens, who worked as a comptometer, who had previously been injured in a no-warning attack on the Electricity Board HQ in Belfast, was killed along with her friend and another 130 were injured. In July 2002 the IRA gave an unprecedented apology to 'noncombatants' killed by them (not including the security forces). But an interview with Martin McGuinness on the US radio station WBAI in July 2002 revealed the true attitude of the IRA to warnings before attacks, in a soundbite played from a previous interview conducted with McGuinness in April 1972 in Derry when he was an IRA commander there:

> Q: Inevitably some civilians are going to be hurt in these explosions.
> A: … But we have always given ample warning, and anybody that was hurt was hurt *through their own fault* [italics added by the author]; been too nosy, sticking around the place where the bomb was after they were told to get clear. It's only been their own fault that they've been hurt.

The WBAI interviewer repeated the phrase 'their own fault that they got hurt'. He then asked whether McGuinness's thoughts had changed, allowing for the fact that things were said thirty years ago that we'd probably want to have back. There was a refusal to answer that question, adding that thanks to the work of those involved in the peace process, we were living in a far better place than thirty or even ten years ago.[58] The 1972 statement may be set alongside another McGuinness made that same year: '… there was an army in our town, in our country, and they weren't there to give out flowers. Armies should be fought by armies.'[9]But of course, in the bombings and shootings of urban guerrilla warfare, other people get in the way.

Some of the early delay mechanisms (see Chapter 6) were deployed in the incendiaries. The ends of the clothes pegs away from the contacts in the device were squeezed together and wrapped with soldering wire. The spring tension of the peg stretched the solder – allowing the contacts to touch and complete the circuit. Some of these devices were concealed in cigarette packs, which would be smuggled into shops and would explode after close of business. Many took life: in February 1977 an incendiary device killed twelve people, all of them Protestants, in the La Mon House hotel in Co. Down where collie-dog club and cycling club gatherings were taking place. These weapons were used throughout the conflict; indeed, similar firebombing techniques were used by the Real IRA in attacks on a number of shops in Newry, Co Down in 2006.[60] The 'blast incendiary' made its mark in 1977, a metal pipe filled with a commercial explosive such as gelignite and aluminium filings which was taped to a petrol container and timing and power unit. The whole package would be bagged and attached to metal security grilles, and when exploded, created an uncontrollable fireball.[61] A further box-type incendiary which used potassium nitrate, chlorate and incorporated commercially available timing chips in a Perspex box was deployed in February 1981 against commercial premises in Belfast, Derry and Armagh,

The incendiary explosive used in the La Mon attack was a mixture of recrystallised ammonium nitrate and aluminium filings attached to a can of petrol.[62] The function room was cascaded with burning petrol and the bomb rendered the whole building an inferno within minutes.

Some had enhanced combustion effects by the inclusion of lighter fuel capsules.[63] Increasingly harassed fire crews were hampered by hoaxes that were mounted at the same time as live devices. So terrible were these incendiaries that one EOD operative, Capt Mark Wickham, who had to deal with one such device left in a pile of boxes in a garage supermarket – and which exploded – said that had he been breathing in rather than breathing out, internal injuries he suffered (as well as extensive burns) would have killed him.[64]

The mailed letter bombs used in the 1930s campaign were updated and became manila envelopes containing two plastic bags filled with a

sugar and chloral hydrate mixture, the first containing a wax container
of sulphuric acid within a rubber balloon or condom, the second, petrol.
The acid container was crushed prior to posting the letter in the slot of
a letterbox or premises, which ate through the rubber and ignited the
sugar and chloral hydrate at some undefined future time.[65]

At first the Provisionals' abilities to construct real improvised explosive devices (IEDs) was hampered equally by lack of materials and
expertise. The lack of stolen explosives meant volunteers had to make
their own. Early attempts often resulted in 'own goals', such as in June
1970, when several members of the IRA leadership blew themselves up
as well as killing two children in the house in Derry where the botched
manufacture took place.[66]

Among the smaller but horrendously deadly devices were nail bombs,
which incorporated 10 grams of dynamite wrapped in corrugated
cardboard, with 70-cm nails embedded in the corrugations and taped
up. A 70-cm fuse attached to a non-electric blasting cap inserted in the
dynamite was ignited with a match and thrown at troops, who would
spot the visible fuse on the bomber. So to prevent detection, matches
were fixed to the fuse end which, when scraped along the pavement and
the device thrown, ignited en route to the target, allowing the bomber to
escape. Another nail bomb type was described by the letter bomber
Shane Paul O'Doherty: ' … a tin can filled with explosives, nails
wrapped around it. We've got a short piece of burning fuse here to get
the delay, and a detonator. And the terrorist would simply light the fuse
and throw this in the direction of a patrol or maybe into a security forces
base where it would explode. Obviously, as its drawbacks, if the fuse
goes out, it's not going to explode.'[67]

A homemade version of the Claymore mine was also used against the
military. These came in long, thin boxes containing a layer of explosives
and a layer of nails or steel rods facing towards the target. It was set off by
a safety fuse and electrical firing, and incorporated a delay mechanism.[68]

TWO BOMBS A DAY

By the end of 1970, the IRA had planted 153 bombs, many of them targeted against Protestant businesses in Belfast city centre, largely avoiding civilian casualties.[69] In 1979 they were averaging fifteen explosions
per month.[70] During 1971 alone, however, more than 1,000 bombs
caused fifty deaths and hundreds of injuries. During the period of
internment and following the Bloody Sunday shootings in January 1972,
IRA recruitment soared, and two bombs were detonated daily, including

a half-day period on 21 July – Bloody Friday – when twenty explosions destroyed banks, shops and pubs.[71] In 1972 there were 1,300 IRA explosions – a staggering total when considered against today's terrorist threat. Hoax bombs and false alarms also caused fear and confusion, and diverted the security forces and bomb disposal squads. At the end of 1971 false alarms had increased from 276 to 939 and hoaxes, from 'only' fifty-one in 1970–71 to a staggering 658 in 1971–72.[72]

In order to make Northern Ireland economically defunct, bombs tore apart its city centres. The campaign peaked between late July and early August, in which ninety riots and attacks on military posts involved up to four petrol bombs and newly acquired high-explosives daily. One Derry volunteer said that ' … It was not so much the physical damage you were doing as the sheer number of attacks. But it was still nice to get a car bomb and then "boom", a whole row of shops would be gone.'[73] The Europa hotel in Belfast was bombed a staggering twenty-six times.[74]

Not only the number, but also the size of bombs increased drastically in the early 1970s: from 2–3 kg in 1971, this rose to 18 kg in 1972; to 23 kg in 1973.[75] The early 1970s saw unprecedented bloodshed. This book does not deal with all the shootings, tit-for-tat killings, but has rather focused on events that reflect particular elements of the IRA's strategy and tactics and use of weapons materials and expertise.

The range of people who died included civilians, members of the loyalist and republican groups, politicians, soldiers, police, hunger strikers, bombers, part-time paramilitaries and UDR men, alleged drug dealers and other criminals, joyriders, judges, armed robbers, individuals under suspicion of collusion with, or aiding through construction and other programmes, the British or the RUC, and alleged informers. The number of casualties reached such a level at this time that many went undocumented. The army did not always release information about casualties whereas the republicans – and also EOD (Explosives Ordnance Disposal) 321 Bomb Disposal Squadron – have long maintained a roll of honour.[76] While this book does not detail the many loyalist bombings and other terrorist crimes, it should be noted that these attacks continued in increasing viciousness throughout the conflict; in one month in 1973 – November – loyalist bomb attacks at twenty-seven exceeded IRA attacks by one.[77]

'BLOODY FRIDAY' AND ABERCORN

On 21 July 1972 ('Bloody Friday'), following the breakdown of a short-lived IRA ceasefire, no less than twenty-two bombs within a two-and-a-half-hour period took a surprisingly low death toll of nine people (from two of the bombs[78]) and 130 injuries.[79] But so intense were the attacks – bodies and body parts were scraped off walls and streets[80] – and in such a small area within Belfast city centre (under 2 sq km), that some were victims of more than one bomb.[81]

The targets were many and various. Here are just three examples. At 3.10 p.m. a car bomb exploded outside the Ulsterbus depot in Oxford Street which resulted in the greatest loss of life and the greatest number of casualties of the day's bombs. The area was being cleared but was still crowded when the bomb, in a Volkswagen estate car, exploded, killing two British soldiers and four Protestant Ulsterbus workers. At 3.20 p.m. a car bomb containing 23 kg of explosive blew up outside a row of shops on Cavehill Road, north Belfast, killing three. Those caught in the blast had no warning of the bomb. At 3.30 p.m. a landmine was detonated on the road to Nutts Corner, west of Belfast, just as a bus full of schoolchildren was passing. The driver saw the device and swerved, avoiding the worst of the blast. The bus may have been mistaken for a British army vehicle. The injured were seventy-seven women and girls and fifty-three men and boys. It was at first thought that eleven had died.[82]

Some twelve explosions had been reported within the Belfast city area with a further blast at Dundrod near Belfast airport. Most of the city blasts occurred outside the security net that had been recently introduced. The front page of the *Belfast Telegraph* recorded the day thus:

> As smoke and dust rose from the wreckage of the blasts, the air was filled with the sound of wailing sirens from ambulances, fire engines and police vehicles … This city has not experienced such a day of death and destruction since the German blitz of 1941.[83]

The same analogy appeared in the *Guardian*, which would have been more sympathetic to the civil rights movement:

> Friday, July 21, 1972, was a day of horror and shame in this stricken city. Even hardened newsmen recoiled with shock from the scenes of carnage witnessed in Belfast as firemen lifted the mangled bodies where bombs ripped through crowds of unsuspecting men, women and children at bus depots and other locations.
>
> In all my years of journalism, which included the worst days of the wartime blitzes, I have never seen scenes so horrible in this city and one felt a deep feeling of anger and shame that such deeds were planned and carried out by fellow Irishmen. All Ireland has been shamed by the events of this terrible July afternoon in Belfast.[84]

Some of the eyewitness accounts are gut-wrenching. A police officer who witnessed the bomb blast in Oxford Street said:

> You could hear people screaming and crying and moaning. The first thing that caught my eye was a torso of a human being lying in the middle of the street. It was recognisable as a torso because the clothes had been blown off and you could actually see parts of the human anatomy ... One of the most horrendous moments for me was seeing a head stuck to a wall ... we found vertebrae and a ribcage on the roof of a nearby building. The reason we found it was because the seagulls were diving on to it. I've tried to put it at the back of my mind for 25 years.[85]

In one of the explosions, a massive car bomb in the Lisburn Road, there were fears that the several thousand gallons stored in the garage's petrol tanks would explode. And on the same day, and reported on the same front page of the *Belfast Telegraph*, a massive 330-lb bread van bomb exploded in Derry – in a street already damaged by bombs – having been driven through a tight army security screen; no-one was killed in this instance.

Bloody Friday confirmed the Provisional IRA as pursuing its aims through terror and as such proved a tactical setback for the rising republican movement. There was clearly a misunderstanding of how chaotic such multiple attacks would be. Telephone warnings had been given for all of the bombs (and many hoax calls, causing bomb scares in many locations). The IRA Belfast battalion insisted that organisations such as the press, Samaritans and Public Protection Agency were informed of bomb positions at least thirty minutes to one hour before each explosion. But the emergency services were overwhelmed. Reports confirmed this:

> As each bomb exploded there were cries of terror from people who thought they had found sanctuary but were in fact just as exposed as before.
>
> On the ground our men had difficulty in controlling crowds of stampeding people in the city centre as bomb after bomb exploded.[86]

This demonstrated the nightmare scenario of the enormous pressure on first responders to simultaneous and multiple attacks. 'The control room was chaotic, and in the streets our appliances were hampered by traffic jams ...'

Republican leaders were themselves alarmed by the extent of casualties. Former IRA leader Seán Mac Stíofáin said that the attacks had demonstrated that the IRA was strong enough to carry out a large number of simultaneous attacks but that the purpose of these was to 'impose a sudden and severe financial load on the British-Unionist system ... This loss of life compromised the intended effect of the whole effort.' But he tried to absolve the organisation in blaming the British for 'failing to pass on the warnings' saying that 'only one man with a loud hailer' was required to clear each target area. It would not be the last time the IRA would accuse the British of disregarding warnings for 'strategy policy reasons'.[87] Some members of the IRA have admitted that they overestimated the abilities of the British army and Belfast authorities to clear areas and miscalculated the extent of devastation that would follow. According to Brendan Hughes:

> What happened on Bloody Friday was a disaster. It was largely the fault of the IRA ... there was never an attempt at any time to kill people with the car bomb because the people who were putting the car bombs there had their own families shopping there as well.[88]

As such, Catholics as well as Protestants were killed, such as Margaret O'Hare, who had driven to north Belfast to collect her children from her mother's after hearing of the bombings. She was killed in the Cavehill explosion; her eleven-year-old daughter sustained facial injuries. Tales of great courage emerged: a fourteen-year-old Protestant boy was killed by the Cavehill Road car bomb when he went out to warn people to get away. He was posthumously awarded the Queen's Commendation for Bravery: his father, on finding him in the morgue, said 'I was able to identify him by his hands, and by a box of trick matches he had in his pocket and by the scout belt he was wearing.' He was said to have told his mother that 'something awful' was going to happen that day.[89]

An interesting disowning of republican actions also appeared in the same issue of the *Belfast Telegraph* as that which reported the bombings: the Northern Ireland Executive of Republican Clubs issued a statement deploring 'dastardly, sectarian bombings' in Belfast, calling for Provisional IRA members to disassociate themselves from the present leadership – which it alleged was being 'financed by big business interests in the Republic'.[90]

It was also acknowledged, nevertheless, by military officials that 'no matter how abhorrent the vast majority of people found this IRA strategy, it was effective. Many could be forgiven for wondering if the security forces were capable of containing the situation and *if the government would be prepared to pay the price for refusing to be intimidated* [italics added].'[91]

TABLE 2.1: TIMETABLE OF BLOODY FRIDAY, 21 JULY 1972

2.10 pm Smithfield bus station. Explosion in a car left in an enclosed yard. Extensive damage to houses in nearby Samuel Street. Many houses damaged.

2.16 pm Brookvale Hotel, Brookvale Ave., Antrim Road. Three men armed with a submachine-gun planted a bomb in the building in a suitcase. The hotel was wrecked and adjoining houses were damaged.

2.23 pm the station interior and the roof was blown off.

2.45 pm Star Taxis, Crumlin Road. The explosion was in a car beside the houses of the warders from the nearby Crumlin Road prison. The blast wrecked the taxi offices and caused damage to the houses.

2.48 pm Oxford Street bus station. Explosion in a car which had been driven into the rear of the station. Extensive damage to the office block and superficial damage to adjoining property. Six people killed and nearly forty injured.

2.48 pm Great Northern railway station, Gt. Victoria Street. Explosion in a Bedford van which was driven into the station and abandoned in the upper yard. Four buses were completely wrecked and forty-four others were damaged. Damage was also caused to the nearby canteen in Murrays tobacco factory.

2.50 pm Corner of Limestone Road. The explosion was in a hi-jacked car and caused damage to the premises of the Ulster Bank, nearby private houses, and six cars. Several people were injured.

2.50 pm York Hotel, Botanic Avenue. The explosion was in a bread van outside the hotel which was badly damaged. The van was blown to pieces. Surrounding property and approximately twenty cars also damaged.

2.55 pm Queen Elizabeth Bridge. The explosion was in a Ford car left on the bridge which normally carries heavy traffic, including bus services. Some damage, which was not extensive, was caused to the parapet.

2.57 pm Liverpool ferry terminus. Explosion in a mini car. Nearby Liverpool Bar extensively damaged. Superficial damage to the terminus itself.

2.57 pm Gas Dept. Office, Ormeau Ave. Explosion in a car left outside the building. Extensive damage.

2.59 pm Premises of John Irwin, seed merchants, Garmoyle Street. The explosion was in a box which had been planted in a store by armed men. The premises were wrecked.

3.04 pm Bridge spanning M1 motorway at Bellevue Arms, Antrim Road. A car believed to have contained explosives went on fire but not all the bombs went off and no damage was caused to other property.

3.05 pm Creightons garage, Upper Lisburn Road. The explosion was in a car which was demolished. Petrol pumps were set ablaze.

3.05 pm Junction of Salisbury Avenue and Hughenden Avenue. The explosion was in a van and caused extensive damage to an electricity substation and superficial damage to the pavilion of Salisbury Bowling Club.

3.05 pm Railway bridge at Finaghy Road North. The explosion was in a hijacked lorry and caused minor damage to the bridge and the parapet.

3.09 pm Footbridge over the railway line at Windsor Park football ground. The explosion was in a bag left on the centre span of the bridge. Concrete sleepers were blown on to the line, blocking it. Windows were broken in many nearby houses.

3.12 pm Eastwoods garage, Donegall Street. The explosion was in a Ford car which had been left on the premises. The damage was extensive and several people were injured.

3.15 pm Cavehill Road shopping centre. The explosion was in a hi-jacked vehicle and caused extensive damage to three shops and lesser damage to several other shops. Three people died – one a mother of seven, another a fourteen-year-old boy.

Source: CAIN Web Service, Bloody Friday (21 July 1972).

Economic targeting took many civilian lives and served to alienate people, including nationalists, from the movement. The bomb attack on the Belfast Abercorn restaurant on 4 March 1972, which killed two and horrifically injured 136 – some Catholic – was a case in point. In a research survey of terrorist bombings producing thirty or more casualties, the Abercorn bomb was found to have caused the highest rate – 81 per cent – of tympanic membrane rupture in victims from having been exploded in a confined space.[92]

The headline in the *Belfast Telegraph* – 'For God's sake, what sort of people are you?'[93] – reported as a statement made by a surgeon, John Robb, reflected what many were thinking: that 'even those who make up the ranks of the Provos know only too well that their image wouldn't withstand this kind of outrage at this stage in the terrorist campaign'.[94]

The accompanying photo on the front page of a dead victim is heralded with:
'What does this picture mean to you? If it appalls, if it is too shocking by far, it will have served a grim purpose.'[95] That purpose was to give the republican movement its worst publicity to date. The piece goes on to ask rhetorically:
'Is she Protestant? Is she Catholic? Is she Unionist? Is she Nationalist? For her and 135 others the bomb did not draw any distinctions.'

Of course, bombs and bullets will always claim the lives and limbs of the innocent. Many hundreds of times the innocent – the 'wrong people' – died. (Examples abound in the monumental work *Lost Lives*, which relates two such tragic examples: that of a nine-year-old Derry boy who caught a tripwire in his garden while playing and set off a bomb that killed him; and a man who burst into a Belfast house, shot the occupant dead, then realised he was in the wrong house.[96])

According to the pro-unionist *Belfast Telegraph* reports, a call was traced to a 'well-known pub on the Falls Road' – that the bomb had been placed in Castle Lane but with no mention of the Abercorn. The report states:

> One theory is that a man planted the bomb and then strolled from the car to the nearby pub, where he dialled the GPO operator to give the vague warning. What happened after that is mere speculation.
>
> The question is: Was the bomb meant to go off when it did? Probably not. Even those who make up the ranks of the Provos know only too well that their image couldn't withstand that kind of outrage at this stage in the terrorist campaign.

Security chiefs then were not surprised at the immediate denials from Dublin. The Provos would certainly have been playing a different tune if the dead and injured were soldiers or policemen.[97]

In the days when bomb attacks were increasing in their intensity, the reporter and many other observers and ordinary people could be forgiven for assuming that the IRA got the target wrong or that the bombing misfired – and that this was only to be regretted by them because of its bad PR consequences rather from any true moral regret for loss of civilian life. As Patrick Magee states in his book, quoting from a novel by fellow IRA man Danny Morrison that defended his organisation:

> The Belfast Brigade during the 1970s curfew had set off bombs outside banks in Anderstonstown in an attempt to overstretch the British army and RUC and lure them away from the Falls. It had also planted incendiary devices in city centre shops to create a similar diversion. As units proliferated a very low level [*sic*] campaign of bombing commercial and business premises in the centre of Belfast was begun. It took the war out of the Nationalist ghettoes and forced the extra deployment of soldiers in city centre checkpoints who would otherwise be engaged against the IRA in its bases.[98]

Of course, a retrospective apology in 2002 was expressed by the IRA, but such a strategy of bombing in civilian areas was bound to take innocent lives, laid bare by stories about some of the victims of the Abercorn bombing:

> Two sisters, Rosaleen McNern (22) and Jennifer (21), have both been seriously maimed. Rosaleen, who planned to marry a Co. Donegal man, has lost both legs, an arm and an eye. Her sister has lost both legs … A male victim lost two legs, and a female lost one leg and one arm. Another female lost one limb and three of the injured have lost eyes …
>
> The surgeon who has taken the unusual step of speaking out about the explosion is Mr John Robb.
>
> 'What do they (the bombers) think they are going to achieve?' he asked.
>
> 'When it is over, do they believe that they can put the bits of our society together any more than we surgeons can put the bits of a human body together when they have been destroyed irrevocably?'[99]

The IRA often lost people in this period and would go on to lose more. The frenetic pace of bomb planting meant there were often simultaneous attempts at multiple targets. On the day of the Abercorn blast, it was reported that:

Police shot dead an 18-year-old youth and injured another while trying to escape after planting a bomb at a Belfast factory – the Olympia Business Machines factory on Boucher Road – when a car with four men in it drew up outside the works. Two men got out of the vehicle and walked to the front of the building carrying a parcel. They set it down and then lit a fuse … While two men in the car drove off, the police challenged the two left behind, but they ran some 150 yards to the seven-foot perimeter fence. One of the bombers was shot dead by police as he attempted to scale the fence. He was later identified as Albert Kavanagh … His companion succeeded in getting over the fence but was shot and wounded … he was taken to the Royal Victoria Hospital, where he is understood to have undergone an emergency operation.

The bomb exploded at 7.40, breaking windows and bringing down ceilings …[100]

There were other reports of a shooting of an ex-UDR officer on the same day. And a short report two days later recounted poignantly how a room in a Belfast police station had been set up to store belongings of people who were maimed and injured: ' … handbags, wallets, coats, shoes, boots, have all been laid out … a child's furry dog … was nearly burnt to a cinder … detectives have been using every means at their disposal to trace owners.'[101]

An interesting postscript appeared many years later, in an article in the *Irish Times* by Fintan O'Toole who said he was a teenage Provo (Provisional IRA) supporter from Bloody Sunday until the Abercorn bomb, and questioned whether republicans ever looked back and wondered how they lost the moral authority that the Bloody Sunday massacre gave them.[102]

TARGETING THE MILITARY

Military targets were executed with maximum ruthlessness, to take maximum life. About half the total of 500 or so British soldiers to die in the conflict were killed in the years 1971–73.[103] There are too many ambushes on the British army to document, but two stand out from 1988: in June of that year a bomb under a van carrying British soldiers through Lisburn killed six, and a further bomb attack on soldiers returning to barracks near Ballygawley, Co. Tyrone using an astonishingly large amount – 91 kg – of Semtex high explosive (see Chapter 5) killed eight.

Such bombs were usually booby trap devices that would be placed under drains in country roads – the 'culvert bomb' – which proved so dangerous for British army patrols that all troops in the area began to be transported by helicopter, a policy which has been continued in theatre to the present. Two culvert bombs were used in the IRA's most deadly attack against troops – on 27 August 1979 on a three-vehicle convoy at Warrenpoint, Co. Down, killing eighteen British soldiers from the most hated regiment by republicans, the Parachute regiment. The first half-tonne bomb was planted under hay on a flat-bed lorry beside a dual carriageway and killed the first six soldiers in one of the convoy trucks. Twenty minutes after the first explosion, as the helicopter took off carrying some of the injured, the second device was detonated, killing twelve more soldiers who had been taking cover in a nearby gate house.[104]

The IRA started to booby trap bombs with anti-handling devices. If the package was moved, a tilt switch would trigger the electrical circuit and set off the bomb. The army became adept at using a hook and line to pull suspect parcels away from buildings. They then placed a small amount of explosive next to the package. It provided enough force to blow the bomb's circuit apart, but not enough to set off the main charge. Booby trap devices were also built into beer kegs, which were used for quite a while as the container for the main charge, or main explosive charge.[105]

Non-military targets would also often be of great strategic value, however, such as the Northern Ireland Forensic Laboratory, which was attacked several times (see Chapter 3). One such was a 'sting' in which the IRA planted a car for the lab's investigation but which contained a bomb that exploded and destroyed much forensic evidence to be used against the IRA. In September 1992 a 1,600-kg bomb, one of the largest used in Northern Ireland, almost totally destroyed the lab.

DEATH ON WHEELS: ADVENT OF THE CAR BOMB

The first car bomb was probably deployed in September 1920 in New York city, when an Italian anarchist's horse-drawn wagon packed with dynamite and iron slugs exploded in a fireball of shrapnel near the corner of Wall and Broad Streets.[106] The IRA was to hone and perfect the use of inconspicuous vehicles through crowded urban settings to transport large quantities of homemade and military high-explosive into precise range of high-value targets. Gas cylinders were often used both to store the large amounts of explosives and to hold the devices within the vehicles.

The Provisionals invented the ammonium nitrate-fuel oil (ANFO) car bomb.[107] These immensely powerful bombs, also known in military jargon as vehicle-borne improvised explosive devices (VBIEDs), elevated urban terrorism to industrial-level manufacture and would, in the 1980s and 1990s, destroy skyscrapers and whole blocks of buildings. Their use has been compared to aerial bombing in their ability to cripple cities and knock out military installations. One IRA man described Derry during 1971 as looking 'as if it had been bombed from the air'.[108] Another realised the car bomb's potential for destruction: 'We could feel the rattle where we stood. Then we knew we were onto something, and it took off from there.'[109]

Many inventions are the result of accidents or incidental observation, and such may have been the case with the car bomb. Before its emergence, volunteers had to courier crude volatile devices – rather like those deployed in the 7 July 2005 London bombings – to the point of deployment. After the PIRA's quartermaster general, Jack McCabe, blew himself up while mixing fertiliser-based explosive (the 'black stuff') with a shovel[110] in his Dublin garage, a consignment of the explosive had already been received by Belfast, and someone had the idea of disposing of it by dumping it in a car with a fuse and a timer and leaving it in the city centre.[111] Maybe not a car bomb as such, but a bomb in what turned out to be the ideal urban delivery mode for the terrorist: a car.[112]

The first car bombs were deployed by the IRA operative hijacking a car and parking it with the bomb inside. This posed problems of synchronising warnings, so led in turn to the increasingly sophisticated radio-controlled bombs (RCIEDs), the first of which was deployed in Northern Ireland in January 1972 – a month before Bloody Sunday[113]– and other remotely controlled detonation and timing methods (see Chapter 6). 'Sleeper' bombs could be detonated weeks in advance of being planted. Such a device was set to blow up the Queen during a visit to Coleraine University in 1977, but the device went off prematurely, before her arrival. Whereas the then secretary of state, Roy Mason, claimed that the bomb had been tossed over the university wall, the British army head of UXO (Unexploded Ordnance) later confirmed it was in fact a sleeper bomb.[114]

Some 500 kg (over 1,000 lb) of explosives per car bomb was not uncommon. Apart from being a relatively cheap means of attack – the explosives and electronics are usually cheaply bought and home-milled (not such an easy process: see Chapters 5 and 6) – the cars could be criminally acquired and disguised and the bomb itself would leave minimal forensic evidence.

VBIEDs enabled the IRA to increase the amount of explosives in each bomb without the attendant risks of volunteers blowing themselves up or being detected. Vehicles also provided more space to arrange the firing mechanism of the bomb and to booby trap both the bomb and the vehicle. With a vehicle bomb it was far easier to achieve maximum target damage than with a hand-delivered device.[115] You drove the car to your target, parked it, and walked away. But the sheer size of these bombs meant an increase in civilian casualties following bungled incidents or ineffective targeting. In March 1972, two car bombs sent into Lower Donegall Street in Belfast city centre were followed by garbled phone warnings that led police to evacuate people in the direction of one of the explosions: five civilians and two RUC members were killed and 100 others were injured.[116] Nevertheless, the then leader of the Provisional IRA, Seán Mac Stíofáin, knew that the IRA now had the ultimate means to inflict untold damage with the use of the car bomb,[117] foreseeing a bombing offensive 'of the utmost ferocity and ruthlessness' that would overthrow the unionist government.[18] On 21 July, no fewer than twenty-two ANFO (ammonium nitrate-fuel oil mixed explosive as the main charge, see Chapter 5) and gelignite car bombs were deployed around Belfast. The first, which exploded in front of the Ulster Bank at 2.40 p.m., blew off both legs of a Catholic pedestrian. The other car bomb targets on that day were a bus depot, railway junctions, and a mixed Catholic–Protestant district on Cavehill Road.[119] Targets were chosen, as will be further discussed, in this instance to maximise chaos and damage to infrastructure and the economy of the province. One explosion followed another, the booms of car bombs followed by eerie silences broken only by the screams of the injured. Belfast resembled a war zone, and received television coverage around the world equalling that afforded the Vietnam War.

The large amounts of explosives that could be packed into vehicles meant that many civilians would be killed and injured, particularly in carelessly deployed VBIEDs. The horror and disgust expressed domestically and universally at the welter of car bomb explosions led to the IRA no longer being seen as the representatives of a persecuted minority whose fight against the British was justified. The sympathy that had been aroused following the deaths of Bloody Sunday was all but annulled. But the IRA leadership was so enthused by the new firepower afforded by the 'nuclear weapon of guerrilla warfare'[120] that the moral and publicity disasters that would accrue from successive explosions did not figure in its strategy.

While not destroying the northern economy totally, and certainly not having the IRA's desired result of bringing down its government, the car bomb strategy nevertheless continued to wreak havoc, kill and injure, and reduce or terminate inward investment and tourism to Northern Ireland. It also led to further tightened security measures, such as the 'ring of steel' surrounding Belfast city, thereby making it the forerunner of the City of London equivalent set up following the IRA's attacks in the 1990s, and the first example of such enclaves and 'green zones' in other areas of the world affected by insurgents and terrorism.[121]

The IRA's continued use of the car bomb also gave the British army the pretext to launch Operation Motorman, in which 13,000 troops led by Centurion tanks and bulldozers (a scene that would be replicated by Israeli forces in the Palestinian territory, and in Fallujah in Iraq, in decades to come[122]) entered the Derry and Belfast no-go areas at 4 a.m. on 31 July 1972 and forced control of the streets away from the republican movement. The same day, a bloody, bungled car bomb attack in Claudy village in Co. Londonderry killed eight people.

The worsening situation in the North led Sir Edward Heath's 1972 government to consider transferring areas with a Catholic majority to the Republic of Ireland and moving individual Catholic families to the Republic, in a paper released under the thirty-year rule.[123] Containing the statement 'the IRA need relatively small quantities of arms and men to maintain an embarrassing level of violence', it acknowledged how the car bombs had done much to put the province almost on a civil war footing.

Car bombs were not confined to Belfast. Two people were killed and 127 injured when two car bombs exploded in Dublin on 1 December 1972. At 7.58 p.m. a car bomb detonated in Eden Quay close to Liberty Hall, Dublin, with a second at 8.16 p.m, exploded in Sackville Place (near O'Connell Street). Two bus conductors were killed in the second explosion. A warning had been telephoned to a Belfast-based newspaper only minutes before the first explosion; the attacks coincided with the Dáil debate on the Offences Against the State (Amendment) Bill, which would have given the Republic much greater powers against the IRA. It has never been ascertained who was responsible for the two car bombs, but many people in the Republic expressed suspicion that the bombings were part of a British covert operation to influence legislation in the Dáil. If so, it would not be the first or last such operation.[124]

PROTESTANT REPRISALS

Another car bomb in Dublin exploded on 20 January 1973, killing one person and injuring seventeen – believed to be the work of the Ulster Volunteer Force (UVF). In fact, loyalist paramilitaries exacted the highest death toll in one day during the conflict – using car bombs – when their triple attack in Dublin and Co. Monaghan on 17 May 1974 left thirty-three and an unborn child dead. As many as 258 people were also injured. The mid-Ulster UVF were most likely to have driven the cars south, and in July 1993 the organisation claimed sole responsibility for carrying out the attacks. No individual has ever been arrested in relation to the bombings.

In Dublin three car bombs exploded, almost simultaneously – a hallmark tactic of both sides which has been continued by subsequent terror groups, such as Al Qaeda – at approximately 5.30 p.m., in Parnell Street, Talbot Street, and South Leinster Street. Some twenty-three men, women and children were killed in these explosions and three others died as a result of injuries over the following few days. Another car bomb exploded at approximately 9 p.m. in North Road, Monaghan, killing five people initially with another two dying in ensuing weeks. An eyewitness, John Casey, who was walking into a Talbot Street hotel when the bomb went off, said: 'Hundreds of people were in the street. They were running and screaming aimlessly. A newspaper stand was blown into the air past me and the newsboy next to it just disappeared in front of my eyes.'[125]

No apologies or regret was expressed for the attacks. Indeed, Sammy Smyth, then press officer of both the Ulster Defence Association (UDA) and the Ulster Workers' Council (UWC) Strike Committee, said: 'I am very happy about the bombings in Dublin. There is a war with the Free State and now we are laughing at them.'[126] However, on the whole the loyalists did not regularly effect incursions south of the border – mainly because they saw themselves as defenders of their own territory, not invaders of the alien South.[127]

Some believed that such events were not unexpected and that the conflict could spread south. Indeed, the Irish authorities feared that the Provisional IRA Army Council could find compelling reasons to ignore the Republic's Army Order no. 8 and authorise operations in the twenty-six counties.[128] Many Irish citizens, however, wanted the Republic to be as isolated as possible from the northern Troubles and the IRA's armed struggle. Memories of the Irish Civil War were not distant, and Ireland, a relatively new state, was struggling not only to find its identity, but to emerge from centuries of grinding poverty and turmoil.

BLOWING UP BRITAIN

Forced onto the defensive by Operation Motorman and the army backlash to Bloody Friday, but also knowing the political, military and propaganda value of striking at the very heart of British power, the IRA once again turned its attention to targeting 'mainland' Britain itself. Bombs in Britain were aimed at pressurising the government to pull out of Ulster and to wake up the British public and media to the situation in Ireland, about which – despite seeing devastation of their 'province' in daily press and TV reports – many continued to show apathy, ignorance, or both. Placing British voters in the frontline of the IRA's campaign was intended to make them question the role of the British in Ireland.[129]

The attacks in Britain in the 1970s included bombs left in pubs and restaurants; targeting of government and public buildings;[130] litter bins; letter bombs; bookbombs; incendiaries in shops; and firebombs on trains. From March 1973 to March 1974 some 130 attacks in England (unlike previous mainland campaigns, the IRA avoided the Celtic lands of Scotland and Wales) were recorded. Out of eighty-six explosions in 1973 there were eleven in November alone, killing four and injuring thirty-five.[131]

The first use of car bombs in England was deadly, and contributed to what became known as London's 'Bloody Thursday' – 8 March 1973. The Belfast brigade planned to send ten car bombs to London via the Dublin–Liverpool ferry using two young sisters who were to become IRA icons, Marion and Dolours Price (see Chapter 8). Snags arose and only four cars arrived in London. Two of the bombs were defused and two exploded, one in front of the Old Bailey, another close to 10 Downing Street – the 'dynamite war' revisited, but several orders of magnitude more sustained and deadly. Some 200 people were injured in the Old Bailey and one died of a heart attack.[132] The Old Bailey car bomb, a 1968 Ford Corsair packed with 2-kg bags of explosives, amounted to 18 kg of gelignite.[133] The attention of the English media had at last been secured; although there were six bombs in Belfast and five in Derry on the same day, they were eclipsed by the London attacks.[134]

A particularly deadly variation on the car bomb was the under-car bomb, or booby trap car bomb, otherwise known by the military as an under-vehicle improvised explosive device (UVIED) or victim-operated improvised explosive device (VOIED). Noted victims of these devices were Airey Neave, MP, the Conservative spokesman on Northern Ireland, killed by the hardline Marxist republican group the INLA as he left the Commons in his car on 30 March 1979, and Ian Gow, MP, who was killed by a Semtex UVIED on 30 July 1990 (see Chapter 3).

Several other attacks backfired – 'the inevitabilities of war'[135] – in terms of arousing sympathy for the republican cause. There were many examples of these terrible events but the Birmingham and Guildford bombings were arguably the most damaging to the IRA at the time. This was compounded by the conviction of innocent people for both incidents.

The explosive charge of the bombs varied between 1 and 90 kg and most were in the form of booby traps. All the explosions took place in a confined space and at times when there were certain to be crowds.

Some high-profile economic targets, such as Harrods, were targeted several times. On 18 August 1973 two incendiary devices[136] were detonated inside the store. On 18 December 1983, a further attack, this time a car bomb of 13 kg of explosives, killed six – three civilians and three police officers – and injured ninety outside the store.[137]

The December 1983 Harrods bomb came at a time when Sinn Féin was starting to attract more electoral support and international backing. So it was a public relations disaster which put the party on the back foot with the onslaught of media attention – and necessitated a statement from Martin McGuinness, by then an established Sinn Féin politician: 'All Active Service Units in Britain, as in Ireland, are aware of the need to avoid civilian casualties, and indeed, as at Harrods, we do not believe that the IRA set out to cause casualties.'[138] Then a lengthy statement was issued by the IRA:

> … at Harrods a 40-minute warning showed that there was no intention to kill or injure civilians. The British Government has attempted to project the Harrods operations as a civilian bombing, *despite the fact that they know that if the IRA wanted to kill British civilians, it could do so in hundreds.*[139] [Italics added for emphasis – as this is among the most chilling part of any IRA statement issued throughout the entire conflict.]

The other very telling part of the statement claimed British apathy towards Ireland meant that 'some oppressed Irish people and republican supporters, out of desperation, would view no-warning bombs as a way of shaking up the British public and their government.'

SMALL BOMBS, BIG TERROR

Many of the early 1970s London attacks employed book bombs, letter bombs, and bombs in carrier bags (used in the Birmingham bombings) that were smaller devices than those used in Northern Ireland, but nevertheless created injury, carnage and terror – to the extent that opposition to civilian targeting arose among some members of the IRA leadership.[140] In 1973, the IRA deployed eleven letter bombs, forty-one incendiary devices and twenty-seven other timer bombs.[141] Many attacks were carried out by a handful of operatives at a time travelling by sea to England, complete with bomb-making materials and explosives such as gelignite. British intelligence at the time was not geared up to the main-land threat, having invested many resources into finding those responsi-ble for the virtually daily bombing of Ulster.[142]

By 1970 gelignite was still available for use in devices and UXO finds revealed mixed levels of expertise. One unexploded gelignite device, found with burned-out match-heads attached, showed amateurism, while only weeks later a booby trapped 10-kg gelignite device planted in a car door showed that the bomb-makers knew what they were doing.[143]

Letter bombs and small time bombs first appeared in 1969. In an early design, the device was set off when the envelope contents, while being taken out, pulled a pin against a detonator.[144] The next-generation letter bomb featured a small booklet inside the envelope with its centre cut out and filled with a battery, detonator and small amount of explosive – usu-ally gelignite.[145] Two pages of the booklet had two foil strips connected to the battery and the firing mechanism. A piece of card attached to the base of the envelope separated the two pieces of foil. When the booklet was taken out of the envelope, the card remained inside, allowing the foil pieces to touch, complete the circuit, and set off the explosive.

These devices caused mayhem in England and, as mainly the work of Shane Paul O'Doherty (whose work and role as an IRA bomb-maker will be discussed in Chapter 8), were aimed at ministers, magistrates, police and major institutions in Britain and, later, British diplomats abroad. The bombs maimed twelve people, including a security guard who lost an eye and a hand.[146] Devices exploded in postal sorting offices, such as at the Royal Horticultural Hall in London on 18 December 1973, injuring six people, while on the same day another bomb injured fifty-two people in Thornley Street – setting the trend for a typical bad bomb day in London in the 1970s.

Other small bombs targeted shops, clubs, pubs, railway signal boxes, underground trains, and the cars and homes of public figures. The ability of the IRA to place large numbers of small devices in multiple locations was a threat that is now being revisited in the light of the 7 July 2005 London transit bombings. Although the nature of the 1970s devices was different – for example, the IRA did not concoct the kind of crude home-made explosive mixture (triacetone triperoxide – TATP) used for recent suicide missions[147] – the fear generated by the ubiquitous character of its bombings at times such as Christmas 1973, when crowds of shoppers and tourists were plentiful in London, was only alleviated by the fact that the Provisionals could not sustain the campaign indefinitely.[148] However, breaks in the bombings sometimes lulled Londoners into a sense of false security.

A SUSTAINED CAMPAIGN

The aim of the IRA to make its case to the British public was, therefore, ineffective as the unpredictability of the attacks – as any psychologist would know – had the effect of causing more terror. This would appear the ultimate irony – terrorists who don't *intend* to terrorise. They did, but only so far as to focus the British mind on leaving Ireland. But, unlike the small world of Northern Ireland, the British campaign was directed at large populations, so that many areas and inhabitants remained unaffected. Trying to wake the British up to the fact that '1,500 people have died in Ireland and no-one seems to care'[149] did not work, as people either became used to the bombings[150] or more hostile to the whole Irish issue as a result.

It is only in recent times that the combination of the Good Friday Agreement, television documentaries and films has revealed IRA faces behind the masks. This has served to make them appear more human to some observers, as former operatives attempt to explain why they felt they had no choice but to respond to British power and occupation by committing bomb outrages.[151] But few are willing to talk in any great detail, particularly in relation to operational matters.

The bombing events also became less unpredictable in coinciding with landmark dates, such as the September 1973 negotiations in London to form a power-sharing government, when two 1.4-kg bombs at King's Cross and Euston stations and in Oxford Street and Sloane Square injured thirteen people and brought chaos to central London on the tenth of that month.[152] The King's Cross bomb exploded without warning and shattered glass throughout the old booking hall and hurled a baggage trolley several feet through the air.[153] Warnings were often not given or were insufficiently clear to get people away from a target – and more than 100 hoax telephone calls throughout the day forced the evacuation of three other London stations.

The first explosion at King's Cross – which injured five people – occurred seconds after a witness saw a youth throw a bag into a booking hall (a forerunner of today's threat, but now the youth would have likely killed himself with the bag rather than throwing it). One witness described it thus: 'I saw a flash and suddenly people were being thrown through the air – it was a terrible mess, they were bleeding and screaming.'[154]

Whereas 1972 was the height of the bombing in Northern Ireland, 1974[155] was to see an unprecedented number of attacks on the mainland, killing forty-four people. But it was also the year when the conflict in Northern Ireland claimed its one 1,000th victim,[156] and the very heart of the six counties was being ripped apart by bombs – up to three a day – ranging from basic petrol-bombs to high-explosive IEDs.[157] But paradoxically, the ferocity and intensity of the mainland attacks diverted British public attention away from the centre of the Troubles in Ireland.

The letter bomb attacks intensified in Britain and claimed high-profile injury victims, most notably the then Home Secretary, Reginald Maudling, on 2 February, who opened such a device delivered to his home. Most offices had warning notices about what to do if a letter bomb was suspected.[158]

The Guildford bombings (5 October; four dead, sixty-seven injured) and Birmingham (21 November; twenty-one dead, 182 injured)[159] were among the most notoriously misplaced, although Guildford was an explainable target as being close to a number of garrison towns. The bomb in the Mulberry Bush pub in Birmingham was powerful enough to blast holes in 20-cm-thick reinforced concrete and bring down the roof.[160] Five more bombs went off in Birmingham on the same day in public buildings that had been cleared. According to a firefighter who responded to the scene of carnage:

> The crew entered the basement with the searchlight, trying to peer through the darkness and clouds of dust. The images and screams amongst the devastation and rubble would remain forever in the minds of the crew and the two young Police officers who witnessed the scene.
>
> … There was a probability of airborne asbestos fibres due to the nature of the incident and age of the building. Finally, there was the possibility of a secondary explosive device. The casualties' needs would override these considerations. The incident appeared to be basically a major search and rescue operation with a couple of small pockets of fire and a large number of casualties. After a quick, rough head count of the casualties, I allowed up to four casualties to each ambulance. I then decided to make pumps five and request forty ambulances. There were probably less than ten red (emergency) ambulances on duty throughout the City at that time of a Thursday evening. Taking into account other demands on their services, we would be fortunate if even three managed to attend the incident.[161]

The conviction of innocent Irish people following both series of attacks indicated the level of hysteria in the UK as a result of the IRA campaign. The Provisional leadership attempted, unsuccessfully, to acknowledge this by releasing a statement in Dublin on 23 November declaring that

'It has never been and is not the policy of the IRA to bomb non-military targets without giving adequate warnings to ensure the safety of civilians.'[162] The definition of 'economic target' would be wide-ranging and invariably involved civilian victims, and 'military targets' would also include civilians, albeit often connected to the security forces, as in February 1974 when an IRA unit planted a bomb on a coach carrying servicemen and their families, killing eleven people.[163] As with all use of bombs in open warfare and guerrilla warfare, targeting can never be accurate to the point of avoiding innocent victims, although the notion of 'no one is innocent' – as with today's Islamicist groups – was not lost on more hardline IRA elements, for whom British lives were more expendable than those in Northern Ireland.[164]

Most notorious in London was the so-called Balcombe Street gang who were implicated in Guildford and the Woolwich pub bombing. They made headlines when, after a shooting incident at a Mayfair restaurant, they took a postal worker and his wife hostage in Balcombe Street, surrendering after a six-day siege. They had shot Ross McWhirter, co-author of the *Guinness Book of Records*, outside his home in Enfield, north London, because he had offered a £50,000 reward for the arrest of the IRA group that had carried out a string of attacks – which included booby trap devices, one of which killed Captain Roger Goad, an explosives expert, and a car bomb, which mistakenly killed a cancer specialist, Professor Gordon Hamilton-Fairley. Gang members had also thrown shrapnel bombs containing bolts or ball bearings through the windows of crowded restaurants in London. In February 1977, O'Connell, Butler and Duggan were sentenced to twelve life sentences; Doherty received eleven life sentences. They were freed in 1999 under the terms of the Good Friday Agreement.[165] A notable aspect of the Balcombe Street gang was that it took months to apprehend them. But their reign of terror occurred before sufficient intelligence or effective countermeasures had been put in place.[166]

The 1974 campaign was indeed sustained and vicious enough for the British government to fear a possible airborne IRA attack. Middle Eastern terrorist groups at the time were focusing on hijackings, but not bombing from the air or firing missiles at aircraft. A letter in January 1974 from Tony Stephens at the Ministry of Defence (MoD) referred to the urgent desire on the part of the general officer commanding in Northern Ireland to prohibit overflying at low altitudes by civil aircraft 'because of the threat of attacks from the air by the IRA' after the Provisional leader, Seamus Twomey, had successfully escaped from Mountjoy prison by helicopter on 31 October 1973.[167] Suspicions increased when Twomey declared to the German news magazine *Der Spiegel* that 'very soon we shall also fight from the air'. An MoD memorandum also cited 'the possibility of training pilots'. However, the IRA's airborne strategy was confined to attacking helicopters, and the mortar attacks on Heathrow in the 1990s (see Chapter 3).

It is thought that negotiations for a ceasefire came as a result of the Birmingham bombs, despite the constant bombings and other activities in Northern Ireland.[168] The IRA certainly came mighty close to the seat of power in Britain in 1974. On 17 June a bomb exploded at the Houses of Parliament, causing extensive damage and injuring eleven people. As explosions often do, the blast also fractured a gas main and a fire spread quickly through Westminster Hall.[169] The home of the former prime minister, Edward Heath was the target of a 1-kg bomb on 22 December 1974, just ten minutes before he returned. The IRA's audacity was demonstrated by the claims by witnesses who described seeing a man emerge from a car and throwing the device onto the first-floor balcony of the house.[170]

But 'ordinary' civilians were increasingly victims; examples are too numerous to describe, and targets increasingly varied. In late November and early December 1974 a series of explosions – again at mainline stations, with devices this time left in pillar boxes – injured two people, along with other attacks in the same period at random locations in London and Bristol. There are many examples of these haphazard and terrifying attacks: on 25 November several devices – small bombs using pocket watches as timers – were left in pillar boxes at Caledonian Road in north London, Piccadilly Circus and Victoria station. Two days later a 'come on' bomb[171] went off in Tite Street in Chelsea: the London ASU had planted a bomb in a pillar box, while a second device was set to explode a metre away once the explosive experts were on the scene.[172] This form of explosive enticement was to mature into a well-honed IRA technique.

The campaign continued on and off through the 1970s, using a mixture of small and larger devices, with increasing means of disguising them (see Chapter 6). Among many other examples where high-value property was targeted and civilians put in danger was when 160 sticks of gelignite were left outside Selfridges in Oxford Street. After a warning was received at the *Sun* newspaper, Christmas shoppers were evacuated to the basement rooms of nearby pubs. A massive explosion caused substantial damage, but no deaths or injuries.

The rail network was also targeted (see below). For example, on 4 March 1973 a bomb exploded in an empty train near Cannon Street tube station, injuring eight people in a passing train. On 15 March 1976 a device exploded at West Ham station on a Hammersmith & City line train. It has been reported that the bomber, Vincent Kelly, took the wrong train and tried to go back but the bomb detonated before he reached the City area. He shot the train's guard and shot and killed the train's driver, Julius Stephen, who tried to catch him. The bomber shot himself after he was cornered by the police. Almost a suicide mission, but not quite.[173]

It was in this dangerously relentless period of the campaign on the mainland that the Prevention of Terrorism Act (PTA) was passed, allowing the police to detain suspects without charge for up to seven days. The atmosphere reached fever pitch, with MPs debating the return of capital punishment (the motion was defeated) and the wrong people being arrested and convicted of the Guildford and Birmingham bombs.[174]

In the 1980s litter bin bombs returned, leading to removal of bins from many locations.[175] An example was on 18 February 1991, when bombs exploded at Paddington and Victoria stations, the latter of which was planted in a litter bin. It killed a commuter and injured forty other passengers.[176] There were other attacks on the rail network, again harking back to the 1930s campaign: on 16 December the same year, a bomb containing approximately half a kilo of Semtex exploded on the railway line near Clapham Junction, necessitating the entire London rail network to be closed for several hours. In 1992 the IRA placed incendiary devices on several trains. At Elephant & Castle station and Neasden, devices were found and defused; another went off at Barking station.[177] The 1993 Bishopsgate bomb wrecked Liverpool Street station – which was also the first target of the 7 July 2005 jihadi bombers.

RESTRUCTURING AND SMART BOMBS

The early 1980s was best known in republican terms for the Long Kesh hunger strikers and the first moves towards politicisation of the IRA. But in terms of military significance, during this period the Provisionals re-organised their structure away from conventional army units and, along with reduced membership from around 500 to 300, had adopted a 'cell structure' in order to counter security force penetration through the use of informers. This led to the active service units (ASUs) in Britain and mainland Europe, each of which would typically consist of five to eight volunteers who would regularly go to ground to avoid detection. By 1982, the IRA had built up a logistical structure in Britain comprising arms caches, facilities for building bombs and a support network for ASUs, which would often spend long periods blending into the community.[178]

The result was sporadic but deadly attacks. In a few days towards the end of February 1981, the Derry brigade firebombed three shops in the city, blew up the centre of Limavady with a car bomb, and bombed and sank a British coal boat, the *Nellie M*, off the Donegal coast.[179] The early 1980s was also the period when the IRA began to develop sophisticated timing and arming mechanisms for its bombs (see Chapter 6). The 10 October 1981 bomb that killed two civilians and injured thirty-nine outside Chelsea barracks incorporated a remote-control detonation mechanism,[180] marking the start of the IRA's pioneering timer techniques that would enable it to plant devices well in advance of detonation. The introduction of video cassette recorders with (for the time) sophisticated electronic remote-control mechanisms and long-delay timing enabled this development in IRA weaponry. Its most infamous example was the Brighton Grand hotel bomb of 1984, which will be described in the next chapter.

The Chelsea bomb was also a nail bomb, which, as is customary for such terrible devices, succeeded in producing horrendous injuries. This kind of device was also used in the bombings during the changing of the guards ceremony in Hyde Park on 20 July 1982. Apart from being detonated by remote control rather than an easily detected command wire,[181] the 13–15-kg car bomb scattered nail shrapnel, killing four guardsmen and injuring twenty-eight other people in the vicinity – although the deaths of seven horses seemed to cause most horror among the British public. Only two hours later, a second explosion, triggered by long-delay remote control, underneath the bandstand in Regents Park killed six Royal Green Jackets and injured a further twenty-four civilians.[182]

The IRA at this time also began incorporating anti-handling devices in mainland-planted bombs, the first example of which was a device that killed a UXO officer, Kenneth Howarth, in an Oxford Street Wimpy Bar on 26 October 1981 as he tried to defuse it.[183] This also showed deliberate targeting of the security services while simultaneously causing economic damage.

By the mid-1980s the death toll in the North had reached 2,500, with some 750 soldiers and police being killed by the Provisionals. However, more civilians were killed by loyalist groups than by the IRA – 587 as against 524 – while the British by 1986 had killed 166. A staggering number of civilians – some 14,000 – were wounded in bombings in the modern Troubles, most by the Provisionals.[184] The IRA had become the world's most sophisticated insurgent organisation, with an effective intelligence and propaganda machine. And yet, through the 1980s and into the 1990s nine out of every ten IRA operations failed or were aborted.[185] But to that the IRA would say, ' ... we only have to be lucky once'.[186]

Despite maintaining a persistent level of mayhem, the IRA had hit major obstacles. The 'dirty war' had taken its toll in infiltration of units, capture of weapons (most notably the interception of the Libyan consignment on the *Eksund*; see Chapter 4) and shooting of personnel. In May 1987 eight volunteers – the highest number in one action since the 1920s – were killed in an ambush by the SAS as they engaged in a bombing attack on Loughgall police station in north Co. Armagh.[187]

The mid-1980s also saw the introduction of the then most powerful military explosive in use – Semtex – from Libya. Seizures in this period included 43 kg of Semtex and more than 5,500 kg of homemade explosive (HME), some of which was found in bombs that were defused by the EOD squads. And they were not just found in one place, but throughout the North – from the biggest hauls in Belfast to those held in smaller towns such as Castlederg and Limavady.[188]

The 1980s ended with what would become known as a 'spectacular' – a high-profile, multiple-casualty attack, which exacted the highest death toll since the Hyde Park/Regent's Park bombings: on 21 September 1989, a bomb planted at a Royal Marines College in Deal, Kent, killed eleven guardsmen and injured twenty-one others. Apart from destroying the canteen, all three floors of the building, and dozens of nearby houses,[189] it demonstrated the vulnerability of military installations in Britain. The blast was powerful enough to be clearly heard in the centre of Deal over 3 km away.

Overall, although the number of people killed by the IRA declined at the end of the 1980s, the number of injuries was higher than at the start of the decade, among civilians and security force personnel. Some 190 soldiers and 150 police were injured in 1990 while seven army and twelve police were killed.[190] Noted differences in the campaign were the choice of highly skilled operatives and a lessening of central control of operations, which were more carefully planned and less frenetic than in the 1970s. The IRA made use of dry runs and long-term planning of each hit – aided by their still formidable arsenal of weapons and explosives. It was said the organisation was almost over-supplied; IRA volunteers were actually tending to drop their guns when pursued![191] By the end of the 1980s the IRA had used up half of the Semtex from Libya, but still had enough left – three tonnes – to blow up much of central London.

TABLE 2.2: BOMBINGS ON THE MAINLAND 1980s, 1990s

Date	Location	Death/injuries
2 December 1980	Princess Louise Regiment Territorial Army Centre, Hammersmith Road, London W6	Device exploded, injuring five people
10 October 1981	Ebury Bridge Road, London SW1	Device exploded, killing two people and injuring thirty-nine
17 October 1981	London SE21	One person injured in an explosion
26 October 1981	Wimpy Bar, Oxford Street, London W1	One person killed in an explosion
23 November 1981	Royal Artillery HQ, Government House, Woolwich New Road, London SE18	Device exploded, injuring two people
20 July 1982	South Carriage Road, Hyde Park, London W1	Device exploded, killing four people and injuring twenty-eight
	Regents Park, London NW1	Device exploded, killing seven people and injuring thirty-one
10 December 1983	Royal Artillery barracks, Repository Road, London SE18	Device exploded injuring three people
17 December 1983	Outside Harrods, Knightsbridge, London SW3	Six people were killed and ninety-one injured in an explosion
25 December 1983	Orchard Street, London W1	Device exploded injuring two people
12 October 1984	Grand Hotel, Brighton, Sussex	Device exploded during the Conservative Party conference killing five people and injuring thirty
15/16 August 1987	Various	Postal devices were sent to six senior civil servants. No injuries
1 August 1988	Inglis barracks, London SW7	Device exploded, killing one person and injuring eight
20 February 1989	Ternhill barracks, Shropshire	One person injured in an explosion
22 September 1989	Royal Marines School of Music, North barracks, Deal, Kent	Device exploded, killing eleven and injuring twenty-one
15 November 1989	Kensington	Device discovered and defused. No injuries
18 November 1989	Married quarters, British army barracks, Colchester, Essex	Device attached to car exploded, injuring two people

16 January 1990	Army HQ, SE District, Aldershot	Postal device discovered and defused. No injuries
20 February 1990	Combined Services Recruitment Centre, Rutland Street, Leicester	Device attached to a vehicle exploded, injuring two people
25 February 1990	Army Recruiting Office, New Road, Halifax	Device exploded. No injuries
14 May 1990	Service Education Centre, Eltham, London SE9	Device exploded, injuring five people
16 May 1990	Army Recruiting Centre, Wembley, Middlesex	Device exploded, killing one person and injuring four
1 June 1990	Lichfield railway station, Staffordshire	One person was killed and two injured in a shooting incident
9 June 1990	Honourable Artillery HQ, City Road, London EC1	Nineteen people were injured in an explosion
12 June 1990	Hampshire	Device discovered and defused. No injuries
21 June 1990	RAF Stanmore Park, Uxbridge	Device exploded. No injuries
25 June 1990	Carlton Club, St. James, London SW1	Bomb exploded, injuring twenty people
6 July 1990	The Strand, London WC2	Small device exploded in a litter bin. No injuries
20 July 1990	Stock Exchange, London EC1	Device exploded. No injuries
30 July 1990	Pevensey, East Sussex	Ian Gow, MP was killed when a device exploded under his car
6 August 1990	London NW8	Device discovered and defused at the former home of Lord Armstrong. No injuries
13 August 1990	Didcot, Berkshire	Device discovered and defused at the home of Sir Anthony Farrar-Hockley. No injuries
10 September 1990	Army and Navy Recruiting Office, Derby	Bomb exploded. No injuries
17 September 1990	Army Information Centre, Finchley, London	Army colour sergeant shot and injured as he sat in a car outside the office
18 September 1990	Milford, Staffordshire	Air Chief Marshall Sir Peter Terry was shot and injured at his home. His wife suffered minor injuries

27 September 1990	Royal Overseas League, Park Place, London WC1	Device discovered and defused. No injuries
24 January 1991	Territorial Army firing range, Cannock Chase, Staffordshire	Small explosion and a shot fired. No injuries
7 February 1991	Downing Street, London SW1	Three mortar bombs fired. One minor injury
18 February 1991	Paddington station, London W2	Device exploded. No injuries
	Victoria station, London SW1	Device exploded. One man killed and thirty-eight people injured
25 February 1991	Napsbury Lane, St. Albans	Device exploded on a railway line. No injuries
3 April 1991	Preston railway station, Preston, Lancashire	A number of incendiary devices were found on a platform. No injuries
5 April 1991	Arndale shopping centre, Manchester	A number of devices were discovered in shops, some of which caused fires. No injuries
28 June 1991	Beck Theatre, Hayes, Middlesex	Device discovered and defused outside the theatre. No injuries
30 June 1991	Royal Navy and RAF Recruiting Office, Fishergate Centre, Preston	Device discovered. Detonated in controlled explosion. No injuries
5 August 1991	Cambridge public house, Charing Cross Road, London	Fire caused by incendiary devices. No injuries
29 August 1991	London underground depot, Hammersmith, London W6	Three incendiary devices discovered under a seat. No injuries
31 August 1991	Bargain Bookshop, Charing Cross Road, London WC2	Incendiary device discovered. No injuries
15 November 1991	Old Barclays Bank, St. Peters Street, St. Albans, Hertfordshire	Device exploded, killing two members of the Provisional IRA. A member of the public was injured
1 December 1991	The Discount Furniture Store Habitat, The World of Leather, The Reject Shop, Tottenham Court Road	A number of incendiary devices ignited causing damage to property but no injuries
2 December 1991	Littlewoods, Oxford Street, London W1	Incendiary device ignited. No injuries
7–8 December 1991	Various locations in Blackpool	A number of incendiary devices were discovered in locations around Blackpool. No injuries

8 December 1991	Arndale Centre, Manchester	Seven incendiary devices ignited. No injuries
14 December 1991	Brent Cross shopping centre	Four devices found in shops. No injuries
15 December 1991	Sainsbury Wing, National Gallery, London WC2	An incendiary device partially ignited. No injuries
16 December 1991	Railway line near Clapham Junction	Bomb exploded on the railway line. No injuries
23 December 1991	Ilford underground depot Neasden underground deport Train at Harrow on the Hill	Incendiary device ignited. No injuries Incendiary devices ignited. No injuries Incendiary devices ignited. No injuries
10 January 1992	Whitehall Place, London SW1	Small device exploded. No injuries
17 January 1992	Marquis of Granby public house, Shaftesbury Avenue, London W1	Two incendiary devices discovered. No injuries
30 January 1992	Elephant and Castle underground depot, London SE17	Incendiary device found. No injuries
3 February 1992	Neasden underground depot	Incendiary device found under seat. No injuries
7 February 1992	London underground sidings between Barking and Upney stations	Incendiary device ignited. No injuries
11 February 1992	Telephone box, Parliamentary Street, London SW1 (outside the Treasury)	Small device discovered and made safe. No injuries
28 February 1992	London Bridge railway station, London SE1	Device exploded, injuring twenty-nine people
29 February 1992	Crown Prosecution Service, London EC4	Device exploded, injuring two people
1 March 1992	White Hart Lane BR station, Tottenham, London N17	Small device discovered and defused
10 March 1992	Near Wandsworth Common railway station, London SW18	Small device exploded beside railway line. No injuries
6 April 1992	Bridle Lane, near Piccadilly Circus, London W1 various offices.	Device exploded outside a building housing No injuries
10 April 1992	St Mary Axe, City of London EC3	Large improvised explosive device exploded, killing three people and injuring ninety-one. Many properties damaged

11 April 1992	Staples Corner, Junction of M1 and North Circular Road	Large improvised explosive device exploded, causing serious damage to roads and nearby buildings
9–10 May 1992	Metro Centre, Gateshead	A number of incendiary devices ignited, causing minimal damage
7 June 1992	Royal Festival Hall, London SE1	Device exploded, causing blast damage. No injuries
8 June 1992	A64 Leeds–York near Tadcaster, North Yorkshire	Constable Goodman was shot and killed and a PC seriously injured by two gunmen
10 June 1992	Wilcox Place, Victoria Street	Small device exploded in a litter bin near the Army and Navy department store. No injuries
15 June 1992	St. Albans Street, near Piccadilly Circus	Device exploded in a cab, which had been hijacked. No injuries
25 June 1992	Coleman Street, City of London EC2	Device exploded hidden in a brief case under a car. Limited damage. One police officer suffered shock
30–31 July 1992	Milton Keynes (shops, library)	Two incendiary devices discovered, only minimal damage caused
25 August 1992	Shropshire Regimental Museum and two furniture shops, Shrewsbury	A small device exploded at the museum and incendiary devices ignited in the shops. Some damage caused in the museum
6 September 1992	London Hilton Hotel, Park Lane, London W1	Small device exploded in the gents' toilets in the foyer of the hotel. Little damage and no casualties
17 September 1992	Madame Tussaud's, Marylebone Road, London NW1	Two incendiary devices caused a small fire
	The Planetarium, Marylebone Road, London NW1	A small device exploded, causing minor damage
	Imperial War Museum, Lambeth Road, London SE1	Two incendiary devices discovered and extinguished. Minor damage caused
7 October 1992	Junction of The Haymarket and Panton Street, Piccadilly, London SW1	Small device exploded in a litter bin. Five people suffered minor injuries. Minimal damage
	Near Centre Point, Flitcroft Street, London WC2	Small device exploded behind a BT junction box. Slight damage and no casualties

8 October 1992	Tooley Street, London SE1	Device exploded under a car, causing damage to two other cars. One person slightly injured
	Melcombe Street, London NW1	Small device exploded under a car, causing little damage and no injuries
9 October 1992	Royal British Legion, Nursery Road, Southgate N14	Small device exploded under a car in the car park. No injuries
	Car Park, Arnos Grove underground station	Small device exploded under a car. No injuries
10 October 1992	Paddington Green police station, Harrow Road, Paddington, London W2	Device exploded in a phone box outside the police station. One person injured
12 October 1992	Sussex Arms public house, Long Acre, Convent Garden	A device exploded in the gents' toilets, killing one person (who died the following day as a result of injuries) and injuring four
19 October 1992	Novotel hotel, Shortlands, Hammersmith, London W6	Small device exploded under the wheel arch of a coach parked outside the hotel. No casualties
	Oxenden Street, London SW1	Device exploded under a car. Two people treated for shock
21 October 1992	Railway line, near Silver Street station, Edmonton	Device exploded on the track as a train was passing, causing little damage. Two people were treated for minor injuries
	Princess Louise Territorial Army centre, Hammersmith Road, London W6	Device, believed to have been hung on railings, exploded. Three people suffered minor injuries
	Railway line, near Harrow Road (junction with Furness Road), London NW10	Device exploded, causing slight damage to the track, but no casualties.
22 October 1992	Sewage pipe, Wick Lane, London E3	Small device exploded, causing damage to a sewage pipe. No casualties
25 October 1992	London SW1	Device exploded in a doorway, causing some damage to the building and to nearby cars. No casualties
30 October 1992	Whitehall, London SW1 (near Downing Street)	Small device exploded in a hijacked minicab outside Cabinet Office. No one was injured
14 November 1992	Stoke Newington Road, London N16	Van discovered containing a very large improvised explosive device. One policeman was shot and injured confronting two men

15 November 1992	Canada Tower, Canary Wharf	Large improvised explosive device is made safe after security guards challenged two men
16 November 1992	Collingwood Street, Bethnal Green, London E1	Device in van made safe
1 December 1992	Stephens Street/Tottenham Court Road	Large improvised explosive device in van made safe
3 December 1992	Deansgate and Cateaton Street, Manchester	Two small devices exploded under bushes, causing damage to properties and minor injury to sixty-four people
9 December 1992	Woodside Park underground station, London N12	HME device partially detonated in a van in car park. No injuries
10 December 1992	Wood Green shopping centre, London N22	Two devices exploded in litter bins outside shops. Eleven people were slightly injured
16 December 1992	John Lewis department store Oxford Street, London W1	Small device exploded in the gents' toilets on the third floor. One person was treated for shock
	Cavendish Square, London W1	Small device exploded in a litter bin. Three people were slightly injured
22 December 1992	Hampstead underground station	Small device exploded on emergency staircase
6 January 1993	Reject Shop, Plaza shopping centre, London W1	Incendiary device ignited, causing minor damage
	Dillons' bookshop, Northumberland Avenue, London WC2	Very small device exploded, causing little damage
	C&A, Oxford Street, London W1	Incendiary device ignited. Very little damage
	Video shop, 60 Oxford Street, London W1	Incendiary device ignited. Minor
7 January 1993	Dillons' bookshop, Northumberland Avenue, London W1	Unignited incendiary device found
14 January 1993	Top Shop, Oxford Circus, London W1	Unignited incendiary device found
28 January 1993	Harrods, Brompton Road, London SW1	Small device exploded in a litter bin. Two people slightly injured and 30 ft of shop front damaged

3 February 1993	Train at Kent House station, Kent	Small device exploded on train stopped and evacuated following warnings. No casualties
	South Kensington underground station, London SW7	Device exploded in underground passage-way following warning and evacuation. No casualties
10 February 1993	London SW1	Small device exploded in doorway of block of flats. Minor damage. No injuries.
26 February 1993	Warrington, Cheshire	Policeman shot and injured after stopping a van; a car hijacked; and three devices exploded (and unignited incendiary made safe) at gasworks causing extensive damage and no injuries.
27 February 1993	Camden High Street, London NW1	Small device exploded in litter bin. Eighteen people injured, two seriously
20 March 1993	Bridge Street, Warrington, Cheshire	Two small devices exploded in litter bins in shopping area. Two children killed and fifty-four people injured, four extremely seriously
7 April 1993	Argyle Square, London WC1	Small device exploded in builders skip. Minor damage. No injuries
23 April 1993	Esso oil refinery, North Shields	Small device exploded next to pipe carrying heavy oil. No injuries. Some damage
24 April 1993	Bishopsgate, London EC2	Large improvised explosive device exploded, killing one person and injuring forty-four. Extensive damage to properties
	Manor House underground station, London N22	Small device exploded in hijacked minicab. No injuries
	Judd Street, St. Pancras, London WC1	Small device exploded in hijacked minicab. No injuries
9 May 1993	Galleries shopping centre, Bristol	Two incendiaries ignited, in the Reject Shop and Waterstones bookshop. No injuries
12 May 1993	Reject Shop, Cornmarket, Oxford	Incendiary device malfunctioned. No injuries
9 June 1993	Gas installation, Gateshead, Tyne and Wear	Small explosive device detonated, causing fire and damage to gas storage tank. No injuries
	Esso oil refinery, North Shields	Two small explosive devices detonated on pipes leading to storage tanks. Little damage, no injuries

13 August 1993	Locations in Bournemouth	Six incendiary devices in retail outlets in Bournemouth. Some ignited causing damage. Two small devices on the pier. One exploded. No injuries
28 August 1993	Wormwood Street, London (City) EC2	Small device discovered containing semtex. Disrupted by controlled explosion. No damage. No injuries
16 September 1993	Curzon Phoenix cinema, Charing Cross Road, London WC2	Two small incendiary devices found. Had malfunctioned, no damage, no injuries
	MGM cinema, Shaftsbury Avenue, London WC2	One small incendiary device found. Had malfunctioned, no damage, no injuries
2 October 1993	Finchley Road, London NW8	Three devices exploded. Five people injured some localised damage. One device found and made safe
4 October 1993	Tottenham Lane, London N8	Two devices exploded. No injuries. Some localised damage
	Archway Road, London N19	Two devices exploded. No injuries. Some localised damage
4 October 1993 *(Cont.)*	Highgate High Street, London N6	One device exploded. No injuries, some localised damage. A second device discovered and made safe
8 October 1993	Junction of Coles Green Road and Humber Road near the North Circular Road junction of Staples Corner, London NW2	One device exploded. No injuries, some localised damage
	Outside the Black Lion public house at 295 West End Lane, London NW6	One device exploded. No injuries, some localised damage
23 October 1993	Wooton underwood, Brill, Buckinghamshire	Device exploded, damaging footbridge over railway
24 October 1993	Reading station	One device in toilets made safe. Another device later exploded by the tracks; no injuries and little damage
24 October 1993	Basingstoke station	One device in toilets made safe
29 October 1993	Edwardes Square, London W8	Small device exploded beside a car. Extensive damage to car, no injuries
14 December 1993	Railway line near Woking station, Surrey	Small device exploded on railway line. Slight damage to line. No injuries

16 December 1993	Railway line, near Brookwood and Farnborough stations, Surrey	Two devices discovered. Disrupted by controlled explosion
20 December 1993	Sorting office, London EC1	Postal device discovered. Made safe. No damage. No injuries
	Travellers Tavern, Elizabeth Street, Victoria, London SW1	Six devices discovered in a holdall. At least one ignited. No injuries, minor damage
	Mount Pleasant Sorting Office, London EC1	Package ignited. No injuries, minor damage
	Northfields underground station, London W13	Small device ignited in a litter bin. No significant damage and no injuries
27 January 1994	C&A, Oxford Street, London W1	Incendiary device ignited. Little damage
	Mothercare, Oxford Street, London W1	Incendiary device ignited. Little damage
	Silverdale Travel Goods, Oxford Street, London W1	Incendiary device ignited. Some damage
28 January 1994	C&A, Oxford Street, London W1	Incendiary device ignited. Little damage
	Mothercare, Oxford Street, London W1	Incendiary device made safe
29 January 1994	Nightingales, Oxford Street, London W1	One incendiary device ignited and another made safe. Little damage
18 February 1994	Record shop, 157 Charing Cross Road, London WC2	Incendiary device discovered and made safe
19 February 1994	Record shop, 157 Charing Cross Road, London WC2	Very small high-explosive device exploded. Minor damage
	Top Shop, Oxford Circus, London W1	Two incendiary devices ignited. Little damage
	Hennes, Oxford Circus, London W1	Incendiary device ignited. Little damage
	Newsagents, Great Cumberland Place, London W1	Incendiary device ignited destroying shop
	Burtons, New Oxford Street, London WC1	Incendiary device ignited. Little damage. A further device was discovered
	Burtons, Regent Street, London W1	Incendiary device ignited and very small high explosive device detonated. Little damage
	Liberty's, Regent Street, London W1	Incendiary device ignited. Little damage
	Mr Byrite, Oxford Circus, London W1	Incendiary device made safe
22 February 1994	Mr Handy, Edgware Road, London W2	Incendiary device made safe

9 March 1994	Heathrow airport, London	Four mortars launched from a car parked at the Excelsior hotel, landing on or near the northern runway. None exploded and there was no damage
11 March 1994	Heathrow airport, London	Four mortars launched from waste ground, landing on an aircraft parking area near Terminal 4. None exploded and there was no damage
13 March 1994	Heathrow airport, London	Five mortars launched from waste ground, landing in the vicinity of Terminal 4. None exploded and there was no damage
15 March 1994	Railway line near Sevenoaks, Kent	IED discovered. Believed to be left over from the series of attacks in December but had failed to detonate
21 March 1994	Railway line, Orpington, Kent	Timer of IED discovered. Believed to be left over from series of attacks in December but had failed to detonate
6 June 1994	Sevenoaks railway station, Kent	Device made safe in controlled explosion
10 June 1994	Liberty's, Oxford Street, London W1	Two incendiary devices discovered and made safe
11 June 1994	Mr Byrite's, Oxford Street, London W1	Incendiary device ignited, causing little damage. A further device had failed to detonate
13 June 1994	Railway line, one mile from Stevenage station	Device exploded on embankment by railway line. Little damage
12 July 1994	Heysham port, Lancashire	Lorry found to contain approximately two tonnes of improvised explosive device
21 July 1994	Reading railway station	Stolen suitcase found to contain two incendiary devices along with component parts for six high explosive devices
13 August 1994	Shopping centre, Bognor Regis	Explosive device, left in a bicycle, detonated, damaging fifteen shops but causing no injuries
	Brighton pier, Sussex	Explosive device found in bicycle. Made safe by controlled explosion
22 August 1994	Regent Street, London W1	High explosive device found in litter bin outside Laura Ashley shop. Device defused—no injuries and no damage
9 February 1996	South Quay, Canary Wharf, London	Two people killed and some forty injured in an explosion

15 February 1996 Junction of Charing Cross Road and Litchfield Street, London WC2	High-explosive device in telephone kiosk disrupted by controlled explosion
18 February 1996 Wellington Street, London WC2	Improvised high-explosive device detonated prematurely on a bus, killing the terrorist transporting the device and injuring eight people

Source: Home Office, as defined in Section 14 of the Prevention of Terrorism (Temporary Provisions) Act 1989. Until 1989 only those incidents which caused death or injury were recorded.

The IRA in the 1970s had associations with some of the many terrorist groups operating in those turbulent years. British bases and other interests abroad were targets for the organisation. Some IRA actions abroad involved the Palestinian Liberation Organisation (PLO): for example, in August 1979 a bomb attack at Grand Place in Brussels, injuring four members of a British military band and twelve others, was carried out in conjunction with the PLO, according to German intelligence reports to the British.[192]

IRA arms smuggling also came to the attention of Israeli intelligence, whose tip-offs would occasionally lead to arrests, such as that of an IRA leader, Seamus Twomey, in Dun Laoghaire near Dublin in December 1977. This followed information from Mossad to the British authorities that an IRA arms smuggler had been involved with Twomey in an attempt to import weapons from Al Fatah – a prime section of the PLO. The weapons were seized by Belgian police.[193]

The Israelis had already been aware of the exchange of IRA bomb-making techniques with Black September (Al Fatah's armed wing, which disbanded later in the decade). These activities were reported by Mossad as having taken place at a training camp near the Lebanese capital Beirut and also a Syrian-controlled camp in the Bekaa Valley east of Beirut. The techniques involved novel ways of using one of warfare's most ghastly substances: napalm. The IRA operatives in training were said to have been taught how to pack milk churns (a classic IRA disguise for bombs) with homemade napalm to produce a hail of shrapnel on exploding.[194] Made notorious by terrible images from the Vietnam War, napalm is a mixture of fuel and gelling solution combined to produce a thickened mixture that readily adheres to most surfaces, most notably, skin.[195] The British army dismantled several napalm milk churn bombs in the 1970s.

ETA

The IRA also built up connections with insurgency groups involved in conflicts far removed from its immediate goal of Irish independence, but seen as brothers in struggle (as well as useful links in the republicans' military campaign). ETA (Euskadi ta Askatasuna – Basque Fatherland and Liberty) was a noted example; very strong connections were established with the separatist group fighting for the independence of the Basque region from Spain. These links were explained ideologically by an IRA statement in 1936: 'The Irish contingent is a demonstration of revolutionary Ireland's solidarity with gallant Spanish workers and peasants in their fight for freedom against fascism.'[196] Many IRA veterans of the 1918–21 war went to Spain to fight in the 1930s on the republican side in the Spanish Civil War. Both groups signed an accord in April 1972. Gerry Adams visited leaders of Batasuna, ETA's political wing, on several occasions.

ETA has – among many other attacks over several decades – earned notoriety in the UK through a series of explosions aimed at UK holidaymakers and ex-pat home-owners. Since 1968, around 1,000 people have been killed and thousands of civilians injured in ETA attacks. The organisation has bombed cars and carried out armed robberies under the name of 'Revolution Tax'. Similarities have been detected in explosive devices used by both groups – and also tactics, including bombings, kidnappings and targeting of security personnel. Both ETA and the IRA have been engaged in a cat-and-mouse battle with the authorities, with their leaders serving long prison sentences, while each has also developed a strategy subject to constraints according to the moderate preferences of some of their supporters.[197]

Following the Good Friday Agreement in 1998 the slogan chanted in towns and cities across the Basque country was: 'Yes; the Basque Country – Yes too'. And the continued connections were not only symbolic: reports emerged in 2002 that ETA had supplied the IRA with fresh stocks of plastic explosives, according to Northern Ireland detectives. This would seem like carrying coals to Newcastle, but security forces believed there was a distinct reason: the IRA was exporting bomb-making technology in return. The concern was based on monitoring of trips made by the IRA to meet the ETA leadership, conducted by a special task force including serving and former members of 14 Intelligence Company, a unit closely linked to the SAS.[198] Shipments from ETA of the American equivalent of Semtex, C-4, would allow the IRA to make a symbolic gesture by handing over some of its out-of-date Semtex explosive without losing its bombing capabilities – and also claim that it was fulfilling a key demand of the peace process, even though the decommissioned Semtex would be past its 'sell-by date'.[199]

The connections between the IRA and the Colombian FARC (*Fuerzas Armadas Revolucionarias de Colombia – Ejército del Pueblo* – Revolutionary Armed Forces of Colombia – People's Army) will be dealt with in Chapter 10.

THE CAMPAIGN STEPS UP

Aside from the blockbuster bombs, the early 1990s – particularly 1992 – was a time of high alert in London, as evidenced by the account below of attacks and attempted attacks on infrastructure installations. In October 1992, the IRA practically had the city under siege, with bombings as well as bomb threats occurring weekly. In just one week, commencing 10 October, seven bombings occurred at a range of targets: near a bridge, a museum, the maximum security police station at Paddington Green, and a pub.[200] But the campaign on the mainland in the 1990s would later demonstrate the IRA's capacity for unprecedented levels of city destruction since the Second World War, the prime examples of which will be dealt with in detail in the next chapter. In its city 'spectaculars' the Provisional IRA would expand its strategy of bombing 'economic targets' beyond all expectations.

This campaign would have gone beyond large truck- and car-borne IEDs into the realms of borderline conventional weapons had the IRA succeeded in developing devices classed as weapons of mass effect – fuel-air bombs. Claims were made by the CIA that the purpose of an ill-fated visit by three IRA men to Colombia in 2001 was to perfect fuel-air bombs and to use the vast wilderness of a FARC-controlled demilitarised zone the size of Wales to test them. One of the three arrested, James 'Mortar' Monaghan, was believed to be the IRA head of engineering, responsible for developing a range of Provo IEDs such as the 'barrack buster' mortars described in Chapter 7.[201]

Fuel-air bombs use a small charge to generate a cloud of explosive mixed with air. The main explosion is then detonated by a second charge (a fuel-air explosion), or by the explosive reacting spontaneously with air (a thermobaric explosion). The resulting shock wave is not as strong as a conventional blast, but it can do more damage as it is a more sustained explosive wave that diminishes far more gradually with distance.[202] These weapons have been used by the Russians, against the Chechens in the 1999 campaign, and by the US, with the BLU-118, in Afghanistan in 2001. The CIA acquired designs for a fuel-air device from the three IRA operatives arrested in Colombia and it was claimed they were developing such a device in collaboration with FARC guerrillas. However, creating fuel-air devices presents far more challenges than the creation of conventional military bombs or terrorist IEDs; even small errors in the design or choice of materials can inhibit a fuel-air device from blowing up.[203] Also, testing the devices, which produce a vast explosion – even in a remote area – would in these days of satellite surveillance reveal the operation.

But the actual, not planned, weapons in the arsenal continued to be used in classic IRA attacks: bombings and shootings. In January 1992 eight Protestant workmen were killed when the van they were travelling in was bombed at Teebane Cross, Co. Tyrone; the dead were claimed by the IRA to be 'collaborators' in rebuilding a British army barracks at Lisanelly.[104] The killings caused widespread outrage in the province and did great harm to the claim that the fight was non-sectarian; it may have been intended not to be sectarian on the part of the Provisionals, but in practice this would often ring hollow. What was clear from the attack was that the IRA did not tolerate collusion or collaboration with 'crown forces'. That could be defined as ordinary folks trying to make a living in the province, albeit in construction projects funded by the British.

PROXY BOMBINGS

The IRA may not have gone in for suicide attacks, but a particularly sinister and ruthless tactic that emerged in the 1990s took away any voluntary aspect of bombing: this was the 'human bomb', which was also used by loyalists. This involved forcing individuals, often targeted as collaborators with the security forces, to drive to targets with bombs in their cars. The proxy bomber along with members of his family would be detained and the unfortunate 'bomber' coerced to take a bomb and plant it. The attacks became known as 'proxy bombs' or 'human bombs' because three Catholic men, whom the IRA claimed had worked for the security forces, were tied into cars which had been loaded with explosives and ordered to drive to British army checkpoints in Northern Ireland.

At the Coshquin checkpoint near Derry five soldiers and the man who was forced to drive the car were all killed. In a second attack, at Killeen near Newry, a soldier was killed. The third bomb, which had been driven to Omagh, Co. Tyrone, failed to detonate.[205] Other 'human bombs' included the two minicab drivers whose cabs were hijacked by IRA operatives and forced to drive to Downing Street on the evening of 24 April 1993 following the massive Bishopsgate blast earlier that day (see Chapter 3). Neither reached their destination.

A particularly shocking example of proxy bombing was the forcing of Patsy Gillespie, who worked in a lowly capacity as an army base cleaning worker, to drive a bomb to the base on 24 October 1990. From this first mission he emerged uninjured, so his wife, who had been held hostage while he drove his car to deploy the device, thought he was safe – having heard from his captors that he was on his way home. She even heard the explosion and assumed that the car was destroyed, but not her husband.

But it was not the car, but Patsy who had been blown to smithereens. The car was deemed too small for the VBIED the IRA intended to use.[206] So they strapped him inside a van packed with 450 kg (1,000 lb) of explosives and ordered him to drive behind his captors to the Buncrana Road checkpoint on the Donegal border outside Derry. From a vantage point the IRA men watched as he was stopped by British troops – then detonated the bomb in the van by radio control and shot five soldiers dead. Of Gillespie, part of a hand was all that was found. The same day, an IRA unit in Newry tied an elderly cancer patient, James McEvoy, into a van carrying a bomb and forced him to drive it to an army checkpoint in the town. He managed to escape before the explosion and shouted a warning – but one Irish Ranger was killed, with McEvoy sustaining broken limbs. There were other occasions when hoax proxy bombs were also used in an attempt to disrupt everyday life. The IRA ceased this tactic following public outrage and pressure from the Catholic Church.[207]

ATTACKING THE INFRASTRUCTURE

Transport
The early 1990s saw a stepping up of the campaign against railway and infrastructure targets. As mentioned earlier, this strategy had already been tried in the 1930s campaign and others before. The IRA, like terrorist groups since, was well aware of the vulnerability of urban commuters. In its campaign against the London underground, eighty-one explosive devices were placed, of which all but two were hand-emplaced time bombs; they had a failure rate of 50 per cent.[208] Although intended mainly to cause panic, such bombs were real terror weapons. The bomb that went off in a litter bin in the ticket hall at Victoria station on 18 February 1991 killed one person and injured thirty-nine, as well as creating commuter chaos across London with the closure of all fourteen mainline stations.[209] Incendiaries were often abandoned on train platforms. Much of the havoc was caused by the need to close all stations on receipt of either coded warnings or hoax warnings – a truly disruptive tactic increasingly employed by the IRA in Northern Ireland at the time and, later, in Britain. The constant security alerts on the underground would present a situation that Londoners would become all too familiar with in the early 1990s and beyond.

The Provisionals also regularly hijacked petrol tankers. This tactic reached a peak in 1976, and included one which exploded while being neutralised by an EOD team south of Newry on the road from Belfast to Dublin. A building and five cars were engulfed in flame and the truck cab was hurled across a field. Many similar attacks occurred with abandoned trucks which would often be accompanied by subsidiary and secondary devices to be detonated by command wire laid well in advance.[210]

Like other terrorist groups which regularly targeted airports and aircraft, the IRA tried to disrupt the vital air link between Northern Ireland and the English mainland by focusing on Belfast Aldergrove airport, which was also used by the RAF and for troop convoys in and out of the province. The airport pub and restaurant were bombed in July 1970 and the fear of hijack led to the introduction of increased security measures and overnighting of aircraft and crews, which were instead flown out to Glasgow from mid-1971. In December 1972 bombs exploded on runways within the 'secure' perimeter fence – a forerunner for the notorious mortar attacks on Heathrow in the 1990s. A truck bomb driven into the cargo terminal bay exploded in July 1973.[211]

But it was the Belfast–Dublin railway – a symbol of some kind of Irish unity and connection between the North and the Republic – that came in for a concerted campaign of IRA attacks. There were eight such attacks in 1974 and many false alarms. In March a signalman was held up and two devices – one in an oil drum, the other in a dustbin made of galvanised iron – were deployed, the latter on the line itself. An EOD squad disrupted this device but found the oil-drum bomb was booby trapped with a pressure plate (see Chapter 6), which was also rendered safe – an operation that took no less than fifteen hours and earned the particular EOD operative, Lt Col John Gaff, the George Medal.[212] Radio-controlled devices were used in a subsequent attack in August, placed on the train at different points. Attacks would come within days and sometimes hours of each other. IRA operatives would watch EOD operations from a vantage point – often across the border – and then adapt their attack methods. Often devices housed in milk churns would be placed on the line to attract the attention of the bomb squad, with another hidden beneath the line.

Power and communications

The attempts on disrupting electricity supplies in Northern Ireland and London was a true indicator of long-term planning and strategy aimed to wreck vital infrastructure – in a concerted aim to force the British to withdraw. This type of targeting is among the greatest of all terrorist threats; efforts to disable the most essential services that keep society and the economy working came perilously close to fruition on many occasions during the conflict, and had they totally succeeded, would have proved disastrous. As it was, attacks on many supply facilities were a regular menace in Northern Ireland, particularly during the 1970s; there were many examples, such as in August 1971 when three HE devices were placed against each of the three main oil-fired boilers at a power station at Larne, cutting off 25 per cent of the province's generating capacity.[213] Earlier, in 1970, the cross-border electricity interconnector in south Armagh had been severed, isolating the Northern Ireland grid from the Republic's equivalent, leading to dependence on internal generating and distribution of electricity in the North.[214]

Many sporadic attempts at bombing substations had been made, such as a landmine attack near a substation outside Stewartstown, Co. Tyrone, which killed an ATO named SSgt V.I. Rose of 321 EOD squadron in November 1974.[215] But in September 1996, a much more concerted plan of attack was uncovered when thirty devices were intercepted in London and Dublin. These standardised devices were to have been deployed at twenty-two named electricity substations linking the National Grid to London (see also Chapter 6). The devices, which used Semtex high explosive and central-heating timer units, were meant to take out the transformer units, along with two spare units per substation. The devices were seized, and attempts to deploy a subsequent batch failed only because the IRA needed more than forty operatives on the ground in London – two per device – to deploy them all, and there was nowhere near that number available. Had just three to five substations been knocked out, electricity supply to large areas of London would have been interrupted.[216]

In 1997, an IRA member on trial for explosives offences, Gerard Hanratty, testified about an elaborate attack that was planned to bring chaos to London using fake bombs containing icing sugar.[217] The plan was to attack six electricity substations and to trick the electricity company into turning off the power. Hanratty said that 'the electrical impact would be total disruption in London. All the traffic lights would be out. It would result in chaos. All industries would be starved – rail, Tube and travel.' Some thirty-seven boxes containing electrical timing devices were planned for deployment; the authorities would have had no option but to deal with the boxes, placed in the substations, as if they were real. 'Any bomb disposal officer called to deal with such a device in the vicinity of 100,000 volts would have to turn the electricity off before. The result would be no electricity in London for however long it took to deal with the devices. It would take a minimum of hours – we felt they would be dealt with in a day and a half.' Hanratty added that it was too risky to place explosives in the power stations.

An ingenious way to confuse EOD squads included the use of wooden dowels the IRA had used for arming the devices since the 1970s, and safety pegs, which would have indicated the devices were fully armed. Icing sugar was used in this instance because when x-rayed it looks like Semtex.[218]

The telephone system was also targeted. In one day in January 1972 eight rural exchanges and a telephone exchange in Belfast were severely damaged.[219] Much of the IRA's campaign pre-dated the computer/communications revolution, and so did not include cyber-terrorism – but the substation attempt would have been much more effective had the IRA moved an operative into the London electricity generating control centre and left him there for an indefinite period. At the appropriate moment, he would have been ordered to destroy the computer system. This would have been more devastating and would have occurred rapidly. As with most cyber-attacks, there would have been less chance of discovery, because the IRA would not have needed to store cars and explosives in highly visible urban areas.[220] Water supplies were also targeted; in October 1971 the IRA blew up a pump house at a reservoir, flooding Whiterock Road in Belfast with a million gallons of water.[221]

NOTES

1. The 9/11 attacks led to 2,973 deaths ('US troop deaths in Iraq exceed 9/11 toll', CBS News, 26 December 2006). Total IRA killings amount to 1,928 (Belfast Independent Research group, 'Deaths directly linked to the political conflict in Ireland, July 1969 through 31 December 1993'). Based upon the revised figures of the Belfast Independent Research Group, http://www.inac.org/irishhistory/deaths

2. A. Garrison (ed.), *Terrorism: Past, Present and Future – A Training Course* (Wilmington, DE: Delaware Criminal Justice Council, 2002), p.46.

3. *Handbook for Volunteers of the Irish Republican Army: Notes on Guerrilla Warfare* (Boulder, CO: Paladin, 1985, reprinted from IRA HQ 1956), p.16.

4. J. McPherson, *Terrorist Explosives Handbook, Vol 1: The Irish Republican Army*, Intelligence report from Northern Ireland (Arizona: Lancer Militaria, 1979), p.1.

5. See K.R.M. Short, 'The dynamite war: Irish-American bombers in Victorian Britain', *The American Historical Review*, 85, 2 (April 1980), p.12.

6. Ibid., p.172.

7. G. McGladdery, *The Provisional IRA in England: The Bombing Campaign 1973–1997* (Dublin: Irish Academic Press, 2006), p.17.

8. See C. Campbell, *Fenian Fire: The British Government Plot to Assassinate Queen Victoria* (London: HarperCollins, 2002), p.61, cited in McGladdery, *The Provisional IRA in England*, p.23.

9. See T. Geraghty, *The Irish War* (London: HarperCollins, 1998), p.313.

10. See C. Campbell, *Fenian Fire: The British Government Plot to Assassinate Queen Victoria* (London: HarperCollins, 2002), p.115, cited in McGladdery, p.22.

11. J. Durney, *The Volunteer: Uniforms, Weapons and History of the Irish Republican Army 1913–1997* (Dublin: Gaul House, 2004), p.62.

12. Ibid., p.63.

13. P. Hart, *The IRA at War 1916–1923* (Oxford: Oxford University Press, 2003), p.158.

14. *Irish Times*, 29 November 1920.
15. See Hart, *The IRA at War 1916–1923*, p.158.
16. Durney, *The Volunteer*, p.65.
17. See R. English, *Armed Struggle: The History of the IRA* (London: Macmillan, 2003), p.60.
18. IRA declaration, 16 January 1939, cited in T.P. Coogan, *The IRA* (London: HarperCollins, 1970), p.126.
19. IRA Army Council to the People of Ireland, October 1938. Files of the Department of the Taoiseach, NAD S11564A.
20. 'The Oul Alarm Clock': 'Wit' me coupla sticks o' geliger-nite and me ould alarum clock' – one of the few rebel songs actually about explosive devices.
21. *A History of IRA Activity in England*, special branch report, PRO HO 144/214358, cited in McGladdery, *The Provisional IRA in England*, p.40.
22. See English, *Armed Struggle*, p.61.
23. Coogan, *The IRA*, p.120.
24. Tom Barry among them, cited in McGladdery, *The Provisional IRA in England*, p.32.
25. Coogan, *The IRA*, p.127.
26. Ibid., p.123.
27. *A History of IRA Activity in England*, special branch report, PRO HO 144/214358.
28. McGladdery, *The Provisional IRA in England*, p.45.
29. See M.L.R. Smith, *Fighting for Ireland? The Military Strategy of the Irish Republican Movement* (London: Routledge, 1997), p.15.
30. Coogan, *The IRA*, p.124.
31. S. Boyne, 'Uncovering the Irish Republican Army', *Jane's Intelligence Review*, 1 August 1996.
32. T. MacCurtain, interviewed on 'Secret History of the IRA 1956–62', History Channel television documentary, summer 2007.
33. 'Secret History of the IRA 1956–62', History Channel television documentary, summer 2007.
34. See Coogan, *The IRA*, p.305.
35. 'Secret History of the IRA 1956–62', History Channel television documentary, summer 2007.
36. C. Ryder, *A Special Kind of Courage: 321 Squadron – Battling the Bombers* (London: Methuen, 2006), p.20.
37. Ibid., p.21.
38. 'Secret History of the IRA 1956–62', History Channel television documentary, summer 2007.
39. Durney, *The Volunteer*, p.50.
40. Including the legendary Seán South, whose death with the 'lorry load of volunteers' in the disastrous raid on the RUC Brookeborough barracks in Co. Fermanagh on New Year's Day 1957 produced arguably the most rousing of the rebel songs, 'Seán South from Garryowen'.
41. 'Secret History of the IRA 1956–62', History Channel television documentary, summer 2007.
42. Durney, *The Volunteer*, p.51.
43. See R. English, *Armed Struggle*, p.74.
44. Ryder, *A Special Kind of Courage*, p.18.
45. Ibid., p.19.
46. Durney, *The Volunteer*, p.50.
47. See English, *Armed Struggle*, p.76.
48. Durney, *The Volunteer*, p.51.
49. PBS Interview with John Kelly, at 'The IRA & Sinn Féin', Frontline online, http://www.pbs.org/wgbh/pages/frontline/shows/ira/inside/kelly.html
50. Ryder, *A Special Kind of Courage*, p.35.
51. B. Hoffman, 'Responding to Terrorism across the Technological Spectrum', US Strategic Studies Institute, 15 July 1994, paper presented at the US Army War College Fifth Annual Strategy Conference, 26–28 April 1994.
52. My father, having grown up in Belfast during the first (1922) Civil War, used to insist that it was indeed a civil war in all but name that was unfolding before our eyes each night on the news in the late 1960s and 1970s.
53. L. Clarke and K. Johnston, *Martin McGuinness: From Guns to Government* (Edinburgh: Mainstream Publishing, 2006), p.166.
54. McPherson, *Terrorist Explosives Handbook*, p.4.
55. Ryder, *A Special Kind of Courage*, p.156.
56. Ibid., p.35.
57. Ibid., p.55.

58. Excerpt from WBAI interview with Martin McGuinness, 18 July 2002, in Clarke and Johnston, *Martin McGuinness*, p.14.
59. Clarke and Johnston, *Martin McGuinness*, p.38.
60. 'Real IRA admits city bomb attacks', BBC News, 11 August 2006.
61. Ryder, *A Special Kind of Courage*, p.190.
62. Clarke and Johnston, *Martin McGuinness*, p.120.
63. Provisional IRA IEDs, Ulster Intelligence Unit document (restricted information).
64. Ryder, *A Special Kind of Courage*, p.202.
65. G. Styles, *Bombs Have No Pity* (London: William Luscombe, 1975), p.75.
66. K. Toolis, *Rebel Hearts: Journeys Within the IRA's Soul* (New York: St Martin's Press, 1995), p.304.
67. 'Bomb Squad', Nova television documentary, US Public Broadcasting Service, PBS (Public Broadcasting Service) Airdate: 21 October 1997.
68. McPherson, *Terrorist Explosives Handbook*, p.13.
69. 'Behind the Mask: The IRA and Sinn Fein' (Peter Taylor, PBS (Public Broadcasting Service) Frontline, 21 October 1997).
70. Ryder, *A Special Kind of Courage*, pp.30–1.
71. CAIN Web Service, 'Bloody Friday', 21 July 1972, Northern Ireland Office news-sheet.
72. Ryder, *A Special Kind of Courage*, p.50.
73. Ibid., p.306.
74. See Geraghty, *The Irish War*, p.211, which tells of the twenty-sixth bomb being exploded during a party at the Europa – to 'celebrate' its twenty-fifth bombing!
75. Ryder, *A Special Kind of Courage*, p.124.
76. D. McKittrick, S. Kelters, B. Feeney, C. Thornton and D. McVea, *Lost Lives* (London: Mainstream Publishing, 2007), p.15.
77. Ryder, *A Special Kind of Courage*, p.144.
78. McKittrick et al, *Lost Lives*, p.229.
79. CAIN Web Service, 'Bloody Friday', 21 July 1972, main events.
80. See English, *Armed Struggle*, p.159 and Geraghty, *The Irish War*, p.71.
81. See Geraghty, *The Irish War*, p.71.
82. CAIN Web Service, 'Bloody Friday', 21 July 1972.
83. 'Bomb-a-minute blitz in Belfast: many injured', *Belfast Telegraph*, 22 July 1972.
84. 'A day of horror and shame', *Guardian*, 22 July 1972.
85. McKittrick et al, *Lost Lives*, p.229.
86. Ibid., pp.229–30.
87. Ibid., p.230.
88. Brendan Hughes, interviewed on *Provos*, BBC television documentary, by Peter Taylor, 1997.
89. McKittrick et al, *Lost Lives*, p.232-233.
90. 'Dastardly act', *Belfast Telegraph*, 22 July 1972.
91. Lt. Col. Michael Dewar, quoted in D. McKittrick, S. Kelters, B. Feeney, C. Thornton and D. McVea, *The British Army in Northern Ireland: Lost Lives* (London: Mainstream Publishing, 2007), p.31.
92. J. L. Arnold, MD et al., 'Mass-Casualty, Terrorist Bombings: Epidemiological Outcomes, Resource Utilization, and Time Course of Emergency Needs (Part I)', *Prehospital and Disaster Medicine*, 18, 3 (2003), pp.220–34.
93. 'For God's sake, what sort of people are you?', *Belfast Telegraph*, 6 March 1972.
94. 'Police pin blame on Provos', *Belfast Telegraph*, 6 March 1972.
95. 'For God's sake, what sort of people are you?', *Belfast Telegraph*, 6 March 1972.
96. McKittrick et al, *Lost Lives*, p.14.
97. 'Police pin blame on Provos', *Belfast Telegraph*, 6 March 1972.
98. P. Magee, *Gangsters or Guerrillas?* (Belfast: Beyond the Pale, 2001), p.157, citing from D. Morrison, *West Belfast* (Cork: Mercier Press, 1989).
99. 'Seven people seriously ill', *Belfast Telegraph*, 4 March 1972.
100. *Belfast Telegraph*, 4 March 1972.
101. 'Personal belongings in room of horror', *Belfast Telegraph*, 6 March 1972.
102. 'What the papers say', BBC News, 29 January 2002.
103. B. O'Brien, *The Long War: IRA and Sinn Féin* (2nd edition) (Syracuse, NY: Syracuse University Press, 1999), p.135.
104. BBC News, 'On This Day', 27 August 1979.

105. 'Bomb Squad', PBS Airdate, 21 October 1997.
106. M. Davis, *Buda's Wagon: A Brief History of the Car Bomb* (London: Verso, 2007), pp.1–3.
107. The US National Nuclear Security Administration chose ANFO – 700 tonnes – for the second most powerful conventional weapons test ever to be conducted at the Nevada Test Site in 2007, which was cancelled due to local opposition that it would release radioactive debris from previous tests.
108. Éamonn McCann quoted in interview with K. Toolis, *Rebel Hearts* (London: Picador, 1996), p.305.
109. Quoted in Davis, *A Brief History of the Car Bomb*, p.56.
110. NB: never use metal implements when mixing explosives.
111. E. Moloney, *A Secret History of the IRA* (London: W.W. Norton & Co, 2002), p.115.
112. A preceding, but nonconventional, example of a 'bomb in a car' having been the core of the first plutonium weapon being transported by car from Los Alamos to Trinity Site, New Mexico, in July 1945.
113. See Geraghty, *The Irish War*, p.208.
114. See Coogan, *The IRA*, p.431.
115. Ryder, *A Special Kind of Courage*, p.65.
116. CAIN Web Service: 'A Chronology of the Conflict', 1972 http://cain.ulst.ac.uk/othelem/chron/ch72.htm
117. Davis, *A Brief History of the Car Bomb*, p.57.
118. Smith, *Fighting for Ireland*, p.99.
119. Davis, *A Brief History of the Car Bomb*, p.58.
120. Moloney, *A Secret History of the IRA*, p.116.
121. Davis, *A Brief History of the Car Bomb*, p.58.
122. S. Grey, 'US learns the Bogside lessons', *New Statesman*, 8 March 2004. Lessons have emerged from Operation Motorman, such as the need to clear any zone where a guerrilla feels safe. Duncan Spinner, whose Argyll and Sutherland Highlanders battalion came to Iraq after three years in Belfast, said: 'Above everything else, there is the need to dominate the ground – to prevent the insurgents being able to prepare and manoeuvre with ease. Only then can you get about and start gathering the sort of intelligence you need.' The second lesson is the famous one about operating within the law and winning 'hearts and minds'.
123. 'Redrawing the border and population transfer', Public Record Office, BBC News, 1 January 2003.
124. 'Dublin and Monaghan Bombs – Chronology of Events', CAIN Web Service http://cain.ulst.ac.uk/events/dublin/chron.htm
125. BBC News, 'On This Day', 17 May 1974.
126. 'Dublin and Monaghan Bombs – Chronology of Events', CAIN Web Service http://cain.ulst.ac.uk/events/dublin/chron.htm
127. J. Bowyer Bell, 'In Dubious Battle – The Dublin and Monaghan Bombings 1972–1974', CAIN Web Service. 'To bomb Dublin required an adjustment of perception, not an easy matter for defenders, parochial and strong in habits; that sort of march could not easily be set to Lambeg drums.'
128. J. Bowyer Bell, 'In Dubious Battle – The Dublin and Monaghan Bombings 1972–1974', CAIN Web Service.
129. See McGladdery, *The Provisional IRA in England*, p.60.
130. When I worked as a civil servant in London in 1974, the office I was in had a bomb scare every week for several months. Bomb drills became a regular feature of office life throughout London. (There was an on–off resentment of Irish people as a result of the attacks and hoaxes: my best friend at the time was from Belfast and was beaten up at least once, and used to be stopped in the street by the police because of his accent.)
131. C. Walker, *The Prevention of Terrorism in British Law* (Manchester: Manchester University Press, 1992), p.32, cited in McGladdery, *The Provisional IRA in England*, p.61.
132. Davis, *A Brief History of the Car Bomb*, p.60.
133. 'Behind the Mask: The IRA and Sinn Féin', PBS, produced by Andrew Williams, reported by Peter Taylor.
134. See McGladdery, *The Provisional IRA in England*, p.66.
135. See Coogan, *The IRA*, p.514.
136. See McGladdery, *The Provisional IRA in England*, p.69.
137. See Coogan, *The IRA*, p.165.
138. Clarke and Johnston, *Martin McGuinness*, p.163.

139. Ibid.
140. P.Taylor, *Brits*, BBC 2 series, 2000.
141. See McGladdery, *The Provisional IRA in England*, p.71.
142. Ibid., p.73.
143. Ryder, *A Special Kind of Courage*, pp.30–1.
144. See McPherson, *Terrorist Explosives Handbook*, p.14.
145. S.P. O'Doherty, *The Volunteer: A Former IRA Man's True Story* (London: HarperCollins, 1993), from p.138. This to my mind remains the most impressive account ever written by a former IRA man of his activities.
146. K. Cullen, 'The Redemption of Shane Paul O'Doherty', *Boston Globe*, 7 August 2005.
147. Most notably the London July 2005 bombings.
148. McGladdery, *The Provisional IRA in England*, p.73.
149. Ruairi Ó Brádaigh, interview with Steve Jones, cited in McGladdery, *The Provisional IRA in England*, p.75.
150. Illustrated by various jokes that did the rounds at the time, including this one: An IRA man is killed in action and goes up to Heaven. When he gets to the Pearly Gates, St Peter asks him who he is. He says, 'I am a volunteer and bomb maker in the Irish Republican Army.' So St Peter says, 'Ah, then you can't come in here my son.' And the IRA man says, 'Aye, and you've all got three minutes to get outa there!' Such jokes reflected the British spirit of laughing at adversity [although this may have been an Irish-generated joke].
151. Frontline Online: The IRA and Sinn Féin, Press Reactions to Peter Taylor's 'Behind the Mask: the IRA and Sinn Féin', W. Goodman, *New York Times*, http://www.pbs.org/wgbh/pages/frontline/shows/ira/etc/press.html
152. BBC News, 'On This Day', 10 September 1973.
153. Ibid.
154. Ibid.
155. The year I came from Liverpool to London I worked in a government office that would be evacuated every few days due to bomb hoaxes. The pub round the corner was bombed twice.
156. BBC News, 'On This Day', 20 April 1974.
157. See Geraghty, *The Irish War*, p.45.
158. With jokes like 'throw it in a bucket of water' persisting to this day. Not a good idea. Suspect mail should always be left on a horizontal firm surface, the room left immediately, the door closed, the building evacuated, and the police called. (Sussex Police Advice & Information: Suspicious Post, http://www.sussex.police.uk/campaigns/suspicious_packages.asp
159. CAIN Web Service, Events: Birmingham Six; Sutton Index of Deaths.
160. Personal communication, Ulster Intelligence operative, July 2007.
161. A. Hill, 'The Birmingham Pub Bombings – a personal account', FIFireE. http://www.birmingham999.co.uk/
162. CAIN Web Service, 'The Birmingham Framework', Fr D. Faul and Fr R. Murray (1976).
163. 'The IRA Campaigns in England', BBC News, 4 March 2001.
164. See McGladdery, *The Provisional IRA in England*, p.92.
165. 'Balcombe Street gang's reign of terror', BBC News, 9 April 1999.
166. Personal communication, garda ex-EOD operative, Dublin, February 2007.
167. 'Whitehall worried by possibility of airborne attacks by Provisionals', *Irish Times*, 7 Jan 2005.
168. See K.J. Kelly, *The Longest War: Northern Ireland and the IRA* (London: Zed Books, 1988), p.228, extracts on CAIN Web Service.
169. Bombings in United Kingdom, Emergency Management Net, Emergency and Disaster Management, Inc. (EDM).
170. BBC News, 'On This Day', 22 December 1974.
171. Intended to lure the emergency services and bomb disposal squads, who would be subsequently targeted by a secondary device.
172. Channel 4 History – *The Year London Blew Up*, http://www.channel4.com/history/microsites/H/ history/t-z/year02.html
173. N. Cooper, 'Terrorist attacks on the London Underground', 27 November 2006, http://en.wikipedia.org/wiki/London_Underground_terrorism
174. Channel 4 History – *The Year London Blew Up*.
175. Causing stand-up comedians to opine that the IRA was responsible for Britain being a nation of litter louts (the jokes being a classic example of the 'Brits muddling through', 1940s Blitz-fashion, and being able to laugh at themselves and others in the face of adversity).

176. PC K. Gordon, BTP History Society, *A Thin Line for Policing the Railways*, 13 January 2003. http://www.btp.police.uk/History%20Society/Publications/History%20Society/The%20history/Printable/A%20Time%20Line%20for%20Policing%twentiethe%20Railways%201670%201899%20printable.htm

177. N. Cooper, 'Terrorist attacks on the London Underground', 27 November 2006, http://en.wikipedia.org/wiki/London_Underground_terrorism

178. S. Boyne, 'Uncovering the Irish Republican Army', *Jane's Intelligence Review*, 1 August 1996.

179. Clarke and Johnston, *Martin McGuinness*, p.143.

180. P. Bew and G. Gillespie, *Northern Ireland: A Chronology of the Troubles 1968–1999* (Dublin: Gill & Macmillan, 1999), p.159.

181. See T. Harnden, *Bandit Country: The IRA & South Armagh* (London: Hodder & Stoughton, 1999), p.239.

182. BBC News, 'On This Day', 20 July 1982.

183. P. Gurney (the former head of the explosives unit of the Metropolitan Police until 1991), *Braver Men Walk Away* (London: HarperCollins, 1993), p.194, and personal communication, Weapons Intelligence Unit operative, British army in NI.

184. RUC and Irish Information Agenda, update 1986, London.

185. O'Brien, *The Long War*, p.157.

186. IRA statement after the 1984 Brighton bombing: 'Today we were unlucky, but remember we only have to be lucky once. You have to be lucky always' (see Chapter 3).

187. See O'Brien, *The Long War*, p.141.

188. Ibid., p.157.

189. BBC News, 'On This Day', 22 September 1989.

190. O'Brien, *The Long War*, p.203.

191. Ibid., p.239.

192. Clarke and Johnston, *Martin McGuinness*, p.130.

193. Ibid., p.118.

194. Ibid., p.130.

195. Burn victims of napalm do not experience first-degree burns due to the adhesive properties of napalm that stick to the skin. Severe second-degree burns such as those suffered by someone hit with a small splash of napalm are the severely painful ones, the ones likely to be survived, and likely to produce hideous scars called keloids [which also bring about motor disturbances]. Napalm is actually harder to ignite than might be expected: thermite is typically used but some forms of modern napalm cannot be ignited by a hand grenade. Various sources, including Napalm, Global Security.org military files.

196. F. Ryan, statement on BBC News, 'The IRA's foreign connections', 14 August 2001.

197. I. Sànchez-Cuenca, 'The Dynamics of Nationalist Terrorism: ETA and the IRA', *Terrorism and Political Violence*, 19, 3 (September 2007), pp.289–306.

198. I. Wilkinson, 'British unit in Spain to track ETA and IRA', *Daily Telegraph*, 31 July 2002.

199. D. Bamber and T. Oliver, 'Basque bombers top up IRA's terror arsenal', *Daily Telegraph*, 30 June 2002.

200. M. Daugherty, 'Successful implementations of guerilla warfare: the IRA', Ireland's Own, Part I, http://irelandsown.net

201. L. Clarke, 'How IRA trio were able to disappear', *Sunday Times*, 19 December 2004. Monaghan and the other three IRA men were accused in 2001 of training the FARC in bomb-making and other weapons training – including truck-mounted mortars and other devices. The 'Colombia Three' were first acquitted of these charges, then, following the rescinding of the acquittal by an appeal court and subsequent seventeen-year jail sentence, in August 2005 turned up in Ireland – at an embarrassing time for the Irish government following the IRA announcement of an end to its armed campaign. Monaghan has since campaigned for Sinn Féin in Dublin. M. Sheehan, 'Colombia Three agitator offers no details to gardaí', *Irish Independent*, 14 August 2005.

202. D. Hambling, 'Experts fear terrorists are seeking fuel-air bombs', *New Scientist*, 21 March 2004.

203. S. Murray, Canadian defence research and development agency (DRDC), in *New Scientist*, 21 March 2004.

204. O'Brien, *The Long War*, p.219.

205. Proxy Bomb Attacks, CAIN Web Service, 'A Chronology of the Conflict, 1990'.

206. Clarke and Johnston, *Martin McGuinness*, p.207.

207. P.J. Bradley, Member, Northern Irish Assembly, 'Living and Functioning under Terror', Confronting Terrorism, Workshop held at Los Alamos National Laboratory, 25–29 March 2002. McEvoy was his neighbour.

208. P. Belton (president of the Foreign Policy Society), Terrorists and the Tube: Lessons to be Learnt from the British Experience in Critical Infrastructure (forthcoming in an edited volume by Praeger Press). http://www.patrickbelton.com/writing/Terrorists_and_the_Tube. html

209. News bulletins, 18 February 1991.

210. Ryder, A Special Kind of Courage, p.184.

211. Ibid., p.130.

212. Ibid., p.162.

213. Ibid., p.38.

214. Ibid., p.129.

215. 321 EOD, Felix Memorial Garden, Thiepval barracks, Lisburn, Co. Antrim, Roll of Honour for Northern Ireland 1971–1988.

216. Personal communication, Irish police EOD operative, November 2007.

217. As will be described in the chapter on explosives, icing sugar was certainly not harmless, but was used as a viable ingredient for bombs to enhance their incendiary effects.

218. J. Bennett, 'IRA planned sugar bomb hoax on capital', Independent, 5 June 1997. On a lighter note, one Christmas in the 1990s saw several instances of suspected explosives packages being carried through security at Manchester airport. They turned out to be Christmas puddings, which have similar density to Semtex. BBC News, 'Christmas pudding alert at British airport', 24 December, 1997.

219. Ryder, *A Special Kind of Courage*, p.53.

220. Michael Mates, Conservative MP for East Hampshire, quoted in Hansard, 29 March 2001, column 1158.

221. Ryder, *A Special Kind of Courage*, p.129.

Three

Spectaculars:
'We have only to be lucky once'

13 Gone But Not Forgotten,
We Got 18 and Mountbatten
         Provisional IRA, following Mountbatten assassination

Today we were unlucky, but remember we have only to be lucky
once; you will have to be lucky always.
         IRA statement following the Brighton Bomb

And these bombs were occurring … when there were secret negotia-
tions going on between Martin McGuinness and the British … and
this was a classic example of the IRA saying look, if you think
you're going to hoodwink us, just you realise how militarily power-
ful we are.
         The IRA Conflict, PBS/WGBH Frontline

By the early 1980s the IRA had restructured itself into five- to eight-member cells and had acquired large quantities of arms and explosives from Libya. Its bomb-making capacity had also come on in leaps and bounds since the frequent 'own-goal' premature detonations of the early 1970s,[1] and it was developing and deploying sophisticated timing and detonating techniques using modern electronics.[2] The IRA's strategy still appeared incoherent: a mixture of attacks on troops and civilians, and the types of device ranging from incendiary bombs on shops to 1–2-tonne VBIEDs.[3] But the effect of this incoherence was deadly, far-reaching, and entirely fitting for the world's most experienced terrorist group. Its improved ability to carry out 'spectaculars' – the term used by the Provisionals to describe a massive attack with maximum impact that would receive blanket media coverage – not only enhanced their reputation as a real guerrilla force, but, most important, enabled them to aim at the heart of the British government (Grand hotel, Brighton; mortars on Downing Street) and the financial heart of Britain (the City bombs: Baltic Exchange; Bishopsgate; Canary Wharf) with full force and increasing precision, details of which, along with the explosives, timers and detonating mechanisms, appear in subsequent chapters.

But the IRA's spectaculars did not begin in the 1980s. Before then, when bombs were exploding on an almost daily basis, each attack often caused millions of pounds worth of damage. As early as March 1969, when Northern Ireland's infrastructure was the main target, a vital electricity transformer at Castlereagh in Belfast was blown up, costing a half a million pounds' damage and showing an expert level of device deployment: four linked explosive charges around the complex had been laid after perimeter fencing had been removed.[4]

And in the 1970s much larger devices began to be used, particularly in rural areas, where heavy loads of explosives were planted and connected by command wire, often in places that were almost impossible to detect. In the 1980s less became more: fewer attacks were causing more damage. Devices also became more varied, so that in one day a car bomb would go off, along with incendiary devices elsewhere, the culmination of which could equal a 'spectacular' level of damage, as on 20 April 1982 when attacks occurred in several places in the province, including incendiaries with a new electronic initiation system and seven-hour timers. A bank in Strabane was hit by a 900-kg car bomb; a garage in Armagh was burnt down by three blast incendiaries; another car bomb went off at the Linen Hall, Ballymena; two more 900-kg devices exploded in Derry and Bessbrook, only minutes apart, with a third 40-kg device going off later in the day in Bessbrook town centre; and a car bomb just before midnight in Magherafelt.[5] The amounts of explosives cited here and beyond must be qualified, as it is almost impossible to accurately determine how much explosive has been used once it has gone off.[6]

HITTING THE FORCES: WARRENPOINT AND NEWRY

The first major spectacular came in August 1979, when there were two in one day: the assassination of the queen's cousin, Earl Mountbatten, on his boat in Mullaghmore, Co. Sligo in the Irish Republic, and the ambush bombing of British army troops at Warrenpoint, Co. Down.

Travelling from an army depot towards Newry on 27 August, British troops were virtually unprotected in four canvas-sided trucks and a Land Rover. A trailer with 227 kg of ammonium nitrate explosives packed in milk churns covered with bales of hay – a classic IRA means of concealment –

was parked beside the road close to the border and blew up the second truck in the convoy, killing six soldiers from the Parachute Regiment – the most hated by republicans – and a British holidaymaker, Michael Hudson. Petrol cans surrounding the hay bales enhanced the ferocity of the explosion.[7] IRA snipers positioned in the Irish Republic opened fire on the convoy.

The surviving troops in the other two vehicles were immediately deployed to cordon off the area and call for reinforcements. A second, 450-kg bomb containing a mixture of south-Armagh-origin ammonium nitrate, nitroglycerine and coal, to boost its firepower, had been planted at the gates of Narrow Waters castle, where in an earlier attack in 1976, troops had sought cover under a similar, but unsuccessful, IRA attack.[8] When a battalion from nearby Bessbrook base, the Queen's Own Highlanders, moved in to conduct a helicopter rescue from behind the castle gates, the second massive ammonium nitrate bomb was waiting for them – and blew up and vaporised a further twelve soldiers, including the Queen's Own Highlanders commanding officer, Lieutenant-Colonel David Blair, the most senior officer to be killed by this time in the Troubles.[9]

It was activated by a radio-control receiver-decoder device hidden in a Tupperware lunchbox, and armed with a memopark timer (the type used in parking meters) that Volunteer Brendan Burns set for thirty minutes just moments after the first bomb did its job. This was the amount of time the IRA calculated, based on repeated recce of the area and the failed 1976 attack, would allow as many soldiers as possible to gather at the spot following the first explosion, and thence be killed by the second bomb.[10]

The explosions were so loud they were heard across the Mourne Mountains over 16 km away in Kilkeel. According to a surviving soldier who was keeping lookout from the back of the first truck to be attacked, Private Tom Caughey, 'All I remember is a flash and a rumble … Then there was a sensation of flying, of losing vision … There were bits of bodies around me, some of them on fire … There was this terrible silence, then it suddenly clicked that my legs were on fire.' Three soldiers could only be identified by their shoe sizes and blood groups.[11] The castle building was totally destroyed and its granite blocks blasted hundreds of metres from impact.

The IRA issued a statement: 'This operation is one of the discriminate ways we can bring to the attention of the English people the continuing occupation of our country.'[12] IRA graffiti proclaimed: 'Bloody Sunday not forgotten, we got 18 and Mountbatten.'[13] As the eighteen

British soldiers at Warrenpoint happened to be British paratroopers, the regiment whose members were largely responsible for Bloody Sunday, their being blown to pieces was seen as a particularly appropriate victory for the IRA.

It was the most deadly IRA attack against the British army to date. It was also a hallmark rural IRA attack, in which a large amount of explosives was expended – some 680 kg – as they could be easily concealed in the countryside as large amounts of agri-materials, such as fertiliser, would normally be moved around in farm vehicles. South Armagh, which came to be known by the authorities as 'bandit country',[14] was the heart of the IRA's rural bomb-making operation. Its strategic location on the border, and the implicit support of the staunchly republican population, meant this area became a haven for planning and executing IRA operations. The South Armagh unit had a degree of autonomy from the main body of the Provisionals and included some of its chief, and most deadly, veteran operators.[15] Semtex bombs, radio-controlled devices and mobile phone-detonated devices[16] were pioneered in south Armagh and the big ammonium nitrate car bombs – the 'city destroyers' which are detailed in this chapter – and mortars (see Chapter 7) were constructed there.[17] The remoteness of the area also provided ideal ambush conditions for the Provisionals – and the army found it the most difficult area to negotiate, move troops, and maintain their bases.

The Warrenpoint bomb marked a sea change in bombing techniques: it used a remote-controlled trigger, enabling the bomb to remain unseen before it exploded – whereas the earlier attack in 1976 had been prevented by the discovery of the command wire, the triggering method then used, that trailed across the road to the detonator of the bomb.[18] According to IRA volunteer Pat Thompson, 'it was military precision. It was thinking about what the British army would do after the first bomb went off.'[19] According to an army spokesman at the scene of the Warrenpoint massacre, 'We don't have eighteen identifiable bodies. We reached this count by the only method we can – taking the numbers missing away from the survivors.'[20]

Another spectacular against Her Majesty's forces involved the use of one of the IRA's most deadly weapons, the timed mortar. An entire series was developed, from extremely erratic and unreliable experimental models up to the 'Mark-10' that succeeded in blowing up Newry police station on 28 February 1985, and which was aimed at 10 Downing Street in 1991.[21]

Before the Newry attack the IRA had tried out early mortars, which were another striking example of its technical teams' ability to create home-made weapons – this time, an improvised missile system – and to keep on developing them until they got results.[22] An attack on Carrickmore police station in November 1983 was the first success with a mortar attack, injuring several officers. But earlier attempts were wildly off target, and were more likely to injure civilians.

For the attack on Newry the IRA used the heavy mortar that became known as the 'Mark 10' by the British army and first used in 1979.[23] The biggest of all the mortar weapons deployed by the IRA,[24] it consisted of mortar tubes fashioned out of an oxy-acetylene cylinder with the top chopped off,[25] that were bolted onto the back of a hijacked Ford truck. The tubes each contained an 18-kg fertiliser-explosive warhead[26] preloaded into ten tube barrels[27] and aimed at different angles to ensure the target would be hit. A timer connected to a battery in the tubes was set by the truck's driver before he exited the vehicle. The battery inside the shells sent an impulse to an electronic detonator to explode each bomb. Just one shell was needed to crash through the roof of the police station canteen, killing nine officers.

ASSASSINATIONS: MPS NEAVE AND GOW

Assassinations were high, if not top, of the IRA's targeting strategy. Airey Neave, MP was the first of two high-profile killings in 1979. Neave was actually killed by the INLA (Irish National Liberation Army, which although a separate armed group associated with the Irish Republican Socialist Party was believed to have benefited from IRA bomb expertise). Neave's position at the time of his assassination was as opposition spokesman on Northern Ireland (before the Thatcher election victory later in the year), and as such did not seem to be a prime Irish republican target, although he was committed to policies to counter the IRA. But claims were made in recent times that he was involved with British intelligence. In 1987 Ken Livingstone, then a Labour MP, suggested in the House of Commons that Airey Neave was a co-conspirator with MI5 and MI6 in disinformation activities involving the controversial whistle-blowing spies Colin Wallace and Peter Wright.[28]

Airey Neave was killed by an under-vehicle movement-sensitive booby trap device which exploded as he drove up the exit ramp of the House of Commons car park – a testimony to the astounding lack of security in those days, even after a decade of IRA bombings. The bomb, which was said to be constructed from less than 2 kg of Soviet-origin explosives (possibly Semtex), was specifically set to go off with the movement of the car up the ramp. Neave's legs were blown off and he was unrecognisable, dying in hospital one hour later.[29]

The bombing was credited to the INLA's 'director of intelligence', Ronnie Bunting, who it was said had gained inside information from the House of Commons – allowing the bombers to infiltrate the car park. But it is just as likely that the device was planted, with a time delay, outside Neave's home, where security was equally inadequate. The *Sunday Telegraph*, on 5 September 1982, named three INLA members as being linked with Neave's murder: Michael Oliver Plunkett, Stephen King, who had just been arrested in France, and Mary Reid. Charges were dropped against them in 1989. Neave's alleged association with British intelligence also sparked rumours that senior figures in the intelligence establishment had decided to get rid of him before he was to become Thatcher's intelligence co-ordinator.[30]

The bombing followed a renewed Provisional IRA campaign, aimed mainly at bank premises in Northern Ireland, and was accompanied by IRA warnings that a new blitz was about to hit the mainland.[31] Margaret Thatcher's 1979 election victory, and her policy on the subsequent hunger strikes in Long Kesh, gave the IRA a vital catalyst for that renewed campaign.

Ian Gow, parliamentary private secretary to Prime Minister Thatcher and MP for Eastbourne, was the other notable MP to be assassinated. The Provisionals claimed he was targeted as a 'close personal associate' of Margaret Thatcher and because of Northern Ireland policy role, specifically as a fierce critic of Dublin's handling of Britain's extradition warrants against IRA suspects. Also of importance was his resignation following the Anglo-Irish Agreement of 1985, saying that the pact would 'prolong and not diminish the agony' in the province.[32] But being a symbol of the British establishment was enough to spell his end. And the IRA did not confine their targets to the top brass – Thatcher and the royal family – but also whoever in public office was vulnerable.

Gow was killed on 30 July 1990 by a 2-kg under-vehicle booby trap device after he reversed his Ford Montego out of his driveway in Hankham, Sussex. He was still alive when an ambulance reached his home within ten minutes of the blast but died as his wounds were being treated.[33] Gow's widow, Dame Jane Whitely, expressed her outrage at the release of eighty-six IRA prisoners from the Maze in 2000.

HIGH-PROFILE ASSASSINATION: EARL MOUNTBATTEN

A matter of hours before the Warrenpoint massacre, the IRA assassinated its most high-profile figure. A 22-kg radio-controlled bomb planted on his boat, *Shadow V* in the waters off Mullaghmore blew up Earl

Mountbatten of Burma and several family members – his daughter, Lady Brabourne, grandson Nicholas Knatchbull, and Paul Maxwell, a crew member on the boat. Mountbatten had been a summer visitor to the Mullaghmore area and did not use a bodyguard,[34] and his boat was left unguarded in the public dock in Mullaghmore where it was moored. Mountbatten was a softer target for the IRA as he was unguarded, unlike more prominent members of the royal family.[35] Despite security advice and warnings from the Garda Síochána, Mountbatten decided to go sailing without security protection, and the IRA's intelligence took advantage of this. Mountbatten had always scorned a major security presence, saying that he 'was used to giving orders, not taking them'. As early as 1960, Mountbatten's estate manager, Patrick O'Grady, raised questions with the gardai about the earl's safety. The police response was: 'While everything points to the fact that no attack of any kind on the Earl, by subversive elements, was at any time contemplated … it would in my opinion be asking too much to say in effect that we can guarantee his safety while in this country.'[36]

Although soldiers were the IRA's main targets (the death of one British soldier was worth at least, in propaganda terms, ten policemen from Northern Ireland),[37] high-profile figures were also on a long list of intended victims. But lesser figures were also targeted, including an isolated Protestant farmer on the border of Northern Ireland, who was a member of the local security force on a part-time basis.[38] And those in the vicinity of high-profile targets were often caught up in the attacks: as well as Mountbatten, two young boys (his fourteen-year-old grandson, and a friend of his grandson) on his boat were also killed. Bombs do not discriminate.

Mountbatten's legs were blown off and he drowned. Eyewitnesses described a roaring explosion which blew the boat high in the air, smashing it into tiny pieces of wood. A local farmer, Martin Dowdican, was working his hay and, watching from his field on the heights overlooking the bay, saw the Mountbatten boat sail towards the lobster-pot markers outside of Oilean Ruadh. He then saw the fragments of boat blown into the air in the huge explosion, along with the shattered bodies. Other people miles away in Cliffoney and Bunduff also looked up in surprise, as their windows shook when the shock waves hit. Joe McGowan, who has written about the attack, described the reaction:

> Dowdican was frozen on the spot. It was too much to take in. Those in the vicinity looked toward the sound in time to see the splintered remains of *Shadow V* fall back into the sea in a tumultuous fury of

water. Paul Maxwell's father, John, hearing what he recognised as an explosion, rushed to the pier … Fragmented, shattered wood, pieces no bigger than matchsticks and barely recognisable as part of a boat, were picked up by fishermen for days after the explosion. Gardai collected them and pieced them together in an effort to discover exactly what had happened.[39]

Other testimonies from witnesses and boat-owners who tried to help on hearing the explosion can be viewed on YouTube (as can official and unofficial republican videos of other IRA actions).[40] One said 'the boat was non-existent. It was just in very small pieces. Blown to small bits.'[41] The IRA detonated the bomb within five minutes by remote control from the coast.[42] One of the leading bomb-makers and leader of the South Armagh brigade, Thomas McMahon, who had been responsible for many bomb attacks, was later arrested and convicted of preparing and planting the bomb (see Chapter 8). He was released in 1998 under the terms of the Good Friday Agreement. Together, Warrenpoint and the Mountbatten assassination realised the highest death toll since the Northern Ireland conflict erupted ten years earlier. A man named Dessie Ellis, who later became a Dublin Sinn Féin councillor, is also reputed to have made the Mountbatten bomb[43] and was jailed for eight years in 1983 for possession of bomb-making equipment.

It has been said that the IRA assassinated Mountbatten not only as 'a discriminate operation to bring to the attention of the English people the continuing occupation of our country' and to 'tear out their sentimental imperialist heart'[44], but also in return for £2 million from Syria, arranged by a Palestinian Liberation Organisation contact in Cyprus. This emerged in the *Sunday Times* article which brought a libel action against the newspaper by Tom Murphy. It was based on revelations by one of the most damaging informers against the IRA, Seán O'Callaghan. Syrian military intelligence was claimed to have 'rewarded' the IRA for the Mountbatten murder and other actions.[45]

Eight years after the Mountbatten killing the IRA targeted the lord chief justice of Northern Ireland, Lord Justice Maurice Gibson. He and his wife Lady Cecily, were blown up by an under-vehicle device in a parked car which exploded close to where they drove across the Irish border on 26 April 1987. The bomb had been detonated by remote control some 200 metres away. The explosion happened on his way towards a heavily guarded police checkpoint and also injured three men and three women in nearby cars. Lord Justice Gibson became a target when in 1984 he acquitted three policemen charged with killing an IRA man. In

January 1983 the Provisionals shot dead another senior judge, William Doyle,[46] and shot the daughter of Tom Travers, a Catholic magistrate, while attempting to gun him down.[47]

STRIKING AT THE HEART OF GOVERNMENT: THE BRIGHTON BOMB

On 12 October 1984, the IRA set out to destroy Prime Minister Margaret Thatcher, whose intransigence it blamed for the death of the Long Kesh hunger strikers in 1981. They hated her with a passion. The bomb that blew out the front of the Grand hotel in Brighton during the Conservative party conference was also intended to destroy the British government. It was arguably the Provisionals' most politically significant spectacular – and, one possible exception being the mortar attack on 10 Downing Street, their most outrageous. Although it did not assassinate the cabinet, the IRA got so close as to send shock waves of tsunami proportions through the government, the British public, and beyond.

At 2.45 a.m., as Margaret Thatcher sat down in the armchair of her hotel room with her back to the window, the bomb exploded with devastating effect. The device did not kill her or the cabinet, but instead claimed five lives: Sir Anthony Berry; Roberta Wakeham; John Wakeham; Muriel Maclean; Jeanne Shattock; and Eric Taylor. It injured thirty-four, a figure that would have been substantially exceeded had the explosion taken place during the day. Television footage focused on the pulling from the wreckage of the Trade and Industry Secretary, Norman Tebbit, grimacing in pain. His wife Mary was left permanently disabled. The bomb was placed in such a position as to cause five of the hotel's eight storeys to collapse.[48] However, it remained standing despite the central section collapsing into the basement. Eyewitnesses to the bombing saw a piercing flash light up the seafront that triggered a chain of awesome destruction. Masonry was flung into the night, ripping the heads off parking meters and shattering a seafront shelter across the seafront. A chimney at the top of the hotel crashed through ceilings and floors, taking with it sleeping guests who were plunged into the foyer and basement. Guests were trapped in a mangled mountain of wreckage, while others staggered into the street.[49]

In terms of weapons expertise, the Brighton bombing was both very simple and very complex – a terrorist 'masterpiece'.[50] In bomb-making terms, it was a truly pioneering operation – employing for the first time a long-delay timer based on that most popular entertainment innovation of the 1980s, the home video recorder. This enabled operatives to plant the bomb months in advance,[51] providing the IRA with many new advantages: bombs could be planted at high-profile targets before suspicion could arise.[52] A parking memo timer, already an established item of IRA technology, was also used.[53] Libyan-origin Semtex was designated as the explosive used in the 13.6-kg bomb, although the IRA claimed it was fashioned from 30–50kg (160 lbs) of gelignite[54] – primed to go off twenty-four days, six hours and thirty-six minutes later. In its statement addressed personally to Mrs Thatcher the Provisionals said, in a quotation that has been oft repeated in assessments of terrorist success: 'Today we were unlucky, but remember we only have to be lucky once. You will have to be lucky always. Give Ireland peace and there will be no war.'[55]

The Brighton bomb was the work of arguably the IRA's most infamous bomb-maker, Patrick Magee, who checked into the hotel on 15 September 1984 under the name of Roy Walsh. The choice of pseudonym was daring, as it was the name of a volunteer who had been involved in the 1973 Old Bailey bombing.[56] He unscrewed the hardboard bath panel of Room 629, which was within range of the prime minister; inserted the bomb inside, wrapped in cellophane to disguise the tell-tale marzipan aroma of gelignite; and set the long-delay timer.[57] He then checked out three days later.

Magee calculated that the prime minister would stay in a room higher up the building in case protesting miners occupied the hotel, and the higher it was planted, the less likely it would be discovered.[58] Sussex police could pinpoint the date on which the package was primed and placed behind the bath panel of Room 629. A fingerprint expert matched a palm print and fingerprint of a man called Roy Walsh, which was extracted from the registration card for Room 629. The same prints were found at the London Rubens hotel, where a bomb was discovered and successfully defused. Incredibly, these prints matched those taken from Magee when he had been arrested for a teenage driving offence many years earlier.[59]

The technological ingenuity involving the bomb's placement at the conference site weeks before the event and the use of a detonation timing device powered by a computer microchip brought to the attention of the security forces, and the wider world, the sophisticated level of weapons construction the IRA had achieved.[60]

But this audacious attack, above all, demonstrated the vulnerability of the British security system. Basic security precautions were not applied to the Grand hotel itself, although some attention was given to the Brighton Centre, where the conference was being held.[61] According to a Belfast volunteer, Kevin McKinley: 'We had done security on that for weeks before Maggie got into it.'[62] Although Thatcher was not killed –

'she was in the toilet when it happened … That's why she wasn't killed, she went to the toilet'[63] – it was a huge propaganda victory for the republican movement. According to Magee, it led to negotiations with the British government.[64]

GETTING CLOSER: DOWNING STREET

The mortar attack on Downing Street at 10.08 a.m. on 7 February 1991 was arguably the most daring attack ever planned by the IRA. It is one thing to attempt to plant a bomb in Prime Minister John Major's government residence, but to fire a series of them with a home-made missile system from a mere 150 metres from the prime minister's office indicated the extent to which the IRA was prepared to stage a political spectacular for maximum propaganda value.[65]

An IRA operative drove a white Ford transit van into Whitehall, got out and drove away on a motorcycle. The van had been bought in London the previous July by three men who paid cash. In the back were installed three 1-m-long Mark-10 mortars, first used in 1979 and which had killed officers in the Newry attack. The mortar warheads incorporated Libyan-origin Semtex with a short-fuse timing device. Launched through a hole in the van roof, the mortars' trajectory sent them in an arc over the roofs of the Horse Guards buildings on Whitehall. One landed in the garden behind the prime minister's house and the others in Mountbatten Green behind the Foreign Office in Downing Street.

The round that landed in the garden at 10 Downing Street dug a crater, scorched the rear wall of the house, shattered windows, and destroyed a cherry tree, causing John Major's Gulf War cabinet to rapidly take cover.[66] The van burst into flames after the mortars were fired. A round that landed behind the Foreign Office exploded and the other disintegrated without blowing up.

According to press reports, as the loud bang of the explosion resounded, a startled John Major said with customary aplomb: 'I think we'd better start again somewhere else,' and moved their meeting to a room in an adjoining building. It was the first use of mortars by the IRA outside of Northern Ireland. The IRA statement on the attack said: 'The operation had been planned over a number of months. Its inception predates both John Major's coming to power and the beginning of British involvement in the gulf war.' Less well publicised was the fact that three people were slightly wounded.[67]

According to the UXO officer in charge of defusing the other two mortars, Peter Gurney, the IRA had worked out the firing range and angle from scale maps and photographs of the location during a dummy run.[68] The mortars were just five degrees off target; had they been more accurately aimed, the assassination of the entire cabinet would have been the result.

A twenty-four-year-old construction worker, Chris Swanscott, who helped put up the scaffolding around Banqueting House, said he was having a cup of coffee when he heard the first explosion. 'It made us jump, and then there were more, about four altogether,' he said. 'The last two were really big. You could see curtains, like, hanging outside the back of the van and it was burning.' An official present at the war meeting, on the second floor, said later: 'There was a loud bang, but *fortunately we've got shatterproof glass in the cabinet room* (italics added – they probably saved life and limb) and nobody got hurt. We were a bit surprised, but my mental process told me it was a bomb rather than a firecracker, and there was some blast effect. My office is covered with flakes of paint and plaster.'[69]

Head of the London Bomb Squad, Peter Gurney, tried to render harmless one of the bombs that failed to explode. Working alone, to avoid placing others at risk, he locked the bomb between his legs and tried to remove the fuse. It turned out the explosive in both mortar bombs had burned away without detonating. (See Chapter 9 for a full account of this incident.)

DEATH AND DESTRUCTION BY ROAD

As mentioned earlier, single bombs were not the only large-scale attacks. Combined and multiple devices wrought havoc, as in the late 1980s and early 1990s in Ulster, when a range of conventional and improvised devices using advanced IED technology coincided with growing politicisation of the republican movement and an embryonic peace process. And the car bomb continued to reign supreme as the IRA's prime weapon of mass effect. Belfast was hit by successive car bomb attacks that exceeded previous levels of devastation, aimed like the 1970s at hitting the infrastructure, army bases and institutional buildings. In six months alone one EOD operator carried out no less than 111 render-safe operations.[70]

The explosions kept getting bigger in the early 1990s. On the last day of May 1991 a heavy Mercedes truck was seen reversing in the street outside the house of a UDR lance corporal in Glenane, Co. Armagh. The truck knocked down a fence as it careered across a field, while two armed IRA men got out of a blue van near the house. The lance corporal alerted the local army base, which was the target of the downhill-bound truck and through whose perimeter fence the vehicle smashed. When the 900-kg (2,000-lb) bomb in the truck exploded, the conflagration killed two soldiers sent to investigate it and a third soldier inside the building. All the building's forty occupants were injured; cars outside were mangled to a pulp.

The blast was heard 80 km away – in other words, many parts of the small area that is Northern Ireland.[71] A 60-metre deep crater was left by the blast; debris was hurled as far away as 300 metres.[72] Ceilings of near-by houses fell in on the heads of residents and their windows were blown in; cows in nearby fields were killed (such effects were redolent of many a 1950s atomic bomb test).

But the IRA intended to blow up even bigger bombs, in the same year. In August 1991 a 450-kg (1,000 lb) HME bomb was driven in a white Nissan 'ringer' van to Markethill RUC station in Co. Armagh, together with two cars (for escort and getaway purposes – a classic IRA car bomb modus operandi). When the van blew up the entire village of shops, people in nearby houses and vehicles felt the blast wave. Although there were no fatalities – an amazing fact in itself and one that was oft repeated in some of these large bomb attacks – the effects for the people of Markethill were disastrous. Businesses closed; houses were demolished; families had to leave or live in temporary accommodation – their own gardens, in some cases. Long delays for compensation occurred.[73]

On 3 September 1991 hijacked trucks were driven to the border to block the roads. Hostages were taken in nearby houses, and a silage trailer attached to a tractor was loaded up with explosive, then rolled down a hill to the border checkpoint – with a captured 'human bomb' driver forced into the vehicle to steer it. But the vehicle was so full of explosive and silage it rolled off the track and became stuck in a swamp. Another enforced driver failed to move it. The IRA unit left the scene, and an EOD squad located the vehicle. After a waiting period of thirty hours (leaving the mobile bomb to possibly go off without harming anyone), several oil drums were removed from the vehicle after a controlled explosion to crack open the tailgate. It took twelve hours to remove eleven black plastic sacks of HME from the trailer weighing a staggering 3,650 kg (8,000 lbs). It would have been the biggest IRA bomb to date. [74] Thanks to the customary bravery of the EOD squad, it wasn't.

CITY DESTROYERS

The term 'city destroyers' has been used to describe hydrogen bombs, the ultimate spectaculars. It may be used, as the 'superbomb' terrorist equivalent, to describe the massive city bombs deployed by the IRA at the Baltic Exchange (10 April 1992); Bishopsgate (24 April 1993);[75] and Canary Wharf (9 February 1996). Total damage from the three City of London explosions was at least $3 billion.[76]

All the bombs were truck bombs. After the 1983 Beirut truck-bombings, physicists at the United States' third nuclear laboratory, Sandia National Laboratory in New Mexico, began an intensive investigation into the physics of truck bombs. Researchers were shocked by what they discovered. In addition to the deadly air blast, truck bombs also produced unexpectedly huge ground waves. 'The lateral accelerations propagated through the ground from a truck bomb far exceed those produced during the peak magnitude of an earthquake.'[77]

BALTIC EXCHANGE

Like the Brighton bombing, the attack on the Baltic Exchange, London's leading shipping market, on 10 April 1992, was planned months in advance and showed how far the organisation had come on in terms of logistical planning and explosives manufacture.[78] At 9.20 p.m. a home-made explosive (HME) bomb in a white Ford transit van parked in St Mary's Axe, 115–160 metres from the thirteen-storey tower block, exploded, killing three people (Paul Butt, Thomas Casey, and Danielle Carter) and injuring ninety-one.

The Baltic Exchange bombing heralded a new and dangerous advance in the IRA's use of large amounts of HME as truck bombs – ammonium nitrate fertiliser and sugar, ground and dried to weapons-grade consistency and wrapped in clear plastic bags. The HME was ignited by 45 kg of Semtex detonating cord wrapped around one tonne of explosives, which were mixed in south Armagh.[79] As Semtex military high-explosive is an ideal booster for bulk bombs made from ammonium nitrate, which will support and promote combustion initiated in another material, the IRA increasingly used it in combination with HME rather than solely, increasing the lifetime of supplies (see Chapter 5). The HME was shipped from Ireland (the sea route was, and is in terms of all weapons-related goods, always the easiest as it is the least secure) – and was assembled in England. It incorporated a US-made Ireco detonator, which was the type used in all three City bombs (and the Real IRA Omagh bomb of 15 August 1998).[80]

The building, which was of modern concrete and slab construction with non-bearing masonry walls on the lower three floors, was directly shielded from the explosion by another building and did not suffer significant structural damage.[81] But tremendous amounts of glass were broken over an extensive area – more than 400 metres in each direction. Glass and fragmentation cause most of the injuries in such situations, as tonnes of glass fall, often from great heights.[82] After the Baltic Exchange bomb some 500 tonnes of glass shards and debris had to be cleared from the street. The bomb blast damaged substantial portions of the windows and dome in the Exchange Hall, which were restored in June 2005. In shattering the tall buildings surrounding it, due to the canyon effect that funnelled the force of the blast into them, the bomb provided the high level of visual impact that exemplifies an IRA spectacular.

Among the injured was John George Brooks, whose daughter Vanessa was unable to work again as an intensive care unit nurse because of the constant memories of her father's injuries following the attack. Brooks subsequently sued the Libyan leader, Col. Gaddafi, for supplying the Semtex explosive the IRA used in the blast.[83]

Of forty-six bombs causing £1,200 million worth of damage in 1992 alone,[84] this one bomb exacted a staggering cost of £800 million,[85] compared with £600 million in total damage caused by twenty-two years of IRA bombing in Northern Ireland.[86] Some 200 buildings were affected, many of which would be badly damaged again in the 1993 Bishopsgate bomb – a level of damage exceeded only by German bombers during the Blitz. Whereas the British taxpayer paid for damage claims from Northern Ireland bombings, claim costs for the City bombings had to be borne by the commercial industry.[87] A total of 325,000 square metres of office space was damaged by blasts in 1992, which resulted in the government paying out £800 million worth of claims.[88]

Companies had to install contingency security measures as a result.[89] The City of London became the most spied-on space in the UK – if not, in those pre-9/11 days, the world – with over 1,500 operating surveillance cameras throughout an area of 2.6 sq km.[90] It was, above all, an alarming sign that the IRA had upped the ante in its mainland campaign in successfully selecting and seriously damaging high-prestige British economic targets. As with the other City bombs, the Baltic Exchange operation conveyed the message that the alternative to negotiation was bomb-borne destruction on an unprecedented scale. As in the past, it was timed to coincide with an event of political significance – in this case, the recent Tory election victory.[91]

The unpredictability of the blast – in fact, of all the City blasts – was key in its shock value. A coded warning incorrectly stated the bomb had been left at the Stock Exchange, half a kilometre away from the actual target.[92] A subsequent bomb attack detonated at Staples Corner in north London, which left a crater in the middle of the A406 motorway and damaged a DIY store, exemplified the use of a long-established terrorist tactic – multiple and/or near-simultaneous attacks. However, as with the other two City bombs, the Baltic Exchange device was detonated at a time when the City was virtually deserted.

BISHOPSGATE – A 1-KILOTON BOMB

The 1-tonne ammonium nitrate bomb that exploded at Bishopsgate on 24 April 1993[93] was the most costly (possibly £1.45 billion)[94] of three blockbuster City explosions. Although it was arguably the IRA's most successful military tactic since the start of the Troubles, in once again striking at the heart of Britain's financial centre, the IRA afterwards called a halt to the English bombing campaign because its leaders believed such attacks threatened to stall the Hume–Adams peace talks and further alienate the Irish government – not fully understanding its real present, and future potential, impact.[95]

Like the other City bombs, the Bishopsgate device was mixed and fabricated in south Armagh. The 30-tonne Ford Iveco[96] tipper truck used for the bombing was obtained via the London criminal underworld rather than the mainland-based IRA network.[97] It was stolen from a yard in the midlands and re-sprayed dark blue, then driven by two Irishmen with criminal records and parked at Bishopsgate – on double yellow lines, a concession allowed on Saturday mornings to building vehicles,[98] within the so-called 'ring of steel' of vehicle surveillance and restrictions that had been set up after the Baltic Exchange bomb.

Eight warnings were telephoned to avoid civilian casualties in the wake of the Warrington bomb, which notoriously killed the schoolboys Jonathan Ball and Timothy Parry in the town's shopping centre.[99]

Despite the warnings, one man – a *News of the World* photographer, Ed Henty – was killed and forty-four injured, mainly security guards, builders and maintenance staff, and those who had come into their offices to work at the weekend.

The Bishopsgate and St Mary's Axe bombs in the heart of the city were the most costly acts of terrorism on British soil. The Bishopsgate attack exceeded the Baltic Exchange bomb in terms of damage caused, an estimated £1 billion: it blasted the Stock Exchange, along with an the ancient Wren's church of St Ethelburga, which had survived the Great Fire of London, and the Blitz, and has since been restored,[100] while another church and Liverpool Street underground station were also wrecked. Repairs to the Baltic Exchange had just been completed, and the building re-opened.[101] All the City bombings had major effects upon small businesses, most of which had poor contingency planning, a very long period of inaccessibility, and a very large cordon (around 1 km in diameter).[102]

The main effect was political and economic damage; the prestige target, the NatWest tower, was shattered, its many windows blasted out.[103] As with the other 'city destroyers', the explosion shook buildings and shattered hundreds of windows, sending 500 tonnes of glass showering down into the streets below. The explosion affected an area of 278,000 square metres, while an estimated £300m worth of damage was inflicted on the buildings and businesses in the surrounding area. Some seventeen companies had to abandon their premises and 137 buildings were damaged within a 400-metre radius of the bomb.[104]

Bishopsgate was at the time the most powerful device ever exploded in Britain. It went off with the power of 1,200 kg of TNT, the equivalent explosive power of a small tactical nuclear weapon ('mini-nuke') – but without the radiation.[105] It was primed by the simple action of switching on the hazard warning lights of the vehicle.[106] A US-made Ireco detonator was used, and possibly a parkway timer (see Chapter 6). These readily available timers were used to set the length of time for car parking. The timer was incorporated into a small plywood box which contained the power source – usually AA batteries or a 9 volt cell as well as the timer. A hole would generally be drilled through the box and a dowel pin inserted to hold the timer at the required delay. The pin was removed to allow the timer to run down.[107]

The IRA attempted multiple attacks on that day. Two minicabs were hijacked, their drivers ordered – as proxy bombers – to drive bombs once again to their prime mainland target, Downing Street. Both drivers stopped short of their destination; one got out of his cab in Judd Street, Bloomsbury, kicked the IRA man out of his cab and called the police; the bomb exploded shortly before midnight.[108] The other exploded at Manor House tube station.

The Bishopsgate bomb was seminal in the history of the republicans' military strategy in its power to wreak dents in the British establishment and ratchet up the process of negotiations. Unlike present-day jihad-inspired attacks, the IRA attempted to avoid maximum civilian casualties. Instead it focused on what it perceived to be a major weakness in the UK economy: the faltering British and European insurance industry. Following the Baltic Exchange bomb, the insurance and reinsurance markets realised that they could not accurately calculate their potential loss exposures for terrorist events, particularly since they could not know the tonnage of the explosives used or where they would be planted. This situation was aggravated by the fact that the insurance industry was reeling from the enormous losses from various events, such as Piper Alpha and the 1987 hurricane in southern England. Significant premium increases followed the Bishopsgate bomb, and the government realised that once they made a commitment to re-insurance, there would be no money in their budget to pay for losses.[109]

CANARY WHARF: THE IRA'S 'HIROSHIMA'

But Bishopsgate was overtaken in terms of explosive power and damage by the Canary Wharf bomb of 10 February 1996. The bomb came just over a year and a half after the IRA had declared a 'complete cessation' of military operations – the first ceasefire of the 1990s, declared on 31 August 1994. Although it was hoped it would be permanent, several factors worked against it. Many IRA members believed that the Major government, in the tradition of Conservative administrations, would only negotiate with Sinn Féin cautiously and would be less willing to budge in negotiations unless the IRA showed its strength. The demands made by the unionists and the UK government for the IRA to decommission were also seen as a request for total surrender.[110]

During the seventeen months of ceasefire the manufacture of explosives and stockpiling of weapons had indeed continued apace, serving to confirm British security services' suspicions that IRA ceasefires were called mainly in order for the organisation to re-arm and re-group. Reconnaissance of future targets was being carried out.[111] In the intelligence community, the breaking of the ceasefire was no surprise, but information available to UK and Irish authorities was insufficient to pinpoint the time, location or exact nature of an impending attack.[112]

Therefore, on 10 February 1996 the IRA exploded another massive truck bomb at a high-prestige target. This time it was Britain's highest building, Canary Wharf, which housed newspaper, television and merchant bank offices in the then newly developed showpiece area of London, Docklands. The attack was preceded by a series of coded messages to the Irish broadcasting service, Radio Telefís Éireann, which, assuming the ceasefire would hold, failed to notify the security services for over an hour.[113] The authorities were no longer on full alert – the 'ring of steel' had been suspended – and so were unprepared for an attack. Attention following the warnings was centred on Prime Minister John Major and the government, while a truck was being parked in the underground car park of the Canary Wharf building – a chilling echo of the first Al-Qaeda bomb attack on the New York World Trade Centre on 26 February 1993.

After driving the transporter down the A13 motorway, the IRA oper-atives linked the timing and power unit containing timers and connecting wires (TPU – see Chapter 6) in the vehicle's cab to the bomb compart-ment in the back. They then set the two-hour kitchen timer. Confusion over the location of the bomb resulted in evacuations and subsequent reoccupations of offices and other Docklands buildings. Then the police spotted the blue car transporter parked outside South Quay Plaza but, realising that it contained the bomb, did not open the car – which would have activated its booby trap mercury tilt switch anti-handling device, connected to a parking memo timer, causing the bomb to explode there and then.[114] As the police attempted to evacuate people in the nearby shops, the one-and-a-half-tonne fertiliser bomb blew up, killing a newsagent, Inan Bashir, his assistant, John Jefferies, and injuring forty others. It also devastated the area surrounding Canary Wharf. The scene of the aftermath resembled a segment of Hiroshima.

As with previous car bombs, the combined half-tonne of ammonium nitrate-sugar HME was packed in plastic sacks, having been lovingly crafted and mixed in south Armagh, like all the IRA's other fertiliser blockbusters. But this was a highly sophisticated device, with several deadly additions: the sacks were packed around booster tubes hidden in a compartment in the transporter specifically cut and welded for the operation[115] and made of scaffolding poles, which had been drilled and filled with 5 kg of that most effective high-explosive kick, Semtex. Its detonating cord was fabricated from plastic tubing filled with the main constituents of Semtex, PETN and RDX military high explosives. A kitchen timer was attached to a nail, which once time had run out at 7 p.m. set off the bomb by completing the electrical circuit. This sent power to the US-made Ireco detonators, which in turn activated the PETN/RDX detonating cord, which set off the booster tubes, triggering the main explosive charge.[116]

The blue flash of the explosion was seen several kilometres away. The two victims were blown through two walls. Office workers in the Canary Wharf building thought it was going to collapse. Windows in council flats and other surrounding structures were smashed. Debris was scattered over an area 100 metres wide. The bomb left a crater 10 metres wide and over 3 metres deep. One injury victim, Barbara Osei, was sprayed with so many slivers of glass that she was blinded in one eye and had to have 300 stitches.[117]

As well as causing £100 million worth of damage (surprisingly less than the earlier City attacks), and rendering a cost to insurers of £170 million,[118] the Canary Wharf bombing had a direct effect on the political situation.[119] On 28 February both prime ministers announced the resumption of all-party talks, scheduled for June. John Major was accused of being 'bombed to the table'; he dropped the demand that the IRA begin decommissioning before talks resumed.[120] According to one paper, 'a half-ton of fertiliser, 100 injuries, two deaths, £80 millions of damage: within nineteen days we are within sight of the negotiating table.'[121] And according to the *Independent on Sunday*, 'Not since Hiroshima has a single bomb achieved the dramatic political effect of the IRA's strike against the London Docklands.'[122]

There were many witness accounts of the bombing. Here are just two. Jamie Thompson was a computer consultant living near Canary Wharf:

> Just as I was about to press play (on the video) there was this rumbling noise. The apartment block was shaking and I remember thinking stupidly enough that it was an earthquake. I was focused on my briefcase, because it was just swaying from side to side as the rumbling noise got louder. The windows on my balcony started to flex inwards and just at the point I thought they were coming in, the briefcase fell over and there was this almighty boom. I'd never heard anything like it before. I went to my balcony, looked out the window and saw a huge pall of smoke rising from the direction of South Quay ... I was about 50 m [164 ft] from where the truck had been parked and that whole area was blanketed by smoke – it was absolutely impenetrable, you couldn't see anything down there. People were just running along the road – some were injured, others had bloodied faces from shattered glass.[123]

The second account was given to me by a cab driver who lived a few hundred metres from Canary Wharf at the time: 'There was the biggest bang I've ever heard. I was thrown off the sofa. I thought it was World War III and they'd dropped the ****ing bomb.'[124]

The bombing caused great concern in Northern Ireland, as had many other attacks before and after the ceasefires. Talk of an IRA split also followed; such a big attack during a ceasefire, much against the aims of Sinn Féin in the midst of its negotiations with the British and Irish governments, was seen as having been carried out in order to keep the hardline and rank-and-file elements on board. In fact it turned out the plan to attack Canary Wharf had been long in the making – commencing around June 1995.[125] The bomb was constructed in south Armagh but, unlike previous operations, was taken to England without using the IRA's customary logistic network or existing sleeper units. Because of the ceasefire, security was lessened, enabling the IRA to conduct reconnaissance and at least one dummy run.[126]

MANCHESTER – A TRUE 'CITY DESTROYER'

The van bomb that devastated Manchester city centre on 15 June 1996 – just four months after the Canary Wharf bomb – was England's biggest IRA bomb, consisting of 1,600 kg (3,500 lbs) compared to 1,000 kg (2,400 lbs) used in the Bishopsgate bomb and 500 kg (1,200 lbs) for Canary Wharf. The seventh attack since the end of the ceasefire, it was executed at a time when the security forces had intensified surveillance and countermeasures in London, and coincided with a lack of progress with the 'peace process'. Six months before the attack – in February 1996 – intelligence-gathering led police to believe that the IRA considered no target too sacred to attack. 'In terms of "spectaculars", they would like to hit anything that features on a postcard of London … anything that would be recognised around the world.' But, as before, the Provisionals would surprise the authorities and the world by launching their next blitz in another British city instead.[127]

According to Richard English, the IRA claimed that the British government had effectively squandered the first ceasefire and had been pursuing IRA defeat and the surrender of IRA weapons. So the Manchester bomb indicated that the organisation could still return to war if it wanted, and could display evidence that it still had the military capacity.[128] It was also, like other ceasefire-breakers, indicative of the power of the hardliners within the Provisionals.[129] The bombing also occurred during a peak shopping period.[130]Manchester had been an IRA target several times before, most recently in 1992, when on 3 December two bombs exploded in the city centre, injuring sixty-five people, and a year earlier, when the Arndale shopping centre was targeted with incendiaries.[131]

Like the other 'city destroyers', the fertiliser explosives were mixed in south Armagh. But this time the mix was shipped from Dublin. The vehicle, a red and white Ford cargo truck, was acquired from a Peterborough car dealer and taken to London where the bomb was loaded onto it.[132] The VBIED was taken to the Arndale shopping centre just after 9 a.m. Coded calls to press and broadcast media gave one hour's warning, intended as sufficient time to minimise civilian casualties, and due to new legislation lower-ranking police were empowered to cordon off and evacuate large numbers of people – some 75,000 – from a substantial area immediately.[133] Initially, the evacuated staff and shoppers stood outside, right next to the bomb, but when the emergency services realised this they shunted them to the nearby Victoria station.[134]

While army UXO experts attempted to examine the vehicle with a remote-controlled robot, the bomb exploded at 11.15 a.m., forty minutes after police had begun clearing the centre, injuring 206 people, mostly by flying glass and debris, and causing more than £400 million worth of damage. Many of those injured were outside the police cordon. When the bomb went off, it exploded at 666 metres (2,000 feet) per second.[135] A Greater Manchester Police video of the blast shows a sizeable mushroom cloud that rises at least 300 metres (1,000 ft) into the sky and is visibly comparable to a mini-nuke blast or a large conventional munition as used by the US air force in the early stages of the 2003 Iraq invasion.[136]

Up to 50,000 sq m of retail space and nearly 25,000 sq m of office space had to be reconstructed. Many buildings were damaged or totally destroyed, such as Marks & Spencer's store and the Royal Insurance building. According to John Grieve, the police commander dealing with the bombing, the attack showed flexibility on the part of the IRA, having to adapt their targeting strategy, but was also 'quick and dirty' – lacking the precision of the City of London bombs.[137] Given the scale of the attack, it was surprising no fatalities occurred; much smaller bombings in Britain had caused fatalities.[138] By the turn of the century the whole area of the devastation zone had been completely restored.

THE FORENSIC SCIENCE LABORATORY

Not so well known or publicised was the repeated bomb attacks on a prime IRA target: the Forensic Science Laboratory in Newtownbreda, south Belfast, which developed increasingly sophisticated ways of sup-plying evidence on IRA operations (see Chapter 9). A vast 1,700-kg HME device was placed on 23 September 1992 in an abandoned truck against the perimeter fence of the lab, and a series of coded warnings put the Belfast EOD squad in a frenetic race against time to deal with it.[139]

When the device blew up it destroyed the EOD robot, propelling and shattering its components as far away as 80 metres. It was one of the largest bombs PIRA had ever used. The blast was heard 16 km away and even damaged protected army vehicles, shattering the windscreen and puncturing the radiator of one of them. The lab was totally destroyed and had to be re-located. The bomb left a 13 x 7 metre-wide, 3-metre deep crater and damaged a staggering number of houses – 700 – as well as a church and other buildings, over a 1-km radius: again, a device of mini-nuke proportions.

The total payout for the cost of the damage to the premises came to £6.26 million.There were 490 owner/occupier claims for damages.[140] As intended, all the forensic evidence was lost. As for human injury, the army EOD team all suffered deafness and hundreds of civilians were treated for shock.[141] The lab had been hit before, first in 1975, when an employee was forced by the Provisional IRA to drive a car bomb to the building. It caused moderate damage but operations resumed quickly.

NOTES

1. M. Urban, *Big Boys' Rules* (London: Faber & Faber, 1993), p.85.
2. 'Bomb Squad', Nova television documentary, US Public Broadcasting Service, PBS (Public Broadcasting Service) Airdate: 21 October 1997.
3. T. Geraghty, *The Irish War* (London: HarperCollins, 1998), p.212.
4. C. Ryder, *A Special Kind of Courage: 321 Squadron – Battling the Bombers* (London: Methuen, 2006), p.24.
5. Ryder, *A Special Kind of Courage*, p.208.
6. Personal communication, Ulster intelligence operative, November 2007.
7. See T. Harnden, *Bandit Country: The IRA & South Armagh* (London: Hodder & Stoughton, 1999), p.198.
8. See Urban, *Big Boys' Rules*, p.85.
9. Ibid., p.86.
10. See Harnden, *Bandit Country*, p.199.
11. Quoted in Harnden, *Bandit Country*, p.199, in which another survivor, Constable B, explained: 'We were picking up bits with sticks. People wonder why people are always blown up that way. It's because when a bomb goes off, the air inside the body has to get out somewhere and the easiest way out is the joints.'
12. BBC News, 'On This Day', 27 August 1979.
13. Harnden, *Bandit Country*, p.203.
14. And the title of the Toby Harnden book on the area's contribution to the IRA's bombing campaign (Coronet Books, 1999). Although a quotation in the book looks at the term from the republican point of view: 'The only bandits I ever saw in South Armagh were wearing British uniforms.' Peter John Caraher, Cullyhanna, 1998. Harnden, *Bandit Country*, p.49.
15. Harnden, *Bandit Country*, p.20.
16. Which was the latest, but failed, mechanism for the attempted car bomb attacks in London and Glasgow, June 2007.
17. Harnden, *Bandit Country*, p.19.
18. Urban, *Big Boys' Rules*, p.86.
19. Quoted in Harnden, *Bandit Country*, p.197.
20. 'Huge hunt on as Ireland reels to mass killings', New Zealand Press Association/Reuters, 27 August 1979.
21. Geraghty, *The Irish War*, p.217.
22. Urban, *Big Boys' Rules*, p.206.
23. Geraghty, *The Irish War*, p.192.
24. Harnden, *Bandit Country*, p.41.
25. Urban, *Big Boys' Rules*, p.207.
26. Harnden, *Bandit Country*, p.41.
27. Geraghty, *The Irish War*, p.192.
28. P. Vallely, 'The Airey Neave Files', *Independent*, 22 February 2002.
29. J. Hiddleston, review of P. Routledge, *Public Servant, Secret Agent: The Elusive Life and Violent Death of Airey Neave*, Media Monitors Network, 31 March 2003.
30. Ibid.
31. BBC News, 'On This Day', 30 March 1979.
32. S. Rule, 'British legislator, foe of IRA, is killed by a bomb at his home', *New York Times*, 31 July 1990.
33. Ibid.

34. CAIN Web Service, A Chronology of the Conflict, 1979. http://cain.ulst.ac.uk/othelem/chron/ch79.htm

35. He was also an iconic figure with a legendary past. My particular knowledge of him was that, on 11 May 1979, when he was awarded the Louise Weiss Foundation Prize by the Stockholm International Peace Research Institute, he gave a speech against nuclear weapons.

36. J. McGowan, '13 gone but not forgotten, we got 18 and mountbatten', http://www.thewildgeese.com, Erin's Far-flung Exiles, GAR Media LLC, 22 August 2004. The author kept a piece of the wreckage of the *Shadow V*, Lord Mountbatten's yacht.

37. 'The IRA Conflict', PBS/WGBH Frontline TV documentary transcript, 1998.

38. Ibid.

39. McGowan, '13 gone but not forgotten ...'

40. Irish Republican Media. Some videos are tributes to the IRA, and vary in their extremity. But some are rare examples of authentic training and operational footage, including bombing, and mortar-firing equipment is shown on some of these videos.http://www.youtube.com/profile?user=IrishRepublicanMedia

41. Assassination of Lord Mountbatten, YouTube, http://www.youtube.com/watch?v=9uezlu_LiBQ

42. Relative of Queen Elizabeth became the target of fatal terrorist attack, *New York Jewish Times*, 27 August 1979.

43. Clarke and Johnston, *Martin McGuinness*, p.136.

44. Ibid., p.135.

45. 'Syria helped IRA kill Mountbatten, says paper', Agence France Presse, 18 May 1998.

46. CAIN Web Service, 'A Chronology of the Conflict', 1983.

47. Reuters, 'Judge and wife slain by IRA in car bombing', *New York Times*, 26 April 1987.

48. 'Secret History: Brighton Bomb', Channel 4 Television, 15 May 2003.

49. BBC News, 'On This Day', 12 October 1984.

50. Geraghty, *The Irish War*, p.67.

51. G. McGladdery, *The Provisional IRA in England: The Bombing Campaign 1973–1997* (Dublin: Irish Academic Press, 2006), p.126.

52. 'Secret History: Brighton Bomb', Channel 4 Television, 15 May 2003.

53. Personal communication, Ulster Intelligence Unit operative.

54. A. MacEoin, 'IRA bombs British cabinet in Brighton', *An Phoblacht*, 11 October 2001.

55. Ibid.

56. P. Bishop and E. Mallie, *The Provisional IRA* (London: Corgi, 1987), p.425.

57. Ibid. and personal communication, Ulster Intelligence Unit operative.

58. Bishop and Mallie, *The Provisional IRA*, p.424.

59. Ibid.

60. B. Hoffman, 'Responding to terrorism across the technological spectrum', US Strategic Studies Institute, 15 July 1994, paper presented at the US Army War College Fifth Annual Strategy Conference, 26–28 April 1994.

61. 'Secret History: Brighton Bomb', Channel 4, May 2003, and 'The Hunt for the Bomber', BBC1, 13 September 2004.

62. Quoted in Harnden, *Bandit Country*, p.379.

63. Ibid., p.379.

64. See R. English, *Armed Struggle: The History of the IRA* (London: Macmillan, 2003), interview with Patrick Magee, p.248.

65. Geraghty, *The Irish War*, p.103.

66. Harnden, *Bandit Country*, p.336.

67. C.R. Whitney, 'IRA attacks 10 Downing Street with mortar fire as cabinet meets', *New York Times*, 8 February 1991.

68. Peter Gurney, in 'Bomb Squad', Nova TV documentary, PBS Airdate: 21 October 1997, http://www.pbs.org/wgbh/nova/transcripts/2413bombsquad.html

69. Whitney, 'IRA attacks 10 Downing Street'.

70. Ryder, *A Special Kind of Courage*, p.238.

71. If I, sitting here in my seafront flat in Hove, Sussex, heard what I interpreted or learnt later was a bomb blast 80 km away, I would – at least for an instant – imagine it were a mini-nuclear explosion on the outskirts of London. That's the kind of distance we are talking about here. Only the current (2007) vast conventional bombs in the US, Russian and UK military arsenals come anywhere near this level of explosive power.

72. Ryder, *A Special Kind of Courage*, p.250.
73. B. O'Brien, *The Long War: IRA and Sinn Féin* (2nd edition) (Syracuse, NY: Syracuse University Press, 1999), p.214.
74. And exceeding the largest conventional bombs in the UK military arsenal by a factor of three. Ryder, *A Special Kind of Courage*, p.250.
75. 24 April was the date of the outbreak of the 1916 Easter Rising and the Declaration of the Irish Republic. The IRA also chose that date to try and blow up Hammersmith Bridge with the largest Semtex devices deployed in England, to commemorate the eightieth anniversary of the Easter Rising. The detonators failed (see Chapter 9).
76. M. Davis, *Buda's Wagon: A Brief History of the Car Bomb* (London: Verso, 2007), pp.134–9.
77. Ibid., p.116.
78. See McGladdery, *The Provisional IRA in England*, p.158.
79. See Harnden, *Bandit Country*, p.317.
80. T. Harding, 'Real IRA leader is finally brought to justice after three decades of terror', *Daily Telegraph*, 7 August 2003.
81. 'Protecting Buildings from Bomb Damage: Transfer of Blast-Effects Mitigation Technologies from Military to Civilian Applications', Commission on Engineering and Technical Systems (Washington, DC: National Academies Press, Div. On Engineering and Physical Sciences: 1995).
82. T. Hillier, Operational Support Department of the City of London Police, 'Bomb Attacks in City Centers', *FBI Law Enforcement Bulletin*, 63, 9 (September 1994), pp.13–17.
83. H. McDonald, 'Gaddafi sued by 160 victims of the IRA,' *Guardian*, 23 April 2006.
84. O. Bowcott interviewing IRA GHQ staff member in the *Guardian*, cited in Harnden, *Bandit Country*, p.318.
85. 'Insurers braced for large claims', *Financial Times*, 14 April 1992.
86. Davis, *A Brief History of the Car Bomb*, pp.134–9.
87. See Geraghty, *The Irish War*, p.217.
88. 'The Cost of Terrorism', BBC News, 15 May 2004.
89. Hillier, 'Bomb Attacks in City Centres'.
90. J. Coaffee, *Terrorism, Risk and the City: The Making of a Contemporary Urban Landscape* (Burlington, VT: Ashgate, 2003).
91. See McGladdery, *The Provisional IRA in England*, p.158.
92. Ibid.
93. Ibid.
94. See E. Moloney, *A Secret History of the IRA* (London: W.W. Norton & Co, 2002), p.411.
95. Ibid., p.411.
96. O'Brien, *The Long War*, p.272.
97. Harnden, *Bandit Country*, p.338.
98. 'Take steps to end war', *An Phoblacht*, 29 April 1993, cited in McGladdery, *The Provisional IRA in England*, p.171.
99. Geraghty, *The Irish War*, p.218.
100. The church has been re-designated an innovative Centre for Reconciliation and Peace.
101. BBC News, 'On This Day', 24 April 1993.
102. J. Liebenau, 'Emergency communications; lessons from the World Trade Center disaster', in M. Noll, *Communications on September 11th 2001* (New York: Taylor & Francis 2003).
103. Ibid.
104. 'The Cost of Terrorism', BBC News, 15 May 2004.
105. Various personal scientific sources, including Los Alamos National Laboratory; Home Office pamphlet, 'Business as Usual: Maximising Business Resilience to Terrorist Bombings, case study Bishopsgate'.
106. Home Office pamphlet, 'Business as Usual', p.5.
107. Personal communication, Ulster Intelligence Unit operative.
108. 'Hijacked minicabs signal return of "proxy" bombers', *Observer*, 25 April 1993.
109. A. J. Fleming, 'An Explosive Topic: Terrorism Coverage in the United Kingdom', *Risk Management* (New York: Risk Management Soc Publishing Inc, 1994).
110. McGladdery, *The Provisional IRA in England*, pp.188–9.
111. E. Moloney, 'Rebel units told "Prepare to Resume War"', *Sunday Tribune*, 9 July 1995, cited in McGladdery, *The Provisional IRA in England*, p.189.
112. S. Boyne, Uncovering the Irish Republican Army, *Jane's Intelligence Review*, 1 August 1996.

113. McGladdery, *The Provisional IRA in England*, p.192.
114. Harnden, *Bandit Country*, p.8.
115. Ibid., p.21.
116. Ibid., p.7.
117. Ibid., p.8.
118. 'The Cost of Terrorism', BBC News, 15 May 2004.
119. Geraghty, *The Irish War*, p.221.
120. 'Bombed to the table', *Sunday Times*, 3 March 1996.
121. Cited in Geraghty, *The Irish War*, p.241.
122. Editorial, *Independent on Sunday*, 3 March 1996, cited in Geraghty, *The Irish War*, p.221.
123. BBC News, 'On This Day', 10 February 1996.
124. Personal communication, London cabbie, November 2007. He partially lost his hearing for several days.
125. Harnden, *Bandit Country*, p.22.
126. Ibid., p.22.
127. S. Boggan, 'IRA "may bomb without warning"', *Independent*, 25 February 1996.
128. Prof. Richard English, interviewed by the BBC's 'Inside Out in the North West' regional TV programme, 27 February 2006.
129. McGladdery, *The Provisional IRA in England*, p.204.
130. Harnden, *Bandit Country*, p.345.
131. BBC News, 'On This Day', 3 December 1992.
132. Harnden, *Bandit Country*, pp.343–4.
133. McGladdery, *The Provisional IRA in England*, p.203.
134. The Manchester Bombing, The IRA bombing of City Centre Manchester, June 1996, Manchester UK, A Virtual Encyclopedia of Greater Manchester in the Third Millennium, http://www.manchester2002-uk.com/buildings/bombing.html
135. 'Manchester Bomb, No Justice', BBC News, 15 June 2006.
136. Greater Manchester Police (GMP) website, Manchester Bomb Investigation, http://www.gmp.police.uk/mainsite/pages/manchesterbombing.htm
      GMP website, Manchester Bomb Investigation.
138. Professor Richard English, interviewed by the BBC's 'Inside Out in the North West' regional TV programme, 27 February 2006.
139. Ryder, *A Special Kind of Courage*, pp.244–5.
140. Parliamentary Question by John D. Taylor MP, Forensic Science Laboratory, Newtownbreda, House of Commons Hansard Debates, 1 December 1992.
141. Ryder, *A Special Kind of Courage*, p.245.

Four

Amassing the Arsenal

When the first tranche of decommissioning of the IRA's vast arsenal – reputedly enough to arm two battalions – was announced in October 2001, the extent of its inventory was truly staggering. The total Provisional IRA stockpile was reported as including fifty heavy and general-purpose machine-guns, forty rocket launchers, grenades, mortars, ground-to-air missiles, two to three tonnes of Semtex – enough for a fifteen-year campaign – and for bombs powerful enough to destroy several multi-storey buildings. After its formation the Provisional IRA quickly became the most heavily and effectively armed terrorist group in Northern Ireland and possibly the world.

TABLE 4.1: AMASSING THE ARSENAL: IRA ARMS PROCUREMENT 1969–1996

Type, quantity of arms	Origin	Date	Comments
About seventy small arms: M1 carbines; M3 'grease guns'; some hand guns;	US	1969	Arms acquired originally for the 1950s campaign. Smuggled to Ireland by Harrison network.
60,000 rounds of ammo			
Revolvers x 50	Spain	c1970	Arms reported to have been supplied by Basque group ETA
9 mm pistols x 500 FRG 180,000 rounds		1969–70	Arms bought not for IRA but for defence groups in North, but IRA planned to seize them. Irish authorities foiled moves to import guns. Four later acquitted in famous arms trial.
Armalite AR-15 rifles	US	1970	Consignment smuggled to Ireland by group of republican sympathizers in Philadelphia.

Small arms and ammo	US	1971	Six suitcases full of small arms and ammo seized by police at Dublin port after being landed by ship from US.
4.5 tonnes of small arms	Czechoslovakia	1971	Shipment arranged by IRA leader Daithi Ó Conaill; bought from Omnipol Prague; seized at Schiphol airport.
Small arms	Libya	1972	Unconfirmed reports that two cargoes of arms from Libya reached Ireland.
RPG-7 rocket launchers	Europe	1972	Reported import of RPG-7s from unknown source in Europe.
M-16s and AR-15s	US	Early 1970s	Smuggled to Ireland by Harrison network.
AK-47 rifles x 250, plus other material	Libya	1973	Czech-made arms supplied by Col Gaddafi; cargo aboard *Claudia* seized by Irish authorities. IRA boss Joe Cahill and others arrested.
100 rifles	US	1974	US Treasury Dept agents foil plot to smuggle to IRA cargo of arms bought at Maryland gun shop. Five later jailed in US.
Small arms: AK-47s x 27; SMGs x 29; RPG-7 rocket launchers x 7; Bren Guns x 2; plus grenades, ammo and explosives	Middle East	1977	Arms supplied by Al Fatah section of PLO. Cargo sent by ship via Cyprus; seized at Antwerp. One IRA man arrested by Irish police. Arms believed to have come from Lebanon.
M-60 MGs x 6; M-16 rifles x c100	US	1977	Arms stolen from US army depot; smuggled by ship to Ireland by Harrison network.
Estimated 500,000 5.56 x 45 mm cartridges	US	1973–78	Ammo stolen from US Marine base, Camp LeJeune, North Carolina. Believed sent to Ireland by Harrison network.
Cargo of more than 150 guns and 60,000 rounds of ammo. Arms included: M-60 MGs x 2; M-16s x 15; M-14s; AK-47 x 1	US	1979	Cargo smuggled by ship to Ireland by Harrison network; seized at Dublin port by police.

MAC-10 SMGs x 350; AK-47 x 12	US	1981	Harrison network plot foiled in FBI 'sting'. Leads to break-up of network.
Fifty firearms and ammo; tone frequency switches	US	1982	US Customs find arms in truck at docks in Newark,New Jersey. Four members of IRA cell later jailed.
Two hundred cases of mixed ammo	US	1982	Five men arrested entering US from Canada; suspected of plot to acquire ammo for IRA. 'Shopping list' for two hundred cases found.
Explosives	US	1983	FBI foils IRA bid to buy explosives in Wyoming. Man arrested.
Seven tonnes of arms, ammo and explosives	US	1984	Cargo seized on fishing boat *Marita Ann* by Irish navy. Men jailed in US and Ireland. Arms procured by drugs gang in Boston.
Small arms	US	1985	FBI foils IRA bid to buy small arms in Colorado. Irishman deported.
Forty firearms, including: FN FAL rifles x 13; AK-47 x 1. Also: hand grenades x 2, drums of nitro benzene, 70,000 rounds of ammunition	Netherlands	1986	Dutch police seize arms in raid on apartment in Amsterdam. Two well-known IRA men arrested.
Heckler & Koch G3 rifles	Norway	1984–86	Irish police seize ten G3 rifles in 1986 – part of batch of 100 stolen from Norwegian Reserve base near Oslo, 1984.
Redeye SAMs, M-60 MGs, M-16 rifles, MP-5 SMGs, bullet-proof vests x 11	US	1986	FBI 'sting' foils plot to fly arms cargo by private jet from Boston to Ireland. Several convictions followed.
150 tonnes of arms: AK-47s, SAM-7s (reported), Semtex, RPG-7 rocket launchers, Taurus pistols, plus other material	Libya	1985–87	Four shipments of arms and explosives successfully landed in Ireland by boat skipper Adrian Hopkins.

AK-47s x 1,000, SAM-7s x 20, RPG-7s, 2 tonnes of Semtex .	Libya	1987	French Navy seize cargo on *Eksund*, skippered by Adrian Hopkins, off Brittany. Five arrested.
380 gallons of nitro benzene	Netherlands	1988	Cargo smuggled from Amsterdam aboard truck; seized by Irish police, Kells, Co. Meath. Driver later jailed.
Small arms, described as 'high-powered rifles'	US	1988	US Customs foil bid to buy rifles from gun dealer in Alabama. Two men jailed.
Detonators for bombs; anti-aircraft missile system	US	c1982–88	Group of IRA supporters jailed in Boston in 1990 for trying to smuggle a homemade missile system to Ireland. Member of group is also believed to have supplied detonators in 1982–88.
Stinger missiles	US	Late 1980s/ early 1990s	FBI foils plot to acquire Stingers on black market in Miami. Several arrests made.

Type	Role	Quantity
Webley .455	Revolver	60
AK-47/AKM	Assault rifle	650
Armalite AR-15	Assault rifle	a few dozen
Barrett M82A1	Sniper rifle	1
7.62 mm FN MAG	Machine-gun	12
12.7 x 107 mm DshK	Heavy machine-gun	20
RPG-7	Rocket launcher	40
SAM-7 (may not be serviceable)	Surface-to-air missile	1
LPO-50	Flamethrower	6
Detonators	For use in bombs	600
Semtex	Explosive	3 tonnes

The diversity of weapons and their sources equalled their number in terms of enormity: from the most powerful military high explosive available – Semtex, originally from Czechoslovakia via Libya – to Russian RPG-7 rockets and Kalashnikov rifles; US Armalites and M60 machine-guns; and Chinese Simarol and Israeli Uzi rifles. There are conflicting reports about the total number of handguns in the possession of the Provisional IRA, although security sources estimate an arsenal of some 600.[1] The IRA's adept use of 'homemade' weaponry and ingenious technologies was complemented by the acquisition of these weapons, many of which became more sophisticated and powerful from the late 1970s on – such as the homemade mortar bombs and firing systems and numerous bombs that contained hundreds of kilos of homemade explosives. The creation of these required considerable machine-tool and electronics expertise.[2] From the ramshackle, ad-hoc acquisition of clapped out guns and ammunition that characterised the early rebellions and persisted right through to the 1970s campaigns, the advanced weapons the IRA were seeking by the late 1970s included surface-to-air missiles to shoot down helicopters.[3] The British army had begun increasingly to use this means to transport troops in order to avoid their being blown up by IRA roadside ambushes,[4] and were vital in the re-supply of British military bases.

This did not include arms and explosives stolen by the breakaway dissident Real IRA (RIRA).[5] Irish gardaí had uncovered an arms cache earlier, in February 2001, which included a PRIG (propelled rocket improvised grenade) armed with a 1-lb Semtex warhead in a dangerous condition, which was removed and detonated by an army ordnance team.

The indications were that several tranches would be needed to disarm the IRA, and that – to this day – not all arms may be accounted for. In February 2006 the Press Association reported that security sources claimed some IRA men may have retained weapons. According to the Independent International Commission on Decommissioning (IIDC), however, 'there was no indication that the quantities of arms involved were substantial. We were also told there is no suggestion these arms [purportedly kept for personal protection and area defence] have been retained with the approval of the IRA's leadership or as part of a wider strategy to return to violence.' But the IICD also said that it did not discount the possibility that a small number of the IRA's weapons may have gone astray over the years as custodians died or the locations of some its arms caches were lost.[6]

THE EXTENT OF THE ARSENAL

At the time of the first decommissioning tranche, the IRA had an over-supply of assault rifles – 600.[7,8] Also in the arsenal were some sixty US Armalite rifles; twelve 7.62 mm FN MAG medium machine-guns; twenty 12.7 mm x 107 mm DShK heavy machine-guns; two to three SAM-7 anti-aircraft missiles; forty RPG-7 rocket launchers; forty Webley .455 revolvers; six LPO-50 flame throwers; and 600 assorted detonators, many from the US.[9] According to a British intelligence handbook, the IRA had eight types of pistol, nine types of rifle, four types of machine-gun, and two types of missile systems.[10]

During the 1970s and 1980s – at the height of the Troubles – the two main sources of weaponry for the IRA were the US and Libya. But before, during and after these illicit shipments, the IRA and its forebears had acquired funding for arms from robberies, protection rackets, kidnappings, republican club contributions, local collections and personal donors.[11] But such a plentiful supply of the means of destruction was not always available. The precursors of the IRA – the Fenian Brotherhood, Irish Republican Brotherhood and the Irish Volunteers – had to steal and scrape together anything they could get their hands on.

STORING THE INVENTORY

Storage of the IRA's weapons in modern times, however, much of which was in large dumps in the Republic, was under the auspices of Southern Command. Smaller border dumps were under the control of Northern Command, which had to make arms readily available for the immediate use of active service units (ASUs).[12] The Provisionals have maintained two types of dumps: 'army (or GHQ) dumps', where major reserves of material were stored, mainly in the Republic; and 'unit dumps' containing small amounts for the immediate use of local units.[13] The IRA's quartermaster general (QMG), who controlled the arms dumps throughout Ireland, was reputed to be living just south of the border near Dundalk. The QMG was arguably the most important member of IRA personnel and his department was the biggest in the IRA, accounting for 20 per cent of manpower.[14] The QMG had to not only acquire and smuggle weapons in, but also find secure dumps for them. Responsibility for major arms dumps in the Munster area was reputedly in the hands of an IRA man based in Limerick who reported to the QMG.[15] From the dumps in the Republic, supply lines had to be established and constantly changed by the QMG Department to the units operating in the North, England, and

Europe. Many of the locations still remain top secret, and the IRA leadership have, before and during the 1990s decommissioning phase, remained reluctant to discuss the state of their armouries.[16] However, in the early days of the modern conflict, the whereabouts of IRA camps and dumps emerged. In 1969 there were many weapons secreted in the South, such as in Co. Kerry and farmland areas elsewhere in the Republic.

The larger, more remote and minimally policed areas of the Republic, particularly in the Munster area,[17] provided far greater scope for arms storage than the six counties. To defeat airborne army surveillance, major arms bunkers were located inside farm buildings or under silage pits. The North was replete with surveillance equipment and observation posts, whereas the Republic was not. Dumps were protected from discovery in a variety of ways, such as sound- and light-sensitive devices, which were in use by the mid-1970s.[18] Much of the smaller guns and explosives were stored in barrel-shaped containers for ready collection and use.[19]

Storing weapons in the Republic also meant less chance of them being interfered with – 'jarked' – by the security services, to make them malfunction (see Chapter 9). The Irish forces did not for a long time have the means to monitor weapons or sabotage them.[20]

IRA units in the border areas linked to Donegal and Leitrim would be tasked with moving arms into the 'war zone'.[21] The most staunchly republican border area, south Armagh, with logistical support from Dundalk, operated almost as an autonomous territory, with units moving weapons across the 'invisible' border in a countryside they knew inside out.

The United States became a source of weapons only once the Roman Catholics of Ulster were seen to be victims of violent persecution.[22] This in turn meant the Provisonals had to improvise and acquire or make weapons and explosives from home-grown sources. Explosions that took place during the late 1960s were caused by English-made materials that had been sold to Irish dealers, ostensibly for use in civil engineering and quarrying. Much of these materials would be sent by boat to the north of Ireland; one such consignment of mines was washed ashore at St John's Point, Co. Down, and was spotted by the RUC. These attempts at smuggling explosives across the sea would come a cropper as commercial explosives, being less stable than their military equivalents, sometimes blew the would-be bomb-makers up, and could also be easily traced forensically by the authorities.[23]

Weapons from the US came across the Atlantic in many small, successive consignments. M-60 machine-guns were stolen from the

National Guard military reserve in Boston; weapons would be smuggled aboard the *QE2* by Irish crew members.[24] Once smuggled in, arms and explosives would be held in republican areas – not only farms and remote countryside dumps, but in flats and basements of houses[25] The well-publicised raid on the Falls Road at the end of 1969 demonstrated this tendency; a mixed haul of guns and ammunition, mainly of 1950s vintage, was seized from their hiding places in several houses. As late as 2003 arms were being unearthed – an arms cache discovered in Essex Street off the lower Ormeau Road in south Belfast included six hand-guns, an assault rifle, timer power units for bombs and a 'very large' quantity of ammunition.[26]

TRAINING: IMPROVISED DISCIPLINE

There is no point acquiring weapons without the appropriate training in how to use them. Before the Provisionals could get to the stage where they could train other guerrilla groups in the black arts of explosives and bomb-making, they were trained up to a high standard. As with weapons storage, much of the IRA training was conducted in remote areas of the Republic, such as Co. Donegal. These camps would be uncovered at various times in the history of the conflict; one such was discovered at Scotstown in Co. Monaghan. Demands were made of the Irish government by London to clamp down on, and raid, such training camps.[27]

Training to use the many dozens of gun models that were acquired by the IRA was said to have been superior to that undertaken by the British army, whose soldiers only had to train on one rifle and one handgun.[28] But many mistakes were made due to lack of conventional military training, particularly in the early days of the Provos. Firing ranges were often dug out in farmland areas. There were elements of training that were intended to protect civilians but in practice were not borne out. For example, IRA volunteers were supposedly not allowed to throw bombs until they were eighteen years old.[29] But bomb deployment 'own goals' and civilian casualties were often the result of faulty training and timing (see more on bomb-making training in Chapter 8). Resources were put into training young IRA volunteers, known as the Fianna Éireann, for eventual membership into the IRA at eighteen. They were inducted into action through scouting exercises, message carrying (phone comms[30] were not used to evade surveillance) and riot involvement.[31] In the early 1970s training was rigorous but basic. According to one ex-volunteer interviewed by Brendan O'Brien: 'We did go down below, in Co. Cavan, ending up in a farmhouse somewhere around Lough Sheelin. You done a lot of shootin'. There was no extensive training ...' It also included political induction. 'You were talkin' three days for the most. You can't let politics run a f***in' war.'[32]

And there were mixed feelings. 'I was young and it was exciting, but I didn't like what I seen. I seen my mother's friend being shot.' But training also provided a means for expression of violence: 'There was no one cryin' to get out of it ... No doubt there was a lot of ego too. A lot of people f***ed up in their heads. They found it hard to live with people. You sort of got people who dropped out of society, sat there drinkin'; it's done a lot of psychological damage in their heads.'[33]

The re-organisation of the IRA in the 1980s led to the strengthening of the 'education department', which was responsible for lectures and discussions at the training camps, so that the customary indoctrination lectures were to be augmented by training in anti-interrogation techniques – a vital aspect of preparation of volunteers for the ordeals they would undergo at the hands of their British and RUC interrogators.[34]

The IRA also received some training – as well as tonnes of explosives – from Libya, and at one stage in the 1970s the PLO (Palestinian Liberation Organisation) offered training and weapons but this was declined because smuggling arms out of the Middle East could not be done without alerting Mossad (Israeli intelligence).[35] But on the whole the Provisionals provided their own training expertise to other groups overseas, most notably the Colombian FARC guerrillas (see Chapter 10).

EARLY DAYS: *ERIN'S HOPE*

In 1867, successive Fenian rebellions depended almost entirely on support from the United States. This connection would persist, with some lapses and lulls, right up until the age of decommissioning in the early twenty-first century. In fact, much of the nineteenth-century attempts at freeing Ireland from British rule were US-inspired and US-aided – albeit from those Irish people who had emigrated, in their millions, from their famine- and poverty-ridden homeland. Many Americans also saw parallels with their own fairly recent struggle against the British. In that year, a British MP expressed his dismay at 'a new Irish nation on the other side of the Atlantic, recast in the mould of Democracy, watching for an opportunity to strike a blow at the heart of the Empire'.[36]

Irish Americans had also become rich and politically powerful. This would be reflected in the late twentieth century in failed appeals to an Irish-descent president, Ronald Reagan, to intervene in the growing Northern Ireland conflict. By then, there were more than forty million

Americans of Irish extraction. But in the mid-nineteenth century, optimism from across the Atlantic persisted despite successive Fenian failures. The winter 1867 rebellion was easily quashed, despite an attempt from the US to arm it with guns sent on a ship known, almost mockingly, as *Erin's Hope*. It arrived after the uprising had been put down, but nevertheless heralded a period of shipments emanating from the New Country to the Old – which successfully reached their destination. *Erin's Hope* would be succeeded by far greater and more lethal shipments well into the next century.

ROGER CASEMENT AND THE UPRISING

The notoriously unsuccessful attempt by the British, Dublin-born, former diplomat and pro-Irish idealist, Sir Roger Casement, to bring guns into Ireland from Germany to arm the uprising scheduled for April 1916 was the apogee of Irish attempts to acquire weapons for the republican cause – if necessary, from England's enemies. A renowned human rights campaigner, Casement was knighted in 1911 for exposing the cruelties practised by European traders in Africa and South America. Having retired from the colonial service in 1912, his Irish nationalist sympathies intensified, and he joined the Irish Volunteers the following year.

Along with the extremist US republican group, Clan na Gael, approaches were made to Germany's United States ambassador for help in mounting a well-armed revolt. The Germans agreed with the Clan's John Devoy to smuggle twenty thousand captured Russian rifles and ten machine-guns – then a revolutionary new weapon – on a captured Royal Navy ship, the *Aud*, onto 'the lonely Banna Strand'[37] on the Kerry coast.[38] By early April, Casement believed the arms cache to be insufficient and that the rising was doomed. He therefore persuaded the German authorities to transport him to Ireland by submarine, ostensibly to rendezvous with the *Aud* and supervise the landing of the weapons.

Due to inept planning by the rebel leadership, local volunteers had not been expecting it to arrive when it did. And owing to navigational error, it failed to appear at the agreed rendezvous point. British intelligence had also intercepted messages between the insurrectionists and the German embassy in New York and was ready to intercept the boat. Hours after landing on the Kerry coast, Casement was arrested on 21 April, when the Royal Navy captured the *Aud*, which was subsequently blown up by its crew. Casement was found guilty of treason, and hanged on 3 August. The Easter Rising failed.

POST-INDEPENDENCE GUN ACQUISITION

The main IRA weapon during the Irish Civil War was the Lee-Enfield rifle, which was stolen or even bought from the British army or police. The Mark-1 could fire eight aimed rounds per minute.[39] The explosives used were mainly dynamite and gelignite, as before, which had been stolen from Irish and British quarries. This period marked the IRA's emergence as the world's prime guerrilla force, capable of constructing IEDs when the term was at least two decades in the future. The IRA were using industrial explosives as early as 1921, in hidden culvert bombs (see Chapter 6), one attack having wounded twenty-nine members of a regimental band in that year and the most bloody IRA ambush of the Civil War.[40]

Many weapons of the time came from the US – most notably the Thompson submachine-gun, immortalised in many a rebel song and first used in 1921 in an ambush on a troop train in Dublin. Shipped in their thousands at the end of the First World War as a means of breaking the trenches deadlock, the guns arrived too late for use – so they were sold back to sporting goods shops in the US and then smuggled into Ireland during the Tan War in the 1920s. A consignment of 500 was seized in the port of New York in June 1921 but by October, forty-nine Thompsons were in the hands of the IRA and units were trained in their use in training camps. This remarkable gun was the perfect weapon for the urban guerrilla, firing as it did a .45 pistol cartridge at 800 per minute from twenty-shot magazines holding fifty or 100 rounds. It continued in IRA service well into the 1970s.[41] Most Irish Civil War guns were British in origin, were used in great quantities by the Free State army against the IRA and were of high standard, while the Volunteers depended on purloined weapons, including machine-guns, to meet the challenges of larger-scale confrontations. This constant adaptation to using whatever was available would define the IRA's entire history of weapons procurement; as with any insurgent and, increasingly, covert group it would not have access to the cream of weapons models and would be forever compelled to improvise with captured weapons. Use of captured weapons often gave away individual volunteers, whose coats would become frayed from carrying heavy machine-guns such as the Lewis, a standard British army machine-gun that weighed about 15 kg.[42]

At the end of 1939, with the Second World War already under way, the IRA broke into arms reserves held by the Irish army at the magazine fort in the Phoenix Park, Dublin. They purloined several truckloads of guns and a million rounds of ammunition, but the success of the theft was countermanded by the problems of storing it safely and secretly; this was borne out by the recovery by the gardaí of much of the haul, along with other arms and materials that the IRA had stolen earlier. This had the effect of compromising the IRA's covert networks and, thence, the English campaign. President de Valera then imposed internment in early 1940 under newly passed emergency powers in the Irish Republic, following the introduction of similar British legislation in Northern Ireland.[43] Constant raids on arms dumps meant the IRA had continually to procure weapons from ever-changing sources.

1950s: THE 'BORDER CAMPAIGN'

In the ill-fated 1950s border campaign, arms raids were a vital part of the IRA military command's strategy. A successful surprise raid was conducted by Derry brigade in June 1951, on the Territorial Army's armoury in the joint Royal Navy/RAF Anti-Submarine School at Ebrington army barracks. The haul included twelve modern service rifles, twenty Sten guns and eight machine-guns, along with the requisite ammunition. Neither the RUC nor northern authorities had known about the impending raid, which gave the IRA renewed logistical and recruitment potential. It also enhanced the IRA's position against rival republican groups, most of which were later absorbed into the broader movement.[44]

Two years later, in July 1953, a further raid was carried out by the Derry unit (including the future first Provisional IRA leader, London-born John Stephenson – as he was then called before he Gaelicised his name[45]). But this time it was in England – on a British army training school in Felsted, Essex – and was not a success. A van loaded with around 100 weapons was stopped by police and the three IRA men apprehended, convicted and jailed.[46] This, with other attempts on weapons stores, taught the movement that audacity in launching arms raids may only work once. And their caution was to pay off, in June 1954 – when the armoury of the Royal Irish Fusiliers in Gough barracks in Armagh city was raided, yielding 250 rifles, thirty Sten guns, nine Bren light machine-guns and forty training rifles. Adding to the success was the fact that no-one was injured in the raid. No ammunition was acquired, however, so successive raids were needed.

The raid was a propaganda coup for the IRA, producing increased funds from the US as well as necessitating heightened security in the North. But success was not continuous; in October 1954 an attempt on the Royal Inniskilling Fusiliers armoury in Armagh resulted in the knifing of a sentry, the injuring of several of the thirty IRA men who had been sent north to perform the raid, and several arrests – as this time the B-Specials were mob-handed and ready.[47] The failed raid aroused the further attention of special branch operating in Dublin, which led to increased readiness for possible southern-based attacks – and consequently had a substantial influence on future IRA policy. Operations in the South were to be limited to arms dumps, training, and planning with the North designated the theatre of war. The prime weapons used in the border campaign, however, were imported from the US: mainly stolen Tommy guns and Bren machine-guns.[48]

ARMS FOR THE NORTH

Following the 1916 Rising, the beleaguered Irish Volunteers in the six counties were largely inactive until 1919, when they began frantic attempts at weapons procurement. In those days, guns were the main priority. Arms dealers, soldiers returning from the Great War, and raids on private residences and British army barracks were the main sources.[49] Gunsmiths and quarries – for explosives – were also targeted. During the Civil War, transfer of guns from southern brigades was the main supply for northern fighters, but there were many problems in effecting the transfers due to mistrust between pro- and anti-Treaty units.[50]

Many weapons acquired from the British, destined for the new Provisional Government army (the Free State army), had their serial numbers removed. Thousands of rifles, sub-machine-guns, grenades and ammunition came into northern IRA hands by several routes, mainly by sea to the Down coast. The northern units also began to acquire mines and detonators.

The North still had targets for arms raiding and, to pursue the constant need for weapons, and to amend the previous failed June 1954 raid, a further fifty-man attack on Armagh was set to take place in March 1955. But the enhanced activity of the B-Specials and RUC in the North led to the attempt being abandoned.[51] Therefore, the acquisition of arms would always be a hit-and-miss affair involving a very high level of risk for the IRA. A large number of volunteers and resources were needed for the raids, and once the authorities became more prepared for them, and until the IRA began to use improvised explosive devices on a regular basis, they had only a slim chance of success.

In the late 1950s explosives began to be used in more missions, along with a change of personnel at the top of the IRA command structure and a decision to target one area in a more concentrated fashion for the acquisition of weapons. Many of the operations, aimed at raiding stores in Co. Fermanagh, failed, as did one further attempt in England to seize rocket launchers from a base in Dorset.[52]

FUNDING THE ARSENAL

The need to acquire considerable financial resources not only to acquire weapons, but also to sustain their very existence, would give the IRA, and later the Provisional IRA, considerable problems. Despite the flow of money from the US and other 'rackets' at home, the IRA was not always awash with resources. During the 1950s the movement was poorly organised and had problems with arms acquisition and obtaining funding. Munitions are usually expensive if bought on the open market through arms traders. Training, procuring and buying weapons (including home-made ones), transport and equipment, and securing storage facilities, is costly. In the case of the IRA, the movement's political wing, Sinn Féin, required – and still requires – considerable funding.

Weapons shortages and shortfalls were therefore augmented, and sometimes replaced, by homemade munitions and explosives, and the unevenness of supply of conventional arms actually instigated much of the IRA's inventiveness in manufacturing its own bombs, detonating and timing mechanisms, and mortars. DIY weapons also run fewer risks, as acquisition of their components and materials can be made through legitimate outlets. The security forces believed that between 1996 and late 1997 the Provisionals needed less money for explosives, machine-guns and rifles.[53]

The IRA has obtained funding via legitimately-owned businesses, from private security firms and 'black' taxi firms in Belfast[54] to hackney cab services in Dublin, construction firms, shops, restaurants, courier services, guest houses, social clubs and pubs in Ireland and the US. Apart from illegal funding, money came from support groups such as the US Noraid (the Northern Aid Committee, see below) and FOSF (Friends of Sinn Féin), other Irish-American fundraising bodies, local collections in pubs and clubs in Ireland and voluntary private donations.

ARMING THE PROVOS

Before the IRA split into the Provisionals and the Officials, weapons in quantity or of the required quality were scarce. In 1970 the situation was dire, as evidenced by Martin McGuinness leaving the Officials – an organisation that 'aimed to blow up electricity pylons with four ounces of gelignite'. [55] In an interview on the US Public Broadcasting Service (PBS), John Kelly, who became a Provisional IRA leader in the 1970s, described the shortage of weapons at the time.

Q: Did you help defend the area?

A: I did, yes.

Q: With what?

A: Oh, shotgun, hand gun, whatever was available.

Q: And how effective was it?

A: Well, it was effective in the sense that it gave people encouragement within those areas to know that there was someone there. I also think that it, on the unionist side, on the special side, on the RUC side perhaps they were not aware just of how bereft republicans were in terms of weaponry, so therefore it might have steered their hand to some extent.[56]

We had literally no weapons. Shotguns, hand guns, very, very few weapons.

Q: Why were there no weapons?

A: Well, again, that goes back to the whole argument that existed within the republican movement, that the demilitarisation of the IRA ... with which the more traditional republicans disagreed, that's basically why there were no weapons available for the defence of nationalist areas in '69.[57]

The emergence of the Provisional IRA brought the North into sharp focus as the 'war zone' – which included the border counties – requiring a steady supply of arms. Southern Command became Quartermaster – procurer and supplier of weapons – to Northern Command, This coincided with the establishment of the new, tight cell structure and the abandonment of the older, less closely organised army structure. Southern Command's logistical support in providing safe houses and storage for arms in areas of the Republic that were, for a time, not as closely monitored as in the North was vital to Northern Command's operational successes and for the supply of arms to southern and northern ASUs.

However, support for covert Provisional activities such as weapons storage varied in its intensity in the South. All insurgent and terrorist movements need the passivity and implicit support of local communities to safeguard, keep quiet, or actively support activities such as storing weapons and protecting personnel. The Irish population had throughout history not been anywhere near unanimously behind the republican insurgency – both before and after Irish independence. Whatever support was available could also waver; for example, if the IRA killed a garda – an Irish police officer – practical assistance for the movement would be curtailed in that area or even turn against the IRA. This was exemplified in the anonymous disclosure of the Clonaslee bomb-making factory in Co. Laois.[58]

By 1970 the US connection was the IRA's main supply source of funding and weapons, stolen mainly from US army bases. Handguns also came in from the ETA Basque separatist group.[59] According to the Derry bomb-maker Michael Clarke, testifying at the Bloody Sunday enquiry in December 2003, in January 1972 the IRA had about six M1 Carbines, one or two Garrand rifles, two Thompsons and a variety of hand guns. He did not recall possession of any .303 riles; the Thompsons were virtually obsolete because it was very difficult to get ammunition for them. If a particular operation was planned weapons would be made available. Typically, patrols in his area of operations, the Creggan estate, consisted of one car with two weapons or two cars and four weapons. Clarke claimed there were only ever four to six weapons available in the Creggan at any one time and the cars patrolled at night to discourage army incursions.[60]

Because the Provisionals neither had the men nor the weapons to take on the British army, they concentrated on causing economic damage by blowing up buildings in the city. This is a vitally important point in judging the entire armed struggle; it sets the scene for what the US military was to call 'asymmetric warfare'. And as the buildings the IRA destroyed and damaged could not be insured, the British exchequer had to foot the bill. This would, if the IRA's aims were met, drive the British out of the North.

In the 1970s the arms famine ended, at least until the end of the decade. The Provos did deals with arms suppliers in the US, Libya, with Palestinian terrorist organisations and other sources in eastern Europe.[61] A monstrous array of weapons was acquired – from rifles, explosives, detonators and machine-guns to RPG-7 anti-tank rocket launchers and surface-to-air (SAM) missiles. Some shipments, such as the *Claudia* from Libya (see p.163) bringing several RPG-7s and thirty-six rockets,[62] were intercepted, mainly due to transnational intelligence collaboration, but many got through, finding no obstacles at customs. The IRA's ability to conduct deals in many countries stretched the world's intelligence services, pushing to the limit their attempts at co-operation. The IRA's favourite gun, the Armalite, made its appearance during this period. The Armalite M16 and the AR180 version are high-velocity weapons that – unlike the older guns that wore away the coat material on volunteers' shoulders – weighed less than 3 kg. It was superior to its British equivalent, the Stirling rifle. Acquiring Armalites was particularly in the forefront for Derry brigade, which was very short of weapons in the early 1970s. A contact from a left-wing group, Saor Uladh, promised to set up a link with the US for Martin McGuinness, then the Finance Officer for Derry, to buy Armalites – returning with a car boot-load that was to more than adequately arm the Derry IRA.[63]

The light US-made, belt-fed M60 had also been brought into IRA use by September 1977. One of the guns was held aloft by two masked IRA men at the Bloody Sunday seventh anniversary in January 1978, and groups of volunteers were trained to use them in camps in Co. Kerry – by a former Irish army captain. In March they were brought to the North and one such made its debut in the conflict in the shooting of a British soldier, Gunner Paul Sheppard, in Belfast. Another M60 was used to shoot at soldiers in Crossmaglen, three of whom were killed at that location in a later attack at the end of 1978 after a temporary abandonment of the guns' use following weapons seizures.[64] But it wasn't until 1985 that it made a dramatic contribution – along with two truck-mounted Browning .50 heavy machine-guns – to the IRA effort in an attack on a British army Wessex helicopter flying near Crossmaglen barracks. The US procurer for the IRA, George Harrison (see p.155), managed to acquire M60s for a bargain price of £677 apiece.[65]

By the end of the 1970s the intelligence services had greater penetration and disruption of the IRA's supply of arms from the US, with the help of the SAS and a virtual licence to dispense with legality in dealing with the Provisionals. The 'long war' had become the 'dirty war', in which high-risk killing missions and evidence of a shoot-to-kill policy became apparent. Arms were not in sufficient supply or modern enough to escalate operations – which the new early 1980s strategy demanded. There were by then no M16 heavy-calibre machine-guns and few RPGs. The US had supplied 80 per cent of the guns for the IRA, and this network had been broken up by the FBI. This also meant a loss of vital funding from the US, at least 75 per cent of which was raised for weapons.[66] After the restructuring of the IRA, weapons and explosives were to be under the complete control of the brigade's or command's quartermaster and explosives officer respectively.[67]

THE US CONNECTION

Pro-republican fundraisers in America (Noraid and others) have put some $11 million a year into IRA coffers.[68] Noraid – which began as the Irish

Northern Aid Committee – evolved out of the various support organisations in Irish America from the nineteenth century onwards, including the Friends of Irish Freedom during the 1919–21 War of Independence.

The Northern Aid Committee was set up by republicans following the 1969 riots.[69] As such, the committee saw its main role as providing support and financial assistance to the republican movement during the conflict in Northern Ireland. It was founded in 1970 – after the modern Troubles had begun in earnest and the emerging Provos badly needed arms, as well as money, to support the families of jailed volunteers. Its key founder was Michael Flannery, who was born in Ireland, had been an IRA volunteer in his teenage years and fought in both the 1919–21 war and the Irish Civil War, and who then became one of the millions of Irish who emigrated to the United States.[70]

Despite denials that Noraid was involved in giving active assistance to the Provisionals' campaign, in 1977 it was forced by the US government to register as an agent of the Provisional IRA. But a direct, verifiable connection between the IRA's weapons and Noraid was not as easy to confirm as were the origins of weapons coming from individual suppliers in the US. Nevertheless, many knew the score, including the British prime minister in the mid-1970s, Harold Wilson – who stated, most likely based on British intelligence information, that 'misguided American supporters of the IRA' were responsible for providing 'most of the modern weapons now reaching the terrorists in Northern Ireland'. By the 1980s, the American press was beginning to expose the connection: the *New York Times* reported in December 1986 that 75 per cent of Noraid money went towards purchasing weapons.[71] But this would be nothing compared to the furore that erupted against US-funded terrorism following the 9/11 attacks.

The IRA's finances actually came under pressure during the 1980s due to further infiltration of the organisation with highly placed informers, as well as demands placed on funding by Sinn Féin's increased political activity. The IRA's subsequent reliance on individual suppliers and contacts like George Harrison appeared to back the argument, from Noraid and republicans, that Noraid funding was not used for weapons procurement.[72] Certainly in the 1970s, Irish Northern Aid's contributions comprised around two-thirds of expenditure on prisoners' dependents, with around £170,000 left – along with other contributions – to spend on arms annually.[73] However, there is little doubt that Noraid funding aided the military campaign. Noraid emissaries visited Ireland in 1971 to set up financing of arms procurement in Europe with members of the Army Council.[74]

While the US had for a long time been a good source of handguns and assault rifles, it did not provide 'heavier' weapons such as RPGs and SAMs. And by the early twenty-first century the supply of weapons from the US had become increasingly restricted due to US federal agencies' policy of stemming the flow of illegal weapons to Ireland.

George Harrison's contribution

George Harrison was the US-based Irish republican chiefly responsible for the IRA's US supplies.[75] He and another security guard, Liam Cotter, supplied guns for the 1950s border campaign until 1962 and beyond, and from the late 1960s until the early 1980s, when the FBI broke up his network. Weapons supplied by him, however, remained in use until the ceasefires in the 1990s.[76]

In 1970 the IRA Army Council chief, Daithí Ó Conaill, visited Harrison in New York to procure weapons.[77] A network of US arms smugglers, with contacts in many parts of the US, continued to supply arms throughout the Troubles. The first consignments were taken from old arms dumps collected for the border campaign, comprising twenty carbine rifles with folding stocks, handguns, and grease guns – a Second World War submachine-gun that was reputed to be as effective as the Thompson, but harder to operate.

Harrison, Cotter, and the IRA set up a supply line of guns – including hundreds of the compact and collapsible Armalite (AR-15) rifle – which continued throughout the 1970s. These and the other weapons were used to kill 285 British army personnel and Northern Ireland police officers between 1970 and 1974. One female Volunteer claimed so many army victims she was nicknamed 'the Armalite widow'.[78] Acquisition of Armalites began in 1971 mainly from another link in the network, George De Meo, who acquired the weapons from US army soldiers, who smuggled out guns and ammunition and sold them to local arms dealers.[79] A range of other guns was supplied, including Colt 45s and German P.38 handguns, Schmeisser submachine-guns, Thompson machine-guns, and standard Second World War – but highly accurate for the sniper – Garand infantry rifles, as well as the Garand's successor, the less bulky M-1 carbine rifle.[80] By 1973 the US network was supplying the IRA with up to 300 guns a year.[81]

In 1979 Harrison acquired a large consignment of arms stolen from Camp Lejeune, North Carolina. Arms were often stored in smugglers' homes, and before shipment to Ireland the weapons were stored in a garage belonging to Barney McKeon, a Northern Ireland-born US citizen who was active in Noraid. Before the arms shipment left New York, one of the conspirators telephoned IRA contacts in Dublin and gave details of its arrival. Irish detectives recorded the call from a wiretap and immediately informed their counterparts in America of the gun-running scheme.[82] When the weapons arrived in Dublin in late October 1979, Irish authorities laid a trap for the IRA but the Provos had already learned about it, so no one turned up to collect the weapons. The gardaí were forced to seize the arms on 2 November 1979. Some of the rifles had intact serial numbers and could be traced. A shipping document linked the weapons to McKeon, who received three years' imprisonment and a fine of $10,000.

But it was in the 1980s that the Provisionals really needed more heavy weaponry to take on the British army, with whom its arms race was gathering pace – and the US appeared to be the likely source for such weapons. During the 1970s George Harrison had shipped over 2,500 weapons and a million rounds of ammunition to Ireland, at a cost of an estimated US$1 million[83] – but it was not to him that the IRA turned this time.[84] The idea was to beef up the IRA's firepower in the wake of the hunger strikes in Long Kesh (which had aroused further pro-republican sympathy in the US). So changes were made in the shipping network, and a Belfast republican, Gabriel Megahey, and a Tyrone brigade Volunteer, Gerry McGeough, who had money – $80,000 – to pay for arms, were dispatched to the US. Megahey became the IRA's number one in the US.[85] The driving force behind this replacement in 1978 was said to be Martin McGuinness, who set out to bring the Harrison network of arms dealers and funders under his control and tried to convince Harrison to formally join the IRA. But Harrison refused, and it was shortly after this that McGuinness chose to replace Harrison with Gabriel Megahey.[86]

But the IRA's US operations were already known to the FBI, which was on higher alert following the Warrenpoint and Mountbatten outrages in 1979; the Reagan government was increasingly aware that these and other attacks were US-funded. Therefore, Megahey was placed under heavy surveillance, and went to Florida to procure weapons. McGeough had earlier secured a consignment of Heckler & Koch HK19s and Armalite AR 15 assault rifles, so Megahey tasked him with a far bigger operation – to acquire surface-to-air (SAM) missiles to shoot down British army helicopters. The CIA-supported Nicaraguan war meant that such weapons could be acquired, and the deal was set up for a shipment of five SAMs to be made from New Orleans, the shipping point to Latin America.[87] The machinations involved are revealed in Peter Taylor's account:

Megahey introduced himself as the IRA's 'Number One man in the USA' and was surprised to find that before business began, he was given an intensive interrogation by the arms supplier. Panicky's suspicions were aroused when the man said delivery of the missiles would be handled by the dealers. Megahey would have none of it. 'You're gone. The truck's hit. Money's gone. Missiles gone. I'm gone. The only one to lose is us.' Megahey suggested that they both offer themselves as hostages to secure the deal. 'I myself will personally go as the hostage,' he said. 'Wherever you want. I'll sit with whoever you want me to sit with. If I'm going to gaol, somebody's going down the hole. I know one thing for sure, if any of my men get nicked, you're dead!' But Megahey also offered a sweetener. 'What we're dealing with here moneywise is chicken shit,' he said. 'If this goes OK, then we're prepared to come in with a lotta big money.' It seemed the missiles were almost home and dry and Megahey and McGeough had pulled off the most important arms deal in the IRA's history.[88]

The FBI arrested Megahey on 21 June 1982, having discovered that the arms deal would have also involved sixty high-velocity rifles and a large number of remote-control detonation and timing devices for bombs that would have enabled them to be triggered up to a mile away. The arms dealers the two IRA men met in New Orleans were actually FBI agents and the missiles themselves had been de-activated. Gerry McGeough went on the run in the US before returning to Ireland. Megahey was sentenced to seven years.

In July 1999, US police discovered that weapons were being smuggled from Florida to Ireland hidden in children's toys. The plot was revealed by accident when a parcel containing a 375 mm Magnum revolver destined for the Irish Republic went astray and was detected by an x-ray machine at Coventry airport. Within days, twenty-three packages containing handguns were found in Ireland, mainland Britain and the United States.[89] Irish security sources discovered that more than 100 weapons may have been smuggled into Ireland, including small-calibre revolvers, easily concealed machine pistols, submachine-guns, Barrett 'Light Fifty' M82A1 sniper rifles and pump-action shotguns.

The drive for rockets

Attempts to acquire rockets were driven by the IRA's desire to shoot down army helicopters, which had been adopted for troop movements and other operations to avoid roadside bomb attacks and ambushes. But the search for portable rocket guns began in the 1950s border campaign, which was characterised by 'flying column' attacks on police stations and countryside ambushes. Some bazookas were acquired, but they did not function well and were not used until 1972, when one was fired at a police station in Belfast, scoring a direct hit.[90]

In the early 1980s, a plan to design and produce its own anti-aircraft rockets in the US – possibly the IRA's most ambitious arms project – involved various highly qualified American pro-IRA sympathisers, at least one of which, the electronics engineer Richard Johnson, had the highest level of security clearance.[91] Together with an IRA engineering and explosives team, Johnson and other US engineers designed – and even test-fired – a mortar that would be fired from a 2-metre tube and radio-command-guided to the target (see Chapter 7).

Johnson aroused FBI suspicion and was eventually jailed for ten years. One of the IRA design team, Éamon McGuire – identified by the CIA as the IRA's chief technical officer – was a senior engineer with Aer Lingus and in his spare time bought equipment and designed bombs, landmines, rockets and technology to shoot down British army helicopters in 'bandit country' (see Chapter 7).[92]

The South Armagh brigade was heavily involved in importing weapons and technology from the US in the early 1980s, just before the IRA began to benefit from Libyan shipments. It would also be the subject of the biggest weapons 'sting' to be inflicted on the IRA during the 1980s – the FBI's discovery of a plot to acquire five Redeye portable anti-aircraft SAM missiles from Florida. This occurred following the first IRA attempt to obtain Redeyes in 1985, when another Boston IRA deal was set up to purchase fifty Armalites, Heckler and Koch sub-machine-guns and belt-fed M-60 machine-guns. The Boston intermediary for the IRA, along with an IRA representative who was actually an FBI plant, also requested Redeye missiles, and those involved in the thwarted deal were arrested.

The Marita Ann *interception*
Also in the early 1980s, a pro-Provo, New-York-born US Marine, John Crawley, with connections with Boston arms dealers, arranged a shipment of weapons on board a freighter, appropriately named *Valhalla*. The shipment included ninety mostly Armalite rifles; sixty machine-guns; pistols, grenades, night sights, flak jackets, and over 71,000 rounds of ammunition. But unbeknownst to Crawley, the FBI, Irish intelligence and Britain's MI6 already knew and were planning to thwart the shipment, so they tracked the *Valhalla* by surveillance satellite on its journey from the US in September 1984.[93]

Five days later, when the arms were moved mid-Atlantic onto another, Irish-registered ship, the *Marita Ann*, a Royal Navy Nimrod aircraft photographed the operation with special magnifying cameras. Two Irish Republic naval vessels, the *Emer* and *Aisling*, intercepted the *Marita Ann* on the following day as it sailed back to its home port laden with weapons. On board, the Irish authorities found Crawley and Martin Ferris, a prominent Kerry republican and suspected member of the IRA Army Council. As with the series of shipments obtained from Libya described on page 163, the final shipment was the one that was intercepted. The *Marita Ann* seizure was allegedly effected with the help of a tip-off from arguably the most prolific IRA informer, Seán O'Callaghan.

Despite international security cooperation, the *Valhalla* slipped past US authorities on its homeward voyage with two IRA men on board. The trawler was in port for three days before its discovery by customs officers on 16 October 1984. The FBI investigation eventually linked the gunrunning operation to organised crime in Boston and to drug trafficking. It was not until April 1986, however, that a grand jury indicted a group of men accused of involvement in the conspiracy.[94]

Nevertheless, US authorities successfully undermined the transatlantic arms network. The seizure of the *Marita Ann* and the subsequent convictions against the IRA–US gunrunning network caused serious problems for the IRA in the mid-1980s. So, although the Provos continued to procure weapons from the US, they turned increasingly to Europe and the Middle East. There was also an outcry against the organisation and a subsequent quietening of US support following various fatal IRA bombings, most notably the 1982 Hyde Park bombs and the 1983 Harrods bombing (which killed one American and injured three others), which – along with the Noraid connection to the attacks – received prominent media coverage in the US, as did the Enniskillen Remembrance Day attack in 1987. A classic reaction was the *Chicago Tribune*'s editorial on the Hyde Park attack:

> IRA front groups ... claim that they are raising funds for the families of slain or imprisoned IRA men. They lie. The money goes for arms, ammunition, and bombs. It buys the high explosives and the remote control detonators that blew up in London. The money bank rolls the sort of sub-humans who can pack six inch nails around a bomb and put it in a place where women and children and tourists will gather.[95]

The Stinger sting

Despite the Redeye fiasco, the IRA tried for many years to acquire a working ground-to-air missile system to match and overcome the army's use of helicopters to transport troops and equipment, which it adopted chiefly to avoid ground convoys being blown up by the IRA. For such missions, it once again turned to the US. In 1994 the FBI monitored and blocked an IRA attempt to acquire Stinger missiles from the US. These missiles, weighing under 16 kg and just under two metres in length, can be shoulder-mounted. Their 5-km range and supersonic speed makes them the ultimate anti-aircraft terrorist weapon. They had been used to bring down some 270 Soviet aircraft in the 1980s Afghan war.[96]

The South Armagh brigade tried on one of many procurement missions to the US to get hold of the 1987 model, which was designed to overcome an aircraft's antimissile jamming system. 'Can you get a Stinger?' Patrick McKinley, one of the IRA men from South Armagh brigade asked an undercover customs officer in a bar in Florida on 20 November 1989. 'That's number one on our list.' McKinley was later sentenced to four years for his part in the arms conspiracy.[97] The FBI's undercover video footage of the meeting to buy the Stinger showed a fake weapon, with its warhead and rocket fuel removed, being handed over.

Ireco detonators

Despite the failure to acquire the Stingers, IRA operatives managed to buy from the Ireco Inc. mining supply company in Tucson 2,900 state-of-the-art electric detonators in November 1989. Although bought ostensibly for 'mining operations', this lie was not the limit of the IRA's efforts at deception in their arms procurement operations: the detonators were packed in boxes marked as 'clothing' addressed to a terminally ill AIDS patient.[98] Four of the buyers were arrested in New York in November 1992 and were indicted by a federal grand jury in Tucson, but were acquitted in May 1994.[99]

The IRA operative, Kevin McKinley of the South Armagh brigade, purchased two types of Ireco detonators in Tucson – 2,500 with 3-metre leg wires (electric detonators) and 400 No. 8 fusecaps, all of which were shipped to New York city, from where they were mailed to Ireland. In March 1992 and July 1993 Republic of Ireland officials discovered caches of the detonators.[100]

The detonators became vital to the IRA's bombing missions, being used first in Northern Ireland in 1991 and in the later London City bombs, the first instance possibly having been in a bomb that exploded at London Bridge station in February 1992. They were also used in

London's Docklands, Bishopsgate and Baltic Exchange bombings.[101] Some of the devices were stolen by the Real IRA when they split from the Provisionals and one was used in the Omagh atrocity in 1998.[102]

Weapons continued to come in from the US during the 1990s, most notably shipments of Barrett high-velocity rifles (Light 50 and Model 90), destined for south Armagh.[103] More than 100 pistols and machine-pistols were bought and sent to Ireland from Florida. The three men responsible were convicted of smuggling offences – the deal was denied by the IRA – but were acquitted of aiding terrorism.[104] The US Barrett Model 90 rifle claimed nine lives before the second ceasefire in 1997. It could fire a .50 bullet at nearly three times the speed of sound. Designed for target shooting, its bullets could pass through a standard flak jacket. Its use coincided with the infamous 'Sniper at Work' signs that sprang up in the border counties.[105]

ARMS FROM THE REPUBLIC

TABLE 4.2: WEAPONS OF THE IRA

SMLE ((Short Magazine Lee Enfield)) No. 1 Mk. III .303 inch

Capacity: 10 rds; Calibre: .303; aka: Smelly, Three Naught Three

The standard issue British Service rifle of the First World War, these were carried by all crown forces and police in Ireland. Highly prized and sometimes given individual nicknames, they were the typical weapon of the IRA up to the 1940s.

Webley Revolvers

Mk. V and VI .455 inch, Capacity: 6 rds
aka: Long and Short Webleys.

While many models of revolvers and automatics were used by the IRA, these were the common sidearm on both.

Mills Grenades/Bombs

Various patterns of hand grenades and bombs were used during the War of Independence. In IRA hands these and the homemade versions were often lobbed into the open-top transports of the enemy, which led to the addition of chicken wire cages over transport vehicles. This was countered by the addition of iron hooks welded to the grenades with the purpose of catching in the wire.

It is now well known that the Provisionals obtained arms and financing from elements in the Irish Fianna Fáil government. What happened in similar conflicts in other countries – that the nation with newly won independence launched a military operation to take over that part of it still under colonial dominance – did not happen in Ireland. Although the Republic maintained a territorial claim to the six counties until the Good

Friday Agreement, instead of trying to invade the North the Irish government lent its support to the republican movement so that it would carry on the fight to get the British out as its proxy. Guns came to the North, money was channelled through a fund 'for the relief of distress', and some training was provided in Co. Donegal.[106]

Evidence emerged in 2001 that Irish government ministers had funded IRA weapons procurement during the 1970s. A particular shipment that did not materialise was destined for Dublin in spring 1970, having been procured in Vienna. A Belfast IRA man was involved in hijacking the weapons' transfer from a monastery in the South to the northern Provisionals.[107] Files released in Dublin revealed that the taoiseach in May 1970 sacked Charles Haughey, the then Minister for Finance and Neil Blaney, Agriculture Minister, who were later charged with smuggling arms to the IRA. They were acquitted due to lack of evidence, but it was viewed they had acted with state approval.

It turned out that some of the funding intended for Catholic victims of 1969 attacks was directed towards IRA arms purchasing.[108] An Irish army intelligence officer, James Kelly, was also involved, having visited Belfast in September 1969 when the northern Catholics were most beleaguered and there appeared to be no adequate defence for them. It is claimed he appealed to the Irish government to supply arms to the North. The implications for Anglo-Irish relations were considerable, as by 1970 the Provisionals were at war with the UK.[109] The renowned poet and playwright, and former IRA man, Brendan Behan, had also been involved in arms smuggling. George Harrison and his arms-supplying colleague, Liam Cotter, sent Behan a truckload of Thompson submachine-guns, handguns and 2,000 rounds of ammunition to a fake Dublin address.[110]

In the mid-1970s Irish-origin explosives were still being used in IRA devices and were occasionally turning up on the English mainland. Some could be traced by decoding the markings on the explosives wrappers – pinpointing exactly from which quarry in the Republic it had been acquired. And not only explosives; other bomb components such as casings and micro-electronic switches, timer components and initiation circuitry equipment were found to be in production in factories in Co. Cavan, Dublin and Dundalk respectively. Some components would be intended for recreational or other use – such as video-gaming machines. Other items in production were a more advanced timing and power unit that could delay an explosion for over five days.[111]

SHIPLOADS FROM GADDAFI

Most of the material in the decommissioned IRA arsenal, particularly the 3–5 tonnes of Semtex military high explosive, was shipped from Libya in the mid-1980s. However, the IRA had made earlier attempts to procure from that country, which under its headstrong and bombastic leader, Colonel Muammar Gaddafi, was seen by the US as a prime 'rogue state'. Between 1972 and 1975 it is estimated that Libya supplied the IRA with weapons and funds – some $3.5 million ($10 million at 2005 prices) to the organisation through City of London banks.[112]

It has been said that Gaddafi chose to continue to send the IRA weapons as a form of revenge on Britain for facilitating the 1986 attack by US bombers on Tripoli and Benghazi, in which his adopted daughter was killed. Already in the early 1970s, the IRA was developing links with a plethora of revolutionary movements in Europe and the Middle East. It is thought that a pact signed in April 1972 with ETA, the Basque separatist movement in Spain, created ties with a number of smaller terrorist groups such as the Breton Freedom Front, the Corsica Liberation Movement and the armed wing of the Kurdish Workers Party. The Bretons are said to have advised the IRA to approach Libya, which intended to assist groups conducting insurgencies against old imperial powers that had controlled areas of the Middle East and North Africa.[113]

On 28 March 1973 the Irish navy arrested a leading IRA player, Joe Cahill, on board a ship, the *Claudia*, sailing towards the Irish coast and carrying 5 tonnes of weapons[114] – including 750 rifles, handguns and sub-machineguns, 500 hand grenades, 100 anti-tank mines, 100 *cases* of anti-tank mines, 230 kg of gelignite explosive and Cordtex detonating cord and over 24,000 rounds of ammunition – from Libya.[115] But the main Libyan shipments were to come. The mid-1980s hauls substantially increased the IRA's firepower. Following Cahill's arrest, relations between the IRA and the Libyans progressed, and an increasingly anti-British Gaddafi began to supply rifles, machine-guns and Semtex, which greatly enhanced the IRA's ability to construct undetectable and highly powerful IEDs (see Chapter 5). This increased capability cannot be overestimated; Semtex was impossible to detect, stable and malleable, and enabled the IRA to build ammonium nitrate (fertiliser) 'city-busting' bombs with a substantial boost.

A cooling-off of the Libyan connection occurred in the late 1970s because the Libyans were said to be uncomfortable about the activities of the IRA go-between involved in procurement. But by the mid-1980s the relationship was restored as part of Libya's response to renewed conflict with the United States and the UK.[116] In July 1985, a British-registered ship, the *Casamara*, later renamed the *Kula*, sailed from Malta with 10 tonnes of assorted weaponry which it had loaded from a Libyan ship, the *Samra Africa*, off the island of Gozo. The first of four shipments, it contained AK-47s, Brazilian Taurus automatic pistols, Soviet-made RPG-7s and three Russian DShK (Degtyarev) 12.7-mm heavy machine-guns.[117]

Two of these huge Russian machine-guns were used in 1988 to bring down a British Lynx helicopter flying from Crossmaglen barracks to Bessbrook, and to riddle Coalisland police station with bullets on an audacious IRA mission in February 1992.[118] The Lynx was hit fifteen times, forcing it to crash; the IRA unit was filmed carrying out the attack, which was to culminate in it shooting the crew and destroying the helicopter with machine-guns and an RPG. But the Lynx crashed far enough away for army colleagues to come and rescue the crew.[119] A DShK was also used to pierce the armour of an RUC car in south Armagh[120] in October 1989, when seventy bullets were fired from one of the weapons mounted on a truck, exploding the car's petrol tank and killing Constable Michael Marshall, whose body was burned beyond recognition.[121]

A subsequent shipment of machine-guns to be used against army helicopters came in aboard the renamed *Kula*. The South Armagh brigade, arguably the IRA's deadliest unit, was the main recipient of the consignment, which was landed, transported in trucks, and secreted in farmhouses and bunkers in several Irish locations. British intelligence failed to intercept the *Casamara* despite it having been used for drug-running operations.[122]

The fourth shipment, destined to be the IRA's biggest to date, came in on a Swedish oil-rig boat, the *Villa*. Eighty tonnes of weapons were landed, including seven RPG-7s, ten SAM-7s and a tonne of Semtex, enough to blow up an average-sized city centre and which supplied all Semtex bombings after 1986. The *Villa* landed off Clogga Strand, on the Co. Wicklow coast in the Republic, and was unloaded onto farmers' tractors and duly secreted in IRA bunkers. The Libyan arms were stored in Southern Command area – mainly Limerick and other parts of Munster. Extensive underground bunkers were also built to house weapons in several locations, such as counties Longford and Galway. Because the orders to construct the bunkers came from Northern Command, intelligence in the Republic did not at first realise their origin, although informants in the RUC had wind of an escalating military campaign.[123]

Much of the Semtex ended up in south Armagh, where it would be used to boost the vast ammonium nitrate blockbuster bombs. The county's closeness to ports meant that finished bombs and bomb materials could be speedily shipped over to the mainland. The Semtex was used sparingly – mainly for smaller devices for directional explosions where the target had to be taken out precisely (very much an original, non-terrorist role for Semtex). Among the best-known attacks using Libyan-origin Semtex were the 1987 Enniskillen bomb which killed eleven, the Ballygawley bus bombing in 1988 which killed eight soldiers, and the 1991 mortar attack at Downing Street; it also featured in about 250 other bombings, usually involving booby trap devices.[124]

Saving the Semtex, however, was an aspect of IRA strategy that has puzzled many. It was likely because the IRA wanted the precious explosive to last through the 'long war' despite growing hopes for the on-off peace process. Half of the Libyan supply had been used up by 1992, leaving three tonnes. But maintaining the capacity to carry on waging war, and the capability to adapt to a seemingly endless variety of targets, meant economies were necessary.

The store of guns remained abundant, with more than 50 per cent of the 1,200 imported AKM fully automatic rifles still held in dumps and volunteer possession. Of classic irony (such as is often found in examples of weapons acquisition) was the fact that the Webley revolvers and general purpose machine-guns the IRA had obtained from Libya were British-made – and that much of the training of the Libyan forces in these and other weapons was conducted by the British army.[125]

The Libyan-supplied arsenal vastly compensated for problems in acquiring weapons from the US, and armed the IRA to the level of a conventional army.[126] It was well in place by the time the last shipment – on the *Eksund* trawler – was intercepted by French authorities on 1 November 1987. The Libyan shipments, which came in relatively quick succession, revealed almost unparalleled technical lapses in intelligence, both in Ireland and abroad. Despite the fact the gardaí had investigated an IRA controller of finance for alleged misappropriation of funds, with secret meetings taking place in the Arklow area, they mistakenly assumed that drugs, not arms, were involved. The intelligence failure was so catastrophic that it resulted in the restructuring of garda intelligence-gathering.[127]

The haul was impressive: seven tonnes of weapons in August 1985; ten tonnes in October 1985; fourteen tonnes in July 1986; and a mighty 105 tonnes in October 1986.[128] These shipments, which were hidden in bunkers mainly in Munster, ensured another twenty years of armed struggle.[129] But there was a catch: none of the arms were supposed to be used until the fifth and largest shipment, weighing in at 120 tonnes, came in. And that was on the *Eksund*.

The *Eksund* was found to be carrying 150 tonnes of arms, one of four final consignments due from Libya – but was reportedly being monitored by French and British intelligence services and was tracked by a Royal Navy hunter-killer submarine.[130] When the French customs officials boarded the ship it was already being scuttled, but not in time for a vast armoury to be discovered: two tonnes of Semtex, 1,000 mortars, the same number of Romanian AK-47s, 600 Soviet F-1 grenades, 120 RPG-7s, twenty SAM-7s (including the coded cards needed to fire missiles supplied in earlier shipments),[131] ten DShKs, 2,000 electronic detonators, 4,700 fuses and over a million rounds of ammunition. Some 600 AK-47/AKM assault rifles – Czech and Romanian versions – were smuggled from Libya between 1984 and 1987.[132]

It also had great implications for the direction of the IRA and Sinn Féin, because having a fully supplied inventory of weapons meant that the military campaign would continue despite growing politicisation of the republican movement, the arms actually providing this process with the necessary back-up muscle.[133]

But the *Eksund* seizure had serious adverse consequences for the republican movement, sparking off as it did major arms searches by the Irish police for the earlier shiploads, some of which unearthed large supplies. This, together with a security clampdown following the Enniskillen bombing, severely disrupted arms supplies. The *Eksund* seizure also had great political implications; from this time on, the republican movement would become inexorably politicised and would take forward the policy of the 'Armalite and the ballot box'.

Of great significance was the advantage gained by the authorities' having taken possession of the final massive shipment en route, as they knew what would be used in future attacks and could be prepared to pre-empt and respond.[134] Some of the weapons would never be used: among the higher-tech examples of weapons imported from Libya was a SAM-7 surface-to-air missile system which was reportedly not used, giving rise to speculation that it was faulty.[135]

Nevertheless, the Libyan shipments were an enormous boost to the IRA's war-fighting capability, enabling the Provisionals to keep on board the rank and file. And, practically speaking, it no longer needed infantry weapons and was able to go to the US and Europe for electrical components for the increasingly sophisticated IED-making operation.[136] But by the early 1990s Libya's Colonel Gaddafi had decided to give no further aid to the IRA and informed the UK authorities as to what material was being shipped to the Provos. Because Libyan supplies ceased, and it became more difficult to procure arms from the US, the IRA during the mid-1990s ceasefire resisted pressure to decommission its precious armoury.

WEAPONS FROM EUROPE

When home sources of gelignite dried up, as well as homemade explosives based on ammonium nitrate, commercial or military explosives were sourced from overseas; traces from some attacks revealed Russian military explosive was being used. The IRA managed to acquire highly dangerous and effective RPG-7 rockets from European sources in the early 1970s. These replaced the clumsy bazookas, and had a 500-metre range. Contacts were opened up behind the 'iron curtain' – but with little success. One particular shipment was ordered via a tortuous route of contacts from the Czech arms manufacturer Omnipol, and included modern sub-machine-guns, rifles and bazookas.[137] The Dutch authorities swooped on the shipment of guns, which bore false labels, at Schipol airport on 16 October 1971; one of the most famous arms seizures destined for the northern conflict, the arms were paraded on television for the world to see. Even more damaging for the IRA was the revelation that it had been dealing with eastern European communists at the same time as appealing for funds from the Irish-American community, itself among the most conservative in America.

In the 1980s, however, the IRA had restored weapons supplies from the communist bloc. In January 1986 the gardaí raided dumps in Roscommon and Sligo and made a vast seizure of weapons of Russian and eastern European origin worth £1 million on the black market. These included ninety-five semi-automatic rifles manufactured in Russia, Romania, East (and West) Germany, plus pistols and 21,500 rounds of ammunition. But a consignment of Yugoslav-made AK-47 rifles had markings indicating that the weapons were meant for Libya.[138] This led to a renewal of intelligence vigilance in the IRA–Libya connection. These garda seizures, revealing the Libyan connection, were cited as a prime reason for Mrs Thatcher's support, through the US Air Force use of British air bases, of US President Reagan's bombing of Tripoli and Benghazi.

A shipment from Antwerp containing thirty-six RPG-7s was seized in late 1977. And following the seizure by Dutch police in 1971 of the Omnipol consignment from Prague, the British embassy in The Hague was tasked with monitoring the underground operations of IRA sympathisers in Holland, who assisted in arms smuggling and provided safe houses in the countryside for Provisional leaders to lie low. The IRA would also take reprisals for arms seizures, and one such took place in the Netherlands when, on 22 March 1979, British ambassador Sir Richard Sykes, a much-decorated war hero from a strong military background, was shot dead in The Hague.[139]

In the 1980s, more Belgian FN FNC rifles were acquired via the Netherlands and AK4 rifles from Norway and Sweden. Although offered weapons by the PLO, the IRA were reluctant to accept as they feared interception by Mossad (the Israeli intelligence service).[140] Bomb-making equipment found in Amsterdam in the mid-1980s was destined to be used in a seaside bombing campaign.[141]

Attempts to build up arms stocks were often thwarted by raids. There were too many raids and seizures of IRA arms to fully document, but some leading examples are mentioned here (and in Chapter 9). Once weapons had been taken, they had to be secretly stored in dumps. Raids carried out following Irish independence, during the sporadic IRA campaigns between the wars, and in the 1950s campaign, resulted in an upsurge in raids on dumps. So no sooner had the IRA stolen weapons than the authorities had tracked them down. In the late 1950s the very occasional success in seizing weapons came to an end. Successive failed attacks on police and raids on armouries, with subsequent heavy prison sentences, resulted in the decision in February 1962 to dump all arms.[142]

The early 1960s saw the seizure by the authorities of large hauls of IRA weapons. These seizures battered IRA morale to the extent that the movement sank into obscurity until the phoenix of the Provisionals rose[143] from the ashes of 1950s failed campaigns.

Once the British troops had moved into the six counties, regular, often brutal, raids were made on suspected stores of arms, most notably in the Falls Road area of Belfast and other republican strongholds. On 3 July 1970 one such raid, following riots and during a military curfew, uncovered an Official IRA haul of over 100 firearms, the same number of homemade IEDs, over 100 kg of explosives and 21,000 rounds of ammunition.[144]

Between mid-1972 and the end of 1973 the British army and RUC seized 1,400 weapons – including over 600 rifles, ten rocket launchers, fourteen mortars and over 155,000 rounds of ammunition. In 1974 alone a further 600-plus rifles, handguns, shotguns and mortars increased the total seized to 2,000 weapons. Following these losses, the connection with George Harrison was stepped up. But seizure statistics showed that the IRA was losing more than it was procuring from the US. This was compounded by the shooting dead of Liam Cotter by gunmen in New York in April 1976.[145]

Between 1985 and 1993 the gardaí and Irish army seized around 800 firearms of all types, including heavy machine-guns and 300,000 rounds of ammunition.[146] The gardaí had begun a full-scale series of searches throughout the Republic in November 1987 for Libyan arms. Other Irish measures to prevent arms acquisition included the passing of a new Extradition Act in December to prevent IRA operatives from being extradited back to Northern Ireland or Britain through the long-held argument that their operations were 'political'.[147] But the *Eksund* find and the Enniskillen atrocity forced the Haughey government into a harder anti-IRA stance. As a direct result of the Anglo-Irish Agreement this change in legislation was a victory for the British government and a considerable obstacle for the IRA's activities in the South.

By the late 1980s a reverse in the IRA's arms procurement fortunes meant many operations were not carried out or effective. Seizures of arms continued after the *Eksund* capture as the Provisionals continued to move arms already procured from Libya from the South to the North, with Southern Command supplying Northern Command. The Irish police stepped up raids, and in January 1988 five machine-guns, 100 Kalashnikov rifles, 50 kg of Semtex explosive and 50,000 rounds of ammunition were found at an arms dump at Five Fingers Strand near Malin, Co. Donegal.[148] In February 1988 a raid in Portmarnock, Co. Dublin uncovered thirty AK47s, three machine-gun tripods, twelve RPGs, 31,000 rounds of ammunition and over 227 kg of Semtex.[149] Other seizures took place at Ballivor, Co. Meath, Patrickswell, Co. Limerick, and at the IRA's training grounds in Co. Donegal. Many dumps were uncovered, and an informer at the heart of the IRA's operations – none other than the Belfast Brigade's quartermaster.[150]

It was proving harder for the IRA to transport weapons North; in February 1988, for example, twenty-eight rifles were seized by the RUC as they were being transported on the road to Belfast in a stolen ice-cream lorry from Tipperary.[151] Weapons were, however, still tightly maintained in the border areas. Many were handed down within families, apart from larger, heavier weapons such as machine-guns used in attacks on helicopters.

In all, from 1985 to 1993 the garda arms raids increased to the point that one would be forgiven for thinking there were few left for operational continuity. Not only were seizures made in Co. Donegal but also in many other parts of the Republic. Some 800 guns – from handguns to heavy machine-guns – were recovered, along with 300,000 rounds of ammunition. A major arms hunt, codenamed Operation Silo, uncovered some of the underground bunkers. The gardaí concluded that the major hiding place for Libyan weapons was Munster, with the chain of command originating with the quartermaster in Dundalk and radiating out into the Limerick hub, where the OC conducted operations.[152]

TABLE 4.3: IRA WEAPONS 1993

---

650 Kalashnikov AK47 semi-automatic rifles

>12 general-purpose machine-guns

20 DShK Russian heavy-calibre armour-piercing machine-guns

1 SAM-7 surface-to-air missile

>40 RPG rocket launchers

6 flamethrowers

60–70 Webley revolvers

600 detonators

3 tonnes Semtex

But despite the recovery of all these weapons, by 1993 the IRA still had a vast arsenal at its disposal – about half of the original Libyan supplies (see Table 4.3).[153] Continuing procurement was reported in 2001, when MI5 and the RUC claimed evidence that the IRA, in the midst of its ceasefire, was involved in attempts to purchase weapons from the US. This all changed after 9/11. But until the decommissioning of Provisional IRA weapons began in earnest, the movement had to prove that it could return to an armed campaign. Therefore procurement continued with the help of fund-raising and criminal activities. However, significant problems arose from the defection of members to the dissident groups, including the 'director of smuggling' and sixty other operatives who had border contacts and specialist expertise in transporting explosives to Britain – such as the bulk explosives used in the Canary Wharf bombing.[154]

Sometimes a seizure would reveal new developments in IRA weaponry. Models of mortars were being made in quick succession during the mid-1970s and a find of twenty-eight Mark 6 mortars in a Belfast bakery in October 1974 enabled whole weapons to be test-fired at a British army range. The level of advancement revealed by the tests indicated that the weapons would have had to have been manufactured in a light engineering workshop or very well equipped home workshop to include metal lathe and heavy welding equipment.[155] The factory in Dublin making firing tubes from industrial piping and mentioned earlier was discovered by Irish police in 1975, as was the light engineering works in Co. Cavan in 1976, where metal casings for mortars were being made.[156] These finds indicated professional levels of invention and manufacture of weapons, and an IRA defence industry in the making.

STEALING THE INVENTORY: THE REAL IRA

In 1997 the Provisional IRA lost a substantial load from its inventory when its quartermaster-general, Micky McKevitt – who controlled the arms dumps – walked out of the IRA and set up the dissident group, the Real IRA, having denounced the IRA leadership and called for an end to the ceasefire. The Real IRA took small quantities of small arms and some Semtex, as well as detonators and timing devices. Having had control for fourteen years of all IRA arms dumps and the movement of weapons, ammunition and explosives across the border into Northern Ireland, McKevitt was well set up to keep a supply of weapons and explosives flowing to the dissident group.

Sources in south Armagh believe that the Real IRA took material only from certain IRA unit dumps; it is possible that dissidents were quietly filching arms since the IRA ceasefire of 1994.[157] It is also possible that entire units and their equipment defected to the Real IRA, which would be an offence punishable by death under the rules of the IRA. However, IRA chiefs would have desisted from eliminating the defectors so as not to lose more members to the new organisation. This may explain why a small number of weapons were taken. The fact that the Real IRA has made bombs from HME with only a small Semtex charge to boost them rather than devices made with a higher proportion of Semtex supports the possibility that the dissidents did not acquire a substantial supply of the explosive. Nevertheless, some Semtex has been used in Real IRA mortar warheads.

Not all the weapons were stolen, however. Evidence for co-operation between the Provisionals and the Real IRA emerged when Semtex-based detonating cord and two Ireco detonators were found in a 230-kg bomb defused at Banbridge and attributed to the IRA.[158] The Real IRA also proved they were capable of launching Provisional-style attacks; in February 1998 two major attacks were mounted, one against the Moira RUC station in Co. Down, and the second in Portadown town centre. They also kept the authorities busy trying to track the whereabouts of their weapons. Movements of IEDs home-made to Provisional-level sophistication were found on both sides of the border.[159]

In September 2000 a Real IRA plot to acquire arms from a Croatian general suspected of war crimes was reported as being at the centre of the Real IRA's arms smuggling network in the Balkans, where during the successive conflicts, and since, a black market in cheap weapons, controlled largely by members of the Croatian and Albanian mafia, has flourished. A paramilitary group can equip itself from these sources with all it needs – handguns, assault rifles, explosives, heavy machine-guns and anti-tank weapons. Weapons acquired from this source included the RPG-18 fired at MI6 headquarters in London earlier that month. The general was believed to have received explosives training from Irish republicans in the 1990s and, since then, to have helped to procure weapons for the dissident Real IRA.[160]

Police seized weapons in Croatia in July 2000, including seven RPG-18s. Irish intelligence discovered that Micky McKevitt had travelled to the former Yugoslavia to establish an arms supply network, and weapons were smuggled into Ireland, including an RPG-18.[161] It was by then easier to smuggle weapons back to Ireland from Croatia than from across the Atlantic. The open-border policy of the ever-widening European Union means arms hidden in the backs of vehicles could be smuggled back to Ireland by road and ferry without detection.[162] This is of prime current importance, as although the Provisional IRA has, as of 2006, all but stood down, the Real IRA remains a threat[163] – although not to the extent posed by Islamicist groups.

Nevertheless, caches of weapons were seized. In October 1999, a garda raid on an arms bunker in Co. Meath turned up RIRA arms of a type never before seen in Ireland. A cache seized in a truck parked in a warehouse in Dobranje, Croatia, included seven RPG-18-type weapons, AK-47 rifles and ammunition, an anti-aircraft machine-gun, twenty packets of Yugoslav-made Cortex military high-explosive and detonating fuses. It is believed the weapons were smuggled in cars or vans across the border from Bosnia-Herzogovina. Balkans-origin weapons are cheap: AK-47s are sold at around US$100, which is low compared with prices in many other countries. It is likely that the Provisionals and other dissident groups continued to maintain their arms dumps to the last tranche of decommissioning, after so many generations of armed struggle and decades of building up the arsenal.

INLA WEAPONS

The Irish National Liberation Army (INLA), although guilty of vicious attacks, never posed anything like a force equal to the Provisional IRA. But it did amass weapons and continued to do so after the IRA ceasefire in 1994. In 1995 the gardaí seized an INLA consignment of twenty-six weapons, including five rifles, several thousand rounds of ammunition, twenty new Belgian-made 9-mm Browning-type automatic pistols, two FN Belgian rifles, two Hungarian AK assault rifles and two submachine-guns. This cache was believed to have been planned for INLA attacks during the first IRA ceasefire. The INLA never formally declared an equivalent but it was assumed it would cease operations after the IRA did. Apart from the Airey Neave killing, the INLA killed twelve soldiers and five women in the bombing of a disco in 1982. While the weapons seized were greased, indicating had either been stored or not intended for immediate use, they still could have been used in attacks once degreased. The INLA did not benefit from the shipments of Libyan-supplied arms and explosives sent to the IRA in the 1980s.

Further complicating the republican faction problem was the emergence of a splinter group, the Irish National Republican Army (INRA), opposed to the IRA ceasefire, in October 1994 following the Joint Declaration of September. A garda raid on an INRA cache revealed ammunition, handguns and radio equipment hidden in a shed near Dundalk.[164]

NOTES

1. D. Sagramoso, 'The proliferation of illegal small arms and light weapons in and around the European Union: SALW among terrorist groups in Europe', Centre for Defence Studies, King's College, University of London, July 2001.
2. See T. Geraghty, *The Irish War* (London: HarperCollins, 1998), p.77, who describes the IRA's armoury as 'a sophisticated armaments industry tailored like a bespoke suit for the Irish War'.
3. M. Urban, *Big Boys' Rules* (London: Faber & Faber, 1993), p.128.
4. Ibid.
5. S. Boyne, 'Uncovering the Irish Republican Army', *Jane's Intelligence Review*, 1 August 1996.
6. Press Association, 1 February 2006. General de Chastelain, his American colleague, Andrew Sens and Finnish Brigadier Tauno Nieminen also said: 'The Garda informed us that what they regard as reliable sources in relation to the IRA and its weaponry have produced no intelligence suggesting any arms have been retained.'
7. Boyne, 'Uncovering the Irish Republican Army'.
8. CAIN Web Service, 'Membership and Arsenals of Paramilitary Groups, Estimates of the Strength of Paramilitary Groups, the IRA'.
9. Ibid.
10. British Weapons Intelligence Unit, *The Terrorist Arsenal*, 1993 edition.
11. R. English, *Armed Struggle: The History of the IRA* (London: Macmillan, 2003), p.344.
12. Boyne, 'Uncovering the Irish Republican Army'.
13. S. Boyne, 'The Real IRA: after Omagh, what now?' *Jane's Intelligence Review*, 24 August 1996.
14. J. Durney, *The Volunteer: Uniforms, Weapons and History of the Irish Republican Army 1913–1997* (Dublin: Gaul House, 2004), p.79.
15. Boyne, 'Uncovering the Irish Republican Army'.
16. Geraghty, *The Irish War*, p.170.
17. Boyne, 'Uncovering the Irish Republican Army'.
18. C. Ryder, *A Special Kind of Courage: 321 Squadron – Battling the Bombers* (London: Methuen, 2006), p.126.
19. B. O'Brien, *The Long War: IRA and Sinn Féin* (2nd edition) (Syracuse, NY: Syracuse University Press, 1999), p.280.
20. L. Clarke and K. Johnston, *Martin McGuinness: From Guns to Government* (Edinburgh:

Mainstream Publishing, 2006), p.180.
21. O'Brien, *The Long War*, p.58.
22. Geraghty, *The Irish War*, p.170.
23. G. Styles, *Bombs Have No Pity* (London: William Luscombe, 1975), p.87.
24. Geraghty, *The Irish War*, p.172.
25. My father lived next door to one in Belfast – which blew up one day when the explosives in the cellar caught fire.
26. BBC News Northern Ireland, 24 March 2003.
27. Ryder, *A Special Kind of Courage*, p.109.
28. Durney, *The Volunteer*, p.67.
29. Ibid., p.70.
30. IRA-speak for 'communications'.
31. Durney, *The Volunteer*, p.79.
32. IRA man interviewed by O'Brien, *The Long War*, p.40.
33. O'Brien, *The Long War*, p.40.
34. Clarke and Johnston, *Martin McGuinness*, p.116.
35. Boyne, 'Uncovering the Irish Republican Army'.
36. J. Holland, *The American Connection: US Guns, Money and Influence in Northern Ireland* (Boulder, CO: Roberts Rinehart, 1999), p.2.
37. One of the most beautiful of Irish rebel songs, to my mind, despite its iconisation of a British traitor.
38. Geraghty, *The Irish War*, p.320.
39. Durney, *The Volunteer*, p.63.
40. Ibid., p.64.
41. Ibid., pp.65–7.
42. Ibid., p.66.
43. B. O'Brien, *Pocket History of the IRA* (Dublin: O'Brien Press, 2005), p.47.
44. Ibid., p.52.
45. To Seán Mac Stíofáin.
46. O'Brien, *Pocket History of the IRA*, p.53.
47. Ibid., p.55.
48. Durney, *The Volunteer*, p.67.
49. R. Lynch, *The Northern IRA and the Early Years of Partition 1920–1922* (Dublin: Irish Academic Press, 2006), p.20.
50. Ibid., p.138.
51. O'Brien, *Pocket History of the IRA*, p.55.
52. Ibid., p.61.
53. J. Horgan and M. Taylor, 'Playing the "Green Card" – Financing the Provisional IRA: Part 1', *Terrorism and Political Violence*, II, 2 (summer 1999), pp.1–38.
54. One co-operative of over 300 taxis on the Falls Road is estimated to have had an annual income of about one million US dollars which was reported to the British taxation authorities. Horgan and Taylor, 'Playing the "Green Card"', p.8.
55. K. Toolis, *Rebel Hearts: Journeys Within the IRA's Soul* (New York: St Martin's Press, 1995), p.302.
56. PBS interview with John Kelly, 'The IRA & Sinn Féin', Frontline online, http://www.pbs.org/wgbh/pages/frontline/shows/ira/inside/kelly.html
57. Ibid.
58. Horgan and Taylor, 'Playing the "Green Card"', p.19.
59. Durney, *The Volunteer*, p.67.
60. Bloody Sunday Enquiry, Week 111, 8–11 December 2003.
61. Urban, *Big Boys' Rules*, p.123.
62. Ibid., p.123.
63. Clarke and Johnston, *Martin McGuinness*, pp.48–9.
64. Ibid., p.126.
65. Ibid., p.125.
66. O'Brien, *The Long War*, p.121.
67. Clarke and Johnston, *Martin McGuinness*, p.116.
68. Jane's Sentinel Security Assessments, 'Ireland: Security and Foreign Forces, 2003'.
69. Holland, *The American Connection*, pp. 30–1.
70. English, *Armed Struggle*, p.117.

71. *New York Times*, 16 December 1986.
72. Holland, *The American Connection*, p.62.
73. Ibid., p.61.
74. English, *Armed Struggle*, p.117.
75. Holland, *The American Connection*, pp.70–113.
76. Boyne, 'Uncovering the Irish Republican Army'.
77. English, *Armed Struggle*, p.116.
78. Holland, *The American Connection*, pp.82–5.
79. Ibid., p.83.
80. Ibid., p.73.
81. Ibid., p.83.
82. D. Blundy, 'US lawmen uncover provo arms pipeline', *Sunday Times*, 18 May 1980.
83. E. Moloney, *A Secret History of the IRA* (London: W.W. Norton & Co, 2002), p.16.
84. 'Behind the Mask: The IRA and Sinn Féin' (Peter Taylor, PBS (Public Broadcasting Service) Frontline, 21 October 1997).
85. S. O'Driscoll, 'US republicans find their struggle was run by an informer', *Irish Times*, 2 January, 2006.
86. Clarke and Johnston, *Martin McGuinness*, p.125.
87. Taylor, 'From Behind the Mask'.
88. Ibid.
89. Sagramoso, 'The proliferation of illegal small arms …', p.33.
90. Holland, *The American Connection*, p.73.
91. Urban, *Big Boys' Rules*, p.128.
92. 'IRA expert tested bombs in Bahrain', *Sunday Times*, 8 October 2006.
93. Urban, *Big Boys' Rules*, p.129.
94. W. Doherty, 'Five charged in hub with exporting weapons to Ireland', *Boston Globe*, 17 April 1986.
95. 'Where aid to the IRA goes', *Chicago Tribune*, 22 July 1982.
96. See Harnden, *Bandit Country*, p.373.
97. T. Harnden, 'Taliban still have Reagan's stingers', *Daily Telegraph*, 26 September 2001.
98. Harnden, *Bandit Country*, p.377.
99. 'Six men acquitted in arms conspiracy case', *New York Times*, 15 May 1994.
100. US Government's Response to Defendant Brannigan's Motion in Limine Regarding Recovery Of Detonators Overseas, United States District Court, District of Arizona, No. CR 92-587-TUC-JMR. VS. et al.
101. T. Harding, 'Real IRA leader is finally brought to justice after three decades of terror', *Daily Telegraph*, 6 August 2003.
102. Ibid.
103. Harnden, *Bandit Country*, p.372.
104. M. Ellison, 'IRA arms trial ends in confusion', *Guardian*, 14 June 2000.
105. Durney, *The Volunteer*, p.71.
106. O'Brien, *Pocket History of the IRA*, p.76.
107. Ibid., p.76.
108. English, *Armed Struggle*, p.119.
109. Ibid., p.119.
110. Holland, *The American Connection*, p.74.
111. Ryder, *A Special Kind of Courage*, p.176.
112. Families Acting for Innocent Relatives (FAIR) petition against the Libyan government, 26 May 2005, http://www.victims.org.uk/petition.html
113. Ibid. The relationship with Libya gave added meaning to the old republican catchphrase: 'England's difficulty is Ireland's opportunity', although according to the USA Friends of Ulster, it was really a case of 'any opportunity will do'. Friends of Ulster – USA, 'Drugs, guns and Semtex: any deal will do', http://www.ulsterflash.iofm.net/gadaffi.htm
114. English, *Armed Struggle*, p.161.
115. Ryder, *A Special Kind of Courage*, p.136.
116. FAIR petition against the Libyan government.
117. See Harnden, *Bandit Country*, p.240.
118. O'Brien, *Pocket History of the IRA*, p.127.
119. Durney, *The Volunteer*, p.68.

120. Urban, *Big Boys' Rules*, p.182.
121. Harnden, *Bandit Country*, p.361.
122. Geraghty, *The Irish War*, p.183.
123. O'Brien, *The Long War*, p.131.
124. M. Devenport, 'Why no-one's reading the Libya dossier', BBC News 24, 11 September 2003.
125. O'Brien, *The Long War*, p.239.
126. English, *Armed Struggle*, p.249.
127. O'Brien, *The Long War*, p.137.
128. O'Brien, *Pocket History of the IRA*, p.108.
129. Ibid., p.109.
130. Harnden, *Bandit Country*, p.244.
131. Clarke and Johnston, *Martin McGuinness*, p.188.
132. CAIN Web Service, 'Membership and Arsenals of Paramilitary Groups, Estimates of the Strength of Paramilitary Groups, the IRA'.
133. AP/RN, 7 November 1985, cited in English, *Armed Struggle*, p.250.
134. O'Brien, *Pocket History of the IRA*, p.111.
135. Boyne, 'Uncovering the Irish Republican Army'.
136. Durney, *The Volunteer*, p.68.
137. O'Brien, *Pocket History of the IRA*, p.82.
138. O'Brien, *The Long War*, p.139.
139. P. Keatley and B. Boyle, 'IRA's link in envoy's death', *Guardian*, 23 March 1979.
140. Boyne, 'Uncovering the Irish Republican Army'.
141. O'Brien, *Pocket History of the IRA*, p.105.
142. O'Brien, *Pocket History of the IRA*, p.63.
143. Celebrated as an IRA symbol on a Belfast mural seen first in 1969.
144. English, *Armed Struggle*, p.136.
145. Holland, *The American Connection*, pp.86–8.
146. Boyne, 'Uncovering the Irish Republican Army'.
147. O'Brien, *The Long War*, p.143.
148. English, *Armed Struggle*, p.260.
149. O'Brien, *The Long War*, p.150.
150. Ibid., p.116.
151. Ibid., p.150.
152. Ibid., p.280.
153. Ibid., p.279.
154. O'Brien, *Pocket History of the IRA*, p.190.
155. Ryder, *A Special Kind of Courage*, p.218.
156. Ibid., p.219.
157. Boyne, 'The Real IRA: after Omagh, what now?'
158. Harnden, *Bandit Country*, p.432.
159. O'Brien, *Pocket History of the IRA*, p.158.
160. H. McDonald, 'Real IRA got weapons from war crimes suspect', *Sunday Independent*, 24 September 2000.
161. 'Real IRA arms purchasing in Croatia indicates a change of tactics', *Jane's Terrorism & Security Monitor*, 23 August 2000.
162. Anyone who travels by ferry knows this to be true, and that current anti-terrorist measures, while emphasising airports and main seaports, are still not adequate at ferry ports. Searches of vehicles may be made at ferry ports, but scanning for explosives and radiation portal monitoring is not customary. However, cars travelling through the Channel Rail Tunnel are searched and scanned for explosives and radioactive materials.
163. As of February 2008, further warnings were issued by the PSNI about the Real IRA still posing a threat, necessitating the increase in counter-terrorist measures. E. Moulton, 'Warning after Real IRA issue new threat', *Belfast Telegraph*, 4 February 2008. See also Conclusion to this book.
164. D. McKittrick, 'Seized INLA weapons "meant to restart war"', *Independent*, 6 April 1995.

Five

Explosives: From Gunpowder to Magic Marble

From here on in, this book will deal exclusively and specifically with the bombs of the IRA – known in military parlance as improvised explosive devices (IEDs) – including the many types of explosives the organisation acquired and used; the timing, detonation and booby trap mechanisms deployed to make the IRA's IEDs the most advanced of their time; the people who made them and the expertise they acquired; and how the army Explosive Ordnance Disposal (EOD) units coped with the almost daily challenges of countering these devices and the evolving technologies used. The IRA has used more types of explosives than any other terrorist group to date. They began with commercial explosives and became adept at making their own. The later acquisition of Semtex military high-explosive was used either solely or to boost a growing range of homemade explosives in devices of ever-increasing complexity. At regular intervals in its history, Ireland has been synonymous with bombs and bomb-making. No idiotic and offensive Irish joke about the 'Paddy factor' – Irishmen blowing themselves up with their own bombs, or making bombs that failed to go off – should be taken seriously. Early IRA bomb-makers did blow themselves up. But they quickly learned how not to.

GUNPOWDER AND PIPE BOMBS

The use of explosives for the early Irish republican armed campaign began with the emergence of the Fenians in the mid-nineteenth century, who used at least 200 lbs of gunpowder to demolish the London Clerkenwell jail exercise yard as well as the adjoining streets, killing twelve, permanently disabling fifteen and seriously injuring 126.[1] The response from newspapers highlighted the shock and panic among Londoners that accrued, much in the way the tabloids do today.

In January 1881 a bomb exploded outside a military base in Salford, Lancashire, killing a seven-year old boy. In June 1881 two Clan na Gael men were arrested in Liverpool with a cast iron pipe filled with explosives smuggled from America.

'INFERNAL MACHINES' – FENIAN DYNAMITE

The US-based Clan na Gael began to think big during the 1870s, when, along with factions of the Irish Republican Brotherhood and the 'Skirmishers' considered how future bomb attacks could exceed the limits of the Clerkenwell explosion. Then, in 1863, the Swedish industrialist, engineer and inventor Alfred Nobel discovered by accident how to mix and safely package the highly unstable liquid nitroglycerin explosive into a malleable paste, which he called 'dynamite'. In 1865, he discovered that nitroglycerin could be detonated by a mercury fulminate primer in a copper tube, and the following year that nitroglycerin could be rendered insensitive to shock by adsorption in diatomaceous earth, or kieselguhr. Combining 75 per cent nitroglycerin with 25 per cent kieselguhr produced an explosive that was stable enough to be banged with a hammer without igniting, but would explode with full power when detonated by a fulminate primer.[2]

To be able to detonate the dynamite rods, Nobel also invented a detonator or blasting cap that was ignited by lighting a fuse. Dynamite can be packed in measured charges, transported easily and, with the proper detonator, exploded safely. It is classified as a secondary high explosive, which means a detonator of primary or initiating high explosive (mercury fulminate, for example) is utilised to set off the main charge.

The stabilising of nitroglycerin and the invention of gelignite meant that it was possible to build bombs to cause massive explosions which could be manufactured, transported, and placed with relative ease and security – making it ideal as a commercial explosive for mining, construction and quarrying – and also for terrorists. Indeed, dynamite was seen, in nineteenth-century romantic fashion, by Irish-Americans as the Great Liberator from England's tyrannical colonisation of Ireland.[3]

Only two years after Nobel's invention, Clan na Gael began to experiment with the new explosive under the initiative of their leader, William Mackey Lomasney, who had directed the use and movement of nitroglycerin around the country.[4] Dynamite's greater malleability and stability made it a perfect choice for the illicit bomb-maker needing to move a device quickly and safely to its target and, indeed, to construct it without being blown up. In July 1881 six dynamite bombs, dubbed 'infernal machines' by the press, were discovered aboard the SS *Malta* after it docked in Liverpool on arriving from the United States. The Skirmishing Fund came under the control of an inner circle consisting of three members of Clan na Gael, known as The Triangle, which enabled the movement to begin the 'dynamite war' against England.[5]

Also of prime importance to the terrorist was that Nobel's fulminate mercury detonation process meant that bombs could, for the first time, be set to detonate minutes or hours after they had been planted. It was therefore no longer necessary to be physically present when detonating a bomb. This capability distinguished the 'dynamite war' as the first timed bomb terrorist campaign in history. I will deal in detail with timing mechanisms in the next chapter.[6]

The use of the explosive became prevalent enough for the Fenian campaign to be known as the 'dynamite war'. Between 1867 and 1887 Clan na Gael planted at least sixty bombs, destroyed at least ten buildings and monuments and killed at least 100 people.[7] Between March 1883 and February 1885 thirteen dynamite devices exploded in London. As many as sixty people were injured by just two bombs on the London underground;[8] and 24 January 1885 was dubbed 'Dynamite Saturday' – when great damage was done to the Houses of Parliament and the Tower of London by Fenian dynamite explosions. Other dynamite devices went off in Glasgow and Liverpool.

A plethora of articles on dynamiting were written in newspapers as varied in political and social point of view as *The Times*, the *Spectator* and the *Newcastle Chronicle*, examining the personal consequences of the dynamite campaign and how it altered travel, work and life in general in London – a portent of what was to come in the last quarter of the twentieth century.[9] Dynamiters, Fenians, anarchists, and *agent provacateurs* abounded in 1880s British popular fiction, as well as weightier philosophical treatises.[10] The nineteenth-century anarchist Johann Most said that 'dynamite … is a formidable weapon against any force of militia, police or detectives that may want to stifle the cry for justice that goes forth from plundered slaves. It can be used against persons and things. It is better to use it against the former than against bricks and masonry … A pound of this stuff beats a bushel of ballots … and don't you forget it.' Most said that the use of dynamite should be 'willingly accepted and emphatically recommended from every quarter, with the single observation that rifles, revolvers, and dynamite are better than dynamite alone'.[11]

The *Spectator* mused in 1883 that there was 'an absence of personality in dynamite. We expect it to explode without any man there manipulating it.'[12] And Queen Victoria's response, along with demanding restrictions on the acquisition of the anarchists' favourite explosive, was surprisingly almost redolent of the modern-day weapons 'anorak': 'Just a cupful of nitrate acid and sand mixed with glycerine and you could blow up anything.'[13] The campaign did indeed result in the imposition of new legislation such as the Explosives Act of 1875 and the Explosive Substances Act of 1883.

The IRA's use of explosives in the years following the 1916 Irish Uprising and, following partition, the Irish Civil War was mainly to achieve military objectives. Early in 1920 the IRA carried out concerted attacks against Royal Irish Constabulary (RIC) barracks, attempting to burn them down using inflammable liquids in hit-and-run attacks. The organisation then began using significantly larger attacking forces through pre-arranged drills, which included the virtual holding captive of a town or village by a section of the attacking force, while a smaller, more experienced core, using a variety of improvised explosive devices, tried to penetrate the barrack defences. The attacks on RIC barracks, particularly those that had closed, increased dramatically to number some 350 between January 1919 and June 1920.

'IT TICKS AWAY THE GELIGER-NITE … '

By 1875 Nobel had invented 'blasting gelatin' – gelignite – which created a significantly more powerful explosion than that generated by nitroglycerin, and which the IRA would employ at various times in the next century, such as during the 1939 mainland campaign. Gelignite is made up of over half nitroglycerin, collodion cotton, potassium nitrate, wood meal, and chalk. It is a vasodilator, which makes it cause headaches (the 'gelly' headache as described by Shane Paul O'Doherty, see below),[14] low blood pressure, chest pains, and possible heart attacks.

Attacks and ambushes during the bitter fighting of the 1920s often featured gelignite. One attack, on Newtownhamilton RIC barracks in May 1920, began with the IRA opening fire on the barracks and throwing a volley of bombs onto its roof. They then occupied a public house, where gelignite was inserted in holes the volunteers had made in the building's gable wall, which separated it from the day room of the barracks. The explosives blew a breach in the wall enabling the IRA to enter the barracks, forcing the police to retire to the rear of the building. The IRA then set the barracks on fire, using potato sprayers to soak the front of the building with petrol or paraffin.[15]

During the Tan War potassium chlorate was also used. The Michael Collins arms smuggling network kept regenerating despite arms seizures and by May 1921 a tonne of potassium chlorate was coming over to Ireland from Liverpool disguised as bread soda.[16]

The IRA's 1930s campaign in England – the Sabotage plan, or S-plan – saw the next major phase of explosives use, with 'me coupla sticks o' geliger-nite'[17] being the main choice. When the January 1939 attacks occurred in Manchester, unexploded homemade bombs made from batteries, alarm clocks and gelignite were found, a material also favoured by British safecrackers. The IRA stole much of it from military store-houses. Following the Manchester attacks, twenty Irish suspects were arrested, one of whom was in possession of forty sticks of gelignite. Six barrels of explosives were seized in a raid at Manchester.[18] By September 1939, some 740 sticks had been found in raids throughout England – 332 in Leeds alone.[19]

In the 1970s the Provisional IRA used gelignite for roadside bombs. A favourite tactic was to put gelignite into a milk churn, then stand it by the roadside among dozens of other containers that farmers put out at night to be collected by the dairies.[20] When an army patrol passed by, the churn would be detonated by remote control. This is now a typical mode of attack in Iraq, although milk churns may be replaced by a plethora of other commonplace objects.

An IRA operative experienced in the use of gelignite was Shane Paul O'Doherty, whose exploits were recorded in his autobiography *The Volunteer* and whose expertise will be detailed in the next chapter. He began his bomb-making career using a stick of gelignite in the centre of a beer can full of nails.[21] O'Doherty also used black gelatine.

Although many of the IRA's IEDs in the 1980s and 1990s comprised ammonium nitrate and/or Semtex, gelignite continued to be used. The Brighton bomb was the most notorious example; it consisted of between 13 and 23 kg (30–50 lb) of gelignite, and the bomber, Patrick Magee, had hidden around 60 kg of it in his Glasgow apartment. Gelignite was also used in the Hyde Park bombing of July 1982, where one of the devices contained nails along with the 11 kg of gelignite.

THE 'SINN FÉIN CONJUROR'S OUTFIT'

IEDs of the 1930s and 1940s also used a host of other explosives, including:

- Potassium chlorate – a common chlorate used in combination with gunpowder or to replace its less powerful ingredient, potassium nitrate. It is extremely unstable due to the sulphur present. Mixes of potassium chlorate with plasticisers (such as wax) were the most common type of plastic explosive used in the First World War, often filling grenades and other munitions.[22]

- Carbide – is used in fireworks. To create an explosion, a mixture of carbide and water was put in a milk churn with a lid and ignited with a torch.
- Iron oxide – a black-coloured powder which can be readily ignited.
- Aluminium, magnesium, saxonite – a nitro compound, and sulphuric acid.

Potassium chlorate was used in the 1930s S-plan, which the then chief of staff, Seán Russell, appointed Seamus (Jim) O'Donovan to mastermind as the 'director of chemicals'[23] of the 'old IRA' and an acknowledged expert in the use of explosive material. The campaign was waged in London, Birmingham, Liverpool and Manchester, against civilian and infrastructure targets – such as the electricity supply grid – by volunteers who, according to one, deployed the 'Sinn Féin conjuror's outfit' of potassium chlorate, sulphuric acid, gelignite, detonators, electrical and ignition.[24]

Russell had insider contacts in the Customs Service willing to help smuggle explosives into England, finding dumps on the mainland to secrete several tonnes of potassium chlorate, sulphuric acid and iron oxide in dumps proved difficult due to poor organisation, with the twelve chosen volunteers sent to blow up targets relying on friends who often did not know the nature of the materials they were hiding and were arrested and imprisoned.[25]

As many as eight barrels of potassium chlorate, powdered charcoal and forty sticks of gelignite were uncovered in one raid in January 1939, and there were many more where similar quantities of potassium chlorate and gelignite sticks, as well as saxonite, were uncovered. In one attempt to blow up an electricity pylon in Lancashire, an unexploded package of gelignite and a stopped alarm clock timer were found attached to it.[26] The then Home Secretary, Sir Samuel Hoare, in introducing the Prevention of Violence Bill to parliament in August 1939 that would free the police from ordinary legal restraint when tracking down Irish terrorists,[27] stated that some 127 explosive IRA incidents had occurred and that British police had seized, in a six-month period, fifty-five sticks of gelignite; two tonnes of potassium chlorate and iron oxide; seven gallons of sulphuric acid; and 400 'weight' of aluminium powder.[28]

This haul puts into perspective the relatively small (but no less deadly) amounts of homemade explosive ingredients seized by the anti-terrorist squad in the wake of the terrorist events of 2005 in London.[29] As we shall see in the next chapter, the IRA may not have totally mastered the art of timing mechanisms and IED deployment during the S-plan campaign – but the damage done was testimony to a capacity to learn these techniques starting from a low level of expertise.

An example of the effect of the S-plan IED attacks is cited in *Time* magazine for 7 August 1939:

> Donald Campbell, young Edinburgh University Latin Lecturer, and his wife, returning from a Paris honeymoon, stepped up to the check room in London's crowded King's Cross Station. From beneath the counter came an explosion that destroyed the check room, burst suitcases and trunks, bowled over scores of passersby, stripped the clothes from two women. As the clouds of choking, acrid smoke rolled away Donald Campbell, both legs blown off, lay dying. Sprawled around him, 15 wounded men and women, including his bride, fed the bloody pools gathering on the cobblestones.[30]

Much of the IRA's knowledge of explosives during the 1950s and 1960s sabotage campaign – which often targeted vital infrastructure such as railway stations and electricity supply installations – was said to be based on knowledge of quarrying. By the late 1960s this was still the case. Gelignite-based explosives such as Quarrex ignited by a timing and power unit in a cigarette packet taped with polythene was used to blow up a statue of a tub-thumping Presbyterian preacher called Rev. Hanna at the end of 1969.[31]

To discover which explosives the IRA used from the 1950s to 1970s one only has to refer to the 1956 edition of the IRA's training manual, the Green Book – which, and this is long before the heyday of the Provos, lists a bewildering array of commercial and military explosives the volunteer can expect to use and how to handle them. They included, as well as gelignite:

- 808 – an early plastic explosive, also invented by Nobel, which looks like green plasticine and smells of almonds (like cyanide);
- TNT, the classic military explosive first used in the First World War to fill armour-piercing shells and now used as the standard measure of bombs, and was so hard to detonate that in 1910 it was exempted from the 1875 Explosives Act;
- Ammonal – an explosive first used in the First World War, made up of ammonium nitrate, trinitrotoluene and aluminium powder mixed in a ratio of roughly 22:67:11. The aluminium makes it less sensitive to detonation. The use of the relatively cheap ammonium nitrate and aluminium makes it a replacement for pure TNT;

- Gunpowder gleaned from fireworks[32] and an underwater demolition explosive – 'Tonite' – originally used for fog signals for shipping safety around the British coast.[33]
- Wet guncotton – one part of fine cotton wool immersed in fifteen parts of an equal blend of sulphuric and nitric acids. It is suitable for blasting but highly sensitive. It was used when nitrocellulose had been invented in 1845 as a first step to modern propellants. When used as a bullet propellant in a musket, guncotton created the same amount of velocity as a larger weight of gunpowder;[34]
- Co-op mix – a blend of sodium chlorate and nitrobenzene. This term was also used for one of the IRA's ammonium nitrate mixtures. (Disrupting Co-op mix devices by burning off the mixture by the use of low-velocity bullets proved ineffective, but high-velocity rounds from a standard SLR rifle sometimes worked.[35])

THE EXPLOSIVE TROUBLES BEGIN

At the start of the 1970s, as the campaign in Northern Ireland gained terrifying momentum, it became clear to British army UXO (unexploded ordnance) teams that tighter control of explosives and detonators was paramount. A leading British army EOD (explosive ordnance disposal) expert working in Ulster during the 1970s, Lt Col George Styles, in his book *Bombs Have No Pity* complained bitterly that the Home Office felt the army should look after them better to avoid theft. He and his colleagues were examining and recording every ingredient and component of the growing number and variety of devices being used at the time, which in effect destroyed the Home Office's notion.[36]

Styles asked why the Provisional IRA was obtaining commercial – not military – explosives. The Home Office did not have the answer and explosives were easily acquired under the 1875 Explosives Act. Commercial explosives such as gelignite and Quarrex came to Belfast from the Irish Republic via English manufacturers, raising the controversial issue (and one that resounds still in our current era of explosives and worldwide nuclear-materials trafficking) of border security. Styles and his colleagues also had to closely study commercial explosives, which are totally different from military ones insofar as the latter are much more stable and therefore safer – as they have to endure bullet impact, drops from a great height, and long-term storage without exploding.[37] In contrast, a commercial explosive has a short shelf life of a few months, as it will tend to be used up within that time.

When the Provos first used homemade mixtures and pipe bombs, it was evident that they were on a steep learning curve. Styles encountered the first pipe bomb, a small metal object propped against the wall of a school in Belfast's Ballymurphy estate, and found it contained an unstable mixture of sodium chlorate – weedkiller – and household sugar. In the early days of such devices, several IRA bomb-makers blew themselves up due to, Styles noted, the inferiority of the materials being used; as explosives pioneers, the Provos could not accurately assess how pure they were – for example, explosives were put into plastic containers, with no knowledge that some plastics accelerate the interaction of certain explosives. Nor was their minimal training sufficient to prepare them to accurately solder and wire the timing connections.[38] As a result, many of their bombs went off prematurely.[39]

Other commercial explosives, such as Greencast and gelignite, were in use at the start of the 1970s onslaught.[40] The sheer amount of explosives used rose dramatically in the early 1970s with 1972 arguably the most explosive year of the conflict in terms of numbers of devices and amounts of explosives used. On 'Bloody Friday', 21 July 1972, twenty-two bombs exploded in one day in Belfast city centre and in one month – August – some 2,660 kg (5,855 lb) of explosives were detonated in 126 explosions, but the supplies available to the IRA were at least twice this amount.[41] Even if the authorities seized vast amounts, as was regularly the case, there was so much more available in stock. By mid-1972, some 5,000 tonnes of explosives were being detonated.[42]

FROM 'PAXO' TO ANFO AND ANNIE

The IRA began using ammonium nitrate in March 1972, when traces were detected in defused devices.[43] By the mid-1970s the Provisionals were regularly deploying ammonium nitrate mixtures, most notably ANFO (ammonium nitrate and fuel oil) – boosted by a commercial explosive, at first gelignite and later Semtex. ANFO was particularly suitable for car bombs as more space was available in a vehicle, which when it exploded – particularly with petrol tanks full – enhanced the incendiary effect of the bomb placed within it. These deadly devices became the main weapon against the economic infrastructure of Northern Ireland, and later the City of London. The IRA would store large amounts of homemade explosive (HME) in industrial gas cylinders.

Shane O'Doherty tells of receiving small bags of HME made from benzene and fertiliser, which he had up to then only used as a primer to set off much larger bombs of 'mix' – a lower-grade bulk HME. He did not rate the power of the benzene mix – having to date used commercial explosives, mostly gelignite. The HME was to be used for training devices, to be detonated on a remote part of the beautiful Northern Irish coast in experimental scenes that would not have looked out of place on the mesas of wartime Los Alamos (albeit wetter). As each of eight devices was timed and primed, Shane and the observers retreated to the cliff top in readiness for 'small puffs of smoke and gentle pops'. Instead, the first device went off with a resounding boom. 'Sand and sky merged. We all fell backwards on our arses.' The explosion was heard in the nearest town and Shane and his trainees had to gather up their gear at a nearby farmhouse and evacuate pretty damn quick. As they escaped to the car, the second bomb went off in equally deafening manner.[44]

Ammonium nitrate (NH_4NO_3) has been used in certain dynamite mixes and as a nitrate oxidiser in pyrotechnics. It is very hygroscopic and must be protected against moisture. It decomposes to nitrogen and water, giving very little smoke, by the ideal reaction $2NH_4NO_3 \rightarrow 2N_2 + 4H_2O + O_2$. The excess oxygen can be used to oxidise some organic material mixed with the nitrate, such as wood meal, starch or diesel oil. Explosives of this type have been widely used since 1867. It is rather insensitive, and must be strongly detonated, perhaps by a Primacord detonator or a similar booster. The IRA often used Semtex to boost it. Its density is 1.725 g/cc.[45]

Explosives approved for use in coal mines where there is a hazard of methane (fire damp) explosions often contain mainly ammonium nitrate, sensitised with nitroglycerin so they can be exploded with normal detonators (No. 6), and cooling salts, such as sodium nitrate or sodium chloride, and some wood meal or other organic fuel. It is chosen to minimise the flame on explosion, and keep it below the temperature that will ignite the methane.[46]

On 16 April 1947, the SS *Grandchamp* blew up at Texas city, followed by the SS *Highflyer* the following day. On 28 July 1947, SS *Ocean Liberty* blew up in the harbour of Brest, France. These disastrous industrial accidents demonstrated the power of ammonium nitrate long before it became the favourite among terrorist groups.

A 1930s-vintage IRA explosive was called 'Paxo', as it was mindful of stuffing mixture and could be prepared in a domestic kitchen. It was mixed from common agricultural fertiliser and was a precursor to the massive ammonium nitrate IEDs that were to comprise the biggest IRA bomb attacks in Britain over a half-century later. Attempts to make Paxo were sometimes thwarted, as when an Irishman's English landlady discovered a strange white substance in saucepans in her kitchen and flushed it down the toilet.[47]

Co-op mix, which was relatively easy to prepare compared to ANFO, was also in use in the early 1970s. Compared to gelignite, more HME was needed for the equivalent explosive power – but that simply entailed greater quantities – 200–300 lbs (91–163 kg) – to be mixed. In May and June 1972 this mix was used to deadly effect in milk-churn devices to ambush British troops, one of whom died, and to blow up a furniture shop – which claimed the lives of two men and two children.[48] The April 1993 Bishopsgate bomb used almost 1,000 kg of ammonium nitrate. It was also used in the IRA's 'barrack buster' mortars, which will be featured in Chapter 7. The 1998 RIRA Omagh bombing used upwards of 160 kg of ammonium nitrate. The sale of this commonly acquired and widely used substance is not restricted in many countries. Suppliers are mainly self-regulated and are expected to inform authorities when large amounts are purchased by one buyer. For obvious reasons it is banned in Northern Ireland and the Irish Republic and is tightly restricted in the EU, where a version is made that does not combine well with diesel oil. The Philippines has banned its importation.

Guidelines for the use of ammonium nitrate are outlined in an IRA 9,000-word document written in the 1970s to train volunteers in how not to leave forensic evidence when preparing military operations, and discovered over twenty years later, in 1995. As quoted in Tony Geraghty's *The Irish War*, it points out the messiness of making the raw material into an explosive:

> … The bulk weight [of fertiliser explosives] can be anything up to several thousand pounds. The sheer volume … that has to be processed and turned into explosives means that the *Oglaigh* are involved in a forensically messy operation … the base will be contaminated with raw material and finished product … the Volunteer's clothes would also be covered … Therefore the manufacture of explosives … particularly in an urban populated area … represents a very great danger …[49]

The official reports of the trial and conviction of ammonium nitrate bomb plotters in April 2007 failed to include how much work these inexperienced individuals would have had to do in order to make ammonium nitrate bombs.[50]

The ammonium nitrate fertiliser had to be milled to the correct consistency, then dried to remove water content. The ammonium nitrate was crushed into small particles in anything from kitchen mixers to cement mixers. Electric barley crushers attached to tractors and used to break down animal feed were also used, as farms in south Armagh were the main ammonium nitrate bomb factories, where such agricultural equipment was readily available.[51] Once milled to a fine consistency, other ingredients were added, such as icing sugar – arguably the most ubiquitous bomb ingredient ever – as an incendiary booster (similar to the use of chapatti flour, another polysaccharide, which was mixed into the unexploded devices that were cobbled together by those found guilty of attempting to bomb London tube trains on 21 July 2005).[52]

Fertiliser-based bombs are usually fairly large and are normally placed in a car, van or truck. A small amount of high explosive (HE) is usually used as a booster to detonate a truckload of it. When combined with diesel oil, which is also readily available, the IRA made a mixture known as ANFO (Ammonium Nitrate-Fuel Oil). The other IRA-pioneered fertiliser mix was 'ANNIE' – ammonium nitrate, nitrobenzene and diesel oil, and combined with a booster charge. ANNIE was also known as 'Donegal mix'. The aim in mixing is to minimise the flame on explosion, and keep it below the temperature that will ignite the methane.

The mixes were many and various, and it was possible to identify the bomb-makers from the mix of ingredients. In May 1988 the Derry brigade placed seven plastic dustbins full of ANNIE – more than 720 kg – at Strand Road RUC station, inside a stolen van with false number plates. This enabled the van to get through the RUC checkpoint, which would register the car as legitimate – a classic IRA 'ringer' trick. The bomb was defused, so that the authorities could establish how the explosives had been put together; the ANNIE would have been ground into high-nitrogen fertiliser in a meticulous long-drawn out operation. Coffee grinders were often used, in relays.[53]

Aluminium powder, which has great incendiary properties, would be mixed with soap powder, diesel oil and sawdust. The oil helped the aluminium adhere to the ammonium nitrate. The better the mix, the more sensitive the main charge, the ammonium nitrate, would be to the booster (often Semtex). When it oxidises in the initial explosion, great amounts of heat are given off. The heat also helped to extend the detonation pulse thereby increasing the explosive power. Charcoal could also be used, but to lesser effect.[54] Soap and sawdust would enhance the detonation as they help reduce the detonation velocity and density. The greater the detonation density, the harder it is for the explosion to have maximum power.

Black and white gunpowder and super-amphor were also used to deliver a more powerful blast than ANFO.[55] Ammonium nitrate was also mixed with nitrobenzene, and with 15 per cent aluminium powder. Another mixture consisted of sugar, weedkiller and gunpowder and normally detonated by a small charge of Semtex. The 10 April 1992 Baltic Exchange and the 24 April 1993 Bishopsgate bombs were the largest IRA devices to incorporate homemade ammonium nitrate and sugar combinations ignited by Semtex. The bomb in Bishopsgate is estimated to have weighed between 2 and 4 tonnes.[56]

One south Armagh bomb-maker admitted to making fifteen to twenty ammonium nitrate mixes ranging from 91 kg (200 lbs) to 10 tonnes in a shed in the county.[57] He recalled making a 1,350-kg (2,500-lb) bomb at the same place as the 1996 Canary Wharf bomb. 'The mix was fertiliser and sugar. One tonne was mixed and put into a twin-axle trailer. The Surgeon [the south Armagh master bomb-maker] towed the trailer away with a big red car. The fertiliser and sugar are just bought at normal outlets.'[58] When gelignite supplies ran out, more HME was used. People learned to distinguish the sound of different types of explosives detonating: gelignite went off with a sharp 'crack', while the ammonium nitrate mixes emitted a slower, flatter thud.[59] Already by the mid-1970s no fewer than eighteen explosives concoctions were in use by the IRA – only two of which required complex chemicals.[60] Incendiary bombs and an increasing use of petrol (usually hijacked tankers) were also employed.

THE IRA'S MAGIC MARBLE

Having used commercial explosives up until the emergence of the Provisionals, the IRA during the 1970s acquired and honed their skills in making increasingly sophisticated home-made bombs. Then in the 1980s, one of the most powerful non-nuclear explosives, and arguably the IRA's most significant and infamous weapon, entered the arsenal: Semtex. It takes just a small amount to pack a big blast: only 250 g was needed to down the ill-fated Pan Am aircraft over Lockerbie in 1988; a mere 1 kg is needed to blow up a semi-detached house. It is the conventional explosive equivalent of plutonium. More than three tonnes of it – enough to blow up a sizeable city centre – was among the three substantial shipments of arms that reached Ireland from Libya before the French authorities apprehended the *Eskund* in November 1987.

Semtex became the accepted shorthand for plastic explosive and violent upheaval. By 1993 there were fifty-eight known terror incidents involving Semtex.[61] Even its Czech co-inventor, Bohumil Sole, ended his life, suicide-bomber style, by strapping the explosive to his body and blowing himself up in March 1997.[62] The Czechs named a soft drink after it.[63]

In 1920 the Czechoslovak government established the Czechoslovak Joint-Stock Factory for Explosive Materials, later renamed Explosia, in the Pardubice suburb of Semtin. Explosives were made in the Protectorate of Bohemia and Moravia for the Nazi war effort. Both the Germans and the Allies conducted research into a volatile compound, RDX (Cyclotrimethylenetrinitramine, or cyclo-1,3,5-trimethylene-2,4,6-trinitramine), which was incorporated into plastic explosives with beeswax and later linseed oil to stabilise the RDX, which is sensitive to shock.

Post-war experimentation with PETN (pentaerythrite tetranitrate) led to combinations of either RDX or PETN with binding and stabilising agents to create a malleable explosive. Not only malleable, but the new explosive was more stable and easier to handle than either nitroglycerin or the military standard HE, TNT. Even more appropriately for terrorist use, it is odourless, making it very difficult to detect. Forensic tracing of Semtex-based bombs depends on analysis of PETN.[64]

The combination became part of the US military explosive arsenal as C-4. Back in Czechoslovakia a chemist with Explosia's parent company Synthesia, Stanislav Brebera, developed a version of the combination of explosive and binding agents. This became Semtex – from '*Semt*in' and '*Ex*plosia'.

Semtex is a crystalline high explosive with the same stability and explosive power as C-4, but even more versatile. Like C-4, it is a malleable, putty-like substance.[65] It can be transported, handled and custom-moulded for any application, and can also withstand extreme temperatures. Semtex-1A is 83.5 per cent PETN, 12.4 per cent oil, 4.1 per cent styrene-butadiene rubber binder, and 0.002 per cent dye (Sudan IV). Semtex-H is minimum 25 per cent PETN, maximum 65.5 per cent RDX for a combined total of 85.5 per cent, 11.6 per cent oil, 2.9 per cent styrene-butadiene rubber binder, and 0.002 per cent dye (Sudan I – incidentally, a dye once implicated in a food dye scandal). Some Semtex batches have been found to be contaminated with other explosives, dyes, plasticisers, and a number of organic compounds.[66]

TABLE 5.1 PROPERTIES OF SEMTEX 1A, 1H, 10

Parameter	Unit	SEMTEX® 1A	SEMTEX® 1H	SEMTEX® 10
Type		plastic	plastic	plastic
Colour		red	yellow	black
Explosion heat	kJ/kg	4,980	4,982	5,030
Swath volume	dm3/kg	950	950	790
Oxygen balance	%O2	-66.0	-61.7	-45
Detonation velocity	m/s	7,200	7,400	7,300
Trauzl test	ml	330	330	330
Brisance by Hess	mm	21	22	22
RWS (blasting gelatine)	%	80	85	80
Temperature of explosion	°C	3,800	3,800	3,800
Transmission of detonation	cm	3	5	5
Density	kg/m3	1,420	1,430	1,470
Initiation sensitivity	-	cap No. 8	cap No. 8	cap No. 8
Water resistance	-	excellent	excellent	excellent
Smallest permitted diameter	mm	3	5	3.5

Source: Own library and Explosia website http://www.explosia.cz/en/

Before its devilish potential was realised decades later in the hands of terrorists, it was called 'the magic marble of Pardubice'.[67] After the development period in the 1950s, large-scale production of the explosive was launched the following decade. From 1964 it was produced under the trademark SEMTEX 1A, from 1967 as SEMTEX H (which was exported) and from 1987 as SEMTEX 10.[68] Its first applications were in mining and demolition, where small (250-gram) charges were used to detonate larger explosives such as TNT. From the mid-1970s to the early 1980s, the Czechoslovak government exported up to 700 tonnes of Semtex to Libya – enough to build 1.4 million bombs.

This is where the IRA came in. The Provisionals began using it to create landmines for attacks against soldiers in border areas. But instead of using up supplies as a primary explosive, the IRA used Semtex as a booster – a kilogram at a time – for large homemade bombs, like that which devastated the centre of Manchester in 1996.[69]

The IRA's first use of Libyan-supplied Semtex was on 28 October 1986, in seven Mark 6 mortar bombs fired at an army team guarding a watchtower in Drummackavall, south Armagh.[70] Subsequent attacks were the Enniskillen bomb in 1987 which killed eleven, the Ballygawley bus bombing in 1988 which killed eight soldiers, the mortar attack at Downing Street in 1991 when the IRA tried to wipe out John Major's cabinet, and about 250 booby trap bombings. It was the main explosive charge in the Brighton Grand hotel bomb in October 1984.[71]

It was also commonly used in smaller devices. Around 1 kg of Semtex was used in under-vehicle booby trap devices attached to a car by magnets.[72] One of these, a book bomb, which was wrapped in paper and sent as a parcel through the post, is described in a television documentary featuring EOD experts and the bomb-maker Shane O'Doherty and broadcast on the US Public Broadcasting Service (PBS) in October 1997. An EOD officer, Mick Kettle, describes it thus:

> On unwrapping the device, we find that it's been hollowed out, and inside, there's maybe three or four ounces of Semtex ... And these sort of things have been sent right away through the campaign to all manner of people, army officers, members of Parliament. And that three or four ounces of explosive, if you're holding it close to your body like this, would certainly be enough to kill you.[73]

Such a small amount of Semtex was needed for a big bang that a small device comprising the high explosive, sufficiently powerful to blow up a building, could easily be carried and left at a target. A well-known bomber, Jimmy Canning, was tailed carrying a holdall containing a 13.5-kg (30-lb) Semtex device intended to blow up twenty-seven members of the band of the Blues and Royals, which were performing at the Alfred Hayes Theatre in Hayes, Middlesex, on 27 June 1991. It failed to explode because a micro-switch for the timer failed; had it gone off, it would have brought down the theatre roof and killed many in the audience as well as the army band. It was also twice the amount that exploded at the Royal Marine School of Music at Deal, Kent, in September 1989, which killed eleven bandsmen.[74] On 6 April 1992, Canning was again tailed as he carried a briefcase containing a small Semtex bomb, which he dumped without finding a target for it.

Larger amounts of Semtex were incorporated into the IRA bombs of the 1990s. On the morning of 24 April 1996, the IRA demonstrated that it was prepared to expend a sizeable amount of Semtex in a single attack in its largest ever deployment of the explosive, on Hammersmith Bridge.[75] But the two devices, exceeding 14 kg of Semtex combined, but small enough to fit into two briefcases, failed to detonate completely.[76] The Real IRA stole half a tonne of Semtex from the IRA's arms dumps and used just 2 kg of it to blow up a section of the same bridge on 1 June 2000 – its first attack on London. No-one was injured but the attack, which caused traffic chaos, was widely publicised as it coincided with the first meeting of the Northern Ireland power-sharing executive convened since it disintegrated earlier in the year over the mainstream IRA's refusal to publicly disarm.[77]

It is surprising that the IRA did not use more of the explosive – on decommissioning, some two tonnes were left. But, according to my contact in the Ulster Intelligence Unit UXO, as a prized substance the IRA quartermasters were loath to let too much go to an Active Service Unit in case it was lost through the bombers being caught.[78] There were several reasons: although relatively small amounts of the 'magic marble' could blow up an entire city centre, and its longevity was virtually unlimited,[79] Semtex was highly prized and not easy to acquire. The batches from Libya were a true windfall and the Provisionals, prepared for a protracted conflict, needed to hold onto as much of the explosive as possible and prioritise its use for tactical locations.[80] That is, to use it for boosters rather than as the main charge – particularly when there was so much ammonium nitrate around to make large VBIEDs, for which a Semtex booster of a few kg was enough for a very big explosion. The big fertiliser bombs could also be made in the remote farmhouses of south Armagh with little chance of detection. By the time decommissioning was complete, some three tonnes of Semtex had been put beyond use. Had the Provisionals used it all up, much of London may have been in ruins – or very many more smaller-scale attacks using Semtex could have persisted over many years.

There were exceptions: as much as 22 kg was used in the Mark-10 mortar, but this may have been because new deliveries had been taken from Libya during the 1980s – and also prior to the 1987 seizure of the *Eksund* (see Chapter 4), which had tonnes of Semtex on board. There is also evidence that the IRA was losing confidence in its supply as Libyan-sourced and other batches not only varied in quality, but some had been interdicted and tampered with. This meant the mix was not consistent and therefore unreliable. They therefore had to hang on to what was deemed high enough quality explosive for future actions.[81]

Explosives manufacture and acquisition continued after the August 1994 ceasefire. In June 2002 it was reported that a batch of C-4 had been delivered to the IRA from the Basque separatist group ETA to allow the IRA to make a symbolic gesture by handing over some of its out-of-date Semtex without losing its bombing capabilities.[82] Another 1,000 tonnes were exported to 'rogue states' such as Syria, North Korea, Iraq and Iran. Exports of Semtex were progressively tightened and since 2002 all of Explosia's sales have been controlled by a government ministry. The worldwide stockpile is estimated at 40,000 tonnes.

CURBING EXPLOSIVES SUPPLY

Attempts to block the IRA's sources of explosives were a constant challenge and closely involved the Irish government. By 1972 some 450 kg (around 1,000 lb) of explosives were being used per month.[83] Residues from explosions and dumped explosives revealed that gelignite (and detonators) originated in the Republic. Out of four and a half million tonnes of explosives imported into Ireland annually, all but 130 tonnes were from the UK.[84] Irish legislation only applied to safety of use and the government claimed that any legislation would not prevent smuggling via the long Irish coastline.[85] Then in September 1971 the Irish government appealed to the British to help improve security at sites where explosives were stored, with the result that legislation was proposed for a police licensing system, with a call-in of small suppliers' stocks to be placed under military control. [86]

Other ways of controlling the means of destruction included tagging the supplies from the point of manufacture to enable them to be traced. Most explosives came from an ICI plant on the Ayrshire coast in Scotland. The company, which was, equally significantly, the sole supplier of detonators to the UK, suggested packaging gelignite in sticks but claimed that numbering the sticks was impracticable; alphanumeric codes could also be removed by the recipients. The relationship between ICI and the UK Ministry of Defence was a crucial issue, as was the danger of revealing countermeasures that could alert the IRA to acquire more stocks or acquire alternative stocks.

Changing the methods of manufacture could also be costly and the company could require compensation from the government. So the UK EOD experts had to come up with a foolproof technical solution that could be applied with the company's approval. Legislation would then make the changes compulsory. The Atomic Energy Research Establishment at Harwell – the home of Britain's nuclear weapons research – produced a scheme whereby batches of gelignite would be mixed with 'rare earths' in such a way that they could be traced, even after detonation. More wrangling with ICI resulted in a reluctant adoption of coding detonators with specifically identifiable paints.[87]

Other measures were proposed to ensure that no explosives used in Northern Ireland were from other than the British mainland. Explosives such as Gelamex (which became Frangex) were coming across the border.[88] But once these and gelignite supplies became harder to obtain, and before the influx of Libyan Semtex (also to be used as a booster), the IRA had begun to develop HME to augment supplies.

This in turn meant that ammonium nitrate and fuel oil came under scrutiny for control. But with agriculture a prime industry in both the North and South of Ireland, and the world beyond, the raw materials for HME were readily available. In May 1972 rigid controls were introduced through rushed-through UK legislation to restrict the sale of ammonium nitrate, sodium chlorate and weedkiller, and special licence was needed for the use of nitrobenzene (another HME ingredient).

But in all, restricting by law the supply of explosives across borders was to remain more than just a gelignite headache for the authorities. Nitrobenzene was still available – five tonnes had been imported by a bogus Irish company – and seizure of fertiliser stocks was made problematic by issues of compensation.[89] Even if water were added to the ammonium nitrate it could be boiled off, as it had to be totally dry for a successful explosive (which was a long and arduous task in the wet climate of Ireland). This could be done by heating the fertiliser with Bunsen burners, then cooling and separating the materials to produce the pure ammonium nitrate.

Newer batches of Semtex contain an identifying metallic code and have ethylene glycol dinitrate added as a taggant for detection – giving the odourless explosive a distinctive vapour signature. Efforts to reduce its shelf life from twenty years to three or even less have, however, proved difficult. However, the Explosia website now lists several types of Semtex (see Table 5.2) that have far shorter shelf lives than the type obtained by the IRA, Semtex-H: Semtex S-30 for example has a shelf life of just one year.[90]

TABLE 5.2: TYPES OF SEMTEX WITH SHORTER SHELF-LIVES THAN
THAT PROCURED BY THE IRA

	Semtex H	Semtex A
PETN	49.8 %	94.3 %
RDX	50.2 %	5.7 %
Dye	Sudan I (red-orange)	Sudan IV (reddish brown)
Antioxidant	N-phenyl-2-naphthylamine	1%
Plasticiser	di-n-octyl phthalate, tri-*n*-butyl citrate	9%
Binder	styrene-butadiene rubber	9,4%

Source: http://www.explosia.cz/

TABLE 5.3: SEMTEX: PROPERTIES OF POWDER AND PLASTIC VERSIONS

Parameter	Unit	SEMTEX® S 30	SEMTEX® 10 SE
Type		powder	plastic
Explosion heat	kJ/kg	1,277	3,992
Swath volume	dm3/kg	420	944
Oxygen balance	%O2	-3	-62.6
Detonation velocity	m/s	2,200	7,000
Trauzl test	Ml	—	—
Brisance by Hess	Mm	10	20
RWS (blasting gelatine)	%	12	72
Temperature of explosion	°C	1,023	2,600
Transmission of detonation	Cm	—	—
Density	kg/m3	—	1,450
Water resistance	-	no	excellent
Smallest diameter permitted	Mm		

Source: http://www.explosia.cz/

But the problem remains with 1980s- and 1990s-vintage long-life stocks still in the hands of terrorists, which take up to thirty-five years to deteriorate. Nevertheless, official production and supplies have been minimal since 2002 – which may explain the growing use of liquid and other homemade peroxide-based explosives by Islamic terrorists, such as TATP (triacetone triperoxide), which the IRA has never used.

NOTES

1. K.R.M. Short, *The Dynamite War: Irish-American Bombers in Victorian Britain* (Dublin: Gill & Macmillan, 1979).
2. J. Bebie, *Manual of Explosives, Military Pyrotechnics and Chemical Warfare Agents* (Boulder, CO: Paladin Press, 1942).
3. S. McLemore, *Homeland Insecurity: Dynamite Terror and the Textual Landscape of London*, PhD dissertation.
4. G. McGladdery, *The Provisional IRA in England: The Bombing Campaign 1973 1997* (Dublin: Irish Academic Press, 2006), p.22.
5. Republican Sinn Féin Poblachtach, Jeremiah O'Donovan Rossa – Irish republican Brotherhood.
6. Without, I hope, contravening anti-terrorism legislation.
7. Short, *The Dynamite War*.
8. T. Geraghty, *The Irish War* (London: HarperCollins, 1998), p.313.
9. McLemore, *Homeland Insecurity*.
10. A. Houen, *Terrorism and Modern Literature from Joseph Conrad to Ciaran Carson* (Oxford: Oxford University Press, 2002).
11. J. Most, *The Science of Revolutionary Warfare: A Handbook of Instruction Regarding the Use and Manufacture of Nitroglycerine, Dynamite, Gun-Cotton, Fulminating Mercury, Bombs, Arson, Poisons, etc.* (1881), cited in A.H. Garrison, 'Defining terrorism: philosophy of the bomb, propaganda by deed and change through fear and violence', *Criminal Justice Studies*, 17, 3 (September 2004), pp.259–79. Most and other anarchists used dynamite bombs to try to assassinate Romanov

dynasty notables, including Czar Alexander II, by bombing railway lines, streets and other thoroughfares where he was expected to travel. The Czar was eventually assassinated by a dynamite bomb thrown into the window of a train car in which he travelled on 13 March 1881.

12. 'The Fear of Dynamite', *The Spectator*, 14 April 1883.
13. Quoted in Geraghty, *The Irish War*, p.313.
14. S.P. O'Doherty, *The Volunteer: A Former IRA Man's True Story* (London: HarperCollins, 1993), p.134.
15. R. Abbott, 'Attack on Newtownhamilton RIC Barracks, Co. Armagh – 9 May 1920', Families Acting for Innocent Relatives (FAIR), south Armagh.
16. T.P. Coogan, *Michael Collins* (London: Arrow Books, 1991), p.153.
17. From the old IRA song, 'The Old Alarm Clock'. ' ... It ticks away politely till you get an awful shock. And it ticks away the geliger-nite in me auld alarum clock'.
18. 'The Hour Has Come!' *Time*, 30 January 1939.
19. *A History of IRA Activity in England*, special branch report to the Home Office, 5 December 1939, PRO HO 144/21358.
20. 'Armagh: This is IRA territory', *Time*, 12 January 1976.
21. O'Doherty, *The Volunteer*, p.82.
22. 'Chlorate de potassium. Chlorate de sodium', *Fiche toxicol*, no. 217 (Paris: Institut national de recherche et de sécurité, 2000).
23. This term is strangely similar to the designation of Saddam Hussein's chemical warfare director.
24. B. Behan, *Borstal Boy* (London: Arrow Books, 1990 (first edition, 1958)), p.1.
25. T.P. Coogan, *The IRA* (London: HarperCollins, 1970), p.121.
26. E. Stephan, *Spies in Ireland* (London: Macdonald & Co., 1963) p.41.
27. *Time*, 7 August 1939.
28. S. Plan, Events June 1939 – December 1939, from Wikipedia, http://en.wikipedia.org/wiki/S-Plan#_ref-0
29. C. Gearty, 'It's 1867 all over again', *Guardian*, 29 November 2005.
30. *Time*, 7 August 1939.
31. C. Ryder, *A Special Kind of Courage: 321 EOD Squadron – Battling the Bombers* (London: Methuen, 2006), p.28.
32. Ibid., p.18.
33. Ibid., p.22. The IRA used Tonite in an attempt to destroy a telephone exchange in Northern Ireland in 1957.
34. IRA Green Book, 1956 edition.
35. Ryder, *A Special Kind of Courage*, p.104.
36. Lt Col G. Styles, GC, *Bombs Have No Pity* (London: William Luscombe, 1975), p.86.
37. Styles, *Bombs Have No Pity*, p.87.
38. Ibid., pp.98–9.
39. Again, redolent of the early atomic bomb-making, where experiments with high-explosives for the highly complex plutonium bomb design involved risk to life, limb and facility.
40. Ryder, *A Special Kind of Courage*, p.34.
41. Ibid., p.70.
42. Ibid., p.76.
43. Ibid., p.62.
44. O'Doherty, *The Volunteer*, pp.167–8.
45. Bebie, *Manual of Explosives*.
46. J. Akhavan, *The Chemistry of Explosives* (London: The Royal Society of Chemistry, 1998).
47. Coogan, *The IRA*, p.123.
48. Ryder, *A Special Kind of Courage*, p.62.
49. Quoted in Geraghty, *The Irish War*, pp.85–6.
50. A.R. Oppenheimer, Press Association interview, syndicated worldwide (e.g. 'The carnage caused by fertiliser bombs', *The Metro*, 30 April 2007), but not all the 'operational details' were included for legal reasons.
51. T. Harnden, *Bandit Country* (London: Coronet, 1999), p.12.
52. C. Summers and D. Casciani, 'Bomb would have been "devastating"', BBC News, 9 July 2007. I was asked to make up and blow up mock versions of these bombs for the trial. I declined. In the 7 July attacks, where the bombs tragically did work, the terrorists used ground pepper, not flour.

53. B. O'Brien, *The Long War: IRA and Sinn Féin* (2nd edition) (Syracuse, NY: Syracuse University Press, 1999), p.165.
54. From various verbal military sources and in fiction, e.g. S. Leather, *The Bombmaker* (London: Coronet, 1999), pp.288–9.
55. A.R. Oppenheimer, 'Conventional explosives: the terrorist's choice', *Jane's Terrorism and Security Monitor*, May 2004.
56. T. Hillier, Chief Supt. Operational Support, Department of the City of London Police, 'Bomb Attacks in City Centres', September 1994.
57. Volunteer Bernard McGinn to RUC detectives, April 1997, quoted in Harnden, *Bandit Country*, p.313.
58. Harnden, *Bandit Country*, p.319.
59. Ryder, *A Special Kind of Courage*, p.64.
60. Ibid., p.177.
61. D.M. Chambers, 'Perspectives on Pentaerythritol Tetranitrate (PETN) Decomposition', Lawrence Livermore National Laboratory, US Department of Energy, Claudia L. Brackett and O. David Sparkman, University of the Pacific, 1 July 2002, p.3.
62. K. Connolly, 'Security fears over terrorists' flexible friend', *Guardian*, 23 February 2002.
63. J. Koyen and A. Zaitchik, 'Semtex: The Magic Marble of Pardubice', 27 August 2002, Politics in Freezerbox. There is also a band called Semtex Girls, and no doubt there are others (all redolent of the many atomic references that abounded in culture and the arts during the Cold War).
64. Chambers, 'Perspectives on Pentaerythritol Tetranitrate (PETN) Decomposition', p.3.
65. It feels a bit like Potty Putty (a stretchy substance children used to fashion into very bouncy balls in the 1960s) but not as gooey.
66. Chambers, 'Perspectives on Pentaerythritol Tetranitrate (PETN) Decomposition', p.4.
67. Koyen and Zaitchik, 'Semtex: The Magic Marble of Pardubice'.
68. Explosia website, http://www.explosia.cz/en/?show=semtex, plus personal communication with Explosia representative.
69. 'The IRA's store of weaponry', BBC News, 14 August 2001.
70. Harnden, *Bandit Country*, p.256.
71. Confirmed by personal communication, Ulster Intelligence Unit operative, 2007.
72. A.J. Fleming, 'Terrorism coverage in the United Kingdom', *Risk Management*, http://www.drj.com/special/wtc/w3_065.htm.
73. 'Bomb Squad', Nova television documentary, US Public Broadcasting Service, PBS (Public Broadcasting Service) Airdate: 21 October 1997.
74. Harnden, *Bandit Country*, p.325.
75. And, as mentioned before, the date of the 1916 Easter Rising. This attempt at blowing up the bridge was to commemorate the eightieth anniversary of the Rising.
76. S. Boyne, 'IRA Weapons and Technology', *Jane's Intelligence Review*, August 1996. But the reason why this vast Semtex device failed to go off cannot be revealed in full on grounds of national security.
77. B. Came, 'Irish Peace Process Revived', *Maclean's Magazine*, 12 June 2000.
78. Personal communication, Ulster Intelligence Unit operative, 2007.
79. Ibid.
80. Ibid.
81. Ibid.
82. D. Bamber and T. Oliver, 'Basque bombers top up IRA's terror arsenal', *Daily Telegraph*, 30 June 2002.
83. Ryder, *A Special Kind of Courage*, p.61.
84. Ibid., p.112.
85. Ibid., p.112.
86. Personal communication, former Irish army EOD operative, November 2007.
87. Ryder, *A Special Kind of Courage*, p.115.
88. Ibid., p.118.
89. Ibid., p.121.
90. Semtex on Explosia website, http://www.explosia.cz/en/?show =trhaviny

Six

Deadly Ingenuity: The Bomb Technologies

Groups of EOs – as we called our people, like, explosives officers – came together to discuss 'How do we stop this?' ... And that's when the ingenuity came out. And you found that a lot of people had a lot of ingenuity.

Shane Paul O'Doherty, IRA bomb-maker

Some of the devices I've had to deal with were the result of sheer genius.

Personal communication,
Ulster Intelligence Unit operative

I have said several times in this book that the Provisional IRA became recognised as the world's most proficient bomb-makers. Much of this reputation was earned, albeit nefariously, by the evolution of their skills in fitting timing mechanisms, methods of detonation, and booby trap devices to their improvised explosive devices (IEDs). As with much improvised technology, the sophistication of the timing mechanisms and detonation methods evolved through necessity – the need to fire off a bomb at a designated time and place and the need to avoid being too close to the detonation being uppermost. Today's suicide terrorists do not need advanced delay timers and remote-controlled initiation of their deadly explosions as they intend to go up with the bombs they produce;[1] the IRA, on the other hand, while embracing a culture of martyrdom of a patriotic nature, never had any intention of blowing themselves up.

This chapter will deal with the complexities of how the bombs were set and constructed to explode in specific ways and at specific times. However, current antiterrorism legislation precludes the inclusion of precise logistical details – such as how components are connected, and proportions of explosives – and the 'operational specificity' of terrorist operations. Details on, for example, why devices failed to go off, also remain classified, the revelation of which would endanger operatives on both sides.

By the time the IRA were deploying 1,000-plus bombs a year in Northern Ireland, and had run several campaigns on the mainland, they had developed a research and development (R& D) operation – conducted by its Engineering Department – that was, and remains, unrivalled by any other non-state group. There were, in total, 19,000 explosions and incendiary attacks using a vast array of devices.[2] By the end of the 1970s the Provisionals had learned from early accidents and mistakes and were producing more sophisticated IEDs with more stable explosives and more reliable timers.[3]

The technical innovations the Provisionals made in IED timing and other mechanisms came thick and fast by the mid-1980s. There was also a tendency to introduce a mechanism for up to, for example, three attacks – and then drop it.[4] It was not always clear why this happened: either a kind of 'corporate amnesia' set in, or the IRA was worried they would be compromised and so kept moving on.

EARLY TIMERS: THE FIRST CAMPAIGNS

The first evidence of the Irish republican movement's use of timers comes during the Skirmishers' campaign in the mid-1880s, when bombers, most notably William Mackey Lomasney, undertook research in new technologies and invented a simple timing device for the bombs used on the British mainland in order to make them more effective.[5] These included wire tied around a clock winder, which was used later in the 1930s.[6]

The results were varied, insofar as Lomasney was eventually killed by his own bomb planted under London Bridge in December 1884. There would be many subsequent 'own goals' like this early example, often taking the lives of the bomb planters more than the actual bomb-makers, but honing such a dangerous craft was bound to claim not just innocent victims of the bombs but their own creators, well into the 1970s and occasionally beyond.

The 1930s campaign also included bombs incorporating clothes pegs with pin tacks pushed through the end as the contacts. These crude timing devices were reintroduced in the 1950s. The delaying device in the pegs would comprise a rubber band or soldering wire. The peg spring would gradually overcome the strength of the rubber or the wire and close the end where the tin tacks would meet, completing the circuit. The problem with this was that it was not possible to gauge exactly the strength of the wood or the clothes peg spring – so timing the bomb was haphazard and consequently 'own goals' were common. One example, quoted by George Styles, was an attempt to blow up an electrical transformer in Old Malone Road in Belfast, in December 1969; the tin tacks met in the device before the bomb had been laid, blowing up its planters.[7]

In February 1971 a clothes peg device was set off prematurely when the IRA attempted to blow up a television transmission mast in Co. Tyrone by laying a mine. When BBC engineers following an army patrol were called to fix damage caused to the mast by a previous attempt to destroy it, their Land Rover ran into a trip wire set at knee height across the path of the vehicle and the impact on the wire pulled a plug out from between the jaws of the clothes peg contact. This led to the contact being made and the mine exploding, killing the occupants of the vehicle.[8] Such 'mistakes' –those who were blown up were not the intended targets but victims all the same – would result in the IRA abandoning a specific technique.

Trying to counter clothes peg devices also posed great dangers for the bomb disposal operators. If a fishing line were used to snare a device, pulling it too far could snap the dowel out of the clothes peg and the device would be triggered.[9] A classic 1971-vintage IED used by the Provisionals consisted of a simple timing mechanism, such as the legendary 'auld alarum clock' connected to a 4.5-v battery, an electric detonator and around 4 kg of explosive, often gelignite.

One of the leading 1970s bomb makers, Shane O'Doherty, tells of his early experience with fuse-delay mechanisms. His first, very basic bomb involved a safety fuse which, once ignited, would burn for three minutes before exploding the detonator and then the main explosive charge. Matches taped to the end of the safety fuse had to be struck with a matchbox striker. If struck too early, the six feet (2 m) of fuse wire was meant to be cut, or the detonator pulled out of the explosive. Also, safety fuse in short lengths is unreliable as the filling often becomes loose and the fuse can 'flash through'.[10] Almost in the manner of a man striking a cartoon spherical bomb with 'bomb' written on it and a fuse sticking up out of the top, O'Doherty had to strike the matchbox against the matches, let the sparks fizz, and then run like hell. He tells of running home and thinking that nothing had happened, until 'an incredible roar exploded over the entire city, magnified many times by the intense quiet of the night'.[11]

Another fuse-delay device in incendiary bombs incorporated a condom, supplies of which an embarrassed, young O'Doherty was sent to buy from the local chemist's. Sulphuric acid in the device had to dissolve two layers of condom, after which the acid ignited the incendiary material, producing the fire. This was a highly dangerous and unreliable method of regulating the time when you wanted your bomb to explode, and was replaced by clocks and electronic circuitry, which eliminated the safety fuse.[12] These advances in turn enabled the IRA to build booby trap devices (see below).

Timing mechanisms on incendiary devices, such as the box-type incendiaries used in the 1980s, could be set for up to twelve hours and made from commercially available timing chips. The PPM incendiary device used a timer unit which included a watch or travel clock – potassium nitrate or potassium permanganate would be chosen as the incendiary mix.[13] Apart from letter-bombs, O'Doherty planted cigarette-packet-sized devices with wristwatch timers against the petrol tanks of cars in Mayfair in London, targeting high-profile military, political and intelligence people.

TIMING AND POWER UNITS (TPUS)

The Provisionals pioneered the TPU as a means of initiating its IEDs. These units comprised a timer, a safe-to-arm switch, and a power supply to trigger the detonator. An indicator on the timer state would be visible – either a torch bulb or LED (light-emitting diode) – which would necessitate the inclusion of a resistor into the electrical circuit. A typical timer was the Memopark timer (see below) used to set the time for car parking. This novel timing device would normally be set for sixty minutes.[14] An entire series of TPUs were made; the Mark-15 model used a Biro to keep the timer at a pre-set delay, but problems with these TPUs, which resulted in bombings where civilians were hurt and consequent adverse publicity for the IRA, led to the development of the Mark-16 in 1988. This TPU incorporated two timers, with two separate circuits independent of each other, and with one containing an anti-disruption device. Should one timer fail, the TPU would still be able to initiate the IED.

A subsequent TPU that emerged in 1993 was discovered in car bombs that were intercepted before they could reach their targets. These TPUs, housed in Tupperware boxes, featured the infamous mercury tilt switch (see Booby Trap Devices, below) and a two-hour Memopark timer.[15]

DETONATORS: THE 'KEY TO ALL BOMBS'[16]

No bomb can go off without a detonator – this is the component that triggers the explosion. Styles quotes one of his instructors: 'The Chinese liken a bomb to a dragon; its explosion to a dragon's breath.[17] Thus I call the detonator the dragon's teeth.'[18] In the 1970s most detonators used in the UK were made by ICI. Eventually, on request from the British army, ICI introduced a system which made their detonators more easily traceable and hence enable identification of terrorist IEDs. Detonators are still relatively easy to acquire, particularly since the dawn of the internet. But long before then the IRA had access to electrical detonators from a number of sources over the years, such as Ireco detonators from the US. They also stole them from quarries, mainly in the Irish Republic.[19]

Small metal tubes with wires attached were the detonators used in Styles' time. They cost only 5p and consisted of a match head blob of material which when lit by a flame or electrical spark set off a small chain reaction with lead azide, a chemical which accelerated the explosion in the tube by around 1,300 m (4,000 ft)/sec. This produced the wave of energy which set off the main explosive charge in the bomb.

Detonating cord then became the standard type. It looks like washing line but has explosive powder running through it.[20] The cord ran from the cab where the timing device and detonators were likely to have been, to link the det to the main charge and transfer the detonation wave.[21] This allowed the IRA operatives who put the device together to assemble everything in relative safety before the bombers took it to the target (it is not a good idea to have detonators connected to explosives while the device is being driven into position). They would then have quickly taped the detonators to the cord and pulled a pin holding the timing device to the required delay. This is a very quick and simple operation, and allows maximum control of the device in transit.[22] An incident described by Styles involved bombs tied together with what was supposed to be detonating cord, but on examination turned out to be a plastic clothes line – which led to the army discovering a Belfast housewife hanging out her washing on a detonating cord![23]

The pace of development in detonating techniques was rapid. This was driven by the need to get a device to an area with minimum risk to the deployer of the bomb. The IRA produced the solution: the TPU – a simple electrical circuit, normally consisting of a battery and a timer. As mentioned above, the electrical circuit's incorporation into the devices meant they were more reliable. The IRA operative could deliver them well in advance of the intended detonation time and did not have to be in the area when this occurred.[24] Shane O'Doherty's first letter bombs, although they caused widespread fear and publicity, did not always go off. Within days an electronically detonated letter bomb was developed, with subsequent devices exacting often serious injuries. Electronic detonators then became the norm for IRA IEDs. But, as he himself has said, the arrival of batteries and clocks and electric detonators was only a temporary advance as, very shortly after, the army began to defuse these simple timing devices. O'Doherty also summed up the race between the IRA and the EOD squads in overcoming each other's efforts:

> So then, we had to figure ways to deter the army bomb squad from defusing them during their 55-minute run until they exploded. So, groups of EOs – as we called our people, like explosives officers – came together to discuss, 'How do we stop this?' You know? And that's when the ingenuity came out. And you found that a lot of people had a lot of ingenuity.[25]

In 1993, it was reported that the gardaí uncovered an IRA workshop at Kilcock, Co. Kildare that was producing a wide range of advanced electronic detonators.[26] While the Provos may have dabbled in the actual production of detonators, the production of lead azide or mercury fulminate was very dangerous.[27]

Some detonating cord came from Canada, which was yellow with black stripes, and had been tampered with. Therefore, having lost confidence in the batch, IRA engineers began to make their own by distilling out explosives from the Semtex mix, as Semtex is comprised of several different explosives (detailed in Chapter 5). These explosive components were extracted and washed with solvents, then poured into clear plastic tubing for the cord.[28] Also it was ascertained that in the early 1970s the IRA began to use bundles of detonators instead of gelignite in fertiliser devices.[29]

Detonators often malfunctioned: detached detonators meant no explosion, and many EOD operations depended on, and still depend on, disrupting or detaching the detonator (and the timing and firing mechanism) from the explosive charge. Sometimes bomb-making failures caused detonator malfunction, a notable example being possibly the most audacious – and potentially most damaging – attempt by the Provisionals to disrupt aviation, in 1974. Several MPs and the RUC's chief constable, Sir James Flanagan, were among eighty-three passengers on board a flight from Belfast to London that was diverted to Manchester following a phoned warning that four bombs were on the aircraft. After taking the passengers off, a 1-kg device was found under a seat, its timer a wristwatch (not digital but the analogue type of those days). The only reason why the bomb had not exploded was because a drawing pin fixed to the watch's face was covered by a thin layer of paint – which had acted as an insulator and prevented electrical contact with the hand of the watch. Hence no detonation, and no loss of high-profile life.[30]

COMMAND-WIRE DETONATION

In command-wire detonation a button is pressed or – as seen in many comic and pastiche renditions of people blowing things up – a plunger pushed to trigger the explosion.[31] There were a great number of IRA attacks using command-wire detonation, two examples of which are cited here. On 17 July 1975, four soldiers were killed in south Armagh when they were sent to investigate suspicious milk churns in a gap in the hedge between a main road and a field. A massive booby trap bomb hidden in the ground exploded, having been activated by an ordinary electric light flex command wire from a distance of almost 400 metres.[32] A lieutenant colonel in the Royal Army Ordinance Corps, who was chief ammunition technical officer in Northern Ireland, in giving evidence at the trial of the bombers in 1976 testified that on investigating the seat of the explosion he found the end of the command wire to the detonator on the bomb running parallel to a hedge. It stretched for a distance of 400 metres and was 'well dug in'. The buried bomb was contained in a steel cylinder, which weighed 34 kg. At the end of the command wire was the firing point and the bomb was detonated by a battery from which the wire led to the detonator.[33]

Command-wire detonation was the chosen method for ambushes, and the initiation of the command wire or radio control was from over the border – where the IRA enjoyed virtual immunity at the time from arrest – as, even when evidence was presented in court, the offences were deemed 'political' and they were protected by the Irish constitution.[34]

On 27 October 1982 three RUC officers were killed when a huge landmine bomb detonated by a command wire linked to a nearby hill exploded beneath their armoured police car, propelling it 36 metres into a field and causing a crater 18 metres wide and 7 metres deep.[35] The Ballygawley bus bomb was another example of this method:[36] eight soldiers from the 1st battalion Light Infantry were killed in a landmine attack at Curr near Ballygawley roundabout, Co. Tyrone, on 20 August 1988, while travelling back by coach to base in Omagh from Aldergrove airport. From the verbatim account of a seriously injured army survivor, Private David Hardy:

> The terrorists made a mistake that night, they got their calculations wrong – just a bit. I am pleased that they did as I might not be here to tell you about it. Remember the equation *Time= Distance= Speed* – well that's the one that they got wrong. The bus had already passed the bomb – by the way while I am on it was two fertilizer bags filled with Semtex all 200lb of it, they just laid them on the roadside and put a little dirt on top to cover them up. OK where was I ... good this, isn't it? OK they had used a telegraph pole as a mark when the bus reaches it, we will detonate the bomb, the bus will be doing about 40mph, so what you do is put the bomb just after the pole so by the time the bus gets to the pole and you react and push the button the bus will just be past the pole itself, right were the bomb is. *WRONG* – the bus driver knew that the lads just wanted to get back to barracks and get their head down as they were cream crackered with hanging around all day, so the driver was speeding 50+ (mph), so the bus was well past the bomb by the time they set it off ... unlucky.[37]

Command-wire detonation in rural areas meant very large devices could be used in ambushes on British troops. But these vast bombs would threaten the safety of nearby residents and their properties; homes would be taken over to facilitate such attacks and hours or days of planning the attacks meant such occupation would overturn the lives of those affected. The planning would include the digging in of the command wires to conceal them – an operation that could take up to twelve hours – over distances of several hundred metres, with the positioning of heavy HME loads in culverts and hedges. Wires would be dug in and left for days on end before being connected to the devices. These command wires were often discovered – often from supplies of food and drink found at the sites – for up to two months before they were to be activated, as the IRA operatives would be waiting for an opportune time and target to connect them to carry out an effective ambush.[38]

REMOTE-CONTROL DETONATION

Remote-control detonators rely on radio or other electronic signals to set off the explosion and represent a higher level of technical expertise in the bomb-maker. These techniques became available as electronics expertise and components acquisition emerged in the latter half of the 1970s.

Radio-controlled IEDs

Radio-controlled IEDs (known in military parlance as RCIEDs[39]) were becoming more apparent by the late 1970s, the IRA having experimented with this method as early as 1972.[40] Command-wire detonation had the disadvantage of the command wire attached to the IED being visible and giving the game away. This happened in a thwarted attack in 1976 at Narrow Water near Warrenpoint mentioned earlier in this book and the forerunner to the deadly Warrenpoint attack of August 1979. A bomb that had been planted to ambush a Royal Marines convoy was revealed by the wires trailing to the device through which a command detonation was to have been sent. So the soldiers took cover behind the walls of Narrow Waters Castle some 400 metres away.[41] On more than one occasion, the command wires running through fields were chewed by cows![42]

The first RCIEDs betrayed no evidence of a command wire so they had to have been detonated by another method. Radio-controlled detonation later came into its own once CB (citizen band) radios became legal in the UK. This increased the number of bands and frequencies available.[43] The need to be able to detonate a device while remaining in a concealed position with a clear view of the target location catalysed the development of such remote-controlled mechanisms.

Using model aircraft

Many of the RC devices came from commercially available gadgets or hobby products. The earliest known IRA device triggered remotely by radio command was adapted from a model aircraft system and detonated a month before Bloody Sunday in January 1972.[44] These improvised systems worked when the command passed by the transmitter to the receiver, which was wired in such a way as to activate a switch and complete the firing circuit of the bomb. Another example from this period is given by Shane O'Doherty from one of his operations on the border, where a vast 270-kg (600-lb) landmine bomb was planted in a hole dug in the road.[45] O'Doherty attached an electronic receiver to it by a small aerial that was almost invisible. A signal to this aerial detonated the bomb when an armoured army vehicle drove over it. In similar operations an IRA observer set away from the bomb and the command position would send a radio signal when the target approached the contact point.[46]

Pulse coding was introduced to prevent stay signals from initiating premature detonation and blowing up the bomber: an encoder on the transmitter and a decoder on the receiver enabled the bomber to set the radio-control system to operate on a given code only. But this did not always work, so tone codes rather than pulse codes were introduced.[47] As with so many of these developments, the initiative was made by the IRA.

The model aircraft systems first operated on a frequency of 27 Megahertz (MHz); then the Provisionals suddenly began deploying devices that operated on 35 MHz. The model aircraft would be bought in the Republic. At first it was believed that this was due to countermeasures having succeeded in jamming the 27-MHz system. However, it turned out that the regulations in the Republic had changed to 35 MHz, and the supply of 27-MHz-based models had ceased. So the IRA switched to 35 MHz simply because the former type were no longer available![48]

Another type of transmitter-detonated device adapted from model boats and aircraft was known as the McGregor. Such switches, which could be bought in model shops, were activated to detonate the bomb.[49] At first the transmitter from the model boat would be used to activate a simple switch which would instigate the detonation.

Among the more ingenious and deadly radio-controlled devices, one example incorporated a firing pack connected to a car aerial which had a Staveley Tone Lock transmitter and receiver – which could enable the device to be triggered by radio control. Attempts by the IRA to obtain the Staveley systems from a Manchester supplier were only revealed to the bomb squad when such a device was found on the border in January 1972 – a failure of intelligence sharing that could have had tragic consequences.[50]

REMOTE VS. COMMAND-WIRE

Radio-controlled IEDs (RCIEDs) enabled the IRA to detonate mines and other devices at a time of their choosing, when a target was most vulnerable and at exactly the time it reached the target location. The Warrenpoint attack illustrated only too clearly that remote control was gaining preference. The milk-churn bomb on the trailer set to ambush the Royal Marines convoy in this instance was triggered remotely by a model aircraft transmitter unit. The second bomb blew up anyone attempting to take cover behind the castle walls, who were also attacked by IRA snipers in position. On the same day, a radio control transmitter was used to detonate the bomb on Lord Mountbatten's pleasure boat at Mullaghmore.[51]

But the IRA nevertheless continued using command-wire detonation alongside newer methods until the very end of the campaign, depending on the situation and the target.[52] Detonating with command wire was proven, reliable, less prone to false initiation, and involved fewer countermeasures such as the British jamming radio signals needed to set off radio-controlled IEDs. There was also no interference in frequencies that may prevent these latter devices going off or set them off at the wrong time or place. The wires could be found but on the whole were very easy to conceal in rural settings. This enabled the IRA to bury the devices and the wires weeks or even months in advance, thereby giving them the capability of careful and timely targeting. They were also effective in urban settings, where the wires were sometimes concealed inside telegraph poles.[53]

The IRA's use of radio-controlled detonation necessitated the army to sweep areas of the countryside with jamming signals on the 27-MHz waveband used by the model boat transmitters.[54] An intelligence report at the time described how the IRA realised that aero-modelling equipment had drawbacks because of the many signals emanating from various sources that put the bomb planter at risk. It was also inherently risky as it would detonate the radio-controlled bombs ahead of the IRA setting them off.

To counter the jamming operations, the IRA developed a system that could not be detonated by such sweeping operations – by refining the radio-control mechanism to incorporate encoding and decoding devices.[55] This consisted of using sophisticated electronic switches as initiators,[56] which prevented the army from detonating the devices by jamming the air waves.[57] Such advanced electronic equipment was obtained from the US and elsewhere by the IRA and used to modify both transmitters and receivers by means of a coded signal to activate the IED. But some were also homemade.[58] This meant an attempt by the army to jam the signal, based on transmitting a constant frequency, would fail in either disrupting the bomb or setting it off in advance; the security forces could subsequently not ascertain exactly the modulations in the signal that were needed to arm the device.[59]

This development exemplified the arms race between the IRA and the British security forces – a race that was to become increasingly complex technologically and psychologically. MoD scientists were propelled to develop new countermeasures, which will be described in Chapter 9. The IRA blamed the Enniskillen explosion of 8 November 1987, which killed eleven and injured sixty-three, on army jamming measures, but it turned out the bomb was set off by a timer.[60] The IRA always claimed that the bomb was never intended to kill civilians and that it had gone off at the wrong time, having been primed to explode during a time when soldiers, not civilians, were present. As was customary during this period of the Army Intelligence–IRA arms race, the army had conducted an electronic sweep of the area and it is alleged that this set off the IRA's electronic timer.[61] While this may be true, whatever the reason for the detonation having occurred at the time it did – without warning at 10.45 a.m.[62] – the atrocity was a propaganda coup for the authorities and did the IRA great harm in this respect. And regardless of how and when the device – hidden in a nearby hall – went off, it succeeded in blowing out a wall, showering the area with debris and burying people attending the Remembrance Day ceremony in metres of rubble. Among those killed were three married couples, a retired policeman, a nurse and thirteen children. The head of the Church of Ireland, Archbishop Robin Eames, who was at Enniskillen, said he 'wished the bombers could have seen what I have seen'. The last victim, Ronnie Hill, died in 2000 after having been in a coma since the blast.[63] One of the victims, a fifty-five-year-old truck driver, Harry Donaldson, spoke of his experience from his hospital bed, having been buried by rubble and sustaining head, face and leg injuries. He had given a lift to one of those killed.

> We were both standing with our backs to the wall of the building when there was a huge bang and the wall came down on top of us. I didn't see him again. My head was trapped in the railings underneath the masonry which fell on top of me and I couldn't move. It was just awful.[64]

With the use of disguise and anti-handling mechanisms (see below), these remote-controlled IEDs were deadly and took many casualties, both troops and EOD teams sent to dismantle them. Helicopters used to move troops in order to evade the threat were prone to machine-gun fire from the IRA on the ground.[65] So the RCIED marked a notable military advance, and advantage, for the IRA in the true spirit of guerrilla warfare at its height.

The IRA had also by the early 1980s developed detonation systems they had adapted from radio systems used to monitor the weather.[66] The notorious 20 July 1982 Hyde Park bomb, which killed eleven soldiers and seven horses, was detonated by remote control rather than command wire. This allowed the bomb to be exploded at just the right time and place to blow up a section of the parade. From the mid-1980s on, the IRA developed the RCIED further, having discovered the 'white band' – a wave band that could not be interfered with by jamming – in order to set off bombs using unimpeachable radio signals. This marked a quantum leap in IED development that put the British under increasing pressure to counteract – and it took them over a year to come up with a counter-measure to it.[67] At this stage, the IRA reverted to command-wire detonation which, although visible, could not be jammed.

Projectiles, flash guns and infra-red
The projectile command IED used a novel means of detonation – a bullet fired from a rifle some distance away from the device that would bring together two sheets of copper inside it and begin detonation of a vehicle-borne bomb.[68] This enabled the IRA to set off car bombs merely by firing at them – a level of marksmanship that had been achieved by volunteers over many years.

Explosively formed projectiles, which re-emerged in the numerous roadside bombings during the Iraqi insurgency in 2007, are explosive devices based on a Second World War-era discovery – the Misznay-Schardin effect – and can penetrate the thick armour of a military vehicle using a precisely configured high-explosive charge. The use of a projectile enables the penetration of fast-moving armoured vehicles at distances beyond those normally swept by EOD officers on the vehicles' main routes. The Provisionals learned about developing and using these projectiles during training in Libya and Syria, specifically that precise triggering was vital to the accuracy of these devices.[69]

Pinpoint targeting was a matter of split-second timing, so this in turn led to a further IRA innovation in setting off bombs at an appointed time – by firing a camera flashlight from around 100 metres away, which struck a light-sensitive cell to trigger a car-borne mortar bomb. Photo flash 'slave' units are used by professional photographers to initiate flash units from a signal generated by the camera. They came in two variants – coded, which sends a specific signal, and uncoded, which are less expensive but which can be accidentally detonated by any pulsed light (such as a neon tube).[70] The flashlight method was pioneered by a unit in Newry and was used in a bomb that killed Colleen McMurray, an RUC officer, in 1992. Her colleague Paul Slaine lost both his legs in the attack. He was later awarded the George Cross for his bravery.[71] The police vehicle that was targeted was driving out of its barracks when the IRA operative used his flash gun to trigger the firing of the mortar at the vehicle.

There were also near 'own goals' sustained by the Provisionals using the flash-gun technique. One such was when an IRA operative's flash unit responded to a nearby neon light flashing and went off prematurely in his hand. The investigators examining the incident could work out how the device was made from piecing together tiny items in the microcircuitry – just one of many great forensic achievements during the entire period of the campaign.[72]

Once the intelligence and UXO people caught up with flash gun techniques, the IRA introduced a method that utilised infra-red sensors of the type used for the remote opening and closing of garage doors. This had the advantage of leaving no chemical forensic evidence behind. Infra-red devices allowed IRA teams to refine the flash technique and detonate explosives from up to a mile away.[73] It is believed that the IRA used the period of the ceasefire in the 1990s to upgrade such mechanisms and to develop techniques to combat British army 'disruptive' radio signals by using radar guns and microwave receivers.

Other uses of light as a trigger for detonation were truly ingenious and devilish. A bomb would be placed in a car and attached to a window tax disc that was made to be light-sensitive. The nearby street lights would have been knocked out by a Provisional operative. A policeman on patrol checking the tax disc at night would have to turn on his torch to see it: when he shone the torch at the disc – bang.[74] Other devices could be triggered by the glove compartment light by adapting the electronics and wiring it to the bomb. Such a device was believed to have killed an ATO (ammunition technical officer) investigating an abandoned car in Newry in May 1981.[75]

TIME-DELAY DETONATION

Time-delay detonators use a clock, wristwatch or other timing device to enable the bomb to go off at a precise time. Shane O'Doherty was already using delayed-timing in his early-to-mid-1970s gelignite devices, which were planted in several Oxford Street shops. He carried one such device in a shopping bag the length of London's main shopping street and had the device constructed in such a way as to be able to put his hand into the bag, set the timer on an hour-long delay, and then join two wires that were the final connection – arming the bomb. This he did while crossing the street – the bomb was set to go off in one hour's time. He tells of a sudden last-minute impulse to stop the detonation – necessitating him to divert into a side street and defuse the device. He then found that he had set the timer for only a few minutes instead of an hour – because the clock on the timer was upside down inside the bag! Had he not felt an unknown impulse to defuse it, he and his fellow volunteer would have become among the world's first (unintentional) suicide bombers and mass killers. He then managed to re-set the timer and plant the bomb in a basement boutique before making three calls with his coded message to the police. A small explosion occurred and no-one was hurt.[76] This was not a failure of the timer, but of the detonator – which had exploded but had failed to ignite the gelignite.[77]

By the end of the 1970s the IRA had advanced from hit-and-miss amateur bomb makers with vast resources of ingenuity, audacity and ruthlessness in their ability to improvise, to advanced technologists whose bomb-making skills would not have gone amiss in the top nuclear weapons laboratories of the world. Timers had also become more reliable and explosives, most notably bought-in Semtex (and home-milled ammonium nitrate), more stable. Timer/power units were acquired or made that could be set for as long as forty-eight days – almost four months. A cache of these, discovered in the Glasgow apartment of the Brighton bomber, Patrick Magee, were found to be inaccurate by only a matter of minutes.[78]

The attempted attack on the London electrical substation network in 1996 was a remarkable example of delayed-timing expertise. The IRA tried to attack Britain's infrastructure on many occasions and this aim was a fundamental aspect of its serious strategic thinking. Some thirty devices were intercepted; there were twenty-two named substations in London and the devices were meant to take out the transformer units, along with two spare units per substation. Each device was a timber box with three compartments; the first contained the power unit, which was a large battery used to electrify fences that would be needed in farming areas. In the second compartment was placed the explosive charge, an unwrapped standard-sized 3-kg block of Semtex. And in the third was a central-heating mains-op 9-V timer which would normally be used to turn on central heating at appointed times. A stand-by battery kept the clock going. The central heating timer allowed a long delay from the devices being placed and their detonation – as much as forty hours. Even if only three to five substations had been knocked out, electricity supply to large areas of London would have been interrupted.[79]

The interception revealed exactly where the Provisionals were aiming to deploy the devices. They also tried to deploy a subsequent batch but failed, as they had in the first instance, only because there were not enough operatives on the ground in London to deploy them all – some forty-four volunteers would have been needed, and there was nowhere near that number available.

On other occasions, IEDs deployed on railway lines actually used as their power source the electricity carried by the power lines themselves.[80]

Besides delaying the time before explosion, in the mid-1970s the Provisionals also began to shorten fusing and warning times in order to counter the attempts made by EOD squads to let devices sit ('soak') within cordoned-off areas – until their timers ran down and they went off or failed to go off (see Chapter 8) or to go in and remove or render safe planted devices. The 'wheelbarrow' remote handling device was already in use by 1974, and the IRA's aim was to shorten the time – known as the 'bogey' time – the EOD operative had to set up the 'wheelbarrow' to get at the IED and disrupt it. Shorter warning times meant a hell-for-leather dash to get equipment in place within ten minutes.[81] By 1976, the time available for neutralising IEDs before the timers expired had shortened to twenty minutes – which had previously been the minimum time, and had now become the maximum.[82]

Enter the home video recorder

The 1984 Brighton bomb was arguably the most famous example of the IRA's ability to plant a device on a long-delay timer. The development of these timers, which coincided with the arrival of the soon-to-be ubiquitous videocassette recorder (VCR), meant that operatives could plant the device in the Grand hotel weeks in advance of the designated event. Under the name 'Roy Walsh', Patrick Magee had checked into the Grand on 15 September 1984, selected the precise location for the planting of his device – in the small space under the bath (in the void between the bath tub and the woodwork skirt)[83] of the shower room in Room 629 – and checked out three days later. The bomb was set to explode on 12 October, at 2.54 a.m. This time was chosen apparently to minimise casualties – which brings home the bitter realisation that so many of the IRA's bombs, without remote timing technologies, would have killed and maimed even more victims than they did.

The Ministry of Defence had several years earlier anticipated the greatly enhanced danger of IRA attacks as a result of this invention – that the planting of bombs could be carried out before suspicion arose; that the system was very accurate; and that it could enable bombs to be detonated months or even years in advance – particularly to time with a VIP visit or high-profile event.[84]

The IRA soon cottoned on to adapting the timing modules from videos as these were commercially produced and therefore reliable and very accurate. It did not take a great degree of skill to convert the timer to send an electrical impulse to a detonator rather than turn on the video player. The timer could be procured as a separate unit from a supplier or could be taken out of a working VCR. After being tested for functionality and reliability it would be incorporated in the device. This would be done by one of the IRA engineering units – probably in the South somewhere – before being handed to the IRA operative in charge of weapons, the quarter-master, who would then arrange for the explosives and ancillaries to be made available to the ASU when they were in place in England. The bombers who eventually placed these devices would not be involved with their design or construction, apart from linking the various elements once the device was in place.[85]

Memopark timers were another cleverly adapted improvisation to delaying an explosion to exactly the time you wanted it to occur. These were simple mechanical two-hour timers used by motorists to indicate how long was left before their meter payment for parking their car ran out.[86] These timers were incorporated into a small plywood box which contained the power source – usually AA batteries or a 9-volt cell as well as the timer. A hole was drilled through the box and a dowel pin inserted to hold the timer at the required delay. The pin was removed to allow the timer to run down.[87] The IRA wired these timers up to detonators, which ensured the vehicle IED went off two hours after its timer had been set.[88] One particular type of Memopark timer, the Parkway timer, had a highly reliable timing mechanism – so much so that they became unavailable as the IRA bought up the entire stock![89]

During the mid-1990s ceasefire the Provisionals upgraded their remote-controlled mechanisms and developed techniques to combat British army 'disruptive' radio signals by using radar guns and microwave receivers.[90] There was also evidence that they had become so advanced as to incorporate satellite navigation and GPS (global positioning system) technology. Remote-controlled driving of vehicles, a technique used by the ETA terrorist group in Spain, was also deployed.[91] Tractors, a common sight in rural border areas policed by troops, were remotely driven to a target – usually soldiers – using command wire technology. This enabled the production of a vehicle-borne IED that could be guided like a Cruise missile to its target by remote control. This technique was used in the first Gulf War and did not go unnoticed by the IRA.[92]

That said, any impression that all these methods were neatly co-ordinated and applied rigorously must be tempered with the reminder that even an organised terrorist group like the Provisional IRA had to duck and weave their way through the surveillance and infiltration by the security services, and so the best-laid plans were not always feasible; or they were intercepted before they could really take off. On one occasion, soldiers heard a trailer and tractor start up. Foggy weather prevented accurate remote steering of the front wheels and the vehicles ended up in a ditch, where the trailer blew up.[93] What remains remarkable is the level of even theoretically based achievements in technology that were achieved – albeit by generous funding from the US in particular, but nevertheless through ingenuity and improvisation built on evolving expertise.

ANTI-HANDLING DEVICES: 'BOOBY TRAPS'

As if it isn't hard and dangerous enough to dismantle a bomb, to have to encounter devices fitted with the means to destroy any attempt to do so must be the very limit of diabolical intent. Such additional components revealed an additional set of skills to be countered in IRA bomb making. These would consist of disguising the device as a harmless object – a practice that has reached its ultimate height in the insurgency in Iraq, but well ploughed by the IRA over the decades – and a host of ways of prematurely triggering an explosion if anyone approaches the device, touches it, or tries to dismantle it. Once the UXO squads had begun taking the IRA's bombs apart, the IRA targeted those very people.

Anti-handling mechanisms – the devilish means of making your bomb impossible to disarm or dismantle without it going off – were not invented by the IRA, but had featured in Second World War sabotage operations and in Palestine thereafter.[94] George Styles describes the variety of fusing that he and his colleagues in EOD (also known as ATOs, Ammunition Technical Officers[95]) were trained on: trembling fuses; light-sensitive fuses (which would detonate if light shone on them); anti-disturbance fuses; and second fuses. Many different combinations of fusing could be used. He adds that the initial attempts in the late 1960s and early 1970s of fitting bombs with these complexities often resulted in early IRA bomb makers blowing themselves up.

An example of an early booby trap and timing device in the 1970s Troubles was described by George Styles as a set of cylindrical steel containers surrounding a cement factory, each containing Quarrex explosive connected by detonating cord and to a central timing and detonating device. The central device, if exploded, would create an energy wave through the connecting detonating cord and set off all the containers. It turned out that the bomb's battery was booby trapped and had to be isolated before making the central detonating device harmless. It appeared that booby traps were being built with the help of a US-imported manual.[96]

Later in 1971 an EOD team had to deal with four devices that were booby trapped by having a burnt-out safety fuse on top of cardboard shoe boxes, implying that the bomb had failed to go off. Each device had anti-handling switches which would explode if moved. One device was a salt box packed with sugar and weedkiller with a switch on its base that would set the bomb off if the box were picked up. Rain had rendered the bomb inoperable, thereby preventing injury to anyone trying to lift it, but the fourth device actually claimed one of the arms of its planter – who made the fatal mistake of putting the bomb down too quickly.[97]

The letter bombs that were built and mailed by Shane O'Doherty during the 1970s are described by EOD operative Peter Gurney as being essentially anti-handling devices, all designed to go off when opened. Book bombs were a particularly cunning means of disguise. These devices would be wrapped into paper and mailed as a parcel. On unwrapping the device, it would be seen to have been hollowed out, and inside it was a gram or two of Semtex and a booby trap switching mechanism, actually containing a safety device for the terrorist to protect him from being blown up while constructing the bomb.[98]

As the bombing campaign of the 1970s intensified, more anti-handling innovations appeared which had to be dealt with by British army EODs, including one such device in the town of Castlerobin, which was adopted by the British as the name of a new type of bomb. Any anti-disturbance device was not at first apparent. Such devices had to be muffled so as to lessen any explosive effect, x-rayed, and a line put around it to pull it away. This would activate the anti-handling device, blowing up the device but without harming anyone. The EOD teams later tried to find ways to dismantle the Castlerobins without blowing them up. (This aspect will be dealt with in more detail in Chapter 9.) From the bomb maker's perspective, Shane O'Doherty tells of coming into contact with senior IRA explosives officers (EOs), who were already deploying booby trap devices in the 1970s.[99] Another reason for employing anti-handling devices was the audacious attempts – often successful – by Belfast citizens in shifting bombs out of harm's way. Pub landlords and customers, shop owners and others would use the time given in warnings to pick up suspicious objects, such as those thrown into doorways, and carry them out into the street. Even a seven-year-old boy took a device home from a village hall; its initiation mechanism had functioned, but for some reason the device failed to go off. Once booby trapped, future civilian attempts to shift bombs often resulted in death and injury.[100]

By 1986 the IRA had perfected the highly sophisticated electromagnetic booby trap detonated by command wire. An intelligence report told of how a stone wall attracted the attention of a bomb sniffer dog and turned out to have been rebuilt with fresh stones, partial detonation of which revealed a booby trap device concealed within the wall.[101] A device with a coil of wire had been dug into the ground at the wall base, and the bomb would have been activated when an electromagnetic field of sufficient force was used to intercept the coil. A similar kind of circuit was used to prevent detection with anti-metal detector (AMD) equipment, a set of components that were wired into a circuit and then used in conjunction with a coil to trigger a switch on the bomb whenever an army sweep operation to find metal was carried out.[102]

The booby trap bomb was at the zenith of devilish adaptation of the IRA's IEDs. As one of the EOD men has described in the Nova television documentary, 'Bomb Squad', booby trap devices were built into beer kegs, which were used as the container for the main charge, or main explosive charge. They contained about 45 kg of explosives, and hidden inside was a booby trap switch. The booster bag was on top, which provided the initial kick to get the explosives to function, and was connected to this hidden explosive device. If the operator stuck his hand in and pulled out the booster bag, he would set this device off, triggering all the explosive charge, and be killed.[103]

Entire locations where bombs were planted could be booby trapped. A house would be booby trapped with trip wires and pressure mats. If you stood on the mat, it would complete an electric circuit, triggering a bomb. The tripwires were made out of thin fishing lines, which are very hard to see, but once detected in a glint of light, would lead the EOD member to a homemade bomb.

The IRA began using their bombs as a means of diverting the EOD squads away from a deployed device, so that the squads themselves had become the real targets. The crew would be told that there had been an explosion, but they knew this could be a trap to entice them into the building. An initial small explosion was meant to pull the EOD team in, at which point the bigger device went off.[104]

South Armagh, the area known by the authorities as 'bandit country', became prime booby trap territory. The army had to carry out all operations to move troops and equipment by helicopter, so dangerous was the terrain, consisting as it does of low hills to provide IRA lookouts. Army units would respond to an explosion, suspect or see a second device some metres away by the roadside, go to disarm it and be a victim of a hidden third device. One such attack was described by an EOD man in 'Bomb Squad':

> I was aware of a rushing sound, a roar, and what appeared to be a wall of gray. After that, I passed out. Those who were watching me

say that they saw me fly through the air about 20 feet or so, and then land on the ground again. I came to very, very briefly, and was promptly knocked down by my number two, who had rushed forward to check that I was A), alive, B), in fairly big pieces. After that, I didn't really feel like taking very much more interest in the day.[105]

This particular bomb had been triggered remotely by an IRA volunteer who had been watching the scene from across the border. When the EOD team returned two days later to check the area, they discovered a fourth device. They uncovered some of the wires and found four bags, each containing about 23 kg of HME linked to a detonator. When one of the unit followed the wires, expecting to find maybe a pressure mat or a radio-controlled receiver, the wire was found to end abruptly: one on one row aligned, and the other wire from the detonator on the railway line.[106] The EOD man recounts this gut-wrenching experience:

> At this point, I was having a real problem thinking, what on earth is it here? And then, I just happened to look up the length of the row aligned, and thought, oh, Christ, this is a command wire device. What they had done was use the railway lines as an alternative to domestic cable, which they use as a command wire. At that point, I got out very, very quickly. Despite wearing the suit, I could have beaten Linford Christie at the hundred metres.[107]

A hole was blown in the tracks to break the circuit and prevent the IRA from having a second chance to blow up the bomb disposal man, who was decorated for his bravery. The IRA actually used the mains power from a house in the Republic to initiate the device. The initial impulse blew all the fuses in the house and so they could not have fired the next device.[108]

The mercury tilt switch

The classic IRA anti-handling device was the mercury tilt switch. If the bomb package was moved, a tilt switch would trigger the electrical circuit and set off the bomb.[109] British army EOD teams made a discovery about the Castlerobin devices that revealed the level of insider knowledge that the IRA were acquiring. Having captured one of them, examination of the circuitry showed that the bomb's electrical switching equipment and built-in micro switches at the top and bottom of the device were of Post Office provenance. If the bomb was lifted up, or tilted, or its top taken off, the switches made sure it blew up, and you with it. It also had a unique priming system: When the bomb was put in position, a metal rod was thrust down into the Post Office switching equipment to arm it.[110] According to Shane O'Doherty:

> The idea of putting your bomb inside a wooden box, screwed down all the way around, meant that first of all, it couldn't be easily seen, what was going on inside it. That was the first part. And then, people were saying, you know, 'Well, hell, you know, if it's an army bomb disposal team, let's give them something to work for, like, let's not aim just for the building in which we're trying to get our bomb to explode.' That's reason enough to put an anti-handling device on.[111]

George Styles describes an interesting consequence of this innovation: subsequent media coverage puffed up the IRA's capabilities, which led to some over-reaching of the technical expertise already achieved as bomb makers tried to improve on the methods. This led to more 'own goals', including the Post Office-linked Castlerobin creator. Such booby trap devices were very dangerous to plant, and the best way of delivering such a bomb was in a car. Attempts by the British army to disrupt these devices were often successful (see Chapter 9). So the IRA built bigger bombs, planting bigger booby trapped devices in the boots of cars, which were less penetrable – meaning the army had to resort to controlled explosions, which sometimes set off the whole bomb.[112]

This booby trap method was used for assassinations. The killing of Airey Neave, MP on 30 March 1979 by an under-vehicle IED which detonated as he started the vehicle was the best-known example of a bomb set by mercury tilt switch. As the MP drove up the ramp from the House of Commons underground car park, the angle of the car set off the tilt switch, which then set off the bomb. These bombs were attached to the undersides of cars by magnets, and by 1993 the tilt switch was glued to the outside of the bomb container. The timer was started by a simple wristwatch. Terry Harkin of the INLA, in a surprisingly revealing account (in operational terms) described the inner workings of the Airey Neave device on a television documentary broadcast on Radio Telefís Éireann (RTE):

> A mercury tilt switch is a bubble of glass containing a blob of mercury with two terminals. The INLA could take these things off the walls (from heating systems), mount them on the side of Tupperware boxes, connect detonators and timing devices, attach magnets and clamp them underneath the driver's arch of cars. When the car drove off or went up or down a certain gradient, the

mercury would come forward, make the connection and detonate the device.[113]

This type of 'trembler' bomb was used to kill Neave as he drove out of the car park at Westminster, according to Harkin. 'The volunteers cleaned under the wheel arch of Neave's car and connected the mercury tilt switch encased in a Tupperware box by magnets. They set it to an angle which would detonate as Neave went up the ramp from the underground car park.'[114]

The under-vehicle booby trap (UVBT) until the end of the 1980s used a TPU in a Tupperware box mounted on the exterior of the IED along with a memopark timer, mercury tilt switch with the explosive, batteries, microswitch and detonator on the inside of the box structure. UVBTs became smaller and harder to detect, and were usually placed under the driver's seat end of the vehicle. The explosive charge could comprise as much as 1 kg of Semtex-H. An ingenious feature was an LED (light-emitting diode – a semi-conductor chip for small indicator lights on electronic devices) which would light up when the mercury tilt switch was closed, enabling the bomber to deploy the device with the safe knowledge that the booby trap mechanism would not function while he was arming the device. This also enabled the UVBT to be adjusted for maximum sensitivity.[115]

Lesser-known persons were also victims of the IRA's under-vehicle improvised explosive devices (UVIEDs). One incident described by the Ulster Intelligence Unit occurred in Benburb, about 40 km from Belfast, where a young girl being picked up by her grandfather from dancing class was blown up when her grandfather's car drew alongside a booby trapped vehicle. While he was talking to his granddaughter before she got into the car, the UVIED exploded. Her body was blown in multiple pieces all over a nearby field; the army personnel conducting the clean-up operation discovered her foot still in its ballet shoe.[116]

There are many, less well catalogued instances related by the UXO services of the innocent being targeted, either accidentally because they happened to be near an IED going off, or deliberately. One such was a man with learning difficulties who worked as a cleaner at an RUC police station who was blown up in a street, along with a child bystander. The man survived, but was critically injured; the child did not.[117]

DISGUISED DEVICES

Many ways to disguise devices were employed by the Provisionals: some originated from a ready supply of rural items such as milk churns and haystacks; cigarette packets, books, cassette boxes, beer cans and beer kegs were more urban; and some methods revealed an unparalleled degree of cunning, such as the placing of shop-window dummies in car seats to disguise the fact the car was carrying a bomb – as it was assumed the IRA would not leave someone inside a car that was about to blow up, meaning that an occupied car would escape detection.[118] Traffic cones were used, which could easily conceal an explosive charge and anti-handling device. Other devices would be concealed below fire hydrant covers which, when lifted, set off the device.[119]

Components of IEDs were also disguised. A milk churn (so the device itself was disguised), having first been checked for command wires, was moved by an EOD squad who suspected after several days of leaving it to 'soak' (leave alone with the surrounding area cordoned off until its timer ran down) that it had been attached to command wires and booby trapped. The EOD operative tried to remove what appeared to be Cordtex detonating cord around the churn but turned out to be a coaxial cable attached to the detonator. Severing the cable with metal cutters completed the electrical circuit, detonating the bomb and killing the EOD operative. IRA observers had discovered that the EOD squads often cut Cordtex during EOD operations.[120]

HIGH-TECH ADVANCEMENT: RADAR DETECTORS

In the late 1980s the security forces discovered that the IRA was using radar detectors to detonate car-borne IEDs. The radar detectors – 'fuzzbusters' – were first deployed to combat army jamming countermeasures using radar to sweep for devices. Fuzzbusters were originally devised as an electronic device for motorists to determine if their speed was being monitored by traffic police (who would bounce a radio wave off a moving vehicle with a radar gun that determined the vehicle's speed by the Doppler-effect-moderated change in the wave's frequency). As described on the internet, the detectors are marketed as simple – 'Nothing fancy here, it just goes off when it sees radar and that's it'[121] – but the IRA used both X and K bands and fitted a decoder, enabling them to detect radar at very large ranges – up to five miles (8 km).[122]

These devices were fitted onto car dashboards by motorists to warn them that police were scanning cars in the area with distantly placed radar guns in order to enforce speed limits. The Provisionals adapted the radar detectors by rewiring them to detonators – so that when a radar beam hit the detector, the device exploded. We shall see in the next chapter how such advanced IED innovations were aided and abetted by several pro-IRA US scientists with top-security government clearances.

BREAKAWAY IRA METHODS

A Continuity IRA bomb planted, and later defused, in the Protestant town of Banbridge, Co. Down, on 6 January 1998 contained 500 lb of homemade explosives, a 10-lb commercial booster and improvised detonating cord of the type used by the IRA.[123] There were two detonators, one a Hercules Ireco type from a batch bought by the IRA in Arizona in 1989, the other of the type known by military weapons analysts as a 'Provisional IRA Mark 3 Improvised detonator'.[124] The dissident groups dabbled with making their own detonators, including a few using the primary explosive (lead azide or mercury fulminate), but these were hard to produce as mercury fulminate is highly unstable.[125]

NOTES

1. Although I should, as of early 2008, qualify that timers, remote detonation methods (such as mobile phones) and command wires are being increasingly used in the Iraq insurgency and other theatres as the bombers refine their targeting of troops and security forces.
2. C. Ryder, *A Special Kind of Courage: 321 EOD Squadron – Battling the Bombers* (London: Methuen, 2006), p.xviii.
3. M. Urban, *Big Boys' Rules* (London: Faber & Faber, 1993), p.112.
4. Personal communication, former Irish army EOD operative, November 2007.
5. G. McGladdery, *The Provisional IRA in England: The Bombing Campaign 1973–1997* (Dublin: Irish Academic Press, 2006), p.23.
6. G. Styles, *Bombs Have No Pity* (London: William Luscombe, 1975), p.83.
7. Ibid., p.83.
8. Ibid., p.102.
9. Ryder, *A Special Kind of Courage*, p.xvii.
10. Personal communication, Intelligence operative, Ulster Weapons Intelligence Unit, May 2007.
11. S.P. O'Doherty, *The Volunteer* (London: HarperCollins, 1993), p.70.
12. Ibid., pp.82, 118.
13. Adapted from IRA IED manual, Ulster Intelligence Unit, restricted information.
14. Ibid.
15. Ibid.
16. Styles, *Bombs Have No Pity*, p.62.
17. A similar expression – 'tickling the dragon's tail' – was used to describe the very dangerous 'prompt criticality' experiments carried out at Los Alamos in the making of the atomic bombs, in which scientists would bring together – manually – masses of fissile material to near-critical levels to ascertain how much was needed to trigger a chain reaction. The two major victims of this procedure – not called 'own goals' here, though – were scientists Harry Daghlian and Louis Slotin.
18. Styles, *Bombs Have No Pity*, p.62.
19. Personal communication, Intelligence operative, Ulster Weapons Intelligence Unit, April 2007.

20. Ibid.
21. Ibid., May 2007.
22. Personal communication, Intelligence operative, Ulster Intelligence Unit.
23. Styles, *Bombs Have No Pity*, p.104. Although my Irish EOD contacts confirmed that this was no accident – the washing-line detonating cord was actually booby trapped as deliberately disguised detonating cord. Personal communication, Garda EOD operative.
24. EOD officer in 'Bomb Squad', Nova television documentary, US Public Broadcasting Service, PBS (Public Broadcasting Service) Airdate: 21 October 1997.
25. S.P. O'Doherty, on 'Bomb Squad'.
26. S. Boyne, Uncovering the Irish republican army, *Jane's Intelligence Review*, 1 August 1996.
27. Personal communication, Intelligence operative, Ulster Weapons Intelligence Unit, May 2007.
28. Pers. Comm former Irish Army EOD operatve.
29. Ryder, *A Special Kind of Courage*, p.120.
30. Ibid., p.131.
31. The legendary Irish comedian Dave Allen used to incorporate this, and explosions in general, in dozens of sketches, and at a time – the 1970s, the onset of the Troubles – when it had become very risqué.
32. 'Army expert tells how booby trap killed four soldiers', *Belfast Telegraph*, 15 March 1976.
33. Ibid.
34. Ryder, *A Special Kind of Courage*, p.48.
35. BBC News, 'On This Day', 27 October 1982.
36. Personal communication, Intelligence operative, Ulster Weapons Intelligence Unit, May 2007.
37. D. Hardy, 'My account of the Ballygawley bus bombing, 20 August 1988', http://www.lightinfantryreunited.co.uk/LIIRELAND/Ballygawley.htm
38. Ryder, *A Special Kind of Courage*, p.128.
39. There is a veritable forest of terms for different kinds of IEDs. See Glossary.
40. Urban, *Big Boys' Rules*, p.112.
41. Ibid., p.86.
42. Personal communication, Intelligence operative, Ulster Weapons Intelligence Unit, May 2007.
43. Tony Geraghty, *The Irish War* (London: HarperCollins, 1990), p.210.
44. Ibid., p.208.
45. O'Doherty, *The Volunteer*, p.152.
46. Geraghty, *The Irish War*, p.208.
47. Ryder, *A Special Kind of Courage*, p.194.
48. Personal communication, former Irish army EOD operative, November 2007.
49. Urban, *Big Boys' Rules*, p.112.
50. Ryder, *A Special Kind of Courage*, p.53.
51. Urban, *Big Boys' Rules*, p.86.
52. Personal communication, Intelligence operative, Ulster Weapons Intelligence Unit, May 2007.
53. Ibid., December 2007.
54. Urban, *Big Boys' Rules*, p.112.
55. Geraghty, *The Irish War*, p.208.
56. Personal communication, Intelligence operative, Ulster Weapons Intelligence Unit, May 2007.
57. Geraghty, *The Irish War*, p.208.
58. Personal communication, Intelligence operative, Ulster Weapons Intelligence Unit, May 2007.
59. Urban, *Big Boys' Rules*, p.112.
60. Ibid., p.113.
61. Personal communication, Ulster Intelligence Unit operative, July 2007.
62. BBC News, 'On This Day', 8 November 1987.
63. Ibid.
64. 'Victim's tale of horror', *Belfast Telegraph*, 9 November 1987.
65. Geraghty, *The Irish War*, p.131.
66. Ibid., p.208.
67. Urban, *Big Boys' Rules*, p.113.
68. Geraghty, *The Irish War*, p.210.
69. M. Knights, 'Deadly developments – explosively formed projectiles in Iraq', *Jane's Intelligence Review*, 1 March 2007.
70. Personal communication, Intelligence operative, Ulster Weapons Intelligence Unit, May 2007.
71. E. Leahy, 'MI5 "helped IRA buy bomb parts in US"', *Sunday Times*, 19 March 2006.

72. Personal communication, Intelligence operative, Ulster Weapons Intelligence Unit, July 2007.
73. Leahy, 'MI5 "helped IRA buy bomb parts in US"'.
74. Personal communication, former Irish army EOD operative, November 2007.
75. Ryder, *A Special Kind of Courage*, p.205.
76. O'Doherty, *The Volunteer*, pp.145–6.
77. This common problem with bomb-making has been eerily resurrected with the recent trial of the alleged 21 July London bombers. This was most horribly depicted by the widely broadcast images of homemade hydrogen peroxide/chapatti flour explosive studded with nails and screws that spewed out of the suspects' backpacks onto the floors of the targeted tube trains – images which actually made me physically sick and a stark reminder of how squalid the exercise of making and deploying such devices can be. I was asked to make similar devices for test explosions prior to the trial.
78. Geraghty, *The Irish War*, p.211.
79. Personal communication, former Irish army EOD operative, November 2007.
80. Ibid.
81. Ryder, *A Special Kind of Courage*, p.152.
82. Ibid., p.175.
83. Personal communication, Intelligence operative, Ulster Intelligence Unit.
84. Brig. J.M. Glover, BGS, (Int.), DIS, *Northern Ireland Future Terrorist Trends*, 2 December 1978. Cited in McGladdery, *The Provisional IRA in England*, p.126.
85. Personal communication, Intelligence operative, Ulster Intelligence Unit.
86. Ibid.
87. Ibid.
88. Geraghty, *The Irish War*, p.209.
89. Personal communication, Intelligence operative, Ulster Intelligence Unit.
90. Boyne, 'Uncovering the Irish republican army'.
91. Personal communication, Intelligence Operative, Ulster Weapons Intelligence Unit, May 2007.
92. Geraghty, *The Irish War*, p.212.
93. Personal communication, Ulster Intelligence Unit operative, July 2007.
94. Styles, *Bombs Have No Pity*, p.62.
95. 11 EOD Regiment RLC, British army website, http://www.army.mod.uk/rlc/units/11_eod _regt/regimental_specialists/at_trade/ato.htm
96. Styles, *Bombs Have No Pity*, p.104.
97. Ibid., p.115.
98. Nova television documentary, 'Bomb Squad'.
99. O'Doherty, *The Volunteer*, p.118.
100. Ryder, *A Special Kind of Courage*, p.134.
101. This booby trap method is also cited in K. Toolis, *Rebel Hearts: Journeys Within the IRA's Soul* (New York: St Martin's Press, 1995), p.226.
102. Geraghty, *The Irish War*, p.209.
103. 'Bomb Squad'.
104. Ibid.
105. Ibid.
106. Personal communication, Intelligence operative, Ulster Weapons Intelligence Unit, May 2007.
107. 'Bomb Squad'.
108. Personal communication, Intelligence operative, Ulster Weapons Intelligence Unit, May 2007.
109. 'Bomb Squad'.
110. Styles, *Bombs Have No Pity*, p.122.
111. 'Bomb Squad'.
112. Ibid.
113. R. Harkin in three-part series broadcast on RTE in 2003, in J. McEnroe, 'Bombers' Secrets to be Broadcast', *The Times*, 28 September 2003.
114. Ibid.
115. Adapted from IRA IED manual, Ulster Intelligence Unit, restricted information.
116. Personal communication, Ulster Intelligence Unit operative, July 2007.
117. Ibid.

118. Ryder, *A Special Kind of Courage*, p.82.
119. Ibid., p.190.
120. Ibid., p.168.
121. Various internet sites selling these devices.
122. Personal communication, Ulster Intelligence Unit operative, July 2007.
123. T. Harnden, 'Violence spreads in Ulster as talks move to London', *Daily Telegraph*, 26 January 1998; and personal communication, Intelligence operative, Ulster Weapons Intelligence Unit, May 2007.
124. Harnden, 'Violence spreads in Ulster as talks move to London'.
125. Personal communication, Intelligence operative, Ulster Weapons Intelligence Unit, May 2007.

Seven

Mortars: A Homemade Missile System

... let the British government understand that, while nationalist people in the Six Counties are forced to live under British rule, the British Cabinet will be forced to live in bunkers.
Provisional IRA statement following mortar attack on
Downing Street, 7 February 1991

Seven years after the Brighton bomb, the IRA targeted Her Majesty's government even more audaciously when it fired two mortar bombs at 10 Downing Street – when the prime minister and his cabinet were meeting during the height of the first Gulf War. This attack was the second attempt to strike at the very heart of government. Its series of mortars – in effect, homemade missiles – was arguably the apogee of IRA technology and bravado. [1]

The acquisition of an estimated fifty Russian-made SAM-7s – basic surface-to-air missiles – from Libya in the mid-1980s[2] did not increase significantly the IRA's ability to carry out such operations. One deployment of a SAM-7 in Northern Ireland was against a Wessex [helicopter] at Kinawley on the Co. Fermanagh border in July 1991, but the missile failed to lock on to the helicopter and exploded on the ground.[3] The weapons kept turning up – as in 2001, when an expired chemical battery from a SAM-7 missile was found in a field in Co. Tyrone, but with no information about how it got there or why.[4] There were also attempts, often spiked by the security services, to purchase Redeye portable missiles from the US. But it was in the series of homemade mortars produced by the IRA that its ingenuity was revealed, and its ability to supplement imported war-fighting equipment by developing its own.

The mortar is defined as a means of firing a shell or bomb at low velocities, short ranges, and high-arcing ballistic trajectories. Other types may have higher velocities, longer ranges, flatter arcs, and sometimes, direct fire. The mortar shell is dropped into a tube, a firing pin at the base of which detonates the propellant and fires the shell. A mortar can be carried by one or more people (larger mortars can usually be broken down into components), or transported in a vehicle.

A mortar system can be built using propane cylinders as the launch tube. Adding a simple elevation system and detonator makes a complete improvised mortar system. The mortar bombs were used mainly for firing at army barracks and police stations in Northern Ireland, with the most notorious mainland attack being the 1994 Heathrow airport attacks. The IRA's highly penetrative, high-temperature shaped-charge anti-armour shell was the nexus of this homemade technology – and has become a standard form of attack for Iraqi insurgents.[5] These penetrative weapons were known as HEAT (high-explosive anti-tank) warheads, and they were used in direct-fire weapons rather than mortars.[6] One device – the Mark-12 mortar – was actually incorrectly called a mortar as it was more like a direct-fire missile. All the other mortars relied on pure blast for effect.[7] It has been suggested that crude nuclear fission weapons made by modern-day terrorists could be based on IRA mortars: using a crude gun-method design, such an improvised nuclear device could easily achieve velocities of 100 m/sec or more to bring about critical assembly (when the two pieces of uranium meet and the fission chain reaction takes place).[8] One advantage of the mortar that appealed to the IRA is its ability to drop shells on targets close to the mortar, which also makes it possible to launch attacks from positions lower than the target of the attack. Its main military disadvantage was (like biological weapons, only in a different way) inaccuracy, and hence its tendency to injure friendly forces.[9] By the First World War, it had become an ideal weapon to bombard enemy forces or civilians cheaply and without damage to the mortar operator.

As with the many types of IED, just a small number of experienced engineers were involved in building the IRA's mortars, which became an entire weapon series and the very essence of improvised weapons ingenuity. The earlier models were 'throw-away' weapons that, although crude, had a devastating effect at short range. The mortar tubes are normally mounted on the back of a truck and are fired by a timing device after the bombers have left the scene. The series went as far as the Mark 17. The heaviest type was the Mark 15 'barrack buster', which often contained ammonium nitrate as the explosive.[10] The Mark-10 was used in the Downing Street attack.

The impetus behind mortar development was the need during the early 1970s for a stand-off weapon that could be launched from a safe distance by those firing it,[11] who could remain unseen. Its forerunner was the catapulted petrol bomb, usually aimed at the security forces in

Northern Ireland from rooftops. This was superseded by cans of explosive attached to the ends of dowel rods, which had a safety fuse to delay ignition before the missile was fired from a bow or shotgun. This was highly dangerous and unreliable.[12]

EARLY VERSIONS

Once police stations in Northern Ireland became heavily fortified, this provided the Provisionals with a challenge. The 'spigot' grenade – fired from a shotgun and comprising 2 kg of gelignite inside a 15-cm pipe – was too hazardous for the operator to remain in the IRA's armoury.[13] Enter the first IRA mortar, deployed in June 1972, which was recorded by Technical Intelligence documents from an unexploded weapon as having consisted of a 50-mm copper pipe filled with 25 g of commercial plastic explosive and propelled to the target by a .303 cartridge inserted into the end of a steel tube tail section. The tube was trigger-operated, and the bomb was dropped into the launch tube by driving a pointed striker against a .22 cartridge and igniting the detonator.[14] The mortar would spin once it took off but would fail to explode if the nose fuse – described by EOD squads as 'of ingenious design' – was damaged by the angle it landed at. And the user got blown up if the weapon were dropped, as it lacked a safety mechanism or a delay circuit.[15]

A subsequent series of attacks across Northern Ireland in 1972 involved the Mark 2, which appeared twelve months after the Mark 1 and was constructed from 20-cm length of 57 mm steel pipe filled with up to a kilo of commercial explosive. It was propelled from a base plate by a 120-bore cartridge containing ninety grains of propellant. A split fuse gave a 5-second delay from impact to ignition. The nose-cone fuse had been modified for more reliable detonation. These mortars were often fired through the roof of a target building.

The Mark-3 emerged the following year and was used in attacks on several army barracks. The bomb was dropped into the 60-mm mortar barrel and a launch cartridge struck a static firing pin on the base plate, igniting another domestic item – a J-cloth – which was soaked in sodium chlorate (one of the explosives used in the first part of the century described earlier in this book) and dried. The explosion propelled the bomb some 250 metres.[16] The bomb for the mortar consisted of high-grade crystalline ammonium nitrate, which, like hydrogen peroxide-based homemade explosives used in the London 2005 attacks, was highly volatile. It therefore tended to explode prematurely, such as in August 1973 when two IRA operatives were killed during an attack on RUC

Pomeroy barracks. The accuracy had been enhanced by a strengthened base plate and an aiming quadrant which rotated the barrel and locked it ready for firing. This, together with cutting the main explosive charge down by half and enhancing the ammonium nitrate mixture with aluminium powder,[17] enabled the mortars to fall within 30 metres of a target when fired from 300 metres. But the model was still unreliable and the mortars would tumble in flight, as happened in the attack on Pomeroy barracks.[18]

Progress on mortars continued through the 1970s, but efforts did not always yield the desired destructive results. In the five years following 1973 the IRA used mortars seventy-one times without claiming any enemy fatalities.[19] The homemade tubes and bombs often could not be made to take out their targets accurately, with many veering way off target, and shells also failed to explode[20] – giving them the unwanted potential of being weapons of indiscriminate effect. Added to this was the problem that the more the mortar fragmented, and the smaller the fragments – and added ball bearings for shrapnel – the greater was its penetrating effect on the target.[21]

In February 1974 as many as nine mortar bombs were found in a hijacked delivery van which was parked against a wall at Telegraph House in Belfast. It was found to contain – as well as the mortars connected to Cordtex detonating fuse hundreds of metres in length to enhance its terrible complexity – 230 kg of ANFO as the main explosive charge; a booster made of a commercial explosive – Gelamex; two timed circuits for initiation; and an anti-handling device. Dismantling this lot took eight hours and earned two EOD operatives, St Sgt Graham Wells and Lt Col Malcolm Mackenzie-Orr, the British Empire Medal and the George Medal respectively.[22]

By 1974 the range had been extended to 400 metres with the Mark-4, first used to attack a base at Strabane (although fourteen failed to function) and with the ubiquitous J-cloth impregnated with sodium chlorate again used as the propellant and comprising 80 per cent of the total propellant weight. The J-cloth would be soaked in the warm saturated solution of sodium chlorate and water and hung up to dry.[23] The ammonium nitrate–aluminium powder mix also contained calcium carbonate, indicating that local fertiliser had been used, with the aluminium content as much as 15 per cent.[24] This mixture has been favoured in recent times by Al-Qaeda-affiliated terrorists, and was stockpiled by suspects on trial in March 2007 for plotting to bomb London locations.[25] As well as containing ball bearings the Mark-4 had the safety mechanism removed so that the model was dropped into the launcher tube and fired as a military mortar shell would. If the propellant charge failed to ignite, however, the mortar would explode while still in the launcher tube.[26]

The Mark-5 included a 'bombard', a primitive cannon of around 25 metres range. But it was the Mark-6 that was the first in the series to be a reliable weapon and cause real trouble for the security services. Of 60-mm calibre with a standard launch tube, it was used to fire as many as thirty bombs in one attack on a Co. Armagh army observation post from across the border in 1974, and its range was 1,200 metres.[27] The bombs would be dropped down the launch tube onto a fixed firing pin. The single tube base plates were said to be made to military standards. The .22 calibre cartridge initiated the detonation of the explosive once the bombs reached the bottom of the tube.[28] The wind-driven nose propeller rotated after take-off and exploded on impact, and was less likely to explode before being launched or if dropped. The mortars had re-designed fins – eight rather than three – cut from an aluminium heat-exchanger pipe.[29]

Greater timing sophistication was also added, by a timer/power unit that used electrical, remotely controlled ignition in the form of a photographic flash-bulb instead of a percussion cap. The remote control innovation meant the bomb could be pre-loaded into the mortar and combined with a timer, providing safety for the operator who could escape before the firing of the mortar – a highly dangerous activity that had taken IRA lives.[30] The long range enabled the weapons to be fired without the firer being detected by military observation posts.

When some twenty-eight of these mortars were found in a Belfast bakery in Belfast in October 1974, the EOD officer, Lt Col John Gaff, reported that:

> The equipment and ammunition are the most advanced of their type which have been used up to the present time. Much thought and care has been taken to produce it … Excellent workmanship is evident … The handwritten user instructions give the impression of past military experience of a specialised nature … although the writer does not register as having had the benefit of a high standard of education.

This verdict epitomised the IRA's hallmark of improvised skills. Lt Col Gaff added, however, that a light engineering factory would have been needed to make the Mark-6. In just over a year, the IRA mortar had developed from something relatively primitive to an advanced weapons series.[31]

HEATHROW: LAUNCH OF THE MARK-6

The mortars fired on Heathrow airport in 1994 were based on this principle. They were made from drainpipes, had tail fins, were fired from the ground and ignited by a car battery. Breeze blocks were used to weight the launch frame down.[32] The warheads contained almost 1 kg of Semtex H. This was triggered on impact of the bomb by a .22 percussion cap.[33] Hand-delivery was still favoured by some audacious volunteers (as in the March 1987 Divis flats attack, when the Mark-6 was dropped onto an army vehicle from the rooftops of the flats).[34]

The series of mortar attacks waged by the IRA on Heathrow, which boasts the highest number of international passengers, had the effect of partially paralysing the capital's main air routes and marking a new and potentially devastating leap in its military capabilities. (It was echoed nearly a decade later in uncovered plots by Al-Qaeda to carry out similar attacks with mortars.)

The three attempted mortar attacks on Heathrow airport in March 1994 were the epitome of IRA audacity. Having given a warning of less than one hour, bombs launched on 9 March from a stolen Nissan car kitted out with five mortar tubes and parked at an airport hotel flew over Heathrow police station and landed on the edge of the north runway. Incidentally, when the UXO technicians were clearing the runway, they were asked if they could hurry up as it was costing £45,000 per minute to keep it closed![35]

Although none exploded – the devices would never have gone off as the Semtex filler had been interdicted[36] – the attempted attack demonstrated how far the IRA was prepared to go to show off the extent of its homemade missile technology. The subsequent firings on 11 and 13 March – the fact that the IRA were able to follow up the first attack with two more so soon after the first was distinctly embarrassing for the authorities – came from scrubland near the airport. Despite police and security services searching the area after the first attack for other vehicles containing mortars, they found none. The mortars had been concealed underground and were fired from a wooded area close to the perimeter fence.[37]

In the first attack, one of the bombs landed on the roof of Terminal 4, in which at least 4,000 people were gathered. Had the device exploded, the IRA may have achieved its first weapon of mass effect attack, the likes of which we have come to expect from Al-Qaeda. In the words of David Norris, TD (member of Irish parliament) speaking in the Irish parliament the day after the attack:

Many people are apprehensive about air travel and it is wickedly cruel to add to this apprehension. If these bombs had hit an aeroplane or cratered a runway before a plane took off there would have been enormous carnage and I thank God that there was not.[38]

According to an Ulster intelligence operative, the reason why these bombs did not explode was their instability in flight and the need to hit the target at a precise angle of 90°.[39]

A further mortar attempt was made on a Crossmaglen army base on 20 March 1994, in which a Mark-10 was fired from the back of a tractor hitting the tail unit of a Lynx helicopter at the limit of its range – 150 metres – causing it to spin out of control.[40] The helicopter exploded after all of the officers inside had been able to escape. There was an interesting trigger method for this. It used a collapsing circuit, and the power from a battery charger was used to hold a switch open (safe). This was triggered by the IRA interrupting the power to the entire (fiercely republican) town. The power from the battery charger was interrupted, allowing the mortar's own battery system to activate.[41]

Possession by the IRA of at least one shoulder-launched rocket launcher – an increasingly popular terrorist weapon – greatly heightened the threat. The deadly aspect of such attacks was encapsulated in the difficulty in detecting the mortar firers: evidence of an attack would only become apparent when the growling sound was heard – which is the sound the launcher makes when the missile has locked-on to the heat of the target aircraft's engines. And by then it would be too late to do anything about it.[42]

THE MARK-7 AND MARK-8

The Mark-7 and Mark-8 versions included bigger bombs, which the IRA first used in 1976 against that oft-repeated target, the army–RUC barracks at Crossmaglen. There were problems keeping the bombs in flight and ensuring they went off, as they were too long – made from more than 1 metre of steel tubing.[43] The Mark-8 incorporated earlier warhead features; tail fins from the Mark-3, wind-driven propeller from the Mark-6, and a longer casing of 1 metre to incorporate more explosive – more than 1 kg, and six times as much as that model. However, it was concluded by the Weapons Intelligence Unit that accuracy had been sacrificed for greater destructive power. The Mark-8 was in fact a far less sophisticated mortar, the result of cannibalising the previous models. Inaccuracy would lead to damage to buildings surrounding targets. This

is exactly what occurred in the Crossmaglen attack, in which five soldiers were injured: the mortar penetrated the roof of the soldiers' living
quarters and surrounding buildings.[44]

The Mark-9 included a fatter, short bomb made from a cut-down gas
cylinder fired from as many as ten mortar tubes. In a later, October 1976
attack on the Crossmaglen base, seven bombs managed to get through
and explode.[45] This model continued the high-risk design of the Mark-7
and 8; its warhead, a converted gas cylinder housing 4 kg of explosive,
was fired from a distance by command wire. In January 1977 five such
warheads were fired at a Belfast security base, landing 100 metres short
of the target in the grounds of a school.[46]

THE MARK-10 HITS NUMBER 10

On 7 February 1991, Prime Minister John Major's cabinet met to discuss
the Gulf War crisis. While the meeting was in progress, the IRA
launched three bombs from a stationary van parked on the corner of
Horseguards Avenue and Whitehall, just after 10 a.m. According to Cmr
Steve Churchill-Coleman of the anti-terrorist branch of Scotland Yard,
the van had been stationary for only 'seconds or minutes' when the mortars went off, leaving it in flames.

One of the mortars landed in the back garden of number 10. Heading
straight for the cabinet room, it hit a tree and exploded just 13 metres
short of its target, scorching the rear wall, forming a crater several metres
wide, and shattering the blast windows and their frames protecting the
cabinet room.[47] Had the fired device not struck the tree it would have
shot straight into the cabinet room, almost certainly killing the prime
minister and most senior members of the British government, who had
to resort to diving under a table.[48] Two bombs landed near a police post
on Mountbatten Green, just beyond the garden of number 10 and, in the
bitterest of ironies, near a statue of the assassinated lord. Although failing to explode, these burst into flames, causing extensive damage to
numbers 11 and 12 Downing Street.[49] Two civil servants and two policemen attached to the Diplomatic Protection Squad were injured. It was
the first mortar attack on mainland Britain and a true 'spectacular' in the
lexicon of IRA operations, despite it not having claimed the lives of any
of the cabinet.

The Mark-10 was developed during the 1980s. It fired a 15-cm shell
with around 11 kg of explosive as far as 300 metres.[50] It consisted of up
to ten 1.4-metre, 165-cm wide steel tubes set at varying angles for maximum target coverage and each filled with 18 kg of homemade explosives

– usually ANNIE (ammonium nitrate mixed with nitrobenzene) in gas-cylinder bombs. The mortar was launched by a propulsion charge in the base.[51] By now the IRA was also making very fine black powder; this had very consistent burning profiles, hence the Provisionals' ability to predict ranges.[52] The system was aimed by aligning the vehicle housing the mortars with a permanent landscape feature in the target area.[53] The gas cylinders, used for domestic heating and cooking in the rural areas where much of the IRA's bomb technologies evolved, were made of oxy-acetylene with the tops and bottoms cut off. On launching, the pin, which was held by a wire, was pulled out, and a spring-loaded arming pin popped out, allowing the working parts of the fuse to detonate when it struck a target. Electrical initiation was always used.[54]

But the Mark-10 had already achieved notoriety at least a decade before the Downing Street attack, when it was first used in an attack on a police station in Corry Square, Newry in April 1980. The shells missed the police post but they injured twenty-six and damaged nearby properties. An added tactic was an attempted, but failed, explosion of a blast incendiary in the mortar truck to eliminate forensic evidence.[55] In the Newry attack the mortar tubes were made from oxy-acetylene cylinders with cut-off tops,[56] bolted onto the flatbed of a hijacked Ford truck and reported as being linked to detonator wire and timers. They were mounted at differing angles to maximise the likelihood of the target being hit.[57] But the lack of accuracy of the mortar meant that shells often overshot their target, resulting in civilians and property being on the receiving end, and in Newry, nearby houses were damaged by falling shrapnel.[58] This was because the bombs were not point-detonated, relying instead on the delay caused by the burning of the safety fuse. This caused airbursts or failure to launch – resulting in the bombs going off inside the mortar tubes or not going off at all once they landed.[59]

In a subsequent 'Bloody Thursday' attack on the Corry Square Newry barracks in February 1985, a Mark-10 killed nine RUC officers (more than in any other single attack since 1969) in the barracks canteen and wounded thirty-seven people, twenty-five of whom were civilians. The Mark-10 was the most indiscriminate of the mortar series developed to date. Just after 6 p.m. on 28 February, nine 22-kg mortar shells each containing 18 kg of high explosive soared over nearby houses and crashed through the roof of the dining hall, which was wood-frame only and part of the cramped Newry station house. The bombs were fired from 250 metres away in what the IRA called 'a well-planned operation' that 'indicates our ability to strike when and where we decide'. In a truck that had been hijacked in Crossmaglen, a volunteer activated two one-hour

Memopark timers connected to a battery pack which sent an impulse to launch the shells.[60] The contraption on the truck consisted of nine launcher tubes bolted to the rear concealed under tarpaulin, connected by wires to the detonation unit on the passenger seat containing the timers, twelve batteries, two microswitches, an electrical motor and relay switches. The mortars in the tubes were 22 kg of ANNIE and Cordtex detonating fuse. The igniter and firing pack were US-made; a separate sodium chlorate propellant charge was intended to help launch the mortar shell, at the top of which was a separate fuse to set off the main ANNIE charge immediately the mortar landed at its target. The timers would run down, and the batteries powering the firing switch set off the ignition system – launching the mortars.[61]

The Newry attack led to the army and RUC adding further 'hardening' defences to their barracks, including the 'Mark-10 cube' made from steel and concrete layered panels. But the threat to areas surrounding targets increased; only one in four mortars hit its target, and some 466 had been used in eighty attacks.[62] Army observation posts continued to be the targets of the Mark-11, which had a range of over 500 metres and was used in May 1989 to attack a post at Glassdrumman, south Armagh, and again contained ANNIE as the explosive. The IRA went for bigger bombs to overcome the hardening of military structures, which included 2-metre-thick blast-defecting walls[63] and an empty top room with a reinforced roof[64] to take the force of a mortar attack from the sky.[65]

Again, the use of mortars endangered civilians whose homes were situated below the firing line of the weapons. Some fifty civilians were injured by flying glass, masonry and shrapnel when, on 29 July 1994, Newry was the scene once again of a mortar attack. Three Mark-10 mortars activated by timers were fired from a Leyland tipper truck parked 100 metres from Newry police station and flew over a high street full of shops and residences.[66] The adverse publicity resulting from such attacks did not deter the IRA from trying to improve its mortar technology; it developed a lighter, more mobile and more precise system by adapting a Mark-6 mortar to fire a rocket-propelled missile as far as 1,200 metres.[67]

THE MARK-11, 12 AND 13

The end of the 1980s saw two new mortar models, the Mark-11 and Mark-12. A recovered Mark-11 weapon from an attack on the observation post in Glassdrumman, revealed a rolled steel cylindrical projectile with a range of 500 metres, and which could carry 10 kg of explosive.[68] The Mark-12, like its predecessors, was a direct-fire weapon comprised of largely hand-crafted components. It was 75 cm long and its explosive filler charge was usually 2–2.5 kg of Semtex – which was ideal for mortars as only a small amount was needed to slot into the warhead and pack the required punch.

This weapon was first deployed in an attack on Crossmaglen – a troops-base town often targeted by the IRA with many casualties – on 26 October 1989, although a Semtex mortar had already been used in a combined mortar and gunfire attack on an army observation post at Drummuckavall, south Armagh three years earlier, on 28 October 1986. This was the first use of 'magic marble' in such a weapon and an alarming development for the authorities, who were able to examine an unexploded weapon to discover the most powerful explosive used by the IRA to date.[69] It differed from conventional mortars insofar as it was used entirely for direct fire. It had an inertia fuse and could be initiated by command wire or timer. Its shaped warhead was based on the HEAT (high-explosive anti-tank) principle. The steel cone, coupled with the explosive charge and impact fuse, enabled the Mark-12 to pierce armour on impact. It had a tube of lesser width than the Mark-10 and was fitted with a carrying handle. A pusher plate attached to a spigot propelled the mortar out of the launch tube. A flash bulb inside the spigot initiated a gunpowder charge within it.[70]

The Mark-13 was designed to be fired at the wall of army and security forces bases and an example of the weapon was retrieved after an aborted attack on an RUC station in Dungannon in May 1990. Subsequent attacks revealed the weapon failed to reach its target.[71] It featured a bomb fashioned from a 45-gallon oil drum containing as much as 36 kg of explosives (another ammonium nitrate HME mix). But it could only achieve a 20-metre range, rendering launch sites vulnerable to discovery.[72] So the IRA made the mobile mortar – a kind of homemade conventional version of the Soviet Union's mobile nuclear missile launchers that proved to be so elusive in the Cold War. A tractor or tipper truck would provide the platform for the mortar, which was first used in May 1990 at Dungannon. The IRA also used diesel tanks from trucks as projectiles in the Mark-13. The Mark-14 turned up in May 1992 – again in Crossmaglen.[73] Continuing the improvised school of IRA launchable bombs, it was made from the top halves of two gas cylinders (these readily available items were used in many IRA weapons), which were welded together with several tail fins. It carried over 20 kg of HME.

THE MARK-15 'BARRACK BUSTER'

By the early 1990s, the Mark-14 and Mark-15 had appeared, and increased the IRA's mortar capabilities even further. Again made from gas cylinders, and often disguised as hay bales, as in an attack on Crossmaglen in February 1993,[74] the mortar could be transported to the launch site attached to the hydraulic hoist at the rear of a tractor.[75] It would also be welded into vans and other vehicles. The Mark-15 combined a large – 1-metre long – bomb containing 75 kg of explosives (as well as deadly one-pence coins as shrapnel)[76] with the Mark-10's range, in this version 100–150 metres. It was used in attacks on the Ballygawley army base in December 1992, in Crossmaglen, Newry and in Germany in June 1996 – at the British base in Osnabrück. The mortar would be driven close to its target – as in an attack on Bessbrook police station in March 1993 which not only damaged it but also 100 houses in the area.[77]

The more advanced mortars were used in the years preceding the 1990s ceasefires – at the same time as the 'city destroyer' ammonium nitrate truck bombs. The Mark-16 mortar was first deployed in July 1993, in an attack in William Street, Derry and was used in eleven separate attacks that same year.[78] The Derry mortar was launched from a tube concealed under the car bonnet. It was a horizontally firing weapon whose advantage over the Mark-15 was that it was relatively small and lightweight, enabling enhanced portability; it was small enough to be fitted, along with its launch tube, into a sports bag. With a range of up to 200 metres, most attacks tended to be within the weapon's effective range of 20–25 metres. The warhead comprised a shaped armour piercing charge formed from two opposing copper cones to create a stand-off detonation. The projectile nose cone was designed to explode on impact. The explosive used was some 900 g of Semtex plastic explosive – far less than the amount needed for the Mark-12 warhead.

Unlike the Mark-12, the Mark-16 comprised easily acquired plumbing spares with stabilising fins welded onto its tail, requiring basic welding skill only. It was fired from a simple launch tube made out of commercial heating piping with a base plate welded onto one end. No anchoring of the launcher was necessary – in previous attacks on security force patrols the device was balanced on a pallet or wheelie bin. It was detonated by command wire and battery firing pack as an army patrol passed by. The design specifications were later stolen by the Real IRA and ETA.[79] The Mark-17 mortar, one of the IRA's most destructive weapons ever, was built during the mid-1990s ceasefire. It was believed to have been tested in the Carlingford Lough area of Co. Louth, just south of the border.[80]

Mortars kept turning up after the ceasefires; one discovered by police in a house in the Bogside in Derry in October 2002 was defined as a Mark-16.

A nameless example of these deadly improvised devices appeared in March 1991 – the dawn of the 'city destroyer' weapons. Consisting of a projectile from a roadside launcher, and fired by command wire, it was used to attack two UDR Land Rovers which had stopped at traffic lights on Killylea Road, Armagh; the projectile hit the vehicle and exploded, killing the driver and another occupant and injuring two soldiers. The weapon took a further two lives – a policeman in September 1992, whose Land Rover was attacked in Swatragh, and a soldier in Bellaghy, in November 1992, again in a Land Rover.[81] The array of mortars developed and used by the Provisionals brings to mind what further and lasting damage could have been done had the IRA decided to acquire nuclear fissile material to make an improvised nuclear device (IND) or radioisotopes for radiological dispersal devices ('dirty bombs').

GRENADES: HAND-HELD DESTRUCTION

The improvised anti-armour grenade (IAAG)

The 'drogue bomb', or improvised anti-armour grenade (IAAG), was an underarm-thrown grenade which deployed a small parachute to enable the charge to detonate at the desired angle and penetrate tank armour. It contained about 230 g of Semtex explosive packed into a large baked bean or dogfood tin attached to a throwing handle with a fin to stabilise it – another example of IRA adaptation of household items and the ultimate in homemade weaponry.[82] It was developed to attack the tops of vehicles and explode on impact with them, following the success of an attack on 30 March 1987, when a Mark-6 mortar was dropped onto an army Land Rover from a balcony in the Divis flats in Belfast, penetrating the armour of the vehicle and killing all occupants.[83] The drogue was subsequently designed to keep the device upright when dropped and was the forerunner of weapons being used almost daily by insurgents in the war in Iraq. The IAAG was first used in an attack on an army Land Rover on the Falls Road on 17 July 1987.[84] The hollow cone charge used in the device was proven to penetrate vehicle armour in an attack in January 1988 on a police vehicle, when a drogue was thrown onto a vehicle from a top room in a derelict house, killing the occupant.[85]

The IRA's mortar series was used during ordinary civilian activity; one has a picture of mortars as military weapons used on the battlefield, but the IRA's use of them and Hezbollah's subsequent use of an entire and fairly advanced rocket system has placed the mortar well and truly as a weapon of insurgency, where targets lie within urban areas or are, indeed, actually urban settlements.

ROCKET-PROPELLED GRENADES

The rocket-propelled launcher was a prestige weapon for the IRA and one that would be featured in propaganda footage. The Provisionals received their first shipments in 1972, but the volunteers' lack of experience in deploying and firing these weapons was as a result of not being able to carry out systematic live-fire training, which would have aroused attention because of the noise. This meant that most, if not all, training did not involve actual firing of the weapons, which were also too scarce to be used regularly. As is often overlooked when analysing terrorist capabilities, there were also storage problems which meant deterioration of the weapons.[86] The RPG-7 shoulder-launched model was used first on 28 November 1972 on an RUC station in a border village in Co. Fermanagh, killing a police officer, Const. Robert Keys, when the rocket penetrated a steel window shutter. It was also used in no less than *eight* other attacks the same day on two army bases and a Saracen APC in Belfast, and police stations and a truck in various towns throughout the province, injuring seven. The next day three more attacks occurred using the new weapon.[87]

Along with small-arms fire, the RPG-7 was primarily used in attempts to shoot down army helicopters. The weapon posed a serious enough threat that new countermeasures such as high wire-netting screens and canopies were erected at police stations and army bases, but armoured ground vehicles remained vulnerable until further armouring was completed. It was amazing that 'only' five security personnel were killed and injured in the following two decades.[88]

But disadvantages to the IRA in using the weapons included blow-back, along with the need for the launcher component to be removed so as not to leave vital evidence of an attack. The dangers of untrained operatives firing such weapons led to accidents and wildly inaccurate targeting: the missile would often not function as intended, and would hit another target – resulting in civilian casualties.[89] In February 1984 one attack only just missed a packed school classroom, adding to objections and resistance by local communities to IRA operations.

These operational problems hampered the IRA's use of the RPG, until the 1990s saw improved effectiveness in its deployment – when single attacks using multiple RPG units increased, as did the speed, tactical flexibility, and variety of IRA attacks. The last use of the RPG was in May 1991 after 200 attacks. Until then, the IRA wanted to control its own supply – and hence, manufacture – of anti-aircraft weapons;[90] this imperative, and the earlier difficulties experienced in using the RPG, led to further ingenious improvisation – the Improvised Projected Grenade (IPG).

IPGS AND PRIGS: COFFEE AND BISCUITS

In the mid-1980s a combined 115-g Semtex–TNT grenade launcher was invented that was fired at a target from a launch vehicle. These were similar to military rocket launchers such as the RPG, but were less accurate and had a shorter range. They also had noted advantages over the RPG, such as being disposable, as there were more available.[91] The lightweight IPG was used mainly as a stand-off weapon to be lobbed over perimeter fences and against mobile patrols. The first deployment in 1985 killed the IRA operative who was handling a loaded launcher, but the Weapons Intelligence Unit noted that the projectile itself revealed a 'high standard of machine manufacturing'.[92] It also bruised the shoulders of the IRA men trying to fire it.[93]

There was also an increasing number of attacks that betrayed operational problems with the new weapon.[94] As a result of the IRA fatalities the weapon was modified in 1986 by the addition of a barrel locking nut and a safety bolt to prevent accidental firing. The weapon was, however, unstable in flight and, as a result, prone to fall away from its desired attack angle. As the spent cartridge could fall anywhere, its position was not an accurate indication of the firing point. Its range could be as much as 140 metres.[95]

The projected recoilless improvised grenade (PRIG) was the IRA's second-generation homemade missile system, based on the Russian RPG-7.[96] It was usable in enclosed spaces, and its warhead used a shaped charge design that increased its penetration power.[97] First used in an attack on an RUC Hotspur armoured vehicle in May 1991, the PRIG copied characteristics of earlier versions (such as a German crossbow missile), which reduced the blow-back problem through balancing the forward momentum of the projectile by ejecting a counter-mass to the rear – as well as producing no flash smoke and blast when fired, making it and its firer's location harder to find.

The counter-mass used was two packets of digestive biscuits wrapped in J-cloths. (Added to which the Mark-15 grenade was dubbed the coffee-jar bomb; see page 243.) The biscuits would turn to crumbs on firing and be ejected rearwards.[98] The J-cloths gave the weapon limited backward obturation[99] by increasing the external diameter of the biscuits to match the internal diameter of the launch tube. This shoulder-launched weapon was made of a 75-cm steel tube which had a wooden handgrip and an electrical detonation pack. The launcher was made of steel tubing, which had a propellant chamber added, and at least 500 g of Semtex was packed into a food tin. The initiation system was housed in the tail unit and the propellant charge initiation power supply was contained in the hand grip.

Attacks with both externally sourced and IRA-made RPGs were affected by specific technical problems that caused the warheads either to deflect before detonating or to not detonate at all.[100] The development of all these weapons was significant mainly because it thwarted many efforts to locate and seize weapons from the IRA, which could 'store' the knowledge of how to manufacture mortars or PRIGs and produce them as needed. The PRIG was able to bore a hole in heavily armoured vehicles, as in an attack on a police Land Rover in January 1994.[101]

The mortars and the PRIG were prime examples of the IRA's technological ingenuity, their construction and workings gleaned from military technology handbooks.[102] The PRIG in particular used an advanced military concept, the shaped conical explosive charge, which made the explosive into a high-temperature, high-velocity gas jet that could pierce solid armour plate. The 50-g Semtex charge was fitted at the back of the warhead formed around a hollow cone, which collapses on impact with the target, propelling the base of the explosive to the armour surface, with the fuse igniting the charge at the back. These were high-explosive anti-tank (HEAT) warheads, as described earlier, with armour-piercing power.[103] The PRIG's shaped charge principles were incorporated into the Mark-12 mortar. Packing the extra energy into the charge's explosive output also enabled the IRA to use HME in the charges rather than large amounts of precious Semtex or TNT.[104] Other explosives used were stolen from quarries, such as Gelamex or Powergel.[105]

MARK-14 AND 15 HAND GRENADES

The Mark-14 hand grenade consisted of a piece of steel piping sealed at the bottom with a welded steel plate. The explosive charge inside the piping was 500 g of Semtex-H, which was arranged in grooves so as to maximise the effects of fragmentation. A fly-off lever was held tight into the firer's body, the safety pin removed and the grenade thrown – upon which the fly-off lever would be ejected under the tension of the striker spring – allowing the striker to travel upwards until it struck and fired the rim-fire cartridge. This ignited a short safety fuse, which initiated a plain detonator, which detonated the Semtex.[106]

The Mark-15 improvised grenade – the 'coffee-jar' bomb – appeared in May 1991 and, used in seventy-three attacks, caused, surprisingly, 'only' two deaths.[107] Sweets jars and Lucozade bottles were also used. The Mark-15 held a pressure switch which was held in the open position by the base of the coffee jar. A metal liner was filled with 500 g of Semtex, with an electric detonator and electrical leads running from the pressure switch through a hole in the coffee jar. The detonator was activated when electric leads running from the pressure switch were connected to the detonator, which was inserted through the hole in the lid of the jar into the explosive. An arming switch in the circuitry was mounted in the jar lid – along with a torch bulb, which when illuminated continued the circuit through the firing switch.[108]

Developing subsequent versions of mortars did not mean that the Provos abandoned one type once they developed another. Previous versions were deployed along with newer ones, such as when the Mark-6 was used in the Heathrow attack in 1994. But despite the publicity this particular series of attacks achieved – again, targeting such a high-profile and vulnerable location on the British mainland was bound to attract more attention than the Northern Ireland mortar attacks – the mortars did not achieve the same impact as the big 1990s 'city destroyer' bombs. And, as Tony Geraghty has observed, such attempts to bomb from the air only had the effect – as in the extreme examples demonstrated in the Second World War – of actually hardening the resistance of civilians on the ground; only atomic bombing had achieved the ultimate impact of such a strategy.[109]

The ability to manufacture and modify weapon systems increased the IRA's flexibility and introduced uncertainty into any attempts to assess, predict and counter the organisation's capabilities.[110] As we will see in the next chapter, the IRA recruited high-level US technical assistance to develop an anti-aircraft missile of its own; as a multimillion-pound undertaking, and even though the IRA intended to cut the costs, it would still take years of effort.[111] Despite these developments, compared with attacks using externally sourced RPG systems, a smaller number of attacks using both generations of the improvised weapons resulted in casualties.

NOTES

1. Probably the best word to describe it is a Yiddish one: 'chutzpah'.
2. E. Moloney, *A Secret History of the IRA* (London: W.W. Norton & Co, 2002), p.137.
3. T. Harnden, *Bandit Country* (London: Coronet, 1999), p.371.
4. *Jane's Terrorism and Insurgency Centre website*, 2003, http://www.janes.com
5. M. Urban, *Big Boys' Rules* (London: Faber & Faber, 1993), p.208.
6. Personal communication, Intelligence operative, Ulster Weapons Intelligence Unit, May 2007.
7. Ibid.
8. Various own technical sources, incl. Carey Sublette, Fission Weapon Designs, Nuclear Weapon Archive, Version 2.04: 20 February 1999.
9. T. Geraghty, *The Irish War* (London: HarperCollins, 1998), p.189.
10. A.R. Oppenheimer, 'Conventional explosives: the terrorist's choice', *Jane's Terrorism & Security Monitor*, 23 April 2004.
11. Urban, *Big Boys' Rules*, p.206.
12. Geraghty, *The Irish War*, p.188.
13. C. Ryder, *A Special Kind of Courage: 321 Squadron – Battling the Bombers* (London: Methuen, 2006), p.214.
14. Geraghty, *The Irish War*, p.189.
15. Ryder, *A Special Kind of Courage*, p.214.
16. Geraghty, *The Irish War*, p.190.
17. Which boasted a suitably unpleasant acronym – ANAL.
18. Ryder, *A Special Kind of Courage*, p.216.
19. Urban, *Big Boys' Rules*, p.206.
20. Ibid., p.206.
21. Ryder, *A Special Kind of Courage*, p.217.
22. Ibid., pp.148-9.
23. Geraghty, *The Irish War*, p.190.
24. Personal communication, Intelligence operative, Ulster Weapons Intelligence Unit.
25. Various news reports of London Old Bailey terrorist trial, February–March 2007.
26. Ryder, *A Special Kind of Courage*, p.217.
27. Weapons Intelligence Unit, cited in Geraghty, *The Irish War*, pp.191-2, confirmed by personal communication, Intelligence operative, Ulster Weapons Intelligence Unit.
28. Weapons Intelligence Unit, cited in Geraghty, *The Irish War*, p.191, confirmed by personal communication, Intelligence operative, Ulster Weapons Intelligence Unit.
29. Ryder, *A Special Kind of Courage*, p.219.
30. Weapons Intelligence Unit, cited in Geraghty, *The Irish War*, p.191, confirmed by personal communication, Intelligence operative, Ulster Weapons Intelligence Unit.
31. Ryder, *A Special Kind of Courage*, p.218.
32. T. Harnden, 'IRA linked to mortar bomb attack', *Daily Telegraph*, 11 March 1998.
33. Geraghty, *The Irish War*, p.191.
34. Where a massive surveillance tower was positioned until only recently, but some surveillance systems remain. Personal communication with ex-IRA commander in Belfast, 2007.
35. Personal communication, Intelligence operative, Ulster Weapons Intelligence Unit, May 2007.
36. Ibid., July 2007
37. CAIN: Chronology of the Conflict 1994, Mortar Attacks on Heathrow.
38. *Parliamentary Debates*, Seanad Éireann, vol. 139, 10 March 1994.
39. Personal communication, Intelligence operative, Ulster Weapons Intelligence Unit, May 2007.
40. Geraghty, *The Irish War*, p.199.
41. Personal communication, Intelligence operative, Ulster Weapons Intelligence Unit, May 2007. You can picture the local population experiencing the dimming of their domestic lights and knowing well why. I explained in the Preface that the IRA rigged up the means to trick electricity meters so that power surges did not occur.
42. Cited from J. O'Halloran, editor of *Jane's Land-based Air Defence*, quoted in S. Millar, 'Heathrow a soft target for missile attack', *Guardian*, 12 February 2003.
43. Geraghty, *The Irish War*, p.192.
44. Ryder, *A Special Kind of Courage*, p.220.
45. Geraghty, *The Irish War*, p.192.
46. Ryder, *A Special Kind of Courage*, p.220.

47. 'IRA Bombs 10 Downing Street', *An Phoblacht*, 7 February 2002.
48. Although official government statements claimed a calmer reaction – that the cabinet members quickly adjourned to another room – I doubt if they would have had time to do anything other than 'duck and cover'.
49. S. Cook and M. White, 'IRA shells the war cabinet', *Guardian*, 8 February 1991.
50. S. Boyne, 'Uncovering the Irish Republican Army', *Jane's Intelligence Review*, 1 August 1996.
51. Geraghty, *The Irish War*, p.192, and personal communication, Intelligence operative, Ulster Weapons Intelligence Unit.
52. Personal communication, Intelligence operative, Ulster Weapons Intelligence Unit, May 2007.
53. Geraghty, *The Irish War*, p.196, and personal communication, Intelligence operative, Ulster Weapons Intelligence Unit.
54. Personal communication, Intelligence operative, Ulster Weapons Intelligence Unit, May 2007.
55. Ryder, *A Special Kind of Courage*, p.221.
56. Urban, *Big Boys' Rules*, p.207.
57. Ibid., p.207.
58. 'Northern Ireland's bloody day', *Time*, 11 March 1985.
59. Ulster Weapons Intelligence Unit, in Geraghty, *The Irish War*, p.196, and personal communication, Intelligence operative, Ulster Weapons Intelligence Unit.
60. Urban, *Big Boys' Rules*, p.207.
61. Ryder, *A Special Kind of Courage*, p.212.
62. Ibid., p.221.
63. Urban, *Big Boys' Rules*, p.207.
64. Ibid., p.207.
65. Geraghty, *The Irish War*, p.94.
66. Ibid., p.200.
67. Ibid., p.201.
68. Ryder, *A Special Kind of Courage*, p.255.
69. Ibid., p.225. Semtex, as explained in Chapter 5, left ANFO and ANNIE behind in terms of explosive yield per kg; ANFO was only 70 per cent as powerful, ANNIE and the other ammonium nitrate mixes only 40 per cent (and they caused plenty of damage).
70. Adapted from Restricted Information, Ulster Intelligence Unit.
71. Ryder, *A Special Kind of Courage*, p.256.
72. Geraghty, *The Irish War*, p.194.
73. Ryder, *A Special Kind of Courage*, p.256.
74. Ibid., p.256.
75. Ulster Weapons Intelligence Unit, in Geraghty, *The Irish War*, p.194, and personal communication, Intelligence operative, Ulster Weapons Intelligence Unit.
76. Geraghty, *The Irish War*, p.203.
77. Ryder, *A Special Kind of Courage*, p.256.
78. *Jane's Terrorism & Security Monitor*, Briefing – Improvised Mortars, 30 October 2002.
79. Ibid.
80. Boyne, 'Uncovering the Irish Republican Army'.
81. Ryder, *A Special Kind of Courage*, p.257.
82. Boyne, 'Uncovering the Irish Republican Army'.
83. Geraghty, *The Irish War*, p.192.
84. Personal communication, Intelligence operative, Ulster Weapons Intelligence Unit, May 2007, who defused this first IAAG by hand so that it could be captured intact and examined.. His action was carried out 'regardless of his own safety' and was recognised with the award of the Queen's Gallantry Medal.
85. Ryder, *A Special Kind of Courage*, p.232.
86. B.A. Jackson, et al., Rand Corporation, *Aptitude for Destruction, Volume 2: Case Studies of Organizational Learning in Five Terrorist Groups* (2005), Chapter Five, Provisional Irish Republican Army, p.122.
87. Ryder, *A Special Kind of Courage*, p.215.
88. Ibid.
89. Jackson, et al., *Aptitude for Destruction*, p.122.
90. Harnden, *Bandit Country*, p.366.
91. Jackson, et al., *Aptitude for Destruction*, p.123.
92. Personal communication, Intelligence operative, Ulster Weapons Intelligence Unit, June 2007.

93. Weapons Intelligence officers would look for these tell-tale bruises on the shoulders of rounded-up suspects. In Geraghty, *The Irish War*, p.197, and personal communication, Ulster Weapons Intelligence Unit operative, June 2007.

94. Jackson, et al., *Aptitude for Destruction*, p.125.

95. Edited from Restricted Information, Ulster Weapons Intelligence Unit.

96. Geraghty, *The Irish War*, p.197.

97. Jackson, et al., *Aptitude for Destruction*, p.125.

98. Personal communication, Intelligence operative, Ulster Weapons Intelligence Unit, May 2007.

99. Sealing the rear of the breech chamber to prevent propellant gases escaping.

100. Jackson, et al., *Aptitude for Destruction*, p.125.

101. Ryder, *A Special Kind of Courage*, p.258.

102. Described by Chris Ryder as 'perhaps the ultimate improvised weapon'. Ryder, *A Special Kind of Courage*, p.257.

103. *Jane's Armour & Artillery* and personal communication, Intelligence operative, Ulster Weapons Intelligence Unit, May 2007.

104. *Jane's Armour & Artillery* and personal communication, Intelligence operative, Ulster Weapons Intelligence Unit, May 2007.

105. Personal communication, Intelligence Operative, Ulster Weapons Intelligence Unit, May 2007.

106. Edited from Restricted Information, Ulster Weapons Intelligence Unit.

107. Ryder, *A Special Kind of Courage*, p.257.

108. Edited from Restricted Information, Ulster Weapons Intelligence Unit.

109. Geraghty, *The Irish War*, p.203.

110. Personal interview with a former security forces member, England, March 2004, cited in Jackson, et al., *Aptitude for Destruction*, p.123.

111. Urban, *Big Boys' Rules*, p.128.

Eight

The Engineers:
'If you hit target, there was elation'

Bombs are legitimate weapons of war and the IRA used them against an occupying force.
Marion Price, IRA bomb-maker

If you hit target, there was elation.
IRA volunteer active in bombings, 1970s–1990s[1]

The best technology cannot restrict the outreach of violence.
Shane Paul O'Doherty, IRA bomb-maker

We weren't nuclear physicists, but we were good electricians.
Tommy McKearney, former IRA commander[2]

So far I have focused on the bombs the IRA made and the materials and technologies they acquired to make them. Now I come to possibly the most important part of this work: the people who made them. Bombs do not make themselves; they are constructed, in the most intricate detail and often under conditions of great danger and – in the case of terrorists – extreme improvisation and ingenuity. They are constructed knowing full well that their prime purpose is to destroy buildings and bodies. But on the whole, unlike the terrorists of the twenty-first century, the IRA made devices in such ways as to prevent civilian collateral damage; much of the sophistication of the bombs was due to this basic part of IRA doctrine.[3]

The IRA's Engineering Department was the unit that designed homemade bombs, mortars and rockets, and this chapter will describe how the republican movement acquired the level of IED-making skills and expertise which has been long regarded as the highest ever achieved by a non-state group; what the bomb-makers and their helpers thought about their role in creating the means of destruction, both of properties and lives; and how the business of making and deploying bombs affected their own lives (and not just the long jail terms) and how they enhanced or hindered the progress of the IRA's armed struggle.

The Engineering Department had special status within the IRA. It was an elite division, and tended to operate independently of the front-line organisation. The engineers had to be protected and preserved at all costs as invaluable and skilled personnel. Sometimes many would be used when operations were stepped up – such as when a co-ordinated bombing attack throughout some twenty-one towns in Northern Ireland was said by the British army to have involved 100 IRA operatives.[4]

'ENGLISH DEPARTMENT'

Some of the best talent would be deployed to England according to the maxim that 'one bomb in England was worth twenty in Belfast' – that this engineering talent must not be 'wasted' in the six counties. This was reflected in the existence of the 'English Department' within the Engineering Department, which had great status within the IRA and was kept separate and well concealed.[5] Tommy McKearney has said that the campaign in England, specifically, was draining the Provisionals of resources and expertise, that the best personnel and resources were needed to have an impact in England. This meant reducing those resources in Northern Ireland operations.[6]

There were also different requirements and rules for the engineers who operated on the English mainland. Because many operatives in Northern Ireland were known to the authorities, those sent to deploy bombs in England had to be 'clean skins' – that is, operatives with no criminal records and new on the horizon – and secrecy on the number of units was to be preserved at all times. Recruitment took place over many years, and indicated a long-term strategic thinking on the part of the Provisional leadership. The significance of the bomb-making expertise of the South Armagh brigade in making the big ammonium nitrate bombs for destruction of the City of London was in evidence later in the campaign – by the mid-1980s.[7]

'YOU LEARNT HOW TO DO IT AND THAT WAS IT'

In dealing with the bomb-makers, I should define the difference between 'bomb-makers' and 'bombers'. The media often use the term 'bomber' to mean the person who made a particular device AND planted it. Or either act. I will define these as they are meant in military terminology: a 'bomb-maker' makes a bomb; a 'bomber' plants, throws, or drops it.

I will draw on first-hand statements by IRA operatives who spoke to me about what they did, or from police and army personnel about how they dealt with these violent acts and the people who perpetrated them.[8]

It must be said here that, although the IRA regarded their actions as 'political' rather than military, they always considered themselves to be an army with army discipline and command and control. As such the IRA became the world's best organised guerrilla group. For example, strict adherence to abstention from alcohol was laid down as a rule in the Green Book, and many engineers led monk-like lives as soldiers with total devotion to the cause.[9]

I will endeavour to convey the bomb-makers' inner motives and public admissions; the confused reasoning of some; the absolute, unstinting dedication of others; the failure to admit guilt; and the ready admission of guilt, albeit tempered with continuing belief in the movement and its aims right up until the present, post-decommissioning, day.

In the early 1970s, when the bombings were frequent, many volunteers would be involved. According to one IRA operative, who was interviewed by Brendan O'Brien: 'You had an engineering squad. They were the technical people. It was up to everybody to drive them [bombs] in ... *Everyone had some knowledge of detonators, where a detonator goes* [italics added].' [10] The 'bombers' would in this period take the smaller bombs to the target by hand. 'The engineers had been in before, told you to put it there ...'

Another IRA volunteer described his role: 'I didn't prime it. I'd get to the target and prime it then. I know people who'd make a bomb and give it to someone else. I wouldn't do that. I wouldn't ask anyone to do what I wouldn't do myself. I'd prime it for two minutes, six minutes.'

In the early days many volunteers were killed by bombs that went off – as many as ninety in the first five years of the modern Troubles:[11] 'You may have a safety device, kind of security for accidents. When you were priming it you were connecting two live wires. People started using this timing device for a safety feature. *You learnt how to do it and that was it. I was never nervous* [italics added].'[12] Despite the appalling act of planting bombs, it nevertheless took some courage – especially if you were a foot soldier who was not familiar with a device built by someone else. 'In comparison to today you took more risks. Now there's more surveillance, more undercover operations.'

Volunteers at the time went out in twos on bombing missions, often as boy–girl couples, as told vividly by Shane Paul O'Doherty in his autobiography. (The women's IRA, Cumann na mBan, was still in existence in the early 1970s;[13] its members had remained with the Provisionals after the movement split into the Provos and the Officials.) These 'courting couples' would evade surveillance (which was basic in those days) by acting intimate, and then nonchalantly leave bombs in shopping centres and other business locations.[14]

Expertise later increased: 'It's all about skill. Now they've access to anybody – aeronautical engineers, electronic engineers. There are people that people know nothing about. It's like two levels, it's a good thing.'[15] Ideas and information began to be shared, but this meant vulnerability for the movement – either through imprisonment or death of those with the expertise.

As for the bombs themselves: 'The bombs were anything from a couple of pounds to a couple of hundred pounds. You were just given it, it was just supplied. That's a kind of separate operation in its own right – who supplies an' stuff like that.' And when the bombs became more sophisticated: '… it became more electronic, more compact, the expertise increased … ' A leading explosives officer in Derry, John Joe McCann, had been trained in bomb making and also trained others in the black art:

> At that time, things were very crude. People would put a timer in with a two- or three-minute fuse; at that time it was fuses, people would just light a fuse in their hands, put a bomb in and then run. It became more sophisticated later on. At that stage they were just very simple, very crude devices, you just went up the town with a bomb, lit the fuse and that was it.[16]

Simple the early devices may have been, but they were just as lethal. Nail bombs, which were among the easiest to make, were a terrible example of this: a stick of gelignite stuck in a beer can packed with 15-cm (six-inch) nails and the top sealed with tape, with a small hole left for the detonator, which would have one or two matches attached. The volunteer, who was often in his or her late teens, would have to throw these devices immediately after lighting the matches – or risk losing a limb.

Another Derry innovation was the Durex bomb. This was a test tube full of sulphuric acid sealed in wax and tied in a condom. Then the condom was put in an envelope filled with an old IRA favourite, sodium chlorate. When the test tube is squeezed the acid, after about an hour, eats its way through the condom and ignites the chemicals.[17] The devices posed problems for the Provisionals as devout Catholic members were unwilling to bring condoms to the Irish Republic (where they were banned) – and as there was often reluctance to train volunteers in making bombs using condoms in case they were used for their original purpose.[18] (See the account below on Shane Paul O'Doherty.)

'I TAKE PRIDE IN MY WORK'

But far more serious questions of conscience would arise over the IRA's making and deploying of bombs. Conscience is tempered with unquestioning loyalty to the cause – but also with the thrill – sometimes admitted – in having power over life and death. As happened with the making of the atomic bombs in the Second World War,[19] the thrill of making destructive devices was a prime factor for many of their creators. 'For some at least it was the thrill of fighting, rather than dying for Ireland, that was foremost in their youthful minds.'[20] According to Seamus Finucane, whose brother John was among the first wave of recruits to join the newly formed Provisionals in spring 1970:

> ... There was a sense of adventure about people taking up the gun and the bomb at that time. Yes, it was exciting at times. You got satisfaction out of it.
> ... But when you bring it down to brass tacks, when you are talking about the grief of that person's family, the misery and the anguish that this death will cause to that family – no, it is not exciting and it is not funny, it is real.[21]

Many are non-repentant: one such, Liam Coyle, who was sentenced in 1973 to twenty years' imprisonment following a series of incidents, boasted to police that as the Derry brigade's engineering officer, he was responsible for as many as 200 bombings. When asked if he had kept details of these actions, he said: 'No, but I take a pride in my work.'[22] When asked by Brendan O'Brien about the deaths that resulted, the response from one volunteer was not untypical: 'Too bad ... There was no conscience. Even today there'd be no conscience ... If you believe in it, it can't be wrong. The more Brits we killed the more pressure was on them to get out.'[23] But it was not always 'Brits' or soldiers that were killed, as we have seen. According to my Irish EOD contacts, the half a dozen chief bomb-makers they dealt with had no remorse.

Kevin Toolis describes one IRA man he met as 'having told funny and threatening stories about making big bombs in other people's front kitchens'.[24] Again, this is redolent of the scientists who made the first weapons of mass destruction in the Second World War: the cause is all – the power attained and the excitement and danger experienced during their creation; and the numbing effect of the very process of making something that has the potential to kill and destroy.[25] Brendan O'Brien describes how one IRA man claimed his operations caused injuries only, no deaths – and his statement reveals the lethality of bombings compared to shootings: 'I can quite honestly say I didn't kill anyone with a gun. I hurt people in the bombs.' And he uses the classic rationale for his actions: he felt 'kind of disgusted, remorseful, because it wasn't the intention to hurt anybody. The intention was to destroy property.' But this was overruled by the thrill: 'At the same time, I didn't regret what I did. If you hit target, there was elation.'

But this was also excused by the situation of many volunteers fighting for a cause: '… we were attacking British installations. It was part of a propaganda thing. You'd see it on the news … We're all looking for f***ing jobs. It's a community-based army, people like me, ordinary people. That's the tragedy. I mean, I don't like violence.'[26]

Nevertheless, some felt agonies of conscience which may remain unstated for many years to come, or forever. An example (with no named individual) was recounted by a priest, Fr Denis Bradley, who attended to both IRA operatives and their victims. Inside twenty-four hours he saw a British soldier who had shot dead a young IRA man, Colm Keenan, and an IRA man who had planted a bomb that killed another soldier. The second scene he endured was thus:

> … I was called over to the scene. All I could make out was the top of a torso lying in the back yard and I remember not knowing if it was a human being or not. It turned out to be a soldier blown up by a booby trap bomb. About three hours later the young fellow who had planted the bomb asked to see me. I knew him very well. It was the first person he had ever killed.

The same priest has said that the IRA 'created a myth that they were defenders of the people. That's a lot of bunkum.' [27]

THE 1930s CAMPAIGN

The bombing campaign in England – the first in modern times by Irish republicans – involved the training of specific volunteers to make devices, many of which killed and maimed civilians. Some early bomb-makers learned their craft from involvement in the British army during the First World War and other conflicts. Groups of IRA men were brought back from England in the late 1930s for training in bomb-making in Dublin, specifically by Patrick McGrath, who was later executed for killing a policeman,[28] and Jim O'Donovan – the IRA 'director of chemicals' (a title that was echoed decades later in Iraq's 1980s chemical weapons programme) – who drew up the notorious S-plan to bomb England. The targets included military installations, BBC transmitters and other communications centres, as well as bridges and other strategic points – in the manner of wartime saboteurs. Classes were held in a hall, the Green Lounge in St Stephen's Green in Dublin, as well as Killiney castle.[29] The classes focused on bomb making and the men were expected to spread their expertise.

The most notorious IRA figure of the time, the Nazi sympathiser Seán Russell, actually received bomb-making and sabotage training when he was in Berlin in 1940 – with the Second World War well underway and British cities being pounded almost daily by the Luftwaffe.[30] It was he who brought O'Donovan out of retirement to train up future bomb-makers. Having been an employee of the Electrical Supply Board, O'Donovan later lost his job following the failure of the 1930s campaign and did time in the Curragh.[31]

A Russell associate, Peadar O'Flaherty, in the attempt to blow up Nelson's Column in Dublin, set a precedent by planning to set his explosives – most likely gelignite – and inform the police once he had exited the scene to enable them to cordon off the area and minimise casualties. A group of volunteers carried explosives – which could have gone off had they been jolted or bumped into – the length of O'Connell Street, only to find that the landmark was closed earlier on Saturdays in the winter.[32] An IRA training officer, Christy Quearney, was of the opinion that the bombing campaign was doomed to failure; initially because he believed it would not have sufficient impact on the British government, but later because the training of recruits in the use of explosives was inadequate.[33]

IRA bomb-makers risked their own safety and that of others, and could also be discovered at any time. Another 1930s bomber, Eoin MacNamee, used his rented room in Fulham, west London, to test iron oxide devices by seeing how long it took acid to burn through the rubber of balloons he had positioned in the fireplace – until the landlady discovered his makeshift lab and threw away the stuff, warning MacNamee that she knew what he was up to. He had to find alternative accommodation.[34]

Some associated with bomb deployment were distinctly unstable. Five people died in a bomb attack in Coventry on 25 August 1939 when a device was placed outside a shop, having been transported in the carrier of a bicycle by an IRA man who was later found to be 'a psychopath'.[35]

BUILDING UP EXPERTISE

The business of bomb-making is not learned in five minutes; indeed many lessons are learned along the way. The danger of putting together life-threatening substances with intricate components that, at a time desired by the device's creator, will detonate in a potentially lethal explosion can never be underestimated, regardless of the experience of the group or individual making them. Even the atomic bomb builders made mistakes after their first bombs had been deployed; two notable accidents resulted in the deaths of the scientists experimenting with the prescribed amount of explosives needed for a chain reaction. Terrorists making bombs in secret, using conventional raw materials, ran the risk of learning from scratch – or from stolen manuals – sometimes with no engineering or similar qualifications. They learned on the job. A volunteer who became an engineer or explosives officer (EO) would learn his deadly trade from a supervisor sometimes with marginally more knowledge than himself.

And they started young. In 1972 members of the Fianna – the youth IRA – who had attended St Columb's school in Derry, broke into their old school to raid the science labs for anything they could use against the British troops. One of them intended to experiment with homemade explosives in his bedroom. His local priest caught him and the other lads before he had a chance to use some stolen sulphuric acid to make a bomb. He later became a top explosives officer for Derry.[36]

The road to success in bomb making was therefore paved with danger. Attempts to manufacture explosives at the end of the 1960s were particularly disastrous for the early Provisionals, whose middle-ranking leadership managed collectively to blow themselves up, along with the two children of a homeowner whose house was being used for bomb-making.[37] In 1972–3, literally dozens of IRA volunteers were killed by premature detonation. One noted 'own goal' scored in the process of bomb making was when the IRA quartermaster-general in 1971, Jack McCabe, blew himself up in his Dublin garage while mixing a particular fertiliser concoction known as the 'black stuff' with – of all things – a metal shovel.[38] But out of this period emerged a generation of highly competent bomb-makers who had learned from the early mistakes – and one of the first lessons was to incorporate safety devices into the bombs to prevent them blowing up before they were planted.

The ability to improvise using limited resources can be measured by the IRA's introduction of the car bomb. This appalling machine of death had already been deployed by Zionists in the 1940s,[39] but the

Provisionals adapted it almost by accident; after McCabe's calamity, a consignment of the 'black stuff' that had already been sent to Belfast was deemed too lethal to be put into bombs – and so an unnamed volunteer suggested leaving it in a car, together with fuse and timer, in Belfast city centre. The rest is history.

Although not a car bomb in the true sense, it heralded a new and enormously destructive phase in the IRA's bombing campaign. Not only could car bombs create a larger explosion, but they could be delivered with minimal risk to the IRA. But as a potential weapon of mass effect, car bombs nearly always claimed innocent lives even when this was not necessarily intended. Indeed, one of the first car bombs deployed by the Provisonals, the Little Donegall Street car bomb which killed seven people and injured 100 others[40] on 20 March 1972, was also one of the first of many public relations disasters for the republican movement.[41]

The Provisionals also learned quickly from mistakes. Problems with the 'black stuff' were solved within weeks and new explosive mixes emerged. Along with growing skills came greater care in preventing discovery. Each bombing required the IRA to put in place intelligence teams prior to the operation. By the late 1980s, these usually consisted of six per team.[42] Surveillance and infiltration were always a problem, which necessitated the IRA ensuring that bombers would find a clear, unobserved target and attack it unhindered without the operation being sabotaged.[43] This explains why south Armagh and other rural areas were chosen for bomb-making, as it was quite easy to put these things together in barns without being under surveillance.

As we have seen earlier in the book, booby trap mechanisms were developed to counter attempts at defusing the bombs.[44] Specific expertise would be drafted in to kill EOD operatives. A noted example was when the Belfast brigade found a booby trap specialist from Strabane to kill an EOD operative, Col Derrick Patrick, who had to deal with a petrol tanker booby trapped with an anti-handling switch below just one of several devices aboard the vehicle.[45]

This specific targeting, as stated in IRA documents, led to delays in the security forces acquiring valuable forensic evidence. IRA training documents seized by the authorities contained detailed instructions to bomb-makers in minimising or totally eliminating forensic evidence. The EOs (explosives officers) were instructed to always wear protective outer garments (known in the countermeasures industry as personal protective equipment – PPE), which in the case of the Provisionals would consist of overalls, gloves and a mask. Everything had to be done to prevent traces of explosives getting into the hair, which would be one of the first places the RUC would inspect when an IRA suspect was arrested,[46] and which on young lads in the 1970s would be copious. The Provisionals became sufficiently clued up on forensics – from bitter experience – to know also what kind of fabrics not to wear: never natural or synthetic wool, which picks up particles easily – whereas nylon and denim were favoured.[47] There was also a trend towards using more stable explosives, enabling easy handling and therefore less likelihood of being blown up in the process of putting a device together, and more reliable timers[48] – which would (in theory) ensure that bombs went off at the appointed time with minimal risk to civilians. But it was acknowledged by the IRA trainers that, apart from being dangerous, the process of making explosives was extremely messy. It had to be done quickly to avoid detection, while the bulk of fertiliser-based explosives and the many processes of drying and purifying that were required meant forensic problems, with contamination of premises and clothing.[49] The process also involved health risks, most notably from inhalation or ingestion of particles.

Strange stories emerged from these activities, such as those which appeared in the media alleging that IRA explosives officers could contract cancer from handling nitro-benzene, a major component of HME – and that the nylon underwear worn by women IRA volunteers was prematurely setting off detonators, leading to a *Sunday Mirror* 1973 headline which read: 'Danger in those frilly panties'. A full-time public relations officer based at Lisburn later admitted conjuring up most of the black propaganda stories of this period.[50]

Many technical advances in the size and complexity of improvised bombs took place during the 1970s. The Provisionals' campaign in the early years of the decade moved from a massive, uncoordinated series of bombings to distinctly more sophisticated techniques using modern electronics. As one EOD officer said:

> As we produced a solution, they often produced a countermeasure. If they produced a near threat, we produced a solution, and so on. So, it has been a game of technological leapfrog over the years.[51]

This arms race – which, adapting an old Cold War term, could be called mutually assured disruption – was exemplified by the attempts by the army to jam frequencies used by the IRA in their radio-controlled devices (RCIEDs). The IRA were reaching a level of sophistication that included incorporating advanced electronics into these devices, which had been obtained mainly in the US, and which enabled the bomb-maker to use coded signals to activate a bomb – so that the army EOD teams had to pinpoint modulations in the signals.[52] This and other measures pitted against the growing advancement of IRA bomb-making are dealt with in the next chapter.

As discussed in the previous chapter, the ultimate in homemade devices was the IRA's mortar series. Although these weapons achieved minimal success, they were the hallmark of the organisation's improvisation and ingenuity, while allowing it to develop a degree of indigenous weapons capability. As we see from nascent and would-be nuclear weapons nation states, while it was expedient to obtain help from other countries' militaries, renegade scientists and black market networks, doing-it-yourself was and still is irreplaceable as a sign of prestige and also to keep facilities, construction work and movement of materials hidden from prying eyes.

However, with all this burgeoning expertise there was a lack of long-term or clear strategy. Explosives and bomb components were plentiful, and the engineering skills rising rapidly – but this did not deliver military superiority to the IRA. Alternating between attacks on army bases and shopping centres in English cities may have kept the security forces on the hop, but even those within the movement could see that this betrayed a lack of direction – as well as the repetition of serious errors in public relations (and, of course, losing grasp of any possible moral position) when innocent civilians were killed or maimed.

(NOT SO) STUPID PADDY

The bombing campaign of the 1970s was indeed several orders of magnitude more intense and shattering than anything that had gone before. While the 1930s campaign was shocking, with a high cost in terms of death and injury, there was a level of ineptitude that would provide lessons for future campaigns.

IRA 'own goals' indeed persisted throughout the Troubles. In October 1987 two bomb-makers, Eddie McSheffrey and Paddy Deery, were killed by their own blast incendiary bomb they were constructing in Derry, and in February 1988 Brendan Burns and Brendan Moley were killed by explosives that went off in the van in which they were being transported. At the time there were five bomb-makers attached to the Derry IRA.[53] But by the time the organisation was bombing England on a regular basis, the ethnically offensive stereotype of the 'stupid Paddy' was being revised: 'English domestic opinion … is undergoing change. Not for any shame or moral reasons, but because "stupid Paddy" isn't so stupid and funny when he's bombing the capital.'[54]

THE IRA'S LOS ALAMOS: SOUTH ARMAGH

The bombing campaign in England was carried out as a collective operation and involved literally thousands of IRA engineers, bombers, procurers of the necessary components, sympathisers and criminals providing transport and other facilities.

The ultimate example of this support was the republican heartland of south Armagh. This small but remote and impenetrable rural area was the IRA's Los Alamos, and the storage and test areas in Co. Donegal its Nevada Proving Grounds. There were also training camps in Co. Sligo in the Republic.[55]

South Armagh was the ultimate safe haven for bomb-making – and the heart of Provisional IRA, and later Real IRA, bomb-making operations. What the British termed 'bandit country' was home to farms that provided ideal premises for ammonium nitrate bomb factories and a plethora of bomb-making operations. Proximity to the border, the absence of unionists, easy acquisition of the materials for the fertiliser mix, the rugged terrain and powerful republicanism through the centuries made south Armagh an ideal operating ground for the IRA. The organsiation's South Armagh brigade made the 1993 Bishopsgate bomb, the Canary Wharf and Manchester bombs of 1996 and the bomb that killed eighteen British soldiers at Warrenpoint in 1979; and was behind virtually every other major operation in Britain in the six years beforehand. It was responsible for the lives of 127 soldiers, sixty-seven RUC officers and ninety-six civilians.[56]

But south Armagh itself did not claim its first victims until August 1970 when two RUC men were blown up by a booby trapped car.[57] As the IRA's main big-bomb making unit, the South Armagh brigade perfected the combined use of Semtex and ammonium nitrate. The Baltic Exchange bomb of 1992, which was the first large fertiliser-based device to be exploded in England, killing three people and resulting in an insurance payout of £350 million, was enhanced by Semtex-based detonating cord being wrapped around ammonium nitrate explosives. According to testimonies of former South Armagh brigade members to the police, the Baltic Exchange bomb was mixed in a shed in south Armagh by the brigade's commander and one of the most notorious of IRA men, 'The Surgeon'.[58]

Another bomb-maker, Jimmy Canning, was also a quartermaster who was sent to England by Tom Murphy (infamously known as 'The Slab') in 1990. In the next two years, Canning was involved in at least a dozen IRA attacks across England – including four firebomb attacks on Brent

Cross shopping centre, the National Gallery, Trafalgar Square, Whitehall Place close to 10 Downing Street, Parliament Street in Whitehall, Clapham Junction and London Bridge stations, outside the offices of the Crown Prosecution Services and on two trains to Ilford, Essex.[59]

Canning was eventually caught and convicted when his fingerprints were traced to a holdall containing nearly 30 lbs of Semtex left outside the Alfred Beck Theatre in Hayes. Had a microswitch not failed, over 300 people attending a performance could have died. After confirming the fingerprints, police put Canning under surveillance, and eventually linked him to a garage in Uxbridge containing 76 lbs of Semtex, six Romanian-made AKM rifles, 651 rounds of ammunition, three car bombs, eight detonators and several mercury tilt switches.

The farm complex owned by 'Slab' Murphy at Ballybinaby, near Hackballscross, where the ammonium nitrate explosives were mixed and bombs created for the Canary Wharf bomb,[60] was alleged to have been used for bomb fabrication from the early 1970s. The 1979 Warrenpoint massacre, caused by a radio-controlled device, was claimed by the army to have originated at Murphy's farm. The Murphy farm complex is also credited with the 1970s development of IRA mortars – the deadly Mark-10 in particular. South Armagh was difficult, if not impossible, for the authorities to penetrate. However, the number of 'spectaculars' that emanated from this remote area was limited by the difficulties involved in logistics, transportation and cost.[61] By 1996 resources were almost spent. Therefore, each bomb that came out of south Armagh in the 1990s was a big one.

'AN UNFORTUNATE CONSEQUENCE OF WAR': MARION PRICE

Continuing the tradition of Cumann na mBan, the original Women's IRA, more women were training as bomb-makers and bomb-planters in the 1970s (some also took part in gun battles) and were involved in organising the hiding of arms and safe houses for volunteers. In many cases no regret for their actions has been expressed, at least not publicly, by IRA bomb-makers. Many people have stereotyped views of women, especially women involved in warfare, and the thought that a female would be involved in making bombs – and express no regret for having done so – would prove shocking.

Marion Price, who along with one other woman and six men was convicted of exploding two IRA car bombs at the Old Bailey and the Ministry of Agriculture in London in March 1973, said that she 'wouldn't change my life at all; I don't regret anything and I wouldn't change anything.'[62] Price was convicted at the age of nineteen for her part in making and deploying four bombs; two were defused, but two exploded. A caretaker died of a heart attack and more than 200 people were injured, although it was sheer chance there were not many more fatalities. After going on hunger strike, in 1980 she received the Royal Prerogative of Mercy and was freed on humanitarian grounds suffering from anorexia nervosa (having been force-fed many dozens of times). Born in Andersonstown, west Belfast, she came from a staunchly republican family. Both parents were active in the 1930s, and her aunt, Bridie Dolan, was blinded and had her hands blown off while moving handgrenades in 1938. Marion and her elder sister, Dolours, were believed to have commanded a ten-member Provo cell stationed in London. The idea and planning came from the sisters. Price travelled on the Dublin–Liverpool ferry with one of the four car bombs, which was then driven to London. A detective who questioned Marion Price when she was arrested at Heathrow airport on 8 March 1973 recalled that just before 3 p.m, at the moment the bombs were due to explode, she looked at her watch and smiled broadly at the arresting officer.[63]

Nevertheless, she has tried to avoid responsibility for the London bombings. Price claims that during their 1973 trial, the bombers learned they had been compromised by a high-placed informer in Belfast who knew all the details but didn't take part in the operation.

> It emerged in court that customs at Liverpool realised one of the cars had false number plates. They phoned Scotland Yard but were told to wave it through. The authorities allowed the bombing to happen. They had details of the operation in advance that could only have come from a senior figure in Belfast. We learned that photos of Dolours and I had been circulated at airports and ports across Britain nine hours before the bombs exploded.

It appears that she would have done just about anything for the republican cause, and is quoted as saying: 'I have dedicated my life to a cause and because of that I am prepared to die … I don't expect sympathy. I have no regrets. I joined young but I knew the risks involved. I had thought long and hard. It wasn't an emotional reaction to something that happened to my family or me. It was a question of fulfilling the beliefs I still hold … '

Specifically – and of most significance, on bombs:

> Bombs are legitimate weapons of war and the IRA used them

against an occupying force. The IRA campaign was never about killing civilians, that was not our intention, but accidents happen, that is an unfortunate consequence of war.[64]

In another interview, Price was asked if she ever considered the morality of planting bombs in densely populated areas, to which the reply was: 'The warnings given were twice as long as in Belfast. That was a conscious decision because we knew the English lacked experience of evacuation. We didn't want civilian casualties, from a moral or pragmatic viewpoint.'[65]

'I've never had a sleepless night over anything I've done as an IRA volunteer. *Bombs are weapons of war* [emphasis added]. Western states have used them far more brutally than we ever did.'[66]

With almost 2,000 people murdered by the IRA in the past thirty years, this would appear to be an empty justification – and one that has been oft repeated by military and political apologists of civilian bombing throughout the twentieth century, including the carpet bombings of Germany, the atomic bombings of 1945 and the bombing of Vietnam and Cambodia in the 1960s and 1970s. Words that indicate aspiring to a moral high ground because you are a 'freedom fighter', terrorist, insurgent or pioneering scientist ring hollow in the ears of the victims, their families, friends and associates.

But such rationale can have strong resonances. You fight for your own cause, to the death, with whatever weapons you have to hand, often against a far better-equipped foe. When asked, post-11 September 2001, and after the Omagh atrocity, whether any terrorist campaign was simply counter-productive, Price replied:

> Is Bush a good guy, just because his bombs are bigger and better than mine and he drops them from further away? Does that make him right and me wrong? I don't take moral lectures from the likes of George Bush.

Having continually opposed the peace process, she became chair of the Irish Republican Prisoners Welfare Association and active in the political wing of the Real IRA, the 32 County Sovereignty Movement.[67] Of even greater irony is the fact that she had begun her career as a nurse and denied there was a huge contradiction between IRA membership and nursing.[68] 'One day, a wounded British soldier was brought into casualty. He was wearing a dirty vest. He looked frightened. I felt very sorry for him. That night, I told my comrades and one joked that I should have finished him off. I asked why on earth I'd do that. He was no longer a soldier, he'd been taken out of the battlefield. He was a patient now, I'd have no difficulty looking after him.'

Price was able to compartmentalise her life in this way. Nevertheless, she and her sister had a tremendous impact, not just on their victims and those robbed of their loved ones but on the Brixton prison chaplain, Fr Langan. Her fellow IRA bomb-maker, Shane Paul O'Doherty tells of the chaplain's closeness to the sisters and how their hunger strike in the prison affected him. The chaplain's fondness for the sisters was such that even when his own sister was injured in the Old Bailey bomb, the work of Marion Price, he did not tell her. Even the prison governor had been affected by their hunger strike and died soon after it ended.[69]

'WE ONLY HAVE TO BE LUCKY ONCE': PATRICK MAGEE

By the early 1980s, the EOD expert Peter Gurney noted that IRA bomb deployment expertise was increasing to the point where an explosion would be timed to occur once daily, but at a different place each time.[70]

Patrick Magee, one of the best-known IRA bomb-makers, both made and planted the Brighton bomb in 1984.[71] For a time in the mid-1970s he was the IRA's chief explosives officer. Although convicted and sentenced to thirty-five years in jail, he was certainly no 'stupid Paddy' (unless you regard his failure to assassinate Margaret Thatcher, the IRA's prime target, as 'stupid' – as although the timing was right, the bomb's position was wrong). This failure aside, the operation he executed – from checking in to the Grand Hotel three weeks before, assembling the unit himself, building it in place[72] and setting up the newly invented video-recorder timer – defied official intelligence and resulted in five deaths and thirty-four injuries, some of them lifelong. The meticulous IRA planning and preparation involved, and the relative sophistication of the device itself (described in Chapters 3 and 6), had been largely unexpected. There were four people involved in the Grand Hotel attack but Magee was the leader, technical specialist, and bomber. Magee had checked in as Roy Walsh, staying in room 629 from 14 to 17 September 1984, in which he secreted the 13.5 kg bomb behind the bath panel.

After the bombing, Magee was tailed for months by MI5 and special branch, and finally arrested in a flat in Glasgow. The flat was a base for an ASU involved not in the Brighton bomb but in planning attacks aimed at seaside resorts.[73] Despite days of interrogation Magee refused to answer questions – but a fingerprint on a registration card recovered from the hotel ruins was enough to convict him.[74] His expertise in timers had already been trialled as far back as 1977 – when a small device was placed in a flower pot at the New University of Ulster at Coleraine the week before the queen's planned visit in August. This device was on a long-delay timer and part of the IRA's evolving strategy of using Magee's skills as a leading explosive officer to develop this type of timer.[75]

Magee has refused – as have other IRA engineers or bomb-planters – to disclose the operational details of the Brighton attack. 'There are the feelings of the victims to be taken into account, and I wouldn't want to be giving any offence.'[76] But he was one of the few IRA bomb-makers (or any other bomb-makers, for that matter) to state his feelings openly about what he had done. In a television documentary, in which he agreed to be confronted by Jo Tuffnell, the daughter of one of his victims, Anthony Berry, he stands by his belief that 'Brighton, from our perspective, was a justified act. Your father was a part of the political elite ... In that sense, there's that cruel word, cruel expression: he was a legitimate target.'[77] But then Magee admits some guilt in seeing the close relative of someone who had died at his hands: 'Meeting you, though, I'm reminded of the fact that he was also a human being and that he was your father and that he was your daughter's grandfather, and that's all loss.'[78]

Magee was sentenced to thirty-five years imprisonment a year after the 1984 bombing. He was transferred to Maghaberry prison in 1994 and subsequently to Long Kesh, before being released under the terms of the 1998 Good Friday Agreement. The judge who sentenced him branded Magee 'a man of exceptional cruelty and inhumanity who enjoyed terrorist activities'. He had allegedly honed his skills at Libyan training camps. Magee was born in Belfast in 1951 but moved with his family to Norwich when he was two. He returned to Belfast at the age of eighteen in 1969 and, in the footsteps of his grandfather, who had been in the IRA in the 1920s, joined the Provisional IRA.[79]

He has, like Marion Price before him, stated the legitimacy of bombing for a cause – while expressing a degree of regret:

> ... I deeply regret that anybody had to lose their lives, but at the time did the Tory ruling class expect to be immune from what their front-line troops were doing to us? I have argued that the military campaign was necessary, and equally now I would argue that it is no longer necessary. It's as simple as that.[80]

Jo Tuffnell said in the documentary that within days of the attack, she knew she wanted to have the strength to overcome bitterness – and that that might involve meeting the Brighton bomber. This is a kind of therapy being increasingly encouraged for both criminal and victim remediation, and while being terribly traumatic for the latter, has often yielded positive results. On 24 November 2000 the pair met at a secret location in Dublin, for what was later described as a 'highly-charged three hours', and during the course of 2001 they met several more times with the cameras present.[81]

While remaining a committed republican, Magee is shown 'clearly disarmed' by the generosity and openness of Mrs Tuffnell.[82] 'I think it's very important to be confronted by the consequences – with your pain,' he tells her. 'It is part of my own healing to hear his story,' says Jo Tuffnell. Patrick Magee muses: 'I wouldn't ask them to forgive, why should they? Just the understanding is all I could hope for.'

Having supported the peace process and condemned dissident IRA groups, of great importance is his subsequent involvement in Irish conciliation groups, most notably the Causeway Project, which seeks to facilitate encounters between perpetrators and victims of any action that occurred during the course of the Troubles. Magee is also an accomplished scholar,[83] having used his time in prison to study for a PhD in 'Troubles' fiction.[84] In the manner of needing to make confession, Magee has said that he wanted 'just to be understood, to get a chance to explain'.[85] But in a television interview in 2004, he maintained that, had he not been captured, he would have continued bombing. 'I was a volunteer. I was committed to pursuing the war in England ... the [Brighton] operation on its own wouldn't have achieved the necessary leverage to change the British political establishment's mind to treat the problem seriously ... we had to sustain the campaign against them.'[86]

'WARHEAD': PATRICK GERARD FLOOD

Patrick Gerard Flood was a master bomb-maker who was executed by the IRA in 1990 after he was found to have been an informer. It was claimed, and denied by the authorities, that he had sabotaged IRA IEDs by omitting the batteries, thereby setting up arrests of his colleagues. When various failures and mistakes that occurred during IRA bombings were added together, Paddy Flood took the blame.[87] A police source later claimed that the battery omission was not deliberate but may have been an omission on the forensic report: that there are other ways to prevent bombs exploding.[88] There had also been other informants who could have been implicated. I will not dwell on the ins and outs of how he became an informer here. My focus is on his technical proficiency, which was such that he was promoted to brigade engineer and Derry's top bomb-maker, working with all of the active service units (ASUs). It is said that by 1988 he had made up to 90 per cent of all IRA bombs in Derry.[89]

Other operations failed because of infiltration and informants. It is said that the Derry brigade was poor on security and easily penetrated, and that by the late 1980s IRA operations in Derry were failing repeatedly. Dumps were seized – as many as seventy-six in 1987 – and volunteers were often arrested on their way to locations for planting their bombs.[90] Flood had joined the IRA in 1985 as a passionate republican. In Toolis's words, he 'lived, breathed and, in a bitter twist of fate, died in the company of Republicans'.[91] He became an IRA engineer in the late 1980s, having started off in the BRY (Bogside Republican Youth), during which time he earned the deliciously nefarious nickname 'Warhead'.[92]

As such, he played a dual role – as that most hated of beings, an informant, and that most damaging of beings, a bomb-maker. He admitted in his taped confession before his execution by the Provisionals that he had become an engineer on the instigation of the authorities. That he was told 'to try and get on an explosives officer course and find out where we were trained, who by, and who was the explosives officer trainer'.[93]

His particular skill was in making booby trap devices. One such, a device disguised as a concrete block concealed in a wall and detonated by command wire (described in the chapter on bomb technologies), was designed to ambush soldiers in August 1989. Flood had been assigned by his RUC handlers to make the device, and apart from being the only volunteer to escape when the operation was intercepted by the police, with others arrested and the bomb defused by EOD, the final forensic report on the device revealed that the batteries had been left out (although Flood had told his IRA colleagues that the bomb was primed and ready) – without which the bomb was totally useless. No bomb-maker worth his salt would ever 'forget' to put in the batteries.[94]

Flood is best known for the fiasco that became known as the 'good neighbours bomb': a classic example of how bombs take life indiscriminately, and not the lives that were intended to be taken. To summarise the operation: Flood constructed a booby trap device the IRA planted in the flat of a petty criminal called Laird whom the Derry brigade wanted arrested. After kidnapping the criminal, the IRA tried to lure the RUC to his flat but the police already knew it was booby trapped and did not wish to reveal that they had this knowledge. When two neighbours broke in to see if Laird was still alive, the bomb blew them up.[95] Despite having the flat under surveillance, the police allowed this to happen.

A further disastrous booby trap incident took place in January 1990, again with Flood constructing a concrete-block disguised device and intended to destroy security forces stationed at the ancient walls of

Derry during a Sinn Féin-organised Bloody Sunday commemorative parade. This operation in itself risked killing civilians too, but the IRA (and Flood's handlers) authorised it nevertheless. The bomb exploded, killing a young Sinn Féin supporter in a nearby block of flats, leading to the claim by the Provisionals – once they knew Flood's bombs had been RUC-instigated – that the bomb's Semtex charge had been made so as to blow out from the wall rather than straight at the troops. The security forces were, on this as on many other occasions, prepared to allow targeting mistakes to occur, concluding that if IRA bombs killed innocent people – as bombs tend to do – this was on the IRA's heads.[96]

There were, tragically, so many examples of this, such as the Harrods car bomb of Christmas 1983, in which six were killed and ninety injured but which had been intended to destroy a high-profile London premises. The IRA said that its volunteers who planted the bomb had not been authorised by the Army Council. [97] A coded warning was received at a Samaritans' office at 12.45 p.m. but the device exploded just before 1.30 p.m. when it is believed to have killed four police officers who were approaching it. A second warning call was made to authorities at the time of the first explosion claiming a bomb had been placed in the heart of Oxford Street. Police tried to clear the area crowded with shoppers and cordoned it off but it was later found to be a false alarm. As pointed out later by Scotland Yard, the bomb was an indiscriminate weapon which, despite being on a timing device, could have gone off at any time in a street crowded with people. [98]

Flood's other talent was disguised devices. One such, concealed behind a metal sheet, killed two soldiers on Buncrana Road in Derry. These attacks generated local comment:

> It was made in Bishop Street and people who were there told me about helping with the circuit testing and that it was under a big sheet of steel at the side of the road. I said [to my uncle] 'wait till you hear this coming on the television, listen for a big bang tonight' and wham, there were two soldiers dead. We all felt good about it, it was a success.[99]

'IT DOESN'T GIVE ME PRIDE OR HONOUR THAT I HURT CIVILIANS': SHANE PAUL O'DOHERTY

Shane O'Doherty became the brigade explosives officer for Derry at the tender age of nineteen, having expressed a desire to work with explosives – which he explained in his autobiography *The Volunteer* was rare, as those who volunteered to do this 'were regarded as "nutty professors" or stark raving mad'.[100] Shane was no nutty professor, but a highly intelligent, well-educated young adventurer with a passionate, romanticised belief in the republican cause.

His early bomb-making career was spent in an upper room in an average Derry house – his secret bomb factory where he specialised in making booby trap incendiary bombs and timing devices.[101] He had his first experience four years earlier, when – before he had 'a vague idea of how bombs worked', he was asked to hide a bomb the Provos had failed to plant and was shown how to deploy it. On this first occasion as a bomber, he 'was excited and delighted by my good fortune. I was being given a look into the secret world of the IRA and its operations which would within a day or two grab the attention of the nation by exploding this very bomb.'[102]

He explains how becoming involved in bombs put a volunteer in the elite ranks:

> They said, 'Well, it's a fuse bomb. You light these matches at the top of the fuse. There's a fizz, and you've got three minutes.' So, I thought about it all evening, and thought, you know, well, how many people get this kind of chance to go from, you know, being a 'nobody' in the IRA to actually getting a chance to do a prominent job and get in there, and be up front? So, I decided to kind of break the rules and take the bomb to its target myself.[103]

He continues:

> So at about 3 or 4 a.m. I sneaked out of bed, went back to the back shed, took this bomb, fearfully. You could probably have heard my heartbeat in London. It was a painfully fast heartbeat. And I carried it down the back alley here and up to the doorway of this building, you know, trembling with fear. I nevertheless rubbed the matches on the fuse, and there was a fizz, and I got the hell out of there …
>
> … You were always aware, like making these devices, that any one of them could explode and kill you, and particularly our kind of homemade devices, or that somebody else's mistake could kill, which often happened to IRA volunteers. But no, you just didn't think about it. I mean, you tried not to think about it.[104]

He goes on to describe the feeling of power he felt in experiencing his device (as a bomber rather than a bomb-maker in this case) actually go off:

Then, there was this incredible boom, and there was a vast pool of grey dust and plaster in the air, and an eerie silence. And I looked at it and thought, you know, this is the most incredible hour [*sic*] I had ever seen unleashed. And all from striking a box of matches.[105]

Of arguably even greater importance was the ability – at least in the case of O'Doherty – to imagine what it would be like to be the victim of 'that kind of horrible, massive explosion' while in the course of an operation, which in his case did happen, if only from a small device:

Sometimes, when you were standing with a 1,000-pound lorry bomb or truck bomb, or standing on a lamp made of 1,000 pounds of explosives, you know, it would occur to you, what would it be like if this went off? And in one case when I was blown up by a let-ter bomb device – and I still have some of the damage on my body from that – I remember seeing the detonator of the device on a table in front of me explode. And all I remember seeing is this incredible rainbow of colours going past me, followed by a fero-cious bang that blew me out the window of a house ... And a cou-ple of days later, I was back on the job again.

When O'Doherty was promoted to being a fully-fledged EO, he recalls his excitement when asked how he would feel about going to London and 'really making a splash': 'And I thought, my God, you know, whew!' He makes the process of getting onto the next stage as a bomb-maker sound amazingly simple:

I stuck some four-ounce packets of black plastic explosive in a ruck-sack. I stuck some electric detonators in the tube frame of a ruck-sack. And I just took a flight to London with about 500 pounds in my pocket, went to a flat agency, got a flat, went out and bought a 'Who's Who' and some stuff, and you know, little batteries and pieces of wire and tape, and aluminium foil. And that's it.

O'Doherty was in a whirl of excitement, with events moving rapidly for him – a situation that for IRA engineers, as with bomb-makers in other groups, where a formal series of training may not have been possible, happened out of sheer necessity and enforced improvisation. 'I could not take it all in. There was supposed to be some preparation and training ... there was little or no transition period ... I hadn't had time to catch up with my new self ... '[106]

The race against having their devices discovered was summed up thus:

> We were all the time trying to improve devices and trying to avoid
> Felix (the bomb disposal units) ever getting time to get there and
> defuse it. So, you know, you were always trying to avoid the sce-
> nario where an army bomb disposal guy got there and got time to
> work on it.

As for learning his craft, O'Doherty had a natural instinct towards how
bombs should be made and set. In being tasked with planting a particular bomb, he knew that sharp right-angle kinks in the fuse wire would
break the inner gunpowder core and therefore the burning fuse would
burn out at that juncture. It was not his place to point out this mistake,
and he duly planted the device and lit the fuse. He then tells of his
mounting panic as he assumed the warning had been called in and the
location evacuated, to see no such activity and fearing that people would
be killed ('how could I ever rid myself of the guilt of this slaughter'?).
The bomb, as he suspected, did not explode, and his IRA masters
accused him of not igniting the fuse – rather than blaming the original
bomb-maker who had fouled up. When it was later reported that the
police had discovered that the bomb's fuse had burnt out before setting
off the explosive charge, he was vindicated and the bomb-maker had to
admit his mistake.[107]
    What is telling is that O'Doherty admits that his main concern was
that he wouldn't lose face, rather than that people would be killed by an
inadequate warning.

> There had been no focus on the fact that only a miracle or wild
> chance had prevented the deaths and injuries of very many Derry
> people. And so we went on about our business, troubled neither by
> the catastrophe that had nearly happened nor by the fact that it had
> been prevented only by a fault in the make-up of the bomb.[108]

Preoccupation with the technicalities of bomb-making and deployment,
and the excitement and power that entails, is clearly in evidence here.
However, O'Doherty was possibly the only convicted IRA bomber to
have written letters of apology to his victims while in prison. He later
renounced violence and has co-operated with authorities for many years,
but carries with him chilling memories of his bombing. His feelings are
encapsulated in this statement:

> It's not a manly thing for a politically motivated sort of heroic fig-
> ure to admit that conscience hurts you. You know? I mean, con-
> science does hurt me, you know? It doesn't give me pride or hon-
> our that I hurt civilians, that I hurt innocent people, that I maimed

innocent people, who, while I sit here and move on with my life, are still wounded and maimed. It doesn't make me feel good. And it even grew upon me – and nobody warned me that it would – that later, that hitting so-called 'legitimate' targets hurt my conscience, you know?[109]

Once in jail for the mail bombings he set about trying to justify the violence of his craft. And then came the depositions – the accounts of how each of his mailed devices had affected his victims. O'Doherty was horrified, showing again a parallel with bomb-makers of Second World War vintage – who also felt the necessity to make bombs as a means of winning their war, enjoyed the technical challenge and adventure involved, then were suddenly stunned at seeing the shocking results of their enthusiastic labours. O'Doherty deeply regretted, and still deeply regrets, the 'callous disregard [he] had shown for civilian casualties at a time when I had been cock-a-hoop about my bombing successes'.[110] His feelings of guilt were such that he sent written apologies to 'those innocent working-class persons accidentally and unintentionally injured by my bombs'.

Before this, however, he learned his trade assiduously. His initial efforts were in making incendiary devices, a dangerous activity not only for members of the public going about their business but also for the devices' creator and planter. The work also involved what O'Doherty found to be embarrassing trips to the chemist, because, as mentioned earlier, the devices incorporated condoms. The fuse delay was measured by the length of time it took for sulphuric acid to dissolve two layers of condom, after which the acid ignited the explosive. The devices often burst into flames, not at the appointed time, but in the throes of their construction, causing burns to handlers.

According to O'Doherty, such accidents simply served 'as a mark of our bravado'.[111] On being injured by one of his devices that blew up prematurely, he describes it as ' ... a rainbow rising from it ... and sped past my head, quickly followed by a blue light, then an almighty BANG!'[112] But knowing what even an accidental blast could do to life and limb did not deter him from continuing his work on deadly devices – but, for his own safety, it shortened the time he wanted to work on them. Like other rookie bomb-makers, O'Doherty made early mistakes – as when an ignition component went off prematurely because of a faulty timer setting. On the non-lethal side-effects of bomb making, he describes the characteristic 'gelly headache', the result of over-exposure to gelignite fumes.[113]

When sent to bomb London – after getting through Dublin and Heathrow airports with a rucksack full of explosives and detonators –

O'Doherty began making what became the hallmark of his bomb making career – letter-bombs, of which he was the sole creator during the 1970s. These he made and posted – apparently, there was no problem taking them to post offices and having them weighed. After his first successes he would celebrate with a curry and a bottle of Sauterne at a local Indian restaurant. But other than this occasional treat, he 'lived like a monk' during his London campaign, living 'only for the armed struggle and the IRA'.[114]

His skills were such that, when only nineteen, he was appointed Derry brigade's explosives officer, which 'was not the kind of position for which there was a lot of competition'[115] – revealing that such skills were in short supply. As such, he was responsible for all explosive devices made and used in the Derry area, as well as training and qualification of battalion and company EOs. This would entail the setting up and running of training camps, which were often in local houses.

As well as letter bombs, the IRA during this period placed small devices in shops and other premises. O'Doherty's expertise grew rapidly to the level of making customised devices for specific operations. His first incendiaries incorporated magnesium and lighter fuel with tiny watch-timers. He also specialised in booby trap devices, which would be planted in locations that would then be reported as hosting suspicious activity in an attempt to lure the army. One of these devices was hidden in a copy of *Who's Who*.[116]

O'Doherty also trained women in 'the arts and crafts of explosives'. He took several young women to a weekend training camp – a farmhouse – on a scenic part of the Ulster coast. They were trained to make and set their own devices, with the sound of the sea and the steep cliffs as a backdrop – and also a testing site.[117] O'Doherty was using benzene and fertiliser – the forerunners to the big ammonium nitrate car bombs. The benzene was being used as the primer for the bulk explosive, which had been concocted from low-grade fertiliser (see Chapter 5).

He admits he was unfamiliar with the power of the benzene, his experience having been primarily in commercial explosives such as gelignite. When the women were tasked with making test devices out of benzene, along with the detonating cord and detonators, he thought the devices would make nothing more than a few pops and bangs on the clifftops. Instead, they went off with an ear-splitting explosion, which in the quiet remoteness of the test site 'woke every living being within miles' and was followed by a blast wave that blew him and his trainees off their feet: 'Sky and sea merged.'[118] As they drove away at speed, having thrown the rest of the explosives and the components into the sea, the second bomb went off with equally deafening force.

So perilous was the business of training EOs in the early 1970s that 'own goals' happened often. O'Doherty was livid when one young volunteer whom he felt was not sufficiently qualified was killed planting a bomb. The volunteer's brother accused O'Doherty of sending him out on the mission, which he hadn't – with the result that O'Doherty 'began to wonder if the prize justified the cost'.[119] On another occasion in 1974 a dedicated young female trainee EO, Ethel Lynch, died in a premature detonation in Derry. O'Doherty, who was accused of running away from the flat where the explosion took place, has stated: 'I would have easily given my life to preserve hers.'[120] Indeed, it is notable that part of O'Doherty's role as EO trainer was to ensure the safety not only of the EOs and other volunteers, but of *the population at large* [emphasis added]'.[121] This was clearly to prevent public relations disasters arising from the injury or death of members of their own nationalist community – which the IRA depended on for hiding weapons, explosives and personnel.

Safety measures introduced into bomb-making were revealed during raids in which devices were found and confiscated. In May 1973 a car being driven by a noted Derry IRA man, Thomas McCallion, was stopped and searched. Six 2-kg HME bombs, along with six electric detonators, alarm clocks wired up to batteries as TPUs, insulating tape, nails and nine torch bulbs were recovered.[122] As was described in Chapter 6, the torch bulbs were used by the bomb-makers as replacements for the detonators while the bombs were being assembled – to avoid 'own goals'. The torch bulbs would light up if there was a faulty connection in the circuit; the detonator would be replaced at the last minute prior to planting the device.

On a wider-reaching point, O'Doherty, when facing up to the results of his actions, acknowledges that innocent people are often injured or killed by bombs. In a clear message to all those who practise high-technology warfare, he says: 'The best technology cannot restrict the outreach of violence.'[123] It is this realisation that turns him into a pacifist – just as so many of those who worked on the first nuclear weapons became champions of disarmament.

The truly squalid element of O'Doherty's trade was the making of nail bombs. Comprising a stick of gelignite in the centre of a beer can full of six-inch nails, these were first devised to throw at soldiers during street rioting in Derry. Again, the technical details and effects are uppermost when O'Doherty examines the spot where a nail bomb had landed, observing 'the astonishing pattern which the nails made in the tarmac into which they had been blasted'.[124]

Another observation about British people's notions of what consti-
tutes an IRA (or other terrorist) bomb-maker is pointedly made by
O'Doherty – who did not fit the stereotype: being 'calm, intelligent,
from a good family and … [sat in the dock] in a shirt, tie and jacket and
looked respectable'. This kind of character stereotyping (that people
committing violent acts fit a certain criminal image) brings to mind the
experiments of the US psychologist Stanley Milgram in the 1950s, and
the work of philosopher Hannah Arendt on 'the banality of evil'.[125]

'GOOD EXPLOSIVES OFFICERS REMAINED EXPLOSIVES OFFICERS': MICHAEL DOMINIC CLARKE

The type of IRA volunteer that would be drafted into the Engineering
Department was typified by Michael Clarke, who during the early 1970s
worked as an electrician in a record-player factory in Derry. He joined
the IRA in Derry just after internment was introduced in August 1971.
He did not know the identities of the battalion quartermaster or explosives officer, nor did he know the officers in the Bogside. He became the
explosives officer for the Creggan.[126]

In his testimony before the Bloody Sunday tribunal in December
2003, he said: 'I was self-trained. I studied books on explosives.'
Explosives were very hard to get hold of so he made incendiary devices.
As a Derry explosives officer he began making gelignite bombs to target
British troops during street rioting. These contained nails wrapped in
corrugated paper and were set off by matchsticks attached to fuse wire,
sometimes put in cans but Clarke believed that by 1972 he had stopped
using cans in favour of tape, which was lighter. A detonator would be
inserted into a hole made in the gelignite and then a 90-cm fuse was carefully inserted into the detonator, giving seven seconds between lighting
and detonation. The fuse was then cut at an angle to expose the gunpowder in its core. Matches were taped to the fuse so that the heads met
the open fuse. Clarke always used safety matches because the risk of
accidental ignition was too great with red, non-safety, matches.

These bombs took five to ten minutes to make and were 'anti-person-
nel devices' – intended for wounding and killing troops and police – not
for use against buildings, which required incendiary or blast bombs.
Clarke's testimony also revealed how the Provisionals controlled explosives, which were never kept in or near the house but were generally
used immediately.

… you would make nail bombs as close as possible to that locality.

I took the rest of the materials in my Maxi car. Some of the seats were removed and the car was used as a mobile workshop.

He did not know where the explosives came from or if bombs had to be kept overnight. They were stored on manned barricades. Explosives dumps were only really used later once they had started making home-made explosives. 'Good explosives officers remained explosives officers.'[127]

Nail bombs were generally thrown at the end of a riot since after they were thrown people did not hang around to wait for the army's response. Clarke said rioters were given a 'republican nod' (a shout) to get out of the way before bombs were thrown. Four or five bombs would be thrown at the same time. About 10 per cent of nail bombs failed to detonate, usually because the fuse was damp or the fuse wire was not cut at an angle. Clarke added that a lit fuse would not go out, and to defuse a lit nail bomb you would have to pull out the detonator. Fuses were coated in tar which would melt once the fuse was lit. This meant the fuse would continue to burn even if under water. Detonators were shock and heat sensitive so nail bombs were not carried around for any length of time. The detonator would only be fitted just before a bomb was to be thrown. They were only ever distributed to volunteers. When they exploded, they made a 'loud booming sound like a very big rocket at a firework display'.

Clarke went on to wreak destruction in Derry, and was convicted in Belfast of fourteen counts of causing explosions or possession of explosives during 1971 and 1972, including a bomb at the Guildhall in June 1972, and was sentenced to ten years. The damage to the city from internment in 1971 and June 1972 was estimated at £6 million. The following exchange between Clarke and prosecuting counsel reveals the feelings and rationalisation of their role among many of the IRA's engineers:

> Counsel: Did you know or care about the lethal potential of the various weapons?
> Clarke: I did not, no, I was not going to stand and start measuring out.
> Counsel: Did you really care about the risk to civilians?
> Clarke: Of course I did … We were not in the business of using people for cover; this is our community we are talking about. We were a fledgling organisation at the time. We relied on the people's support. If we had put people, our own people from the area at risk, we would not have lasted very long.[128]

'THE MOST SKILFUL AND PROLIFIC BOMB-MAKER
OF HIS GENERATION': DANNY MCNAMEE

Danny McNamee was convicted and sentenced to twenty-five years in Long Kesh for constructing the 1982 Hyde Park bomb, which killed four members of the Household Cavalry and seven horses. Two hours after the Hyde Park blast, a bomb fitted with a timer exploded underneath a bandstand at Regent's Park as the band of the Royal Green Jackets gave a lunchtime concert. Six soldiers were killed and a seventh died of his wounds two weeks later.

Prosecutors relied heavily on traces of McNamee's fingerprints found on remnants of the bomb and two other arms caches to convict him in 1987. His fingerprints were purportedly found on a tape taken from two arms caches. One print had been on the non-adhesive side of a piece of red tape wrapped around a motorcycle repair kit tin, which had been adapted into a radiowave encoder found in Pangbourne Woods in Berkshire in October 1983. Another was on the adhesive side of a piece of grey tape on part of a radio receiver discovered at Salcey Forest in Northants in January 1984. At the Old Bailey in 1987, the prosecution argued that a comparison between the Salcey Forest receiver and a fragment of the receiver recovered from the debris of the Hyde Park bomb showed twenty-four similarities and had been constructed by the same master bomber. McNamee's defence was that his prints may have been there because he worked in the manufacturing plant in Dundalk (Kimbles Manufacturing) for seven years where some of the parts were produced.[129] At his Hyde Park trial, McNamee took the unusual step of denouncing the IRA in an attempt to be acquitted.[130]

But following his release from Long Kesh in 1998 under the terms of the Good Friday Agreement, McNamee, who had consistently protested his innocence, appealed against his conviction and won. At his Court of Appeal hearing in December 1998, the judges accepted that it might have made a difference had jurors, who ruled the conviction was unsafe, known that many more prints from a known IRA bomb-maker were also on the bomb remains.[131]

Despite this, McNamee was reputed by the RUC to be 'the most skilful and prolific bomb-maker of his generation',[132] having been implicated in supplying bombs for the England campaign in the mid- to early 1980s, when small teams of bombers would cross the Irish Sea on specific bombing missions. As 'chief of PIRA's remote-control bomb technology group'[133] he was said by the RUC to have constructed a 227-kg (500-lb) radio-controlled bomb that blew up a British army major and two RUC officers at Cornoonagh Hill less than three months before his arrest. RUC files listed the suspected bomb-maker as 'D. McNamee, XMG, PIRA, EO [Explosives Officer] DOB 29 SEP '60'.[134]

The police have tried to link McNamee to IRA attacks that killed nineteen people in London, including six blown up by the Harrods bomb, between autumn 1981 and Christmas 1983. It is claimed his devices killed dozens in Northern Ireland and that his expertise covered radio-controlled, command-wire, booby trap, timer, incendiary and electronic devices.

McNamee had achieved no less than eleven O Levels and three grade As at A Level. Having been accepted for a Physics BSc at one of the world's leading centres of physics excellence, Imperial College London, he left after only a week – and because of the aptitude he showed for maths and science was persuaded by the IRA to continue at Queen's University Belfast with his studies in 1979, going straight into the second-year course. Indeed, the IRA sponsored much of McNamee's education at Queen's, where he attended electronics lectures while studying for his physics degree.[135] It was his electronics training that would be vital for IED construction. He was regarded as excessively conscientious for attending these extra lectures, and it is alleged he was trained in bomb-making during vacations. But it was probably due to these extracurricular activities that he failed his second-year course and eventually only managed a pass degree.[136]

'GO HIGHER UP THE SPECTRUM': RICHARD CLARK JOHNSON

The republican movement's long connection with the US was epitomised by Richard Clark Johnson – a Boston-based electronics engineer who worked for NASA on the Voyager and Shuttle space projects and had a high-level US government security clearance.[137] Johnson was the IRA's leading pioneer in radio-controlled devices, and had he not been caught, would have added high-tech systems, such as laser-activated anti-aircraft missiles, to the IRA's formidable arsenal.[138] He tried to move the Provisionals into light-based triggering systems, saying 'you have to go higher up the [electromagnetic] spectrum', but was compromised by the authorities' surveillance and knowledge of his activities throughout much of his time inventing weapons systems for the IRA.[139]

With an electronics engineering degree from the Catholic University in Washington, DC and an MSc from the University of Berkeley, California, Johnson had worked for the Northrop Corporation.[140] He then worked at the Mitre Corporation in Massachusetts on radar, electronic countermeasures, and electronic counter-countermeasures – a highly technical field that would be of great value in constructing advanced IEDs and other weapons systems – and which upgraded his security clearance from 'secret' to 'top secret'.[141] He was a high-level example of the many US-based IRA sympathisers with scientific and technical training who passed information on technical details in bomb-making to visiting IRA operatives – often in Irish pubs and other social gatherings in the US.[142]

Johnson's association with the IRA began when the Provos emerged in the 1970s, although it has not been established exactly why, other than the long American connection with the republican movement.[143] He was known as a social misfit, unmarried and with no friends outside work – probably what we would now call a 'geek' or a 'techie'. His early bomb-making experience was in radio-controlled IEDs, at a time when the original idea of using radio control mechanisms based on model toy boats and planes was proving to be liable to interference from other signals and from static. The RCIEDs could also be detonated by electronic sweeps conducted by the army.[144] The race was therefore on for the IRA to change frequencies in order to overtake army EOD countermeasures – a vital stage in the game of mutual assured disruption.

Enter Johnson: his talents first came to light when an EOD squad investigated a blast that blew up a vehicle checkpoint at Bessbrook near Newry. Part of an electronic switch used in the bomb – an FX401 tone frequency selector switch, operated on a frequency unique to North America and not used previously by the IRA – was traced back to a batch exported to the US by a UK company.

Johnson had bought the FX401s while working for the defence giant Northrop. He had incorporated the switches into an ingenious system he created that was based on a weather alert radio system activated by satellite.[145] He stated under questioning by the FBI that he used the switches for a prototype of a telephone-controlled burglar alarm and that they had not been forwarded to Ireland. But when further FX401s were discovered in unexploded devices in various sites, he had to admit he 'may have sent some to relatives in Ireland'.[146]

The IRA were also at the time developing plans in the United States to actually design and make their own anti-aircraft missiles – to bring down army helicopters. So along with Éamon McGuire, an electronics engineer who worked for Aer Lingus who had filled the breach left after Danny McNamee was jailed in 1987, and a US resident, Martin Quigley,[147] Johnson became involved in the technological challenges of surface-to-air systems.[148] Quigley and Maguire provided the explosives and detonator design expertise, and the team got as far as designing a radio-controlled rocket that could be fired from a 2-metre tube.[149] But Johnson was arrested in 1989 before this plan could come to fruition, following the British army investigation into the Bessbrook device's components and the FBI's suspicions resulting in constant surveillance of the team. Correspondence from Johnson to another Maguire was discovered, and phone calls intercepted, which involved the procurement of radio-controlled detonation and components.[150]

The phone calls revealed that Johnson had been asked to procure a new surface-to-air missile that could bring down army helicopters flying at 1,000-metre altitudes, and to solve the technical problem posed by designing a proximity fuse that could function at low altitudes.[151] Another Second World War invention, proximity fuse shells, enabled the blowing up of land targets at the most effective height above the ground rather than bursting upon impact. This increased the effectiveness of artillery shells by making them explode when in the proximity of an aircraft rather than having to score an actual hit – both to increase the effect of blast and to overcome the protection provided by foxholes and shallow trenches. The fuses work on the basis of built-in sensors, which may be radio, optical, acoustic or magnetic.[152]

Johnson recommended a radar-activated device but his contact Quigley – a Dundalk IRA man who was in the US to take a computing course – wanted to make small, home-grown versions. Johnson said in further eavesdropped meetings that such devices could be made from parts of radar detectors used to warn drivers of police radar guns in speed monitoring operations – and that he could do this in his parents' basement, with the help of supplies readily available from the Radio Shack US store chain. Such a detector, if attached to a detonator, would rely on the signal from a radar gun to set off a bomb.[153] Such a device killed an army ranger at a checkpoint at Cloghogue in October 1990.[154]

In April 1989 Johnson and Quigley got together in the basement lab for the latter to fabricate a surface-to-air missile – having begun work on two computer programs for the guidance system – with Johnson tasked with creating a proximity fusing system to enable devices to explode close to a flying aircraft. Also on the team was a thirty-nine-year-old studying for a PhD in mathematics, Gerald Hoy, whose job it was to calculate trajectories and burn-out rates, and another operative tasked with buying rocket motors. Quigley warned that recruiting such experts in electronics ran the risk of them being infiltrators, saying, pointedly: 'If you were to go out in the morning ... around all the different areas and say "right, I want a guy with some electronics experience, can you recommend somebody?" you might get ten guys but you can nearly bet your arse two of those guys will be put in there ... just to infiltrate ...'[155]

Johnson was being tailed and bugged during most of these encounters, with the FBI bungling one such attempt at bugging Johnson's car and being discovered.[156] There was also discussion of developing hyper-velocity missiles (this is so advanced that it has recently been claimed as a Russian means of countering US second-generation anti-ballistic missile defence systems) and laser detonation systems recommended by Johnson.[157] Army helicopters had been equipped to counteract SAM-7s and were capable of jamming them with infra-red jamming (see Chapter 9). They also carried chaff (which, when released, would deceive missiles fired to home in on the aircraft) and bafflers (to reduce the heat signature of the aircraft), together enabling the helicopters to fly at higher altitudes out of range of SAM attacks. All these measures, albeit in smaller form, are the stuff of ballistic missile defence.

But the FBI moved in before these plans came to fruition and every member of this particular IRA electronics division, except Maguire who had left for Dublin, was arrested. Johnson was sentenced to ten years in jail.[158] The FBI found an almost complete laser detonation system and parts – including an American FX401 switch – for the same weather radio alert system that had been found abandoned by the IRA in a shopping trolley in Armagh city.[159] They even found a shoulder-held rocket launcher prototype at Quigley's premises. Such was the IRA's engineering operations: part advanced technology, part ingenious improvisation – which would so often be ramshackle because of its covert nature; like nuclear proliferating nations, it had to constantly try to keep its bomb making – and concomitant R&D operations – top secret. But the Johnson–Maguire–Quigley trio proved that the IRA was reaching a level of advanced electronics expertise that, if unchecked, could have produced weapons seen only in the arsenals of the world's larger armed forces.[160]

'FORCED THE BRITISH ARMY OFF THE GROUND': ÉAMON MCGUIRE

Éamon McGuire used the deserts of Bahrain to test equipment for use in south Armagh. By day, he was a senior engineer with Aer Lingus, having joined the airline in 1978. In his spare time he bought equipment and designed bombs, landmines, rockets and technology to attack the British army in Northern Ireland's rural terrorist heartland.[161] He claims in his autobiography[162] that he and an IRA team 'forced the British army off the ground and into the air' in south Armagh. Following his extradition to the US in 1992, he was described by the CIA as the IRA's chief technical officer. 'The Americans would claim that I killed more than anyone else. I would accept that,' he said.[163]

McGuire was a trained aviation engineer who worked in countries that were extricating themselves from the last bonds of the British empire, such as Kenya and Malaysia. His mission was to keep ahead of the British army in terms of weapons and detection by procuring and designing systems. His activities forced him to go on the run, hiding in remote parts of Africa and eventually ending up in war-torn Mozambique. He was captured by the CIA in South Africa and subsequently spent several years in various prisons where he started to write his story.

After the outbreak of the Troubles in 1969, McGuire put his expertise at the disposal of the IRA. Working for Gulf Aviation in Bahrain, he tested equipment in the desert. 'You could put equipment on British Army communications bases to see how it stood up to bombardment,' he said. 'I used their communications and radiation systems to check out our gear against it.' He admitted indirect responsibility for the 1979 Warrenpoint attack. McGuire also says he was involved with the IRA bomb attacks in Britain in the early 1990s, even though he was in prison in the US. He also claimed that his biggest achievement was 'the capacity of farmers' sons in South Armagh particularly to adapt to new technology'.[164] 'Bombs constructed there were brought to London. I was involved in the evolution of the training and manufacturing to do that.'[165]

He was posted to the Bahamas and visited Florida, where technical components were produced. His aim was to work as closely as possible to the US – as the nexus of the high technology the IRA needed. But in 1989 one of his cohorts caught FBI agents putting a listening device into his car. This gave them enough evidence to wind up his activities. He then went on the run in Ireland and Africa, was betrayed in Mozambique and arrested by South African police, then extradited to the US and jailed.

STEPHEN CAMBRIDGE AND CIARAN CHAMBERS

Cambridge was one of the main IRA inventors within the Engineering Department, who developed many of the electronic and other higher-tech systems for the bombs. The Engineering Department was able to operate independently of the front-line organisation in Northern Ireland, especially once the five–six-member cell structure was established. Cambridge was a Dublin-based electronics engineer who worked in gaming machines, and provided the means to set bombs on long-delay timers and to construct radio-controlled devices that worked on various frequencies, as well as in light- and radar-initiated devices. Much of the innovations would arise – and this was a general rule in terms of IED development – because the IRA would demand that requirements should adapt to new strategic thinking in bomb deployment. Little is known about Cambridge but his mental health is said to have declined over the years.[166]

Ciaran Chambers was a Dublin bomb expert known particularly for his inventive timing and power units and particular wiring signature.[167] He was arrested at his flat in Ranelagh, Dublin, in November 1993 after gardaí found bomb-making equipment – components for IRA incendiary devices that were deployed in Northern Ireland in 1992, and similar to parts used in some of the major IRA bomb attacks in Britain over a three-year period from 1993 to 1996. He was given a seven-year prison sentence in November 1994 and was later released under the terms of the GFA.[168]

GABRIEL CLEARY

Dublin-born Gabriel Cleary became one of the most skilled IRA bomb-makers in the 1970s and 1980s. He rose rapidly through the ranks of the Engineering Department, to eventually become its head. His experience with Semtex-based devices made him the natural choice for placing precisely positioned Semtex charges on the Libyan vessel that carried a veritable arsenal of weapons, the *Eksund*, so as to scuttle the ship once the arms smuggling operation had been completed (described in Chapter 4). Four earlier shipments, carrying 150 tonnes of weapons and explosives (most notably, Semtex) had already been transported by the ship and transferred to IRA boats off Malta.

The fifth shipment was as great as the other four combined,[169] but the ship ran into engine trouble off the French coast and Cleary, fearing the mission was doomed, decided to scuttle the ship with the weapons cargo on board, the plan being to depart the ship in an inflatable dinghy (the IRA have never been into suicide missions). Cleary was particularly expert at precisely crafted explosive charges; they were put together in such a way that the explosions would not attract attention, but would sink the boat within seconds. But when he set about triggering the timing device and checked the charges, he saw to his horror that the operation had been sabotaged – the timing power unit (TPU) and wiring had been compromised beyond repair. The operation must have been known to the authorities.[170] As the TPU was found to be in perfect working order before Cleary set sail, and connected to detonators fixed into the Semtex slabs, the sabotage must have been carried out by someone on board. With no time to repair the TPU, which was an easily sabotageable bomb component, and a spotter plane circling overhead, Cleary had no option but to surrender when the authorities boarded the ship. The extent of the smuggling operation then became public.

'YOU GOT 18, WE GOT MOUNTBATTEN': TOMMY McMAHON

Tommy McMahon is best known for having made the bomb that killed Lord Louis Mountbatten on his yacht off Mullaghmore in 1979. He had already been behind a series of lethal land mine attacks against British troops in the early 1970s. He was arrested by gardaí only two hours or so after the attack with traces of ammonium nitrate and nitroglycerine on his clothes.[171] He received life imprisonment.

McMahon, a leading light in the South Armagh brigade, was one of the first IRA members to be sent to Libya to train with detonators and timing devices and became an expert in explosives. He later renounced his links with the IRA while serving his time in Mountjoy prison, Dublin.[172] The level of forgiveness for IRA bombers was seen at its height when John Maxwell, the father of a teenager who died in the Mountbatten explosion, publicly backed the Irish government's decision to free McMahon when he was released in August 1998 as part of the Good Friday Agreement. Maxwell said: 'Thomas McMahon has served his time and, if he is no longer a danger to society, then he should be released. Keeping him in prison will unfortunately not bring my son back.' He added that his son's killing could not be excused and when the innocent were deliberately killed, as in the Mountbatten assassination, those responsible were guilty of a crime against humanity. He summed up the bomb-maker's dilemma thus:

> Human beings have a great ability to rationalise their actions but I feel that the enormity of some of the acts carried out by both sides in the conflict here are such that at some point in their lives the perpetrators are bound to see, or perhaps only glimpse, the full horrific nature of their actions. If this is so then to have to live with such knowledge ... is arguably worse than being incarcerated.[173]

DEADLY PROLIFERATION

Attacks by the Real IRA following the Good Friday Agreement revealed that several Provisional members with bomb-making skills had left the Provos and become part of the breakaway hardline group. A large car bomb which blew up in Newtonhamilton, causing extensive damage, and a landmine attack two days earlier aimed at an army foot patrol, which featured a mobile phone remote detonation mechanism, indicated that the Engineering Department had haemorrhaged somewhat – and that several of its members had joined the quartermaster leader of the Real IRA, Michael McKevitt.[174] This was to result in the most deadly and probably the most terrible of all republican bomb attacks – the fertiliser bomb at Omagh on 15 August 1998 which killed twenty-nine people and injured hundreds more.

MI5 learned in the early 1990s that a senior IRA member in south Armagh was working to develop bombs triggered by light beams. IEDs being deployed by insurgents in Iraq today are combining a command wire, radio signal and infra-red beam in a technique which took the IRA twenty years to develop. Although the photographic flashgun unit (see the previous chapter on bomb technologies) was replaced with infra-red and then coded infra-red, they were variations of the same device. The proliferation of this technology and expertise by the IRA extended to the FARC guerrillas in Colombia, the Basque separatist group ETA and Palestinian groups. Among three republicans accused in 2005 of colluding with FARC guerrillas was Martin McCauley, who served a prison sentence for possessing weapons in the 1980s. Irish police regard McCauley as a leading figure in the Engineering Department – and Gabriel Cleary, featured on p.281, was the IRA's director of engineering in the mid-1980s.

It is also claimed that the IRA developed the infra-red beam devices based on technology supplied to an agent inside the Provisionals who was acting on behalf of the security forces as an infiltrator. The very same technology triggered a bomb that killed a policewoman and mutilated her male colleague near Newry before security countermeasures were in place.[175]

While the ceasefires and subsequent political agreements seemingly ended the bomb-making era of the IRA, it is – as with any similar situation of disarmament – pertinent to ask what has happened to all this expertise? Could it be regenerated, or redeployed for a future armed struggle or with movements elsewhere? The materials, to all intents and purposes, may have now been decommissioned, which is dealt with in the final chapter. But as you can never undo knowledge – unless those possessing it die without passing it on, which is highly unlikely in an age of mass communication – proliferation of that knowledge will remain a thorny problem for the IRA's disarmers and those tasked with antiterrorist operations throughout the world. The Real IRA still exist, although at greatly reduced strength, and with hardly any influence to speak of. But it would be complacent to assume that it's all over – and that the IRA's expertise has remained confined within the communities from which it was spawned.

NOTES

1. B. O'Brien, *The Long War: IRA and Sinn Féin* (2nd edition) (Syracuse, NY: Syracuse University Press, 1999), p.57.
2. Tommy McKearney, interview with the author, July 2007.
3. Personal communication, former Irish EOD operatives and Garda EOD expert, February 2007.
4. C. Ryder, *A Special Kind of Courage: 321 Squadron – Battling the Bombers* (London: Methuen, 2006), p.195.
5. Personal communication, Garda EOD operative, February 2007.
6. Tommy McKearney, interview with the author, July 2007.
7. Personal communication, former Irish army EOD operative, November 2007.
8. I tried without success to interview Patrick Magee and Shane Paul O'Doherty – the former not responding (probably due to my military connections) and the latter not found.
9. Personal communication, former Irish army EOD operative, November 2007.
10. Interview of IRA man in O'Brien, *The Long War*, p.41. Having knowledge of installing detonators in IEDs would, despite the ubiquitous nature of information these days, still be regarded as a rare skill.
11. O'Brien, *The Long War*, p.57.
12. IRA man quoted in ibid., p.56.
13. My Irish nanny had two battle-scarred aunts who had been in the original Women's IRA. I met them in my teens at her family functions and they are arguably the toughest women I have ever met!
14. L. Clarke and K. Johnston, *Martin McGuinness: From Guns to Government* (Edinburgh: Mainstream Publishing, 2006), p.49.
15. O'Brien, *The Long War*, p.57.
16. Clarke and Johnston, *Martin McGuinness*, p.49.
17. This deadly little device may be said to have added a new meaning to the definition of 'contraceptive'.
18. Clarke and Johnston, *Martin McGuinness*, p.83.
19. 'I am become Death, the Destroyer of Worlds', arguably the most noted quotation on the subject, attributed to J. Robert Oppenheimer, quoting Hindu scripture on seeing the fruits of his labours at the first atomic bomb test, 16 July 1945.
20. D. Sharrock and M. Devenport, *Man of War, Man of Peace? The Unauthorised Biography of Gerry Adams* (London: Macmillan, 1997), p.42, cited in R. English, *Armed Struggle: The History of the IRA* (London: Macmillan, 2003), p.132.
21. Quoted in K. Toolis, *Rebel Hearts: Journeys Within the IRA's Soul* (New York: St Martin's Press, 1995), p.105.
22. Ryder, *A Special Kind of Courage*, p.135.
23. IRA volunteer quoted in O'Brien, *The Long War*, p.40.
24. Toolis, *Rebel Hearts*, p.209.
25. Much has been written on the subject of forces, scientists and others involved in military or

repressive policies and the making of the means of destruction, by Hannah Arendt and others. R.J. Lifton and E. Markusen *The Genocidal Mentality, Nazi Holocaust and Nuclear Threat* (New York: Basic Books, 1991) is a prime example of this analysis: although dealing with far greater destruction – of whole races, and of the effects of Hiroshima and Nagasaki – and those involved, it explains in great detail how 'normal', bright people become involved – and either rationalise ('the end justifies the means, I haven't actually killed anyone') or enjoy their role ('isn't science exciting') in the machinery of death.

26. In O'Brien, *The Long War*, p.57. Again, this statement is redolent of results gleaned from the psychological experiments conducted by Stanley Milgram following the 1961 Eichmann trial. These revealed how 'ordinary people' could be capable of causing pain and injury to those they do not know, and were able to rationalise that they were 'only taking orders' from authority figures – despite seeing apparent pain and injury taking place before their very eyes. T. Blass, 'The Man Who Shocked the World', *Psychology Today* (March/April 2002).

27. Father Bradley quoted in Clarke and Johnston, *Martin McGuinness*, p.85.

28. T. P. Coogan, *The IRA* (revised edition) (London: HarperCollins, 1995), p.20.

29. Ibid., p.119.

30. English, *Armed Struggle*, p.63.

31. Coogan, *The IRA*, p.120.

32. Ibid., p.121.

33. G. McGladdery, *The Provisional IRA in England: The Bombing Campaign 1973–1997* (Dublin: Irish Academic Press 2005), p.37.

34. Coogan, *The IRA*, p.123.

35. Ibid., p.127.

36. Clarke and Johnston, *Martin McGuinness*, p.42 (this was most likely Shane Paul O'Doherty). Many a young chemist or physicist has done this and if dabbling in the materials on the premises could partially blow up the school lab in the process. Note that sulphuric acid would much later become a staple (and highly unstable) ingredient of the type of HME made by Islamic terrorists – triacetone triperoxide (TATP) – to attack the London underground and a bus on 7 July 2005. The IRA never used TATP but they did use sulphuric acid in the 'Durex bombs'.

37. Toolis, *Rebel Hearts*, p.304.

38. Various sources, including E. Moloney, *A Secret History of the IRA* (London: W.W. Norton & Co, 2002), p.115.

39. M. Davis, *Buda's Wagon: A Brief History of the Car Bomb* (London: Verso, 2007), p.4.

40. Families Acting for Innocent Relatives (FAIR), Co. Armagh, Republican Atrocities During the Troubles, http://www.victims.org.uk/eventsoftroubles.html

41. Moloney, *A Secret History of the IRA*, pp.115–17.

42. O'Brien, *The Long War*, p.165.

43. M. Urban, *Big Boys' Rules* (London: Faber & Faber, 1992), p.113.

44. Ibid., p.33.

45. Ryder, *A Special Kind of Courage*, p.188.

46. IRA instruction manual quoted in T. Geraghty, *The Irish War* (London: HarperCollins, 1990), p.85.

47. Geraghty, *The Irish War*, p.84.

48. Urban, *Big Boys' Rules*, p.112.

49. Ulster Intelligence and EOD sources.

50. In D. Morrison's book review of B. Murphy, *The Origins and Organisation of British Propaganda in Ireland 1920*, 8 July 2006, Campaign for Press and Broadcasting Freedom, and D. Morrison, 'British army strategy in '70s bears an uncanny parallel to Tan War propaganda', *Daily Ireland*, 29 March 2006.

51. 'Bomb Squad', Nova television documentary, US Public Broadcasting Service, PBS (Public Broadcasting Service) Airdate: 21 October 1997.

52. Urban, *Big Boys' Rules*, p.112.

53. O'Brien, *The Long War*, p.165.

54. Arnlis, 'Nature of Strategy, Politics, Revolution, British Withdrawal', *An Phoblacht*, 27 March 1976, cited in McGladdery, *The Provisional IRA in England*, p.105.

55. Toolis, *Rebel Hearts*, p.352.

56. T. Harnden, *Bandit Country* (London: Coronet, 1999), p.11.

57. T. Harnden, 'What now for the fighting men of Crossmaglen?', *Sunday Business Post*, 3 July 2005.

58. Harnden, *Bandit Country*, p.12.
59. Jimmy Canning, 'Taking the War to England', from an article by T. Harnden in the 'History' section of the *Ireland's Own* website, http://irelandsown.net
60. Moloney, *Secret History of the IRA*, p.441.
61. Ibid., p.443.
62. Interview (28 February 2002), cited in English, *Armed Struggle*, p.383.
63. R. Cowan, *Guardian*, 13 March 2003.
64. Ibid.
65. S. Breen, 'Old Bailey bomber ashamed of Sinn Féin,' *The Village*, 7 December 2004. http://www.villagemagazine.ie
66. Ibid.
67. D.M. Gould, 'Marian Price – A Real Republican', *Ireland's Own*: Women Freedom Fighters, http://irelandsown.net
68. Breen, 'Old Bailey bomber ashamed of Sinn Féin'.
69. S.P. O'Doherty, *The Volunteer* (London: HarperCollins, 1993), pp.197–8.
70. Peter Gurney interviewed by Peter Taylor, BBC TV documentary, 'The Hunt for the Brighton Bomber', 2004.
71. Personal communication, Garda EOD operative, March 2008.
72. Ibid.
73. Ibid.
74. J. Wilson, 'Brighton bomber thinks again', *Guardian*, 28 August 2000.
75. Personal communication, Garda EOD operative, March 2008.
76. Wilson, 'Brighton bomber thinks again'.
77. Cited in English, *Armed Struggle*, p.382.
78. Patrick Magee, in 'Facing the Enemy', BBC Everyman TV documentary, BBC 2001.
79. 'Patrick Magee: The IRA Brighton bomber', BBC News, 22 June 1999.
80. E. Mallie and D. McKittrick, *Endgame in Ireland* (London: Coronet, 2002), p.20.
81. Brighton bomb: filming forgiveness, BBC News, 13 December 2001.
82. Ibid.
83. While loyalist prisoners traditionally spent their time in jail doing body-building, Magee followed the oft-trod republican route of studying.
84. P. Magee, *Gangsters or Guerrillas? Representations of Irish Republicans in 'Troubles Fiction'* (Belfast: Beyond the Pale Publications, 2001). A fascinating work, and having read or seen movies of most of the works he cites as being biased against Irish republicans, I mostly concur. But he skips over mention of IRA military activities, bomb-making, and there is only an occasional hint at what he did time for.
85. Magee interview (5 March 2002), in English, *Armed Struggle*, p.384.
86. Magee interviewed by Peter Taylor, BBC TV documentary, 'The Hunt for the Brighton Bomber', 2004.
87. L. Clarke and K. Johnston, 'Paddy Flood', *Ireland's Own*: History, http://www.irelandsown.net
88. Clarke and Johnston, *Martin McGuinness*, p.205.
89. Toolis, *Rebel Hearts*, p.216.
90. Ibid., p.215.
91. Ibid., p.207.
92. Clarke and Johnston, *Martin McGuinness*, p.204.
93. Toolis, *Rebel Hearts*, p.217.
94. Personal communication, Ulster Intelligence operative, April 2007.
95. Toolis, *Rebel Hearts*, pp.216–18.
96. Ibid., pp.229–30.
97. 'Bomb unauthorised says IRA', *Guardian*, 19 December 1983.
98. BBC News, 'On This Day', 17 December 1983.
99. Said to Charlie Coogan in Clarke and Johnston, *Martin McGuinness*, p.199.
100. O'Doherty, *The Volunteer*, p.69.
101. S.P. O'Doherty on 'Bomb Squad'.
102. O'Doherty, *The Volunteer*, p.69.
103. O'Doherty on 'Bomb Squad'.
104. Ibid.
105. Ibid.
106. O'Doherty, *The Volunteer*, p.72.

107. Ibid., p 79.
108. Ibid.
109. O'Doherty on 'Bomb Squad'.
110. O'Doherty, *The Volunteer*, p.198.
111. Ibid., p.82.
112. Ibid., p.135.
113. Ibid., p.134.
114. Ibid., p.142.
115. Ibid., p.154.
116. Ibid., p.161.
117. Ibid., p.167.
118. Ibid., p.168.
119. Ibid., p.176.
120. Ibid., p.177.
121. Ibid., p.155.
122. Clarke and Johnston, *Martin McGuinness*, p.98.
123. O'Doherty, *The Volunteer*, p.214.
124. Ibid., p 82.
125. Milgram conducted experiments in which ordinary US citizens were asked to deliver electric shocks to subjects being asked questions. If the subjects got the questions wrong, these observers were asked to deliver increasingly powerful shocks to those being questioned, who were actually actors being given fake shocks. To the horror of the experimenters, most of the ordinary citizens increased the voltage they approved to be administered (by men in white coats) even beyond lethal levels. The point here, as in Arendt's seminal work on the 1961 Eichmann trial, is the 'ordinariness' of 'nice middle-class' educated people who are capable of inflicting pain and murder simply on orders, or for a mission, or for an ideology, or because they think it is the right thing to do. Not that O'Doherty was the epitome of evil, despite his actions – I am referring here more to the reactions of observers at his trial to his level of education and 'normalness'. See S. Milgram, *Obedience to Authority* (London: Tavistock Publications, 1974) and H. Arendt, *Eichmann in Jerusalem: A Report on the Banality of Evil* (revised edition) (Gloucester, MA: Smith, 1994). Also for an insight into the psychology behind bomb-making on a WMD scale, see R.J. Lifton and E. Markusen, *The Genocidal Mentality* (London: Macmillan, 1990).
126. Bloody Sunday enquiry, Week 111, 8–11 December 2003.
127. Ibid.
128. Ryder, *A Special Kind of Courage*, p.68.
129. Danny McNamee, in L. Ó Comain, 'The Belfast Agreement – An Alternative', *Ireland's Own: History*.
130. Ibid.
131. 'Man wins bomb appeal', BBC News, 17 December 1998.
132. Harden, *Bandit Country*, p.331.
133. Ibid., p.365.
134. Ibid., p.331.
135. Ibid., p.332.
136. Ibid., p.333.
137. Ibid., p.356.
138. USA v. Richard Clark Johnson et al.: 89-CR-221-MA, MIPT (Memorial Institute for the Prevention of Terrorism) Knowledge Base http://www.tkb.org/CaseHome.jsp?caseid=349
139. Personal communication, former Irish army EOD operative, November 2007,
140. Harnden, *Bandit Country*, p.362.
141. Ibid., p.363.
142. Personal communication, former Irish army EOD operative, November 2007,
143. As detailed in Jack Holland's book of the same name – *The American Connection* (New York: Viking Penguin, 1987).
144. Harnden, *Bandit Country*, p.362.
145. Ibid., p.356.
146. Ibid., p.363.
147. Urban, *Big Boys' Rules*, p.128.
148. Moloney, *Secret History of the IRA*, p.32.

149. Urban, *Big Boys' Rules*, p.128.
150. Harnden, *Bandit Country*, p.365.
151. Ibid., p.366.
152. Dr William T. Moye, 'Developing the Proximity Fuze, and Its Legacy', US Army Material Command Historical Office, 19 February 2003.
153. Harnden, *Bandit Country*, p.367.
154. Ibid.
155. Ibid., p.369.
156. Ibid., p.372.
157. Ibid., p.370.
158. USA v. Richard Clark Johnson et al.
159. Harnden, *Bandit Country*, p.372.
160. Johnston was arguably, according to former Irish EOD operatives, the most advanced of the IRA engineers.
161. *Sunday Times*, 8 October 2006. Burns & Moley Sinn Féin Cumann, south Armagh, http://www.burnsmoley.com/pages/archive/eamon.php
162. Review by W. Hughes of E. McGuire, *Enemy of the Empire: Life as an International Undercover IRA Activist* (O'Brien Press, 2006), *The Blanket*, 26 October 2006.
163. Burns & Moley Sinn Féin Cumann, south Armagh.
164. Review of E. McGuire, *Enemy of the Empire: Life as an International Undercover IRA Activist* (O'Brien Press Ltd, 2006), W. Hughes, *The Blanket*, 26 October 2006.
165. Review by W. Hughes of E. McGuire, *Enemy of the Empire*.
166. Personal communication, former Irish army EOD operative, November 2007, who also said Cambridge was among the most highly skilled of the IRA engineers.
167. Personal communication, former Irish army EOD operative, February 2008.
168. B. Carroll, 'Balcombe Street gang moved to Portlaoise - Provos freed from jail as part of peace dividend', *Irish News*, 30 April 1998.
169. Moloney, *Secret History of the IRA*, p.3.
170. Ibid., p.6.
171. Harnden, *Bandit Country*, p.205.
172. 'IRA prisoners released for Christmas', BBC News, 23 December 1997.
173. R. O'Reilly, 'Victim's father backs IRA release', *Independent*, 8 August, 1998.
174. Harnden, *Bandit Country*, p.436.
175. G. Harkin, F. Elliott, R. Whitaker, 'Revealed: IRA bombs killed eight British soldiers in Iraq', *Independent*, 15 April 2007.

Nine

The Countermeasures Arms Race and the 'Long Walk'

It was cold and lonely. Christ, was it lonely! But then it always is whenever you're approaching a bomb for the final attack. It's cold and lonely even at noon on a hot summer's day.
Lt Col George Styles, GC, British army EOD operative[1]

To go up against the best IRA units in south Armagh, it's an extremely brave job ... To go in there for not a very great wage and for a very scant thanks from the community, and risk your life over some of the best devices that the IRA ever did plant and try and defuse them – I mean, you know, they've got unbelievable courage.
... And a lot of people in the IRA would have no trouble at all saluting the courage of these people, because I mean, it must be one of the bravest things that a human being can take on, to take on a bomb.
Shane Paul O'Doherty, former IRA bomb-maker[2]

It was the best job in the world. It was like a drug, you got a high from it.
Maj. Roger Davies, former commander, 321 Squadron[3]

So far this account has focused on the ways the IRA conducted its military campaign; how weapons were acquired and adapted for the Provisionals' missions; how the multitude of improvised explosive devices were built, and by whom; what and who they were targeted at; and the effects of their use. This chapter will deal with the saving, rather than the taking, of life – how the British army and security and intelligence services met the challenges of the IRA's evolving modus operandi; how missions and the weapons to conduct them were intercepted; and how the bombs were dealt with.

From 1970 to the end of the Provisional IRA bombing campaign, there were 54,000 EOD call-outs. Of these, in Northern Ireland alone, some 19,000 explosions and incendiary attacks took place (which included the other paramilitaries), and some 50 tonnes of explosives detonated or neutralised in another 6,300 incidents.[4] The countermeasures amounted to the longest campaign ever conducted by the British army. The examples of extreme bravery in dealing with the IEDs – which, as we have seen, were often booby trapped – are too many to document here, but I have endeavoured to include some notable ones. Some twenty EOD (explosive ordnance disposal) officers died in the process of their work.

There is also a limit to which the detail of countermeasures can be described so as not to contravene current legislation that restricts the description of 'operational specifics' in accounts of security operations, and also to protect those who were involved, and those who are now involved in similar operations.

Countermeasures can be divided into two main efforts. First, attempts were made to pre-empt attacks through intelligence, which was often obtained through the use of informers, either as infiltrators of the republican movement or from members of the republican community; surveillance, which became increasingly sophisticated and pervasive; and raids on weapons and explosives which would not only reduce the capability of the IRA but reveal details of their methods.

Second is dealing with the devices and the technologies and methods involved in making the bombs. Dismantling bombs before they go off nearly always provides invaluable information about the 'trademarks' of a bomb maker's craft and how the devices are put together. Finding weapons caches was another vital means to keep up, and often to overtake the IRA's progress: these finds not only revealed evidence of forthcoming operations, but also provided the opportunity for the security forces to 'spike' the materials so that they wouldn't work. Some of these examples can be found in open-source material, but the majority are not to be revealed.

The IRA pitted their wits against one of the world's best equipped armies, one that had at its disposal weapons such as SA80 assault rifles[5] and armoured vehicles, as well as advanced means of control, command, communication and intelligence (C3I), and still managed to overtake both the army and one of the most heavily armed police forces in the world, equipped with the most up-to-date anti-terrorist equipment. No sooner, however, did the security forces discover a particular method of building and setting an IED – which proceeded at a frantic pace once the Provisionals' campaign of the early 1970s got under way – but the Provos caught up and overtook their enemy.

ARMS RACE

This turned into an arms race of unprecedented proportions in the history of insurrection within peacetime. The IRA's methods increased in sophistication and lethality to the point of – most certainly in the 1970s – the potential to mount a campaign using weapons of mass effect. Although 'own goals' were prevalent in the early days of the Troubles, when the Provisionals were on a learning curve in terms of bomb-making and deployment, their ability to adapt and use what they had to hand meant the race to keep up with improvisation, and the sheer number of devices used soon dispelled any notions of 'stupid Paddy' that had prevailed in the past.[6]

The British army's ammunition technical officers (ATOs) were the experts responsible for defusing IRA explosive devices in buildings and cars and for destroying by controlled detonation those impossible to dismantle. This contest with the terrorists could be won only on a day-to-day basis. Patterns of strategy and tactics emerged, which became the hallmarks of the IRA campaign. Bombs often came in twos, and in close proximity. The first, despite called-in warnings, would often take life and injure anyone who got in the way. The second would be targeted at the very people sent in to respond to the first – in the first decade of the IRA campaign, this would be on foot, with only special suits, shields and gloves for protection. Thus the first bomb came to be called a 'come-on'.[7]

Different targets required different types of bombs. The 'city destroyers' – usually huge car bombs – were aimed at destroying the property, high-profile buildings and economy of Northern Ireland and of Britain itself. The variety of bomb types and the sheer number of devices deployed led to the British EOD squads becoming the world's best, and this great skill has continued beyond the IRA ceasefire into the present-day nightmare of Islamicist terrorism and insurgency in Iraq and Afghanistan, where the pace of IED attacks, and the changes in materials and mechanisms, is relentless.

As mentioned earlier, the IRA would bring in a specific type of device and deploy it up to, say, three times. Then the model type would be discontinued, sometimes for no apparent reason; it was believed that a form of 'corporate amnesia' had set in.[8] This may have been because, as a covert group developing technologies in several locations at once, the IRA was not always able to consolidate and co-ordinate manual-based models of bombs in order to keep developments covert. The 'organic' development of device types could also have been a basic response to availability of bomb components, ingredients and the necessary people to put the devices together – meaning that improvisation was constant in order to keep the authorities on the hop.

The security measures put in place proved to be extremely costly. After the Baltic Exchange bomb in 1992, vast sums were spent in the City of London to safeguard high-value premises and install the 'ring of steel' surveillance and vehicle search system, while companies had to shell out for enormous insurance premiums. The threat to the infrastructure of London's financial heart had never been greater and the Provisionals proved that they could further cripple it.

INTELLIGENCE AND SURVEILLANCE

The IRA campaign in turn produced ever-increasingly sophisticated countermeasures. Surveillance methods were refined, and the technologies used to monitor operatives and the communities which sheltered them enhanced. West Belfast became one of the world's most intensely patrolled sectors; the sound of British army helicopters was forever in the air, with bases and observation posts, equipped with increasingly complex means of spying on the population, to be found everywhere in the nationalist areas.[9] Housing estates were patrolled constantly by armoured vehicles which could withstand rocket attacks (which the IRA later tried).

Sensors were deployed that could record movements near the homes of suspects; cameras at borders could also be used to record illicit activities without the need for staff to be sent on covert operations.[10] Gazelle helicopters were deployed by the army air corps with cameras to conduct constant surveillance over Belfast and republican areas of the province; republican funerals, for example, were highly visible events attended by leading IRA people, who would be observed and sometimes apprehended.[11]

Airborne surveillance, using infra-red imaging, was used to find deployed bombs. Old spotter planes rather than helicopters were used, as the sensitive equipment on board would not work on a bumpy helicopter ride. Command-wire bombs were particularly targeted for such observation, and later sophisticated thermal imaging equipment was deployed, which could produce high-quality images miles from the objects being observed.

These draconian and highly sophisticated surveillance operations had a substantial effect on the IRA and the nationalist community of Northern Ireland. The 'vast array of spy-posts bristling with antennae and communications masts, listening devices … behind this visible presence there is always the frightening level of undercover and covert sur- veillance ... the bugging of cars and open locations in republican strong- holds' was one of numerous responses in *An Phoblacht*. This spying apparatus meant that IRA operations had to be more carefully planned than ever, which consumed sparse and variable resources.

Major attacks were prevented by intelligence operations, among the most notorious being the thwarting of the IRA's attempts to bomb Gibraltar, where an ASU (active service unit) had been sent to car-bomb the governor's official residence during a parade. The target was delib- erately chosen to expose weak defence on what was one of the few remaining British colonial strongholds. The operation was well known to British intelligence, which had installed a substantial number of watchers to trail the ASU. The Gibraltar police knew about the opera- tion but did not know that three members of the ASU would be shot as they were leaving the colony, by the SAS on 6 March 1988.[12]

What was little known at the time of the shootings was that a simul- taneous intelligence operation was under way in Belgium, where the UK Foreign Minister Sir Geoffrey Howe was due to attend an EU/NATO meeting, and was targeted for assassination by the IRA – by a remote- controlled car bomb that would have been detonated as the Howe car passed by. Having been tipped off by British intelligence, the car failed to turn up. But the unusual factor in the operation was the British non- notification of the situation to Belgian authorities – as the operation was occurring at the same time as the Gibraltar one, with the targeted IRA personnel on the island having been part of the Howe plot. The British authorities preferred to show off Prime Minister Thatcher's capability in pre-empting a major IRA operation in the British colony.[13]

THE USE OF INFORMERS

This constant watching, together with the RUC's experience gained over decades of recruiting informers – a constant source of undermining of the republican insurrectionist movement throughout Irish history – meant that taking up arms against the British was not only highly risky, but could be so short-lived as to land many in jail before their objectives could be achieved. There are innumerable examples of informers but only a few examples can be cited here.

The Derry brigade is cited as notoriously prone to informers – 'touts' – including at least one Volunteer who turned 'supergrass' and informed on his comrades, providing accurate information leading to seventy arrests and 180 charges made, including possession of arms and explosives.[14]

Many informers were blackmailed or threatened in ways that forced them to betray their colleagues. This weakness within the movement persisted until the late 1980s – after a decade of what has been called the 'dirty war', in which the British used methods that would have been classed as illegal and which will be dealt with later in this chapter. Operations went wrong or had to be aborted; bombs failed to explode; volunteers were pre-empted before they could carry out bombings; and as many as seventy-six arms dumps were seized in one year alone, 1987, sixty-six in 1988 and more than sixty in 1989.[15]

Some of the informers sabotaged bombs – including some of the bomb-makers themselves (Gerard Flood being a prime example – see Chapter 8).[16] A number of these operatives were encouraged by the police to sign up as explosives officers. Flood was one such, who assembled bombs in safe houses and became Derry's top bomb-maker. In this elevated role, he would have access to secrets and could bypass the internal cell structure in working with the city's ASUs.[17] Some operations that went badly wrong – such as the 'good neighbours' bomb, were also such an embarrassment that the IRA would not reveal the reason why.

Even long after the ceasefires and the Good Friday Agreement, IRA bombs that had been the result of such interference rose from the ashes like the movement's phoenix emblem: it was revealed in 2005 that eight British soldiers killed during ambushes in Iraq were the victims of bombs triggered by infra-red beams, which were first developed by the IRA using technology passed on by the security services in a botched 'sting' operation in the early 1990s as part of the counter-terrorism strategy. It is claimed that the firing devices, based on photographic flash units (see Chapter 6), were used after the Provisionals were given advice by British agents. One trigger used in an Iraqi bombing in 2005 was a three-way device, combining a command wire, a radio signal and an infra-red beam – a technique perfected by the IRA. Army intelligence learned in the early 1990s that a senior IRA member in South Armagh brigade – the heart of the IRA's R & D and bomb-making activities – was working to develop bombs triggered by light beams.[18]

The alarming message from such an operation is the claim that the devices were supplied by the security services to an agent inside the Provisionals – a hallmark of the 'dirty war' between the intelligence services and the IRA which reached a peak in the 1980s. Much of this passing of information – and disinformation – was carried out by an undercover unit, the Force Research Unit, and MI5. But becoming intimate with IRA technology meant that the security forces could develop countermeasures, and thereby keep one step ahead of the IRA. If that meant supplying technology to the organisation, this was one way of doing it. Back then, it was not thought that this technology would be used to kill British soldiers in a future war.

One such example was described by George Styles, in which the army put out an official release about a bombing, giving the poundage of the bomb as far lower than its true weight. IRA operatives were in a bar and were heard to say: 'That stupid army always gets it wrong. Sure and don't we know the bomb was 57 lbs because we carted it up there.'[19] The misinformation was given out and eavesdropped with the knowledge that some IRA volunteers would be more loose-tongued and wanting to thus proclaim the power of their weapons after an action.[20]

The change from the old IRA army structure of companies and battalions to a centralised system tightly controlling covert small cells would lay the organisation open to infiltration by informers. This was because one infiltrator would be at the heart of the organisation and know what was going on in several operations. Big IRA operations would be compromised, such as an ambush on a large British army checkpoint by a single flying column on the border between Co. Fermanagh and Co. Monaghan, in December 1989. Although the attack – involving a truckload of IRA men using automatic rifles, heavy machine-guns, grenades and a flamethrower (believed to be the only use of such a weapon by the IRA)[21] – resulted in the deaths of two soldiers, a 180-kg (400-lb) car bomb that had been primed was abandoned when the IRA column was scared off by the arrival of a Wessex helicopter. The bomb did not explode and it turned out that the detonating mechanism had been tampered with.

The operational information for the attack had been shared with Northern Command – that is, outside of the tight circle of its original planners.[22] It would be the last flying column-style attack and the extent of infiltration, coming as it did after the *Eksund* interception, was so serious that it appeared that the British were at last winning the 'long war'. Much was accomplished in the late 1980s and beyond due to huge increases in spending on intelligence operations, which included recruitment of IRA-infiltrating spies.

By the early years of the twenty-first century, the informer crisis came out into the open with the revelation of a high-ranking IRA officer having spied for the British: the infamous 'Stakeknife' (or 'Steaknife') – whose penetration was so deep that many operations that resulted in fatalities were allowed to go ahead under this watch so as to protect his cover. While this exposure of infiltration of the IRA by the authorities exposed the moral and political expediency of the British, it did far more damage to the IRA – showing up as it did the extent of the informer problem. Stakeknife was said to have operated for twenty years, which would have covered the bulk of the IRA campaign in Northern Ireland and the mainland. Information he had access to included operatives' names; methods; equipment and procurement; explosives and expertise; and how the IRA structure evolved during the period.[23] It is said that he got far enough inside the organisation as to assist in the compromising by his British handlers of the IRA's explosives inventory – from 1986 onwards. The move toward political compromise in the 1980s and early 1990s – so controversial among the Provisionals' rank and file – could now be put down to the damage wrought by this infiltrator.

SEIZING THE WEAPONS

Before having to dismantle deployed devices, the security forces raided and seized IRA weapons and explosives. Many dozens of raids, too numerable to detail, were carried out by authorities in the north and south of Ireland. So-called 'blind' raids were often successful. These opportunistic raids were based on intelligence gathered by local units, which would spot a street that was normally very quiet – a 'vacuum' area where there were no riots or other incidents that would attract attention, but would be concealing Provisional activities. The street would give away its secrets when a warning signal was given that troops were approaching – such as the clashing of dustbin lids or, less well known, the hanging of a pair of coloured knickers on a washing line of white clothes! Based on such signals, troops would carry out their arms raid.[24]

Many raids were conducted based on border and coast patrols. An example of a successful seizure resulting from a patrol was in 1970, when the RUC led by a Captain Brazier spotted boxes floating on the incoming tide at St John's Point, Co. Down. On inspection, they were found to contain gelignite – and the boxes themselves actually mines that would have contained nails. The embryo mines were made in the Republic to be smuggled on a ship bringing supplies to lighthouses in the North. They had been landed, but the smugglers had miscalculated the tides – so that the boxes of mines ended up flowing away on a rising tide into the arms of the authorities, rather than being picked up in a quiet secret cove.[25] The IRA would, however, show initiative in making seizures difficult and hazardous. This was exemplified in the packing of explosives into the tail of shotguns that, if seized, had to be x-rayed before they could be handled.[26]

Arguably the most significant of arms seizures was the capture by French customs authorities of the *Eksund*, the coaster bound from Libya loaded with 150 tonnes of weapons and explosives in autumn 1987 (see

Chapter 4). Many earlier shipments had got through, which had, over the preceding year, aroused the attention of various intelligence agencies. By the time of the *Eksund* seizure, the IRA already had an oversupply of arms, but the impact of the loss of the *Eksund* cargo – itself as large as the four previous arms shipments – apart from robbing the Provisionals of a heightened capability for insurrectionist warfare, also deprived them of the element of surprise.[27]

The betrayal of the IRA in receiving the *Eksund* was realised by its skipper and the IRA's director of engineering,[28] Gabriel Cleary, who – knowing that the ship was being observed constantly by RAF spotter aircraft and was drifting closer to the French coast due to steering malfunction – decided to scupper the ship by exploding Semtex charges after he and the crew had escaped in an inflatable dinghy to the northern French coast. But he discovered that the timing and power unit (TPU) for the explosives had been sabotaged. A traitor had given away the *Eksund* plans to the British. Cleary came to this conclusion after the ship had left Tripoli, as he had checked the TPU when they had set sail and it was working to plan.

The interception of the *Eksund*, apart from bringing worldwide media coverage to the IRA's failure with the attendant embarrassment of betrayal and infiltration, laid bare the details of the arms smuggling operation, links to Libya – then an arch 'rogue state' – and previous gun-running operations. But it also revealed the extent of the IRA's arsenal.

The loss of the *Eksund* had serious consequences for the Provisional IRA. It dissipated its ability to surprise the authorities and it removed from the arsenal potentially devastating weapons such as mortars that could have been used from safe distances against army barracks and RUC stations, and 106-mm cannons that would have sunk boats in Belfast harbour, thereby blocking dock access, and Royal Navy boats patrolling on Carlingford Lough. The ship's seizure also meant the cancellation of a major offensive planned to provoke a return to internment of IRA suspects – and hence drive up recruitment and support for the IRA campaign. Other plans involved a resurgence of the flying columns in border areas and the main towns of Northern Ireland.[29] While some high-ranking IRA people felt this major offensive was not within their capabilities – believing that it would have needed more than just heavy weaponry but a level of successful intelligence and organisation that may have been unachievable – nevertheless any major boost to the overall IRA mission had been thwarted.

And it was not just disruption to the weapons deployment plans that had taken place. The structure of the IRA took a bashing due to the subsequent all-out hunt by the authorities for the earlier shipments. It was then believed that the move towards a tighter cell structure and the ASUs introduced in the early 1980s had made the organisation more prone to infiltration even than the old, looser army-style battalion and company structure.[30]

Judging by the effect the later City of London bombs had, the influx of the *Eksund*'s haul would have at least enabled a push to bigger and more adventurous attacks. Intercepting, locating, moving or interfering with weapons dumps went on after the 1990s ceasefires, as did the interdiction around these points in time of undeployed IEDs, in which real detonators would be replaced with dummy detonators.

BUGGING THEM …

Airborne surveillance, using infra-red imaging, was used to find arms dumps. Aerial photography from helicopters was a prevalent method used to observe the movement of weapons from dumps or the creation of new dumps. When a new dump was discovered, the army would install tiny transmitters inside the guns and bomb-making materials which would monitor the movements of anyone who purloined them, with later devices incorporating microphones to listen in. Once an arms dump was located, the Weapons Intelligence Units (WPUs) and SAS would 'jark' the weapons – install surveillance devices on them to track and apprehend their users.[31] Items located in the arms caches, which were often in remote areas, had to be bugged without the IRA knowing. Photographs of a cache would be taken to ensure that the WPU knew exactly what was stored in case IRA operatives removed weapons. Sometimes the Provisionals discovered the bugs, which would lead to the outing and punishment, often death, of an informer who had aided the army in locating the cache. This would give the IRA the advantage insofar as informers were uncovered. But the enormous technical resources of the British would be constantly put to work in refining the bugging devices so that they were increasingly difficult or impossible to uncover by the weapons' users.[32] But there were limitations; a monitoring station had to be situated close to a weapons cache, as the monitoring instruments planted inside the weapons were of short range only. The jarking period was also limited to the battery life of the devices used.[33]

… AND TAMPERING WITH THEM

The number of ways to render weapons and bomb-making materials harmless, like the surveillance methods, reached a peak in the 1980s.

Sometimes the IRA thought that the failure of bombs to go off properly may be put down to poor ordnance – but there was, increasingly throughout the 1980s, uncertainty as to whether that was the cause or because an informer had enabled the materials to be spiked. But when it was certain that an item, say a gun, had been tampered with, the IRA would have to launch its own counterintelligence operation to find out the source of betrayal. A noted example of this was when a couple living on a Belfast housing estate were 'turned' by special branch (using a common form of blackmail, in promising non-prosecution of petty crimes). Having allowed the IRA to store weapons in their house, the couple – who were being paid £20 a week by special branch – then allowed branch technical experts to come in and spike selected weapons. They were uncovered by the Provisionals, who shot them both.[34]

Several bomb attempts are now known to have been due to tampering with the materials. One such was the attempt to blow up Hammersmith Bridge, on 24 April 1996, with two of the biggest Semtex bombs (17 kg apiece) ever planted on the mainland. Although the detonators went off, the main charges failed to explode, as they had been 'doctored'.[35] Bomb tampering was also believed to be behind the premature explosion of a bomb carried on a London bus by a twenty-one-year-old Volunteer, Ed O'Brien, on 18 February 1996,[36] which killed him but no others. This 'own goal' and the subsequent uncovering of two IRA 'bomb factories' in London indicated that further penetration by the security forces had occurred.

DISARMING THE BOMBS

EOD training and procedures

To qualify for duty in Northern Ireland, British army operatives had to pass one of the world's most rigorous bomb disposal training courses, and which has had one of the highest failure rates in the British army. The course includes knowledge of terrorist tactics, which is vital in making threat assessments at the scene of UXO (unexploded ordnance). The British army set up its own bomb-making units, creating IEDs to exact terrorist specifications and using real circuits and fake explosive to test the skills of the EOD officers who would have to defuse them – rapidly. Making the devices you will have to disarm is a vital way to stay on top of the many technical advances in their complexity, and the great variety of ways in which they can be constructed.

The early methods of response were as improvised as some of the devices the EOD squads had to encounter. Much depended on the sheer skill, bravery, and luck of the EOD operators. When the first EOD squads were sent to deal with bombs in Northern Ireland, their main assets were 'an iron nerve, a steady hand'[37] – and a long, green tool chest containing a stencil kit (for drawing bomb diagrams), brushes, hammers, crowbars, and a selection of drills, screwdrivers, knives, scalpels, fishing hooks and lines, rubber gloves, an electronic stethoscope (for detecting a ticking timer), a Plasma arc cutting torch, liquid nitrogen and a 300-kv x-ray machine with trailer-mounted generator – a cumbersome piece of kit which some operators did not employ.[38]

Later more sophisticated techniques using modern electronics and electrical detonators required the British army to produce intricate countermeasures. Before then, the IRA developed a simple electrical circuit, normally consisting of a battery and a timer. The electrical circuit enabled the operative to deliver it hours or days before he wanted it to go off, and – of great significance for his survival – he could be well away from the area when that happened.

An example of a horrendous scenario that would face EOD people was the IRA hostage bomb, in which the Provos would tie a hostage into a van loaded with explosives and order him to drive to an army barracks. To teach soldiers how to deal with such incidents, exercises were staged to test their ability to assess hidden danger. Similarly vile was the booby trapping of corpses of IRA-targeted victims, such as when, in April 1972, a UDR part-time corporal, James Elliott, was abducted and shot, then his body booby trapped, with red and black wires leading from his body to a milk churn device planted across the border. The ATO seeking out the trap discovered a further six milk churns each containing 45 kg (100 lb) of gelignite – and more: four 5-kg Claymore mines were found that had been intended for any survivors of the initial gelignite blast.[39]

A method to test the skills of the trainees involved a radio receiver wired up to a boot full of homemade explosives. A cable for the receiver ran around the back and joined up with the bomb from the front and onto the detonator. A hostage was strapped in the car. There was no time to put on a protective suit or send in a remote-control robot. In this situation, as the IRA was well aware, the bomb disposal man had to risk his own life to save the victim. If the car was booby trapped, pulling the door open might set off the bomb. He would search for the detonator, looking for a small thin tube of explosive which sets off the main charge and forms the vital link between the electronic circuit and the bags of explosive. By cutting it out, he could reduce the immediate risk, but there could still be secondary devices concealed in the car. The trainee would then find a wire connected to the driver's door. If opened, it could set off an explosive charge, so he would let the hostage out the other side of the car. Once the area was clear, the crew could send in a remote-control robot to finish off the job.[40]

CAT AND MOUSE

The IRA's bombing campaign instigated a deadly game of cat-and-mouse that became the ultimate war of nerves, with the bottom line being one man against the bomb – with booby trap mechanisms and means of disguise to make the dismantler's job infinitely harder. The approach an EOD operative makes to an IED is often described as the 'long walk': he gets so close to the bomb his body armour cannot save him. Beyond this point, only his training and experience will protect him.[41]

The bombing campaign was intended to strike a careful balance. While the main aim was to destroy and damage property, take out troops and police and create a constant level of apprehension, killing too many people would seriously threaten the cause – as often occurred after bombings such as Abercorn and Enniskillen. The former notorious example led to the IRA abandoning the type of bomb used – the blast-incendiary. After such outrages the IRA would change their bomb-making and deployment methods to prevent a repetition of bad publicity.[42]

The practice of coded warnings also came in after Abercorn, to minimise civilian casualties while causing the intended damage to property and disruption to responder services and economic life. But they also enabled the specific targeting of first-responders and EOD squads to continue, with the further introduction of the secondary bombs and booby trap devices to make their already highly dangerous task even more perilous. This policy in turn led to the evolution of rapid response methods to ascertain where the IED was, what type it was, and for its effective disruption before the timer ran down and the detonation took place.[43]

Responding to a bomb warning or multiple warnings would always achieve one of the IRA's main objectives, and those of terrorists throughout history – maximum inconvenience, fear and disruption. In order to learn more about the devices being deployed, EOD squads would try to render them safe without blowing them up, in order to save vital forensic evidence.[44] Therefore, at first, 'hand entry' was the method used to dismantle the IEDs – which required the ultimate heroism and which resulted in the loss of life and limb of many EOD operatives. Dealing with devices rapidly to save lives first and property second – with restoration of normality last – made the job even harder.

But the chief aim of the EOD squads evolved into maintaining normality as far as this could be achieved. Reducing disruption to normal life and shaving off the time needed to get an area back to normal, often at the expense of forensic evidence or catching the perpetrators of an attack, became the main practical means to defuse the aims of terrorists. This included response to the many hoaxes and false alarms which were an essential part of the IRA's aim to disrupt the economy and infrastructure.[45]

An example of extreme bravery was cited by George Styles, when describing how his colleague, a Capt. Stewart, was called in the early 1970s to deal with explosives that had been placed around the power station of a cement factory. The explosives were connected by detonating cord 'like a disjointed spider's web' with a central timing and detonating unit 'as the spider waiting to pounce on its fly who, this time, was Capt. Stewart'.[46] The officer had to check painstakingly all the explosive charges bit by bit, first ensuring that there was no light-sensitive fuse in the mechanism – that is, a fuse that would detonate if light is shone at it. He had to perform the check by playing searchlights on the power station from a safe distance. Once this was clear, he had to look for other traps that would be incorporated into the device – as by this stage the IRA had access to complex bomb-making manuals imported from the US. Stewart then found the booby trap element designed to kill him, thus enabling the device to work: the battery in the central device was the source of the booby trap; this he had to isolate to render the device harmless. He achieved this, and was then able to disarm the entire contraption.[47]

George Styles, as the senior ATO with the army, would often encounter a new IRA design. In October 1971 he was called to deal with a bomb of apparently new design which had been found in a telephone box in the lobby of Europe's most bombed hotel, the Belfast Europa. After clearing the area except for his immediate support team, he examined the bomb. It was not only of a new design, but he saw that, until the electrical circuit inside the device had been neutralised, the slightest movement would detonate the 7 kg of explosive it contained and kill him instantly.

He made a plan to disarm the bomb in stages, each of which had to be meticulously thought out, executed and confirmed as successful before he could plan and carry out the next stage. It took him seven hours of thinking, planning and working on the bomb to render it harmless. Throughout this period, other than for brief pauses for refreshment, his life was at immediate risk. Two days later he was again called to the

Europa hotel to deal with a much larger device, judged to contain 13.5 kg (30 lbs) of explosive with an even more complex anti-handling mechanism. A deliberately confusing system of duplicate circuits, clearly intended to defeat the disarming techniques he had used on the first bomb, was the first obstacle. Styles worked out precisely how the anti-handling device was constructed, thus he was able to counter each threat in a sequence that would ensure that the bomb was defused. Success on this second mission came after nine hours' work.[48]

The main aim of the EOD operative would be to separate the bomb's firing mechanism from the explosive charge.[49] The decision was also made during the height of the bombing onslaught in the 1970s, not to attempt to dismantle every device but – so long as life was not endangered, with the area cordoned off – to allow bombs to 'soak' or 'cook' during a waiting period of around two hours. The time was calculated according to the type of bomb timer thought to be used: thirty minutes for a watch or clock; two hours for a kitchen or parking meter timer. This 'soak' period also enabled EOD squads to search for secondary devices operated by a pressure plate or tripwire. It took some of the pressure off the squads who, up to then, had to rush in wearing only light protective clothing during a 'window' before the bomb went off to try to sever the detonator lead.[50]

PLAYING CATCH-UP

Learning to understand improvised devices is a process that never ends because, unlike standard military specifications for a weapon or bomb, IED designs would change and also vary according to who made them – and those who made them would change designs with successive operations. However, on the whole, the British army kept up with the catch-up game in reactive fashion. The IRA would come up with a new detonation, timing or disguise technique and the army had to catch up rapidly. To do this, a large team of scientists and electronic and explosive experts worked constantly; an entire branch of the Royal Signals regiment was devoted to electronic countermeasures.[51]

The Provisionals would come up with a new device within days, but it would take far longer to develop the appropriate countermeasure. British EOD squads learned their skills the hard way during the 1970s and early 1980s.[52] A particularly difficult catch-up challenge was the Provisionals' use of photo-flash and radar in their IEDs, to which countermeasures would take months to be created. Also, such techniques would be used in one or two deployments and would then be abandoned or changed soon after. So, just as the army came up with a response, they were faced with yet another ingenious device. This was an expensive process – not only in terms of lost lives and limbs, but financially.[53] According to an EOD officer, Colonel 'W':

> We lost operators in doing that early development work. As we produced a solution, they often produced a counter measure. If they produced a near threat, we produced a solution, and so on. So, it has been a game of technological leapfrog over the years ... Twenty lost their lives tackling IRA bombs. Many more have been maimed and injured.[54]

The Provisionals would also shift bomb-making operations from the urban theatre to the rural areas of Northern Ireland. This presented an extra challenge for applying countermeasures.[55] The army would also have to find ways of tracing explosives or preventing their procurement. By late 1971 the Irish government put all gelignite under Irish army control.[56] Thus a ready supply of commercial explosive had to be replaced either by homemade explosives or by those acquired from other countries. The UXO people persuaded one leading manufacturer of detonators in the 1970s to make the handling chain recognisable and traceable once the items left the factory. This meant extra expense for the manufacturers, but a cheaper system was found within a year of the request that helped identification of the devices.[57] The IRA overcame this by acquiring detonators from the United States.

Sometimes ideas for catching up with the bomb-makers came from unlikely sources. One development came from the popular science television programme, 'Tomorrow's World' – which one week showed a device that could detect chemical vapours. The army approached the manufacturers to discover if it could be applied to explosives, especially gelignite, then in common use by the IRA, as it had been four decades before. A machine was purchased and, dubbed the 'Sniffer', dispatched to Northern Ireland to be reviewed by government research chemists and army top brass. The demonstration involved passing a stick of gelignite around and then scanning the handlers' hands for tell-tale chemicals. Each handler had to remember which hand or hands they had used to hold the explosive; the 'Sniffer' worked convincingly and was deployed effectively in the six counties later the same year as a spot-search detector.[58] However, it is likely that no television programme broadcast on official channels featuring such a countermeasure would be permitted today, with the raft of antiterrorist legislation that has been passed to prevent the dissemination of such information.

Catching up with even the technological means the army used to disrupt bombs could be speedy. Once the IRA introduced steel-cased bombs (made in the local dockyard) certain devices used by the army (such as the Pigstick, see p.311) which had worked well in disrupting soft-skinned bombs were no longer useful – necessitating further tools to be brought in by the EOD squads.

Getting the bomb out of its deployed location also posed great problems for UXO squads but, as with so many technical operations, new means of tackling the beasts would emerge by accident. An incident recalled by George Styles involved dealing with a bomb left in a canvas bag outside an RUC station, whose mechanism was visible through the bag's half-opened zip. The bomb had to be dragged away with a pulling line from the police station immediately; when the UXO officer's line broke, and was reattached – with the bomb squad officers crouched across the road pulling on the line – the bomb exploded. Although unharmed – save for feeling 'the hot blast of the explosion and the ringing in our ears' – the officers' frustration was clear: 'Although men have landed on the Moon it is still necessary for us to walk up to a bomb and put string round it. Ridiculous.'[59]

The officers went on to design a mechanical 'tortoise' that would be sent trundling off to the bomb to grab it, and then pulled out with it attached. This would mean that the officers would not have to go on the 'long walk' up to the bomb to remove it. The tortoise proved to be a major breakthrough in bomb disposal methods as it could move bombs, and early models were also able to disrupt them.[60] It was the precursor of the 'wheelbarrow' (see p.317). Modern versions now have remote television cameras, can open and break into cars, fire projectiles at the devices, and disrupt them – but their emergence can be traced back to the broken line of Styles' colleague.

The British also came up with the means to make soldiers safe from gun attacks. By the late 1980s, the killing of British soldiers had declined; by 1991 'only' five soldiers were killed, compared with seventeen in a three-month period in summer 1988.[61] The army brought in new flak jackets that could not be penetrated by IRA bullets, other than the Barrett Light 50 rifle acquired from the US, which could fire armour-piercing bullets at helicopters but which were hardly used in the years leading up to the 1994 ceasefire – one of the three guns that had been lost by the Belfast brigade and purloined by the security forces.[62]

WHEN BOMBS WENT OFF

Bombs often exploded during an EOD operation, particularly those that were so well concealed as to remain undiscovered.

IRA bombs sometimes went off at unintended times due to army countermeasures. The 1987 Enniskillen bomb was said to have been on a timer that was set to explode during the army parade, not during the civilian service – but that an army sweep re-set the timer, either accidentally or deliberately – resulting in the explosion occurring during maximum civilian attendance.[63]

The EOD squads often witnessed the outcome of 'own goals' in the course of dealing with bomb incidents. Targeting the squads with devices containing anti-handling mechanisms sometimes backfired, as when a colleague of George Styles, Chris Carrier, who later won the George Medal for bravery, found the first two of four shoebox devices which had burned out safety fuses on top of the boxes to imply, ingeniously, that the devices had failed to go off. In taking one of the boxes apart, he found an anti-handling device which would have enabled detonation had the box been moved. The third device, built into a Saxa salt box with a switch at its base that would set the device off on picking it up, was found in a pub. When the pub landlord picked up the innocuous box of salt, he was, by a stroke of fate – and the Irish weather – not blown up because the device's inner workings had been rendered harmless by rain. However, it was the fourth device which claimed a body part of its creator; an army patrol had seen a man placing a Saxa salt box outside a building, shouted to him, and the bomber put it down too quickly – so that the anti-handling device inside it blew half of his arm off, which he left behind as he ran away.[64]

These events were matched by the loss of life and limb among the EOD squads. An experienced officer appointed to work with George Styles died in the process of dealing with an incident that was the result of the Provisionals overtaking the army in fashioning a new type of device, which it deployed in a village called Castlerobin, after which the device was named (also see Chapter 6). Comprised of a simple box left on its end, its placing near to a local Orange hall was witnessed by a local postman, who told a local policeman, who contacted the army. When the UXO officer, Capt. Stewartson, arrived, he assumed it would have an anti-handling device and tied cord around it and, from behind a wall, began to rope in the bomb. When it seemed safe to approach the device, he began opening it, and its 7 kg (15 lbs) of explosive detonated and killed him.

There was often enough explosive in such devices to kill an EOD operative but not enough to cause any great surrounding damage. The officer had assumed it was safe on pulling it with the cord without it going off. It had to be dealt with by first not touching it, muffling its effect by surrounding it with sand, taking a radiograph, then putting the line around it and pulling it in. This would activate the anti-handling device, but at a distance – which although not harmful to the EOD squad, often meant resultant damage to nearby premises. Its secret was yet to be discovered. To do this, the EOD team had to 'capture one alive'[65] – that is, risk their lives and dismantle one.

Eventually, two devices – now called Castlerobins – were dismantled safely, and the bomb's new aspect revealed: its circuitry incorporated Post Office micro-switches in the top and bottom of the device, and it was these switches which betrayed its provenance: 'We knew now that the Castlerobin bomb was of a better class than anything we'd met before. It was nicely done, nicely arranged … '[66]

But it didn't end there. The intricate part of discovering who had actually made the bomb – once they knew who its electrician was, the IRA operative who had worked for the Post Office – involved the army 'playing a psychological game' with the electrician. They did this by putting notices out to the media which understated the IRA's abilities – that the army was 'on top' of the bombing operations of the IRA. This message was broadcast repeatedly, with the effect that the Provisionals then tried to improve what was already a sophisticated design. This had the desired result for the army: the IRA over-reached themselves with a new design, and as many as twenty-one volunteers blew themselves up while constructing the devices.[67] Through painstaking work with dummy Castlerobins, Styles managed to unravel how to disrupt the circuitry of the anti-handling mechanism and hence isolate it.

The EOD squads believed they were still on top when operatives were sent to the Europa to deal with a 2 ft-high bomb that had been left in the foyer – a box with 'IRA' and a cheeky 'tee-hee' message written on it.[68] When the device was x-rayed *in situ*, it revealed a mass of wires and micro-switches which could be anti-handling devices, similar to the Castlerobin. The bomb was sandbagged to minimise damage if it went off. It was then rendered safe by dismantling charges – a controlled explosion.

EOD LIVES LOST

The number of lives lost in the process of dismantling bombs increased through the 1970s and 1980s, particularly in the early part of the

Provisionals' campaign. Ammunition Technical Officers (ATOs) had to rely on simple tools in the late 1960s and early 1970s – before the emergence of robots and other equipment – such as wire clippers and Stanley knives. Many were from the 321 EOD Company Royal Army Ordnance Corps (RAOC). As well as Capt. Stewartson mentioned on page 306, WO2 C.J.L. Davies was killed in November 1971, aged thirty-nine, by a device planted in a car showroom in Lurgan. He approached the device, heard it ticking and was leaving the building when it exploded; he was killed by falling masonry. Staff Sgt G.R. Cracknell was killed in March 1972 along with one other member of a bomb-disposal team, Sgt A.S. Butcher, by an IRA booby trap device left in the back seat of a car off the Grosvenor Road. Having been spotted by a foot patrol, a controlled explosion was carried out to open the boot of the car but it did not trigger the main 9-kg (20-lb) device, which then exploded as the team approached the vehicle for a closer inspection. EOD officers were also killed while inspecting explosives caches. One such, found in a Nissen hut in Derry, killed Capt. B.S. Gritten and three other soldiers in June 1973.

Many deaths resulted from encountering new devices. One of the most senior bomb disposal officers in the province, Major B.C. Calladene of the RAOC, died when a car bomb exploded on 29 March 1972 in a tiny side street opposite Belfast City Hall. Having asked to be summoned on the discovery of new devices, and having already defused a 70-kg (150-lb) truck bomb earlier that day, the device in the Austin 1800 he approached for his first inspection exploded. Maj. Calladene was the most senior officer of the army's bomb squad to be killed in Northern Ireland at that time. A cone-shaped Semtex device – a forerunner of the shaped charge that maximised its killing power – killed six soldiers on a civilian minibus on a charity 'fun-run' in Lisburn, Co. Antrim. Disguised devices took their toll: the first bomb-disposal officer to be killed in the dreaded south Armagh, twenty-two-year-old Capt. J.H. Young died while trying to defuse a milk-churn bomb at Silverbridge, near Forkhill in July 1972. As much as five years later, Sgt M.E. Walsh was killed by a similar device that he was trying to dismantle near Newtownbutler.

FORENSIC EVIDENCE

The materials collected both from exploded and dismantled devices and seized explosives and components provided invaluable forensic evidence. The Northern Ireland Forensic Laboratory acquired a reputation over the years of state-of-the-art analysis of world renown that enabled the authorities to track new bomb-making methods and the origins of the materials[69] – so much so that the building was destroyed by a 910-kg (2,000-lb) IRA bomb in 1992 (see Chapter 3).

The first forensic science laboratory for Northern Ireland was set up in Belfast in 1956, with only four forensic scientists working there. In its first year it dealt with 500 cases; total staffing rose during the 1970s bombing campaign and then declined somewhat after the 1990s ceasefires.[70] The lab earned an international reputation for its work in firearms and explosives and became an invaluable source of expertise for police forces around the world. It was mainly concerned with testing debris from explosions. DNA testing increasingly put forensic science at the core of the criminal justice system and the lab was in the forefront of this technology.

At its relocated premises in Sevenoaks, Kent (after temporary relocation at Carrickfergus) the lab is run by the Defence and Evaluation Research Agency (DERA). Just 5 nanograms of RDX – a Semtex ingredient – is enough to link a suspected terrorist to a bombing. However, amounts in excess of this have been found in the laboratory as contamination, not connected with specific cases; for example, in 1989 140 nanograms of RDX was discovered on a bench, and traced to a camera. This led to increased safety measures in the sampling process.

DEALING WITH SPECIFIC THREATS

Car bombs

Early attempts to cope with the growing menace of car bombs – vehicle-borne IEDs (VBIEDs) – involved using a hook and line to pull open the rear door of a car, then to attach a line to the box containing the IED to pull it free of the car. If the EOD operative then approached the bomb, it could go off, as when St. Sgt Christopher Cracknell and his colleague Sgt Anthony Butcher were killed making such an attempt in March 1972. This led to a major change in procedure: the 'one-man risk' rule – which meant that at no time would more than one EOD operator approach a suspect device. The 'long walk' would be a lonely one indeed.[71]

An early example of a car bomb incident that former bomb disposal officer Peter Gurney had to deal with but could not prevent was the Scotland Yard attack in 1969. The police had received intelligence that an IRA unit was active in London. After two separate warnings telephoned to different agencies police discovered a 1968 Ford Corsair packed with explosives outside Scotland Yard before the warnings were given. Gurney described the awesome challenge that faced him:

The explosive appeared to be packed in sort of five-pound bags. We thought the best thing to do was to remove the bags as quickly as possible. Then, if the bomb did go off, at least you would cut down the amount of damage that was caused. We'd removed quite a lot when we came to the sort of core of the bomb, which was about 40 pounds of gelignite-type explosive.[72]

Despite the discovery, two of the other bombs went off, injuring over 200 people.

Various weapons were used to deal with car bombs. The Carl Gustav 88-mm anti-tank rocket was one: firing these disrupted the bombs, especially the anti-handling mechanisms. But – as in many examples of adapting military methods to civilian situations – its use was inappropriate in built-up areas and its success rate patchy.[73]

One way of disrupting bombs left in car boots was to push large amounts of sheet explosive under a suspect car in order to remove the bomb from the boot. Various objects, such as metal lampshades filled with water, or steel shot, would be projected upwards by the sheet explosive to shift the bomb. When smaller devices were left on car seats, small disrupters were used to break the car window to gain access to the car's interior and burst open the suspect package. Disrupters were also used to shoot nails into the car floor to hold open doors – which would normally trap a remote-controlled vehicle as they tried to withdraw.[74]

Locating the car bombs provided just one more obstacle in keeping up with the IRA. Once they had begun placing the bombs in car boots, they would change to hiding them inside the back seat. They would observe how the UXO units worked – the surveillance operation worked on both sides – and put the bomb somewhere not yet thought of or not part of a pattern. One device was planted in a car that had been parked under a railway bridge, which had to be cleared and the car driven away in a matter of minutes; not only were many troops in the immediate area, but crowds were walking to a football match. A search of the boot did not reveal the bomb, until the operative discovered a tear in the back seat; a 2-kg Semtex device with a switching unit made from bellpulls.[75]

Ways of disrupting bombs, specifically its TPU, were undertaken without setting the vehicle on fire. A coal-mining explosive consisting of TNT, ammonium nitrate and salt would be dropped in a can onto the top of the vehicle to disrupt the bomb's TPU from within. Another method – 'hook-and-line' – was used to drag suspect devices from hard-to-access positions so that they could be examined and disarmed.[76]

Another highly significant tool was invented for disarming car bombs. The use of gun-fired water jets, pioneered by military scientists, was developed to fracture the TPU of a bomb before it could detonate the explosive charge. It consisted of a powerful blank cartridge which ejected water from a massive gun barrel. Trials failed at first, with close-range firing required to disrupt timers. The disrupter, known as the Pigstick, then became smaller and lighter – the mini-Pigstick. Subsequent versions were able to penetrate beer kegs and oil drums. Intense secrecy surrounded these developments, and the consequent 'controlled explosions' that would be highlighted in the media were done with no cameras or media intrusion in order to preserve the integrity of this most valuable countermeasure.[77]

Booby traps
The prime area in Northern Ireland for elaborate booby traps was south Armagh, which was controlled and constantly watched by the Provisionals, and where the terrain was so dangerous for British forces to transport equipment by road that all operations were carried out by helicopter. The IRA booby trap bombs had anti-handling devices – the mercury tilt switch being the most ubiquitous and deadly. If the bomb package was moved, a tilt switch would trigger the electrical circuit and set off the bomb. To deal with these devices the army used a hook and line to pull suspect parcels away from buildings. They then placed a small amount of explosive next to the package to blow the bomb's circuit apart, but this was not powerful enough to set off the main charge.[78] Shane O'Doherty, who made and deployed letter bombs in London in the early 1970s, outlined a typical process of IRA bombing tactics, in which they began targeting the bomb disposal operatives:

> The idea of putting your bomb inside a wooden box, screwed down all the way around, meant that first of all, it couldn't be easily seen, what was going on inside it … And then, people were saying, you know, 'Well, hell, you know, if it's an army bomb disposal team, let's give them something to work for, like, let's not aim just for the building in which we're trying to get our bomb to explode.' That's reason enough to put an anti-handling device on. But then, they thought … 'Instead of trying to shoot a soldier on the border or shoot a soldier walking up the street in Derry, let's try and take out the ATO (bomb squad).'[79]

But as the anti-handling devices were much more dangerous to plant, the bombs were delivered in cars – a new threat that the army needed to react to quickly. Some of the first experiments they employed to defeat the car bomb involved the use of foam to try to attenuate the blast.[80] The car is filled with foam, and on firing the charge, there are hardly any visible effects. Foam produced by the two standard fire-fighting generators is delivered through polyethylene tubes directed towards a car bomb 30 metres away. The far end of the street is closed off with nylon mesh screens. The car and the street are smothered in foam, which rises to a height of about ten feet.[81]

Another EOD operative described the method thus:

> The vehicle would drive up towards the car bomb. It was one of our PIG vehicles. It had a nozzle on the top, and it would spew this high-density foam into the street. It was known as Foaming PIG. It was like your washing machine had gone awry and there's all this foam all over the place. And the whole street would fill up with foam, with the intention of stopping the damage. Unfortunately, it wasn't much of a success. It didn't actually reduce the blast damage too much. And if the device failed to function, then someone had the problem of wading through all this foam to try and find where the bomb was in order to deal with it.[82]

Another way to render safe booby trapped, under-vehicle bombs[83] was one of the most significant weapons in the EOD inventory: the Disrupter. As Peter Gurney explained:

> When the current campaign started, the only tool the bomb disposal operator had was really a Stanley knife, a few hand tools, a ball of string, and some detonating cord. But this, of course, meant you had to be with the bomb while you were defusing it, which is not a good idea. And we did lose quite a few operators. And then, along came the idea of knocking the bomb apart. This technique was called disruption.

One technique went thus: a gun, which would usually fire a solid projectile, is filled with water and fired electrically from a safe distance. This is put in the vertical position and once it has penetrated the case of a bomb, the slug of water which it projects bursts in all directions, and it tends to burst the bomb open from the inside. The idea is to knock the bomb apart rather than setting it off, so the components can be gathered without causing the bomb itself to explode. Then the pin is withdrawn. Being able to gather up the components would be an invaluable exercise in learning the bomb's innards. The gun is aimed either to disable one of the vital components – a battery of the parcels within a bomb – or to destroy the circuitry, which will stop the electrical current and get into the detonator, or even blow the detonator away from the explosion.[84]

The dangers of disarming booby trap devices demanded extraordinary courage and inventiveness. Sometimes a beer keg was used to contain a bomb comprising up to 100 lbs of explosives, the main explosive charge. Hidden inside is a booby trap switch connected to a booster bag on top, which provides the initial kick to get the explosives to function. If the EOD operator puts his hand in to pull out the booster bag, he will set this device off, in turn setting off the whole of the explosive charge, killing the operator.[85]

To deal with the problem, a veteran EOD officer, Sidney Alford, who devised new countermeasures to remove bombs from car boots, invented a semi-cylindrical case on the back of which was taped detonating cord. When the detonating cord explodes, it squeezes the water inside the container and projects it at great speed. Propelled by high explosive, the slug of water blasts straight through the gas tank, and without igniting the fuel, lifts the beer keg 50 feet (18 metres) clear of the car. The bomb can then be more completely disarmed.[86]

The beer keg problem surfaced in the early 1970s. George Styles' team were tasked with dealing with beer keg bombs delivered to pubs. The challenge was to enable bar staff to spot which beer kegs were bombs in time for the bomb squads to arrive and deal with the disguised devices. One barman had worked it out for himself; he tapped the barrels with his knuckles, and could tell that those filled with bombs made a different sound than innocent or empty kegs. Such was the power of local awareness which, when communicated to the authorities, contributed to the safeguarding of many lives: the bomb squads could, accordingly, put out public advice to the bar staff of Northern Ireland on how to prevent being blown up by beer deliveries.[87]

Searching a house for bombs would often include booby trap devices laid inside the property. The EOD operative would put on an armoured suit, and carry a disrupter, before checking out the house. He would use a metal detector to locate a classic booby trap: a pressure mat under the carpet. If he stood on the mat, it would complete an electric circuit, triggering a bomb. To search for tripwires, which may be thin fishing lines that are very hard to see, the operative would use a thin, metal wand and a flashlight to scan each doorway. By focusing his eyes along the wand, he could catch the glint of light from a fishing line and follows it to a homemade bomb hidden around the corner.[88]

Army UXO suffered great loss and high casualty rates from dealing with booby trap and disguised devices – even when the nature of devices had been established. One device was planted in a sports centre in Belfast and a UXO clearance team was sent in but found no device. Believing one part of the centre to be clear, UXO officer John Howard was sent in and – in walking on a gym mat – set off a pressure plate in the device and was killed.[89]

As well as car bombs, British army EOD officer Peter Gurney defused many letter bombs, which are essentially anti-handling devices, constructed by Shane O'Doherty (see Chapter 8). He described how this was done:

> Letter bombs are all designed to go off when opened. But fortunately, x-rays have come in, and we were able to use this to make out what the contents of the letters were. These were a great innovation, these machines, the light-weight x-ray machines. This is a suspect package, in this case, which we put in front of it. We stand at the x-ray machine about a measure off, and if we move back, that machine is now functioning. So, we remove the cassette. You pull out the black tag, which pulls out the film, and peel away the cover. This is only a very small x-ray which consists of a detonator and the delayed-action timer. You can see the battery case in here. Oh, so the x-ray was taken in that line with the … you can see the battery pack. The detonator is buried in explosive here. You can just see the edge of the watch. And that was the … as I've opened it, the two wires have come together, which, had it been a real bomb, would have completed the circuit and caused the bomb to fire.[90]

Command wire and radio-controlled devices
It was not always clear when called to a UXO how the bomb would be triggered – by radio control or command wire. Such an operation was described on the groundbreaking Nova documentary 'Bomb Squad' in 1997:

> I started uncovering some of the wires and found four bags, each containing about 50 pounds of homemade explosive linked to a detonator. I then followed the wires, expecting to find maybe a pressure mat or a radio-controlled receiver or something like that, and found that the wire ended abruptly. One on one row aligned, and the other wire from the detonator on the other row aligned … What they had done was use the railway lines as an alternative to domestic cable, which they use as a command wire.

The EOD unit quickly blew a hole in the tracks to break the circuit and prevented the IRA from having a second chance to blow up the bomb disposal man – Warrant Officer 'K' – who was awarded a medal for his bravery.[91]

Urban command-wire detonation was a classic example of the Provisionals combining technical expertise with disguise ingenuity. They would make the command wires very hard to find, thus enabling the device to go off before it could be located and dismantled. Wires would be installed in the type of wooden lamp-post that existed in many areas of Northern Ireland. The command wire would be inserted inside the metal cowling (shielding) that ran from the ground attached to the phone line inside right up to the top of the lamp and across the road to a targeted building. A soldier leaning on one of the lamp-posts realised this was the wire's route.[92]

The British also learned how to counter bombs triggered by command wire as they developed infra-red sensors that could detect the heat being emitted by the detonating cables.[93] They were also able to deal with one of the biggest IRA menaces against troop patrols, the culvert landmine bombs deployed in drains beneath the roads in rural areas. This countermeasure consisted of installing wire mesh to block the culverts – denying the IRA access to bomb-planting.[94]

Sweeping

Sweeping devices were developed to detect RCIEDs; these included the 'bleep', which would, from a nearby EOD squad vehicle, scan the radio frequency spectrum for warning signs that radio-controlled devices were deployed in the area. The 'bleep' worked by creating and preserving an electronic 'bubble' against any incoming radio signal that would detonate an IED.[95] EOD robots were later used to deal with radio-controlled devices. During the IRA campaign, however, the bombs the soldiers were trying to locate were also radio-controlled. Therefore, to avoid triggering the device with radio signals, the robot trailed a wire for firing the weapons that would blow apart the bomb.

The catch-up game reached a peak with the army's methods of disrupting these devices through jamming. As mentioned in a previous chapter, the IRA began in the 1970s to use a transmitter found in model aircraft and boats to trigger a simple switch in an IED and set it off. The army discovered which wavelength was being used to transmit the signals, and jammed them. But, as they were transmitting on the same frequency, the army ran the risk of exploding the bombs prematurely.[96]

The IRA realised this pretty quickly, and began using electronic devices in the IEDs that necessitated a coded signal to activate them.

This meant that the army's frequency not only failed to set the bombs off prematurely, but also to jam the signals or find out which modulations in the signal acted as the trigger – giving the IRA a distinct technological advantage. The use of coded signals led to major research in UK defence laboratories, which resulted in the emergence of inhibitors – the means to disrupt the bombs to prevent them from going off. This cat-and-mouse process resulted in the IRA blaming the army when bombs went off with substantial civilian casualties, such as the 1987 Enniskillen remembrance service bomb, which in fact had a timing device rather than a radio-controlled signal to initiate the bomb. As explained above, the sweep operation of the area was likely to have re-set the timer – resulting in the bomb killing civilians rather than 'just' soldiers taking part in the army parade.[97]

However, the IRA discovered a way around inhibitors: by sending radio signals in a part of the electromagnetic spectrum – the 'white band' – where the inhibitors would not work. This method led to the deaths of a number of army personnel and police, stepped up the arms race several notches and made it imperative that army scientists come up with a countermeasure. This they did; and in response, the Provisionals, having run out of wavebands, reverted to command-wire detonation (which could not be jammed). So the British also won this phase of the counter-measures war, but after a long, expensive process to catch up.

USING SPECIALISED EQUIPMENT

In order not to have to disarm a bomb by the highly risky method of hand entry, attempts were made to disrupt the inner workings of bombs to prevent detonation. Early attempts to disrupt bombs involved the firing of shoulder-launched, recoilless antitank guns with inert projectiles to knock bombs apart before they could detonate.[98]

Disrupters were developed that used water to prevent detonation. The Pigstick was the most commonly used disrupter and produced a controlled explosion to blast apart the IED components, particularly if the IED had a soft skin.[99] The mini-Pigstick would be set up, and the EOD operative would not approach the bomb for thirty minutes to ensure that no secondary device was set to go off. Once the TPU had been fractured, the bomb would be x-rayed and then cleared.

But there were problems. The water that accelerated along the entire length of the gun barrel was projected faster than the increment from its muzzle, so the slug of water projected was basically unstable and burst radially within a few centimetres of the muzzle. This limited its range and penetrating ability despite its considerable bursting power once through the bomb's wall. As soon as the IRA introduced steel-cased bombs (made in the local dockyard) this device was defeated, necessitating further tools to be brought in by the EOD squads. One such device used sheet explosive to project steel blades through gas cylinders and beer kegs (see below).[100]

There was also the eternal problem of anti-handling devices, which could set off the explosive once the bomb was moved, even with its TPU disabled. Or disruption of a first device could trigger a secondary booby trap device. A device was invented, the 'flatsword', which completely severed metal oil drums, milk churns, beer kegs, gas cylinders and other favoured bomb containers so that the explosive would spill out of the device.[101] Then an amazing invention that was remotely controlled, commanded by an electric cable, was used to clatter its way towards a device – enter the 'wheelbarrow'.[102]

The 'wheelbarrow' and 'hobo'

As the IRA's booby traps became more elaborate, the army relied increasingly on robots to assess dangerous situations where remote access was desirable – particularly for dealing with car bombs, with the need to open a car door or boot which could be booby trapped or operated by time-delay devices.[103] The earliest form of remote-control handling and dismantling came about in the early 1970s after an inventive British army colonel adapted his novel way of cutting grass – by tethering his lawn mower to a stake. He imagined using long ropes to steer a remote-controlled tow-hook towards a suspect car bomb. The operator would be far enough away to escape any blast if the bomb was accidentally triggered. The first prototype was actually built from garden machinery, and was thence nicknamed the 'wheelbarrow'.[104]

According to Col. Peter Miller, its first use possibly saved as many as forty cars and a garage from being blown up – at that time, the actual cost of a 'wheelbarrow' was £250. The Mark II 'wheelbarrow' had a remotely controlled arm, which meant it could tackle a car bomb where it was parked. Peter Gurney was one of the first people to try it out in Belfast:

> This machine was really the first of the car bomb killers, because it had on the front an attachment to break a car window. Now, the idea was that you drove up onto this part that actually came in contact with a car window, and so it was forced in. This would spring out and break your car window. There was a lot of trouble with the

early ones on these, because they tended to skid up a window, and you would find yourself unable to break the window. So, you had to withdraw the Wheelbarrow. And then, Colonel Miller modified them by fitting in a tungsten carbide tip in there which actually digs into the glass and stops it skidding.[105]

To disrupt the bomb components without setting off the device, the 'wheelbarrow' delivered an explosive charge known as 'candle' – a plastic tube of 108 g of aluminised explosive and initiated by an electric detonator. When candle is fired, the car is opened up and there is a high probability that the IED will be completely disrupted – a 'controlled explosion'.

The early 'wheelbarrow' models had long umbilical cords to control their movement, but these would become jammed in doorways. So they fired a metal spike into the floor to hold the door open. This was the first 'wheelbarrow' to have a television camera enabling the operator to hunt for the bomb in the car. It also had tank tracks which could climb stairs. But the long umbilical, which contained wires for steering and setting off the explosive, could be dangerous, as Peter Gurney found out when he was dealing with a suspicious car in Belfast: 'Whilst pulling the car out, unbeknown to myself, the car had actually gone over the top of the control cable for the robot, and it had scrubbed all the insulation off the wires.'[106]

Behind the cover of their armoured vehicle, Gurney's men attached the explosive candle to the robot arm. Unknown to them, the bare wires inside the damaged umbilical were touching, so when Gurney flicked the switch to move the robot, he set off the explosive charge – they were standing just a few feet away from the explosion. Although Gurney escaped lightly, his two colleagues were more seriously injured. With the robot wrecked, Gurney risked his life by placing the explosive candle in the suspect car.

The 'wheelbarrow' has come a long way in twenty-five years. In seven out of ten incidents, it acted as the eyes and hands of the operator so that he could work on the bomb from the safety zone. It features a pair of roving cameras to locate the device and a pair of disrupters to destroy it. For more cramped situations, the 'wheelbarrow' had a companion robot called 'buckeye' that could manoeuvre in narrow places like the aisles of trains or steep staircases.

Also in the early 1970s a robot called the 'hobo' was developed by Kentree (now Allen-Vanguard), originally designed by an Irish former EOD operative[107] to clean the submerged hulls of ships while in dock.

The technology was adapted in 1979 for the Irish army to deal with the IRA's IEDs. Many variations of the 'hobo' were subsequently developed, with the most advanced, the 'defender', now being used in a number of theatres of war and insurgency. Many of these technological advances resulted from the Northern Ireland experience and were produced or guided by former EOD experts who served during the Troubles.[108]

The ultimate EOD robot is a hand-held device rather like a Dan Dare ray gun which will detect, perhaps diagnose, and ultimately dispose of terrorist devices. One of the key problems is trying to fit the tools, cameras and weapons on the end of the arm, as they are all competing for the same space. The aim is for the robot to have a selection of different tools and attachments that can be carried on board. The ultimate attachment would be a hand – with a virtual reality gauntlet, so that the operator can slip his hand into a glove and feel, as well as see, what he is doing.

The IRA were not, however, fazed by the army's use of robots. According to Shane O'Doherty:

> If the bomb disposal team are going to send any robot anyway, who cares? Then, you've got to think, where are they going to send the robot in from? What street corner? What part of the street are they going to use as their operations point? What manhole cover, what building, what wall of a building can you conceal something in?[109]

Nevertheless, much of the equipment used to disarm or contain bombs during the Troubles formed the basis of more advanced gadgets and techniques that are being deployed in the Iraq and Afghanistan theatres of war. These range from robotics and electronic countermeasures to vehicles and training. For example, the SNATCH 2 Land Rover, which has enhanced protection against IED blasts, was developed from the threat assessments measured during the Northern Ireland conflict.[110] Other developments came on stream and became vital parts of the EOD operator's inventory. New x-ray equipment – the Scanray system – allowed instant processing for rapid inspection; new explosives detectors emerged that were up to 2,000 times more sensitive to gelignite, nitrobenzene and TNT (and in large spaces); infra-red photography; and lighter, improved EOD suits.[111]

RESPONSE TO ATTACKS

When the IRA attacked 10 Downing Street on 7 February 1991 Peter Gurney, then head of the London Bomb Squad, was on the scene within minutes. The mortars were launched from a parked van, in which a short timer had been set to trigger a set of explosive charges. Gurney saw three large mortar tubes through the flames, having been told there had been an explosion in the garden of number 10. At that point only one mortar shell had exploded. He described his rapid response:

> All I did was tell people to keep in the heart of the building, because there were two bombs possibly unaccounted for. And should these bombs either fire, and then detonate in the area, people would be safer in the heart of the building rather than outside on the streets. Then it comes, being led through the garden, one gave a quick look around and it was quite obvious that the bomb had gone off at the bottom end here.

Gurney dismantled one of the three mortar bombs that failed to explode – it had landed nearby, near the Mountbatten statue. Working alone, to avoid placing others at risk, Gurney locked the bomb between his legs and tried to remove the fuse:

> The bomb was almost red hot, and I got off it rather quickly, found some snow, which was … It was beginning to snow at the time … and packed it into my trousers and then sat on the bomb again, and eventually managed to get the four bolts out. I then found the bomber actually burned – the filling had burnt out, the indication that it was very, very hot indeed. And it was, really in fact, an empty bomb. But anybody who saw me at the time must have wondered what on earth was going on, because I would sit on the bomb, take a couple of turns on a nut and jump up and rush around [laughter] and then come back and then have another go at the fuse. I was somewhat disappointed having gotten the fuse out to find out it was empty … I had gone through all the danger of *excitement* [emphasis added] of getting the fuse off, and then to find out … It was like opening a Christmas package and finding that there's nothing inside.[112]

It turned out the explosive in both mortar bombs had burned away without detonating. The constant need to respond to bomb incidents led to advances in the establishing of cordons and evacuation of citizens[113] – both operations that would cause massive disruption in order to preserve normal life.

The first models of homemade mortars developed by the Provisionals during the 1980s, which were not usually accurate enough to find and take out their targets, nevertheless achieved certain success – as when nine police officers were killed on 28 February 1985 when a mortar fired from a lorry hit a station canteen in Newry, Co. Down. Subsequently, a costly programme was initiated to reconstruct bases to make them less vulnerable to mortar attack – such as building blast-deflecting walls and reinforced roofs. Army patrols were also increased, mainly to serve as a deterrent.[114]

Amazing anecdotes emerged from EOD operations. One involved a mortar attack on an RUC station in Pomeroy, Co. Tyrone. An IRA unit had hijacked a truck which they had loaded with advanced mortar on a short timer. They parked it outside the station and began to fire AK-47 rounds on the station to distract its inhabitants. The timer on the mortar ticked down and the propulsion charge went off, but the bomb failed to detonate. The IRA unit sped off and the army EOD squad choppered and defused the mortar. The EOD operatives discovered that the bomb had a one in a million chance of not detonating. They also discovered that, despite the empty magazine cases from the AK gun fire, there were no strike marks anywhere in the station's structure. It turned out that the police station was on consecrated ground that had been due to be deconsecrated but this had never taken place. The EOD members, while trying to avoid paranormal or religious conclusions, never solved the riddle why both elements of the IRA attack had failed.[115]

At the time of the 1990s ceasefires the intensity of countermeasures development had flagged and some EOD squads had lost basic skills, as had the IRA itself. The Provisionals had conducted recce operations in between the ceasefires, and the intensity of the old catch-up game began to increase once more. Roger Davies, who was commander of the Northern Ireland bomb squad from 1991 to the second ceasefire in 1996, ran a small, four-man team. Its members were close, and soon regained (and exceeded) their former expertise during this period. Lessons had been learned from the early hellish days of the 1970s, and continue to provide the Gold Standard for EOD operations.[116] The three pillars of EOD remain equipment, procedures and training. The first two cannot work without the third; if a piece of kit is developed to disrupt or disarm IEDs, the time taken to use it properly remains key to successful EOD.

Maj. Davies described his role as 'the best job in the world'. The ATOs were in sole control of a situation – over the local police, army brigade and local population. They stopped IEDs from going off and risked their own lives in the process. They minimised disruption as well as saving lives, and in doing so reduced the threat from terrorism, and thereby its main aim – to disrupt economic and daily life.

NOTES

1. G. Styles, *Bombs Have No Pity* (London: William Luscombe, 1975), p.134.
2. Shane Paul O'Doherty, interviewed in 'Bomb Squad', Nova television documentary, US Public Broadcasting Service, PBS (Public Broadcasting Service) Airdate: 21 October 1997.
3. Maj. Roger Davies, MBE, QGM, former commander of the Northern Ireland bomb squad, interview with the author, November 2007.
4. C. Ryder, *A Special Kind of Courage: 321 Squadron – Battling the Bombers* (London: Methuen, 2006), p.xviii.
5. K. Toolis, *Rebel Hearts: Journeys Within the IRA's Soul* (New York: St Martin's Press, 1995), p.127.
6. Personal communication, Ulster Intelligence Unit operative, June 2007.
7. S. Alford, 'Disruptive Influences', *Intersec*, June 2007, p.19, and personal communication in my journal, *NBC International*.
8. Personal communication, former Irish army EOD operative.
9. Toolis, *Rebel Hearts*, p.127.
10. M. Urban, *Big Boys' Rules* (London: Faber & Faber, 1993), p.117.
11. Ibid., p.117.
12. The shootings would become the subject of one of the most controversial political television documentaries ever made in the UK, Thames Television's 'Death on the Rock', 28 April 1988.
13. E. Moloney, *A Secret History of the IRA* (London: W.W. Norton & Co, 2002), p.333.
14. Toolis, *Rebel Hearts*, p.214.
15. Ibid., p.215.
16. Ibid., p.192.
17. Ibid., p.216.
18. G. Harkin, F. Elliott and R. Whitaker, 'Revealed: IRA bombs killed eight British soldiers in Iraq', *Independent on Sunday*, 25 August 2007.
19. Styles, *Bombs Have No Pity*, p.103.
20. Ibid.
21. A. Palmer, 'Tribute paid to soldiers killed in IRA attack', *News Letter*, 14 December 2004.
22. Moloney, *A Secret History of the IRA*, p.334.
23. B. O'Brien, *Pocket History of the IRA from 1916 Onwards* (Dublin: O'Brien Press, 2005), p.187.
24. Styles, *Bombs Have No Pity*, pp.93–4.
25. Ibid., p.95.
26. Personal communication, former Irish army EOD operative.
27. Moloney, *A Secret History of the IRA*, p.326.
28. Ibid., p.3.
29. Ibid., p.326.
30. Ibid., p.330.
31. Urban, *Big Boys' Rules*, p.119.
32. Ibid., p.120.
33. Ibid, p.121.
34. Ibid., p.122.
35. Personal communication, Weapons Intelligence Unit operative, 2007.
36. Moloney, *A Secret History of the IRA*, p.443.
37. Ryder, *A Special Kind of Courage*, p.76.
38. Ibid.
39. Ibid., p.61.
40. 'Bomb Squad'.
41. Ibid.
42. Styles, *Bombs Have No Pity*, p.102.
43. Alford, 'Disruptive Influences', p.19 and personal communication in my journal, *NBC International*.
44. Ibid.
45. Maj. R. Davies, interview with the author, November 2007.
46. G. Styles, *Bombs Have No Pity*, p.104.
47. Ibid.
48. 'Army demolition expert who defused two IRA bombs in two days in Belfast', Obituary, Lt Col George Styles, GC, *The Times*, 2 August 2006.
49. Ryder, *A Special Kind of Courage*, p.42.

50. Ibid., p.49.
51. Personal communication, Ulster Intelligence Unit operative, September 2007.
52. Maj. Roger Davies, interview with the author, November 2007.
53. Personal communication, Ulster Intelligence Unit operative, September 2007.
54. EOD officer interviewed in 'Bomb Squad'.
55. Styles, *Bombs Have No Pity*, p.103.
56. Ibid., p.124.
57. Ibid., p.108.
58. Ibid.
59. Ibid., p.148.
60. Ibid.
61. Moloney, *A Secret History of the IRA*, p.338.
62. Ibid., p.339.
63. Unnamed intelligence sources.
64. Styles, *Bombs Have No Pity*, pp.114–15.
65. Ibid., pp.119–21.
66. Ibid., pp.122.
67. Ibid.
68. The Provisionals actually 'branded' some of their bombs with their logo 'PIRA'. Photo of nail bombs in J. Durney, *The Volunteer: Uniforms, Weapons and History of the Irish Republican Army 1913–1997* (Dublin: Gaul House, 2004), p.15. Pre-1980s examples of product marketing!
69. Ryder, *A Special Kind of Courage*, p.80.
70. Minutes of Evidence, Select Committee on Northern Ireland Affairs, Memorandum submitted by Forensic Science Northern Ireland and The Northern Ireland Office, House of Commons, March 2002.
71. Ryder, *A Special Kind of Courage*, p.57.
72. Peter Gurney, interviewed on 'Behind the Mask: The IRA and Sinn Féin' (Peter Taylor, PBS (Public Broadcasting Service) Frontline, 21 October 1997).
73. Ryder, *A Special Kind of Courage*, p.83.
74. Alford, 'Disruptive Influences', p.20 and personal communication in my journal, *NBC International*.
75. Personal communication, Ulster Intelligence Unit operative, September 2007.
76. Alford, 'Disruptive Influences', p.20 and personal communication in my journal, *NBC International*.
77. Ryder, *A Special Kind of Courage*, p.85.
78. 'Bomb Squad'.
79. Shane O'Doherty, interviewed in 'Bomb Squad'.
80. 'Bomb Squad'. Using foam is also a method applied by the US Nuclear Emergency Search Teams (NEST) to 'contain' a planted nuclear device.
81. 'Bomb Squad'.
82. Mick Kettle, former British army EOD operative, interviewed in 'Bomb Squad'.
83. Known in military parlance as BTUVIEDs.
84. Peter Gurney interviewed in 'Bomb Squad'.
85. Mick Kettle interviewed in 'Bomb Squad'.
86. Sidney Alford, former British army EOD operative, interviewed in 'Bomb Squad'. Also personal communication, Garda EOD operatives, February 2007, who said these were dubbed 'paw-paws' because of the shape.
87. Styles, *Bombs Have No Pity*, p.150.
88. 'Bomb Squad'.
89. Personal communication, Ulster Intelligence Unit operative, September 2007.
90. Peter Gurney interviewed in 'Bomb Squad'.
91. Warrant Officer 'K' in 'Bomb Squad'.
92. Personal communication, Ulster Intelligence Unit operative, September 2007.
93. Ibid., December 2007.
94. Moloney, *A Secret History of the IRA*, p.443.
95. Ryder, *A Special Kind of Courage*, p.xvi.
96. Urban, *Big Boys' Rules*, p.112.
97. Ibid., p.113.
98. Alford, 'Disruptive Influences', p.20.

99. Ryder, *A Special Kind of Courage*, p.xv.
100. Alford, 'Disruptive Influences', p.20.
101. Ryder, *A Special Kind of Courage*, p.xvii.
102. Alford, 'Disruptive Influences', p.20.
103. Ryder, *A Special Kind of Courage*, p.86.
104. 'Bomb Squad'.
105. Peter Gurney interviewed in 'Bomb Squad'.
106. Ibid.
107. Who accompanied me to the IRA inventory in Dublin Garda HQ.
108. About Allen-Vanguard, company press release, 2007.
109. Shane Paul O'Doherty interviewed in 'Bomb Squad'.
110. P. Hobson, Hobson Industries Limited press release for the Defence Systems and Equipment International (DSEi) Exhibition, London, September 2007. Hobson Industries used its extensive knowledge in building vehicles for the RUC in Northern Ireland to develop new armouring solutions for lightweight military vehicles.
111. Ryder, *A Special Kind of Courage*, p.103.
112. Peter Gurney interviewed in 'Bomb Squad'.
113. Alford, 'Disruptive Influences', p.20.
114. Urban, *Big Boys' Rules*, p.207.
115. Maj. Roger Davies, interview with the author, November 2007. He described the incident as 'making the hairs stand up on the back of our necks' when they discovered that the station was on consecrated ground.
116. Maj. Roger Davies, interview with the author, November 2007.

Ten

Decommissioning: 'Not a bullet: not an ounce'

The IRA has formally ordered an end to its armed campaign and says it will pursue exclusively peaceful means.
                    Official IRA statement, Seanna Walsh, July 2005

Republicans are not quitters.

                                        Gerry Adams, October 2003

This was a brave and a bold leap. The IRA's courageous decision was the right thing to do.
                                        Gerry Adams, September 2005

That's how it works. The Bomb Department bombed. This Department talked. That's how it works.
                        Brendan Duddy, secret mediator between the
                                                British and the IRA[1]

Only the Provisional IRA knew the true extent of its arsenal. Despite this, in September 2005 the head of the international body charged with decommissioning paramilitary arms in Northern Ireland, the Canadian general, John de Chastelain, announced to a waiting world that the IRA has now put its weapons beyond use and that original estimates (by Jane's, among others) were accurate. He also said that, given the advanced age of some of the weaponry, and the condition in which it was presented to the decommissioning team, that the IRA itself no longer knew exactly what arms it had in its vast inventory.[2] The Irish police was not involved in the decommissioning process – and did not receive sufficient credit for the process of seizures and EOD that made inroads into taking the IRA's war machine apart.[3]

The locations where the decommissioning took place remain secret.

The process took, each time, several long days that began at 6 a.m. and ended late at night.[4] The final act, in September 2005, was by far the largest. This chapter will deal with the endgame of decommissioning but will not re-visit in full all the political machinations that took place on the way – rather, it will focus on the issues concerning the ceasefires and weapons disarmament.

REVEALING THE ARSENAL TO THE WORLD

General de Chastelain did not, however, at this point in time reveal whether any of the weapons he has seen had been rendered either unusable or unobtainable. But details of the extent of the arsenal became known as each decommissioning act went through. The Semtex became the hallmark explosive for the IRA. Before decommissioning, it was estimated by British intelligence that they had enough of the plastic equivalent of plutonium to build two thousand bombs like the 'city destroyer' which devastated the Baltic Exchange in April 1992.[5] The highly accurate Barrett Light 50 sniper rifles were used to kill British soldiers in south Armagh. Russian-made machine-guns were used to target helicopters in ambushes. But other weapons, such as surface-to-air missiles acquired for the same targeting purposes, and ammunition that had been in storage for many years were never used.

According to the general, many of the guns were old. One he had handled – a 1930s vintage Bren machine-gun – was the same model he had trained with at the start of his military career.[6] Some of the ammunition came in loose, or in ammunition belts, indicating it had been recovered from individuals, local dumps or ASUs.

How did the IRA get to this state of disarmament – seen by many of its supporters as surrender, but many others as a great act of statesmanship – from a fully fledged and well-armed military campaign set to continue for many years? How did they progress from 'not a bullet, not an ounce' and the world's longest war to full demilitarisation?

RE-ARMING TO THE END

The road to disarmament was a long and painful one for the republican movement. As has been detailed earlier, the 1994 ceasefire did not hold and was broken by the biggest mainland bombs ever used by the IRA. It was known that during the ceasefires the Provisionals continued to recruit more members, target locations for bombing, and produce explosives[7] – which countermanded Sinn Féin's efforts to win electoral support from the broader nationalist community and wider acceptance as a legitimate political party. There were reports – mainly second-hand intelligence – to suggest that IRA members had been 'scouring' the six counties and the Republic to gather in weaponry from members in the weeks running up to de Chastelain's formal meeting with the IRA to commence decommissioning.[8]

Other claims were made by City of London police that dummy runs, including movement of weapons and recce missions were being made in early 1995 on potential City targets should a resumption of the military campaign ensue.[9] It was not proven whether these moves were to appease the restive factions of the rank and file who opposed any reduction of the armed struggle, or actual preparations for renewed war. They were probably both.

What was a distinct message from the IRA was that the whole issue of decommissioning was not on the table and was the chief means of exacting its surrender. Much of the membership viewed the dumping of arms as the ultimate sacrifice that would only indicate an all-out victory for the unionists and would place no onus on them to disarm their own paramilitaries.

BEGINNING OF THE ENDGAME

A three-man international body to deal with decommissioning of IRA weapons, chaired by US senator George Mitchell, was set up in parallel to the gradual process towards all-party talks. The IRA expressed its disfavour in no uncertain terms to any move towards decommissioning 'either through the front or the back door'.[10] The Mitchell group recommended that there would not likely be prior decommissioning before negotiations, but that some should take place during negotiations. The IRA was at this time readying itself for the Canary Wharf attack.[11]

This was a period of compromise and counter-compromise during the John Major government which needed unionist support in parliament. Gerry Adams and his supporters in the republican movement were the collective instrumental voice in moving the republican movement onto the track of the peace process and, despite the fits and starts, eventual decommissioning.

While the republicans wanted all-party talks to get underway without decommissioning, the unionists would never accept this. There was already a precarious IRA ceasefire holding, but this was threatening to collapse. According to Anthony McIntyre, the Provisionals would 'create a crater bigger than the one needed to hold all the weapons for decommissioning'.[12] One would be forgiven for thinking at the time that the IRA was threatening to explode an atomic bomb, and a ground-burst at that!

When the bomb came, it may not have been atomic, but it was certainly vast: the Canary Wharf 'spectacular', which exploded at 7 p.m. on 9 February 1996, killed two, injured forty, and caused at least £100 million worth of damage. The crater, created by the detonation of 1,500 kg of ammonium nitrate explosives mixed with icing sugar and boosted by 4 kg of Semtex, was over 10 metres wide and over 3 metres deep. A blue flash could be seen several miles away as the lorry exploded.[13] The IRA's military power, just in case it was doubted, was once again proclaimed.

The IRA said: 'It is with great reluctance that the leadership announces that the complete cessation of military operations will end at six o'clock on February 9th. The cessation presented a historic challenge for everyone and Óglaigh na hÉireann commends the leadership of nationalist Ireland at home and abroad. They rose to the challenge. The British Prime Minister did not. Instead of embracing the peace process, the British government acted in bad faith, with Mr Major and the Unionist leaders squandering this unprecedented opportunity to resolve the conflict.'[14] Talk spread of a split in the IRA and that the bomb had been deployed as damage limitation to prevent such a split taking place and a means of keeping the hardline elements onside.[15] This would eventually happen, with the formation of the breakaway Real IRA and Continuity IRA only two years later.

The security forces were not prepared for an attack during ceasefire, at least not as early as February 1996. The 'ring of steel' around the City of London was not in evidence – even with the vast explosions at Baltic Exchange and Bishopsgate having occurred only two years or so before. Contrast this with the constant surveillance that prevails in the face of the current, more amorphous threat from Islamicist groups.

THE AGONY OF COMPROMISE

However, before the big City bomb attacks, the IRA had already set off on a course of compromise and ceasefire. This posed huge problems within the movement, as ending the armed struggle with the goal of a united Ireland and British exit was not in sight. The Sinn Féin leadership of Gerry Adams and Martin McGuinness had the ultimate mountain to climb in convincing not just the British authorities that there was a chance for peace but the IRA rank and file to abandon war. But force would continue to be the main lever for the IRA to push the British into negotiation on 'Irish self-determination'.[16] Sinn Féin pushed for negotiations on the basis of its growing electoral mandate, at the same time as keeping the military option. But this was also set against a background of secret talks between the IRA and British officials, between Gerry Adams and the SDLP leader, John Hume, and between the Irish government of Albert Reynolds, a new taoiseach who showed unprecedented confidence that the IRA could be delivered in the peace process.[17] These negotiations led to Sinn Féin producing its document 'Towards a Lasting Peace', in 1992. With several IRA attacks having taken place early in the year – such as the roadside bomb attack at Teebane Cross in Co. Tyrone, which blew up a minibus carrying eight Protestant workmen, and two massive bomb attacks in Belfast city centre – the pronouncements about peace appeared increasingly hollow.

But such attacks, albeit seemingly opposed to any cessation of violence, were intended to keep the political process going. That process culminated in the combined Hume–Adams–Reynolds Joint Declaration which was submitted by Sinn Féin to the Irish government. It focused on EU developments as having 'changed the nature and the context of British–Irish relationships and will progressively remove the basis of the historic conflict still taking place in Northern Ireland'. This was indeed a revolutionary step for the republican movement, so different was it in tone and content from previous undiluted 'Brits Out' statements.[18] Instead, the Declaration emphasised the 'ending of divisions … through the agreement and co-operation of the people, North and South, representing both traditions in Ireland …' What was of paramount importance was that a British withdrawal was not included, and that 'Irish self-determination' was based not on British concessions but an acknowledgement by the Irish government of a separate right of consent for the people of the island of Ireland.

But more attacks and bloodshed followed the Joint Declaration. The early 1990s was punctuated by relentless bomb attacks and security scares in Northern Ireland and the British mainland. A plethora of bomb types appeared, including new mixes of homemade explosives following a shortage of nitrobenzene.[19] The impact of attacks, whether successful or not, had to be sustained to prove to the IRA membership that the movement still meant business. These included the 910-kg (2,000-lb) bomb attack which destroyed the forensic science laboratories in Belfast in September 1992; the destruction of much of Bangor city centre in October; the notorious Warrington bombing in March 1993; and the biggest bomb attack on the mainland at the time, the April 1993 Bishopsgate bomb.

In June 1993, after much wrangling between the IRA and the Irish government over the length of time that would be allowed for 'Irish self-determination' to be reached, the Declaration was submitted to the British by the Irish government. Gerry Adams summed it up thus: 'The Joint Declaration contains for the first time ever a recognition by the British, although heavily qualified that the Irish people as a whole have the right to self-determination.' Nevertheless, he said in an interview that: ' ... never does a British government act in anything other than what it perceives to be its own self-interest ... '[20] The distance of its content from the IRA's original aims was seen by many, on both sides, as an admission that the two-decades-plus period of sustained armed operations had not succeeded in attaining them.

Important in this was the Provisional IRA's failure, for many reasons, to acquire sufficient support or make much of an impact in the twenty-six counties. This had long been the situation, even from the days of the War of Independence, and was acknowledged by Martin McGuinness in his speech at Bodenstown in June 1993. It became only too clear how the many twists and turns of the negotiation process had resulted in a massive compromise – chiefly, to keep the support of the Irish government. The IRA had also appeared to submit to the unionist position, and despite the unionists' objections to much of the peace process, they were seen to have won through with no change to the status of Northern Ireland as part of the UK.

The so-called 'Irish Peace Initiative' of June 1993, the result of secret talks between John Hume, leader of the SDLP (Social Democratic and Labour Party), Irish prime ministers Charles Haughey and Albert Reynolds and Sinn Féin president Gerry Adams was intended to skew the path to peace to come from the Irish side, rather than the British, as leading the negotiations. The British position had changed; although the people of Northern Ireland, together with 'the people of the island as a whole', would have to decide on any change as to who governed them, the 'one-island approach' had entered the peace process and was to eventually cement the eventual Belfast (Good Friday) Agreement. No doubt the lack of overall support from the Republic had influenced the British move in allowing for any eventual decision on who governed the North. But the IRA's eventual decision for the 1994 ceasefire came about with the belief that there was a strong nationalist consensus in Ireland backed by the Irish–American lobby, which would ensure political and constitutional change in the Republic and thereby obviate the further need for military operations to attain republican goals.[21]

But beyond the complexities of all the negotiations that finally led to decommissioning was the hard fact that the IRA was viewed as a force that could not be defeated. But neither could it win; its leaders knew it would 'soldier on' in a state of stalemate for years to come.[22] The main intransigence on the IRA side came from the hardline heartlands of south Armagh, Tyrone and Fermanagh. The IRA brigades seemed at odds with the leadership – with ninety votes versus ten against the Declaration. There were bitter memories of the Treaty that led to partition in the 1920s; the IRA could not countenance ceasing operations if the British promised to eventually disengage.

Tension between Gerry Adams and the rest of the leadership emerged, but his strength gave the movement a steadiness that served it well through its turbulent endgame. Considering that back in 1984 – the year of the Brighton bomb – the Army Council had proclaimed in its New Year message that 'this war is to the end. When we put away our guns, Britain will be out of Ireland … '[23], it became startlingly clear how far the movement had matured, as evidenced by Gerry Adams stating:

> You have to find an accommodation, if you had a united Ireland tomorrow and it became the six counties for the last seventy years on an all-Ireland stage, it wouldn't be worth anything because you would have a disaffected minority who would use the same methods as republicans used.[24]

And the hard man of Sinn Féin-IRA, Martin McGuinness, was also seen as taking a pragmatic approach, stating that the IRA could cease actions in 1994 if the British were 'imaginative',[25] in recognising that Irish self-determination was the Irish people 'alone' – echoing the very meaning of 'Sinn Féin' itself.

But IRA attacks still continued throughout 1993, including warnings to foreign-owned financial companies in the City, and many northern republicans rejected the Anglo-Irish Downing Street Declaration of December 1993. While continuing armed operations, the Army Council decided not to reject the Declaration.[26] It had taken the republican movement eight weeks to respond, and during the six weeks following the Declaration's publication there were, as well as a number of shootings and hijackings by the IRA, twenty-two explosions and twenty-four incendiaries – including on New Year's Day, 1994, in eleven Belfast stores[27] (a sinister throwback to the 1970s). Mortar attacks continued in 1994; in March came the Heathrow operations and a string of attacks on British army bases, patrols and RUC stations. Within days of the Heathrow mortars a south Armagh-made 'barrack buster' scored a direct hit on Crossmaglen army/RUC base on 19 March, injuring three soldiers and a policeman while also arousing public repugnance because it affected a surrounding built-up area.

According to British intelligence the IRA were continuing procurement and movement of weapons, bomb-making, and intelligence gathering. Some 150 incendiaries had been moved north, over seventy of which were destined for the British mainland. Arms dumps were being secured, with weapons buried deep in ditches, having been wrapped in plastic barrels and pipes. This indicated that the IRA were either digging in for the long haul or preparing to cease operations. Several Irish police arms seizures yielded twelve 3-kg blocks of Semtex, Russian DhSK machine-guns and assault rifles.

'COMPLETE CESSATION'

The Irish government was indeed greatly instrumental in securing the ceasefires and the eventual three-party agreement, along with the US (Clinton) administration and an Irish-American lobby that aligned itself with republican moves towards non-violence. As well as this thrust for a change in direction, which had been long in the making and carried through by the efforts of Gerry Adams, was the prisoner lobby which had always had a marked influence on the movement as a whole. Nevertheless, any ceasefire would be temporary – three to six months, with no expectation of a complete cessation. The ranks still believed that the armed struggle could be sustained and that a temporary stoppage would give the IRA leverage to extract further concessions.[28] The ceasefire had to be dressed up as something other than 'suing for peace'. Political arrangements and a 'transitional phase towards Irish unity' was an approach that helped to bring on board the more intransigent elements of the movement towards a complete cessation.[29]

When the announcement came of a 'complete cessation of military operations', the culmination of eighteen months of intense negotiations, it was met with predicted scepticism by the unionists, who demanded it should be made 'permanent'. The Reynolds government had intended 'complete' to mean permanent without having to use the word 'permanent'. In the province, loyalist violence intensified while those groups were meant to be considering their own ceasefire.

The Declaration of 6 September 1994 – made televisually real by the triple handshake of Adams, Hume and Reynolds – did not just herald in a 'new era' in which republicans had become 'committed to democratic and peaceful methods of resolving our political problems', but also ushered in a form of constitutional republicanism with the full support of the Irish Republic. Before, the IRA had been declared enemies of the Irish state.[30]

Only one day before the ceasefire a mortar attack was launched on the British army Fort Whiterock base in Belfast. The day after, the statement was greeted by widespread celebrations in nationalist areas awash with processions of cars with tricolour flags waving out of windows and cheering republicans. While saying 'We are therefore entering into a new situation in a spirit of determination and confidence, determined that the injustices which created this conflict will be removed and confident in the strength and justice of our struggle to achieve this,'[31] the IRA was signalling a willingness to endure a non-violent process towards Irish self-determination. But 'A solution will only be found as a result of inclusive negotiations' signalled to all involved in the tortuous peace process and beyond that a resumption of IRA military operations would ensue if Britain refused it a political voice in talks.[32]

However it was viewed, the first ceasefire had come without a British withdrawal from Northern Ireland. The hardline IRA factions resisted its continuation, and would be instrumental in its end. Politics as a means to Irish unity had always been mistrusted. Loyalist groups continued, intent on the IRA getting 'no deal' from the British. But the twenty-five years of armed struggle had won the IRA a place at the negotiating table.

When the Canary Wharf bomb ended the ceasefire on 9 February 1996, it became clear that the Provisionals had maintained a programme of intelligence-gathering, explosives manufacture and training. A major plan had been put in place to assault economic and infrastructure targets on the UK mainland and cause maximum disruption if the talks fell through. Bomb-making continued in south Armagh, as well as at the infamous 'bomb factory' – a remote house in Clonaslee, Co. Laois.[33] The Canary Wharf bombing was followed by an IRA statement that called for an 'inclusive negotiated settlement' rather than its former, overall demand of 'Brits out'. The Clonaslee bomb-making house had made and supplied several of the homemade, primarily ammonium nitrate, bombs and had been at the heart of the engineering operation for seven years. It had remained undetected, and the bombs followed the route via south Armagh to their cataclysmic destinations – London and Manchester, where 'sleepers' awaited their arrival and contributed towards their deployment.

The Canary Wharf attack was not unanimously agreed to by the Provisionals by any means – not all members of the Army Council were present when it was decided. Two civilians died, and republican political activists on the ground who depended on community and electoral support were not warned the bombing was about to take place. The attack was also viewed as tactically successful but strategically flawed, as it threatened the IRA's long-term negotiating position.[34] Nevertheless, it proved the IRA still had the means to destroy, disrupt and continue to wage war.

It did not stop the arrangement for talks to resume in June 1996. In the same month, two IRA members who were in the process of assembling mortar bombs and which included the senior IRA quartermaster who had been arrested in 1987 on board the *Eksund*, were arrested during an Irish police raid on Clonaslee. The materials raided included explosives, timers and electrical components for the mortars; the raid was a coup for the gardaí, resulting from a tip-off received following an appeal for information following the IRA killing of a special branch officer, Jerry McCabe. The response from the officer in charge of Metropolitan Police specialist crime squads since 1991, Assistant Commissioner David Veness, summed up the reality of the abandoned ceasefire: 'Domestically, we are resigned to the long-term threat of the Provisional IRA. We regard ceasefires as periods of terrorist preparation.'[35]

The frequency of IRA attacks increased during the first months of 1997 in anticipation of the British general election on 1 May. By 30 April the Provisionals had carried out twenty-nine attacks as compared with eleven in the whole of 1996.[36] Disruption was wrought on the country's motorways on 3 April 1997, when police found and detonated two bombs, one of which contained up to 1 kg of Semtex, and several hoax devices. On 21 April the police had to close seventeen rail and London underground stations as well as all the main London airports – Gatwick, Heathrow, Luton and Stansted – and the port of Dover's eastern dock.[37]

CEASEFIRE MARK II

A new ceasefire was not to come into effect until 20 July 1997, only three months following the landslide election of the new Labour government which, unlike the Major government, did not need the parliamentary support of the Ulster Unionists. If the ceasefire were restored, Sinn Féin would be admitted to talks. The promise of real political inclusion was to be a prime deciding factor. But the basis for Sinn Féin entry to the talks process was, according to the new prime minister, Tony Blair, 'a permanent and complete cessation of their violence and that they have begun the process of handing over their weaponry'.[38] But the IRA leadership, through statements made by Martin McGuinness, the chief negotiator for Sinn Féin, was assured that the decommissioning issue had been removed as a precondition for talks,[39] that Blair had suggested as much.[40]

Also, the ceasefire prompted an increase in activity among republican (and loyalist) splinter terrorist groups opposed to the peace process. The Continuity Irish Republican Army (CIRA) and the INLA, which had long been sidelined throughout the Provisionals era, increased their attacks to protest against the talks. INLA gunmen murdered a Northern Irish police trainee in Belfast on 9 May and carried out several attacks against the RUC and British troops in July during three days of heavy rioting in Belfast over controversial loyalist parades. A new loyalist group, the Loyalist Volunteer Force (LVF), appeared in 1997 and attacked both republican activists and Catholic civilians who had no paramilitary affiliations.[41] Peace was still a long way over the horizon.

Two days after the ceasefire, Tony Blair said decommissioning should take place during talks from September until May 1998. The unionists wanted weapons to be surrendered before talks started. Therein lay the next great deadlock that would be broken by the Good Friday Agreement in 1998. By 9 September 1997, Sinn Féin had affirmed its commitment to the 'Mitchell Principles' on democracy and non-violence to abide by a peaceful resolution of the Northern Ireland conflict – only to have them rejected three days later by the IRA.[42] Nevertheless, Sinn Féin entered the talks later in the month, having made substantial electoral gains mainly as a result of signing up to the Mitchell Principles. By the end of 1997 the peace process included both unionist and republican parties, including Sinn Féin.

Of supreme importance was the role of the US government in the aftermath of the second ceasefire. US secretary of state Madeleine Albright accepted from the British government that the ceasefire was 'genuine in word and deed', permitting Sinn Féin to join inclusive, all-party talks in Belfast, and said that any resumption of violence by the IRA would have a direct impact on the administration's ongoing review of the ceasefire situation. The days of the armed struggle were numbered, but no-one knew how long it would be before the weapons used to wage it would be actively removed from service.

THE GOOD FRIDAY AGREEMENT

The Good Friday Accord, signed on 10 April 1998, outlined for the first time in history a comprehensive power-sharing arrangement between both communities in a multiparty administration of Northern Ireland. Allowing Sinn Féin to join the new administration as long as its leaders remained committed to 'exclusively peaceful means' set the scene for the highly delicate process that would lead to decommissioning. This was fraught with problems, however; having already conceded so much in order to acquire power-sharing status, republicans would now be at the mercy of their electorate in maintaining support for any of their long-term or short-term aims.

The split in the IRA that led to the formation of the Real IRA and less-important Continuity IRA became a serious problem for the security services and threatened support for the new constitutional republican-ism. The Omagh bomb of 15 August 1997, which exacted the largest death toll from a republican attack in Northern Ireland, followed an attack by the same group in Banbridge on 1 August, which injured thir-ty-five and damaged 200 homes.[43] By November the agreement looked in tatters. The dissident republican groups would cast a shadow over the entire peace process and efforts to decommission: in 2000 the Real IRA was expected to continue its sporadic, but potentially deadly campaign, and the CIRA had called on the Provisionals to hand over weapons that were acquired 'to defend the Republic'.[44]

'NOT A BULLET, NOT AN OUNCE'

As was the situation leading up to the second ceasefire in 1997 and the Good Friday Agreement a year later, the IRA continued to resist what it regarded as a 'surrender' of its arms, particularly as it felt the conditions that caused the conflict remained unresolved. Martin McGuinness had said before the 1997 ceasefire that he did not believe the IRA would hand over a single bullet: 'The IRA have said they will not decommis-sion a single bullet and I have not heard any statement from them say-ing they have changed their position on that.'[45]

By the turn of the century, decommissioning remained the dominant and unresolved issue of the peace process. It was to be part of a solution that would lead to 'all the guns being removed from Irish politics' – giving equal weight to IRA weapons and the presence of the British military. The process towards the three separate acts of disarmament would take a mul-titude of twists and turns that closely resembled a political soap opera.

The first IRA meeting with General de Chastelain's Independent International Commission on Decommissioning (IICD) was in December 1999. At the end of January 2000, with the Good Friday Agreement nearly three years in place and expectations running high, General de Chastelain's first report declared that there had been a stalling in the decommissioning process and that the IRA had stated it had entered no agreements to decommission.[46] The suspension of Stormont and direct rule ensued in February.

A second report followed just eleven days after the first, and implied that progress had been made:

> We find particularly significant, and view as valuable progress, the assertion made to us by the IRA representative that the IRA will consider how to put arms and explosives beyond use, in the context of full implementation of the Good Friday Agreement, and in the context of the removal of the causes of conflict ... The Commission welcomes the IRA's recognition that the issue of arms needs to be dealt with in an acceptable way.[47]

And, most importantly, 'The representative indicated to us today (Friday) the context in which the IRA will initiate a comprehensive process to put arms beyond use, in a manner as to ensure maximum public confidence.' This showed that the IRA was on the brink of rewriting its history once again – although a definitive IRA statement was still not forthcoming.[48] The February 2000 report also reaffirmed the importance of loyalist arms decommissioning, which had been conveniently sidelined, in stating that 'The elimination of the threat posed by loyalist paramilitary arms is clearly within the Commission's remit.' The commission's belief in an eventual solution would be severely undermined by the IRA's withdrawal from the decommissioning body on 16 February 2000 – until the Northern Ireland police force and judicial system were reformed (which would take years to achieve) and the Northern Ireland institutions immediately reinstated.

But the ceasefire held – and a significant turning point came on 6 May 2000 when an IRA statement revealed the organisation's intention to 'begin a process in which its arms would be placed completely and verifiably beyond use', providing the Good Friday Agreement was implemented in full. The statement followed a proposal to restore the Northern Ireland assembly – linked to a firm commitment to decommissioning.[49] Then, in June 2000, the IRA allowed two international inspectors access to some of its arms dumps as a confidence-building measure, and both declared they were satisfied weapons and explosives were secure.[50] President Clinton's December 2000 visit further demonstrated and solidified US support for achieving lasting peace in the North of Ireland. And the turn of events that was to follow the worst terrorist attack in history the following year would be instrumental in propelling decommissioning irrevocably forward.

But in the meantime, the process stalled again. De Chastelain's commission in July 2001 had reported that a second deadline for decommissioning had elapsed. The report stated:

Taken in conjunction with the continued maintenance of the July 1997 ceasefire and the opening of some IRA arms dumps to inspections by the international inspectorate, we believe that this conditional commitment is made in good faith. We have, however, been unable to ascertain how the IRA will put its arms beyond use, except for the assurance that it will be complete and verifiable.[51]

The commission's faith in the IRA was also not, naturally, accompanied by an equivalent from the unionists: the resignation on 1 July 2001 of the Stormont first minister David Trimble over what was widely perceived as the IRA's failure to disarm added another dimension to the crisis and put the delicate state of self-government for the province in jeopardy. Loyalists desisted from disarming, with the main group – the Ulster Volunteer Force (UVF) – stating that it would not consider doing so until it had a declaration that 'the Provisionals' war was over'. The commission concluded:

Given the conditions the IRA, UVF and UFF say they require before they will put their arms beyond use, we believe we cannot influence that activity by making demands or by setting deadlines. But we will continue to do what we can to implement our mandate through continuing contact and discussion with each of the three paramilitary groups, insisting that the objectives of the legislation calling for arms to be rendered permanently inaccessible or permanently unusable are respected.[52]

Even before the events of 9/11, any renewal of terrorist activity was severely threatened by new legislation passed in the UK in February 2001. The Blair government's Terrorism Act 2000 replaced temporary and emergency laws that dealt with Northern Ireland-related terrorism and authorised the government to ban groups involved in domestic or transnational terrorism and to use special arrest powers to prosecute their members or supporters. The Regulation of Investigatory Powers Act, which became effective in July 2000, created a statutory basis for intercepting communications and for covert surveillance. By late 2001, UK authorities had frozen more than £70 million ($100 million) of suspected terrorist assets.[53]

'BEYOND USE' – THE ROAD TO DISARMAMENT

The first real moves towards decommissioning came in June 2000, when the Provisionals opened up some of the arms dumps for inspection.

While holding onto their command structure and not laying down their arms wholesale, the Army Council prepared for the political long haul – to tread a tortuous route of trying to convince their own membership that the IRA was undefeated, and their enemies that 'the conflict was over'. The month before, an IRA statement laid the foundations for future moves, saying that the IRA 'will initiate a process that will completely and verifiably put IRA arms beyond use' – also saying it was working with the decommissioning body to 'resolve the issue of arms'.[54] This raised expectations, which were often unrealistic, that total decommissioning was just around the corner. But the reality was far more complicated and ambiguous: the statement also outlined the 'root causes of conflict' that would have to be solved by removing British jurisdiction from Ireland.

There were still problems with the peace negotiations; the Northern Ireland Executive was suspended from February; few trusted the IRA to fully disarm, and dissident groups still held on to sizeable quantities of arms and explosives and had every intention to use them.[55] The majority of republicans, however, knew they were entering the endgame – and that the journey would be painful and protracted. They knew that any form of self-rule with republican input depended on decommissioning of IRA arms – but were trying desperately to avoid further defections into the dissident ranks. The IRA now had to be seen to be all things to all men: seen to be making peace, while maintaining the wherewithal to make war.

ASSESSING THE WEAPONS

By October 2000 the arms inspectors had confirmed that large amounts of explosives, weapons and related equipment were secure.[56] The IRA leadership was trying to stall the process in the hope of concessions on British demilitarisation and policing arrangements in Northern Ireland.

Meanwhile, the British authorities were in the process of assessing how much firepower the IRA actually had, and what level of weaponry was still available to it if the ceasefire broke down. As with all assessments of weapons capability, this could be simplified in a basic equation: intent + weapons + expertise = threat. The IRA at the beginning of the twenty-first century had low intent, certainly compared to the past. But its capability was high, and possibly higher even than at the height of large-scale operations that bombed the City of London.

As stated at the beginning of this book, it was estimated that the Provisionals held enough weaponry to equip two battalions and destroy through bombing at least one sizeable city centre, as shown in detail in Table 4.1 (see Chapter 4).[57] In February 2001 a sizeable amount of arms had been uncovered in Co. Donegal, including a projected recoilless improvised grenade (PRIG) that had been armed with a Semtex warhead and was in a dangerous condition. The existence of the PRIG – an advanced improvised weapon – identified the cache as Provisional IRA rather than Real IRA.[58]

The 2000 capability assessment, based on intelligence, insider information, arms seizures and knowledge of arms deals, was used to justify maintaining high troop and surveillance levels in Northern Ireland – which, in turn, did not contribute towards speeding up the decommissioning process. Therefore, by May 2001, no weapon had been put out of use.[59] The sign on the Belfast wall that read: 'NOT A BULLET – NOT AN OUNCE' held true.

The deadline for decommissioning (22 May 2000) set by the GFA had already been extended to June 2001. Arrangements had been made between the IRA and the IICD to agree locations for weapons decommissioning and record weapons that would be made 'permanently inaccessible or permanently unusable'.

THE IMPACT OF 9/11

Enter the Americans. By May 2001 the US government was becoming increasingly concerned about the pro-Irish republican following, which had resulted in some $11 million contributed annually into the IRA's coffers, to the extent that it banned the Real IRA as a 'foreign terrorist organisation'. Also in May 2001 came the FARC scandal, with the arrest of three Irish nationals under suspicion of training the Colombian guerrilla group in bomb technology. Furthermore, after the Colombia arrests a leading figure in Irish–American politics and chairman of the Mutual Bank of America, Bill Flynn, called on the IRA to disarm.[60]

With the Bush administration less inclined towards support for the Irish cause than its predecessor, the coup de grâce came with the Al-Qaeda terrorist atrocities on 11 September 2001, resulting in a seismic shift in US policy. The 'war on terror' had begun – waged by a country with little experience of terrorism, either home-grown or foreign. In the minds of millions of Americans, the Provisional IRA were no different to those who had attacked them on 9/11: 'one man's terrorist was ... another man's terrorist'. All assets of listed terrorist groups – including dissident republican groups and their political wings (and later, many of their loyalist equivalents) – were blocked and all US-based funding banned, and pressure on the Provisionals to disarm grew by the day. Having paid visits to Washington, DC during the Clinton years, and still dependent on political support from the powerful US lobby, the Sinn Féin leaders grabbed whatever was left of the political initiative and announced, in the full glare of the world's media, the first act of IRA decommissioning – in Washington – on 23 October 2001.[61]

What the world wanted to know, of course, was what the IRA had put 'beyond use' when the first cache of weapons had been concreted over in bunkers north and south of the border.[62] The decommissioning was accompanied by the installation of satellite surveillance to spot tampering. But no indication of what exactly went under concrete was revealed. Much of the arsenal had been under the control of the South Armagh brigade – the most hardline in the IRA – and stored in remote areas of the Republic.[63] This was significant in itself for the republican movement insofar as it indicated the extent of the upheaval – the giving up of weapons – taking place at its very heart.

'LITTLE EARTHQUAKES'

The unionist and British army commanders predictably said that too many concessions had been made in order to propel the IRA into commencing decommissioning: pledges by the British government to scale down troop numbers in Northern Ireland; dismantling of army installations, particularly in the republican border areas; and a proposal before parliament for an amnesty for OTRs (on-the-runs). However, decommissioning caused what Gerry Adams called 'little earthquakes' among the IRA leadership and republican community.[64] But the Northern Ireland Executive had been restored – and although the word 'historic' was well worn in the reports following the IRA's announcement, it was hard to deny that its first act of decommissioning was groundbreaking not only in the history of the republican movement, but in the history of insurgency movements worldwide. No bullet or ordnance had ever been surrendered by the IRA previously, while in making this first commitment, the movement was no nearer to its ultimate goal, a united Ireland. Much wrangling, however, was to follow, the complexities of which will not be dealt with here. Suffice it to say that the IRA had to avoid at all costs appearing to be in the process of surrender. The acts had to be conducted as an overall effort to demilitarise Northern Ireland. There was still no formal acceptance of the GFA and moves to disarm were seen as coinciding with eventual British withdrawal. But the real crunch was yet to come, and until it did, the process dribbled along in fits and starts.

THE SECOND ACT: 2002

Then, on 8 April 2002 a further 'substantial and varied' IRA cache, according to the IICD, was decommissioned, 'so that the peace process can be stabilised, sustained and strengthened', according to the accompanying Provisional statement – with still no equivalent moves from the loyalist groups. Once again no details on numbers or types of weapons were released.[65] The sites of the arms dumps and the method of putting the weapons beyond use remained a secret, except for having consisted of plastic explosives, mortars and assault rifles thought to be buried in locations around the Irish republic.[66]

This act was vital in order to show that the IRA's first, groundbreaking move was more than a mere act of political symbolism and opportunism. Gen. John de Chastelain said: 'I believe they are on the path to peace.' Most significant was David Trimble's statement that critics who argued that this would never happen now looked 'foolish', and that they ought to be directing their attention instead to Protestant paramilitary groups, which had shown no interest in destroying their weapons.[67] However, de Chastelain added that more actions were needed to dispel lingering doubts about the IRA's commitment to abandon its weapons. This would commit the republican movement to an unstoppable and irreversible process of disarmament. But throughout the process until the very end, it was clear that the mainstay of the IRA's organising structure – the Army Authority – which claimed that force of arms was to be maintained in order to secure a thirty-two-county Irish Republic[68] – remained in place alongside the political moves to increase support for Sinn Féin.[69]

But this was not apparent for the rest of 2002. The second act was followed by a series of crises and setbacks. Gains by Sinn Féin in the Irish general election in June 2002 were offset by the arrests of several Sinn Féin figures in September, accused and charged with espionage activities at the Stormont government offices. Decommissioning remained the major stumbling block in talks between all parties seeking to restore devolution after the Northern Ireland Assembly was suspended in October 2002, when the IRA announced it had broken off contact with the IICD, having accused the British government of not keeping the promises it made in the GFA. Nevertheless, the IRA announced it was still committed to the 'search for a just and lasting peace' and the 1997 ceasefire remained intact – but that recent events showed unionist leaders had 'set their faces against political change at this time'.[70]

Then in December 2002 a confidential Irish government document was inadvertently leaked stating the IRA was still recruiting, acquiring weapons and gathering intelligence.[71] This was no surprise to those who knew that the IRA, having waged the 'long war', would ensure that it held onto the means to restart it if political initiatives failed and promises were not kept. The accusations centred on the IRA having a network of spies – most of them in low-key jobs such as clerks, cooks and chauffeurs – in areas of government, many of them 'sleepers' who only jumped into action when a particular piece of information was needed. It was claimed that the IRA had been doing 'exactly what MI5 used to do during the Cold War – they used to try and "turn" or get into place people in fairly low positions who nevertheless had access to documents and so on'.[72] The Provisionals were merely continuing the tradition of intelligence and planting insiders established by Michael Collins in the War of Independence.

DEADLOCK

By 2003 the continued ambiguity of IRA statements and all-round deadlock in the Northern Ireland peace process brought matters to a head. The republicans had come to a fork in the road, with one route taking them further along the path of politicisation, talks, and compromise – and the other, to continue what was enshrined in the IRA's doctrine, 'to guard the honour and uphold the sovereignty and unity of the Republic of Ireland, *primarily by force of arms*'.[73] The extent of that dilemma was seen in the ambiguous nature of the IRA's statements. With the start of the Iraq War of 2003, a US presidential visit and constant calls for the Provisionals to disarm amid continuous back-room talks, the pressure was on like never before. Yet another statement was rejected by the British and Irish governments. It had said the IRA was not party to the GFA, and that a third act of decommissioning was under way 'for a complete and final closure of the conflict', but there was no timescale for the process. And it would only take place once the GFA had been fully implemented by the UK government. Did that mean a united Ireland? If so, then it would likely never happen in the lifetime of any of the protagonists.

The wrangling continued and the deadline extended once again, to April 2005. There was continued ambiguity over precisely which paramilitary activities would cease. Activities included military attacks; training; targeting; intelligence gathering (which continued apace); acquisition or development of arms or explosives; other preparations for terrorist campaigns, punishment beatings and attacks and involvement in riots. Elections for Stormont were put back and some demands were made on the unionists to implement their part of the GFA. Moves towards full demilitarisation by the British would only come with more decommissioning. But big changes in the Northern Ireland political landscape were also in train, including devolution of policing and judicial powers. Equally groundbreaking was the agreement that 'on-the-runs' would be allowed to return to Ireland without prosecution.

But Sinn Féin faced exclusion from Stormont if the IRA did not deliver on their commitments under monitoring by a special US–UK–Irish four-person independent body, the Independent Monitoring Commission, which could respond with such sanctions. So in order to continue in the government of Northern Ireland, the IRA had to sign up fully to the GFA and hope that the political process would in the end lead to a united Ireland – but give up its arms within the context of continued partition.[74] In October the IRA refused again to decommission, with all-party agreement once more set for November 2003.

There followed a series of revelations that were to further complicate the process. The highly controversial issue of collusion between the RUC and British intelligence in loyalist murders of republicans was confirmed. This had long been suspected, and revealed the extent of the 'dirty war'. 'This is not about rogue elements within the British system,' commented Alex Maskey, the Sinn Féin lord mayor of Belfast: 'It's about a state policy sanctioned at the highest level.'[75]

Then a high-ranking IRA operative – codenamed 'Stakeknife', who had been deputy commander of the IRA's much-feared internal security unit – was unfrocked as having been working inside the movement for twenty years as a British agent. He would have passed on vast amounts of information of all operations, arms expertise and equipment, and would have aided the sabotage by the British of many planted devices. As the bitterest of ironies, as an IRA intelligence chief, he was himself betraying intelligence about the IRA to the British. But it also revealed how far the British had gone to infiltrate the IRA. This was truly a scandal for the British as his activities included participation in IRA murders of policemen and soldiers. The extent and implications of Stakeknife's role were so serious that it is likely that the resultant compromising of IRA operations would have contributed greatly towards the admission that the military campaign would have to end.[76]

THE THIRD ACT: BRINGING DOWN THE CURTAIN

Meanwhile, the Real IRA continued to be a thorn in the side of all involved. Defections to the dissident group had led to losses of personnel, weapons and funding. Even the Provisional Army Council was in danger of splitting over whether to resume military operations. The political aims of the republican movement were greatly enhanced; Sinn Féin made considerable inroads in the postponed November 2003 elections – emerging as the largest nationalist party in Northern Ireland. This produced the irony of ironies: a Sinn Féin deputy minister, Martin McGuinness, sitting alongside the head of the Democratic Unionist Party – which had become the biggest unionist party in the province – the Protestant firebrand who had been dubbed 'Dr No' due to his repeated, high-volume intransigence, the Rev. Dr Ian Paisley.

A third act of decommissioning a month before did little to assuage the unionists, who demanded to know details which Gen. de Chastelain was not at liberty to disclose, other than that the latest tranche was 'considerably larger' – an estimated 200 tonnes, up to 70 per cent of the IRA's arsenal[77] – than the previous two.[78] It was made clear by the IICD that the decommissioning rules had been followed; that disclosure of information was only necessary for reasons of public safety; to confirm the legitimate participation in the decommissioning process by those eligible to do so; and to fulfil the commission's duty to report to the two governments.[79] In other words, the rules did not have to satisfy unionist demands.

PROBLEMS OF DISCLOSURE

The commissioners stated that disclosure of details without IRA agreement would make their positions untenable.[80] Of great significance is that the agreement made with the Provisionals that details would not be revealed was a vital factor in the IICD achieving the successive acts of decommissioning. What was revealed from the third act was that 'light, medium and heavy ordnance' had been decommissioned – which was taken to mean more of the same: mortars, rockets, machine-guns, rifles and Semtex. That there were so many successive acts of laying down of arms indicated just how much there had been to begin with, and how much was left to go – of arms that were known about. Also, it became clear that setting the original deadline for total decommissioning to two years following the GFA had been totally unrealistic. After decades of armed insurrection, which had not achieved its original goals, the agonising process of giving up weapons was not likely to be compressed into such a short space of time.

But at the time of each of the first three acts, much talk was of these being symbolic rather than actual surrender of arms. It was well known that further arms could be brought in from the Balkans, awash with illicit hardware, and elsewhere. As mentioned earlier, a consignment of Russian Special Forces AN-94 assault rifles had been reportedly bought in late 2001. Also, the improvised nature of much of the weapons meant that replacing them would not necessarily involve smuggling and extensive and observable overseas procurement. These included the timer and power units (TPUs) for bombs, which would themselves have been improvised; 800-metre range mortars containing up to 400 kg of explosives; radio control mechanisms for command-detonated IEDs; and the euphemistically named 'victim-operated devices' – booby traps.[81] Bomb-making expertise in the Provisionals also remained, despite the RIRA defections; this was a 'knowledge they could not lose'.[82]

Therefore, until all the weapons were apparently decommissioned, the tranches of arms put 'beyond use' – by pouring concrete onto the bunkers – in the first acts of decommissioning were viewed as gestures (even though similar 'gestures' were not forthcoming from the loyalist paramilitaries). Such judgments overlooked how significant the abandonment of any weapons was when viewed against the entire history of the republican movement. And the essence of decommissioning under the aegis of a respected independent body was that it created a climate to facilitate an ongoing peace process, and this trend was virtually irreversible by 2003. In some ways it could be compared to the successive nuclear weapons reduction treaties negotiated between the US and the Soviet Union during the Cold War; many weapons remained and still remain, but the treaties marked a complete reversal of years of arms build-up and, despite ongoing panics over nuclear proliferation, had enormous political implications for world peace.[83]

THE FARC CONTROVERSY

Arguably the most damaging incident to threaten the delicate negotiations surrounding decommissioning was the FARC-linked IRA arrests. Jim Monaghan, Martin McCauley and Niall Connolly were accused in August 2001 of training FARC (Revolutionary Armed Forces of Colombia) guerrillas in Colombia. Jim Monaghan was reputed to be the IRA's leading mortar-maker who had escaped explosives charges in the 1970s but became a member of the Sinn Féin executive in the 1980s. Niall Connolly was Sinn Féin's Cuban envoy.

The effect on the peace process was seismic: although it was common knowledge that the IRA had established links with foreign paramilitary organisations such as ETA in Spain and Palestinian groups, the FARC connection was a surprise to all except those close enough to be in the know. It also had a catastrophic effect on the republicans' connections with, and support from, the US when the country was collectively traumatised by the events of 9/11 one month after the arrests.

An IRA statement eight days after the Al-Qaeda attacks insisted that it had not sent anyone to Colombia nor interfered in its internal affairs. Then as the deadlock tightened in October, the day before the first IRA decommissioning act Gerry Adams admitted that Niall Connolly worked for Sinn Féin in Cuba, but that he and other party leaders had been unaware of this.[84]

The 'Colombia Three' were acquitted in Colombia in April 2004 on all charges except travelling on false passports; but their acquittal was overturned by an appeal court in December 2004 and they were sentenced to seventeen years in prison. However, the three Irishmen were reported in August 2005 to have fled the country while awaiting the appeal, and to have returned to Ireland.

It is alleged that the FARC were trained in the construction of shaped charges, roadside mines, propane-butane gas cylinders,[85] triggers/initiators for hand grenades, and in IED deployment. A FARC defector was said in May 2005 to have told the commander-in-chief of the Colombian army, General Carlos Alberto Ospina, that the IRA team trained him in the use of explosives, landmines and mortars. Ospina said IRA-style techniques are now being used all over Colombia by FARC.[86]

A British military attaché and other British experts who travelled to Colombia to compare explosive devices and sniping techniques (using high-tech sighting equipment) also found IEDs that they confirmed had been used by the IRA. An Irish army expert claimed that 'The Provos increased their weapons' size and range ... That's standard enough, but if the FARC were using 0.5-in rifles that would indicate some similarities. With a 0.5-in rifle you can engage from three-quarters of a mile and if you hit the target you'll take it down.' Multiple mine-laying methods were also tied into Provisional operations – such as that which killed eighteen British soldiers at Warrenpoint in 1979. The noted tactic was to detonate a bomb, wait until a larger patrol arrived, and then detonate an even larger bomb where it was likely the unit would muster. Another classic IRA technique, remote proxy-bomb detonation (see Chapter 6), was exposed when in Colombia a child was paid to ride a bicycle loaded with 4 kg of dynamite to a road block before it was detonated by a FARC operative nearby, killing the boy and two policemen.

THE FINAL ACT – 'A VERY BRAVE AND BOLD LEAP'

TABLE 10.1: DECOMMISSIONED TRANCHE OF WEAPONS, SEPTEMBER 2005

1,000 rifles
2 tonnes of Semtex
20–30 heavy machine-guns
7 surface-to-air missiles (unused)
7 flame throwers
1,200 detonators
11 rocket-propelled grenade launchers
90 hand guns
100+ grenades

Source: Security estimates/Jane's Intelligence Review

The talks dragged on through the last part of 2003 amid the feeling that both sides felt short-changed. Gerry Adams had spoken further about the future peaceful intentions of republicans. In September 2004 Sinn Féin agreed to allow two clergymen, one Protestant and one Catholic, to witness decommissioning. But this still wasn't enough for the unionists as it fell short of their demands for visual proof – photographs – of the destruction of weaponry. In December 2004 Sinn Féin said republicans would accept the complete decommissioning of IRA arms as part of that deal. The measures included other changes addressing nationalist concerns. However, Sinn Féin said photographing IRA arms was unacceptable because unionists might use them to humiliate republicans.

In February 2005 the end still did not seem to be in sight. The IRA withdrew its offer to complete all arms decommissioning, following accusations that the organisation was behind a £26.5m bank raid in Belfast in December 2004. In April, Gerry Adams again said he had told the IRA that there was now an alternative to violence and that the climate was right for republicans to 'fully embrace and accept' democratic means of achieving their goals.

But it appeared that delays in full disarmament signalled to the unionists and the world beyond the republican and nationalist people of Ireland that the war had not been totally ended. They also showed that the IRA was trying to hold onto operational capabilities. But discussions within the IRA carried on through the first half of 2005, until July – the month in which the most lethal terrorist acts were committed on British soil: the attacks by home-grown Islamic extremists on the London transit system, on 7 July, killing fifty-six people and injuring 700.

It was therefore vital that the IRA were seen to be moving in the right political direction. The 7/7 attacks made bombing and terrorism even more abhorrent than before, and although the methods used differed from the IRA's, this meant little to anyone affected in any way by the attacks and the subsequent attempted attacks later in the same month. If 9/11 had brought pressure on the IRA from America, the 7/7 atrocities brought far closer to home the need for the 'old' terrorism to end and the message that there was no room in the mainstream of politics for the use of violence.[87]

But the IRA did not want its internal consultations on decommissioning to be sidelined as a result of the attacks, while wanting to differentiate themselves from what was taking place elsewhere.[88] The various reports indicating IRA criminality – the McCartney murder, the Northern Bank robbery, and so on, continued to undermine attempts by Sinn Féin to achieve respectability. Shootings and other acts were seen as inevitable snags during a difficult and total transition of an armed and violent organisation with a political wing into a political party which had left behind its violent history. Acts of giving up weapons that had been amassed, seized, then amassed again over many years were not to be underestimated by any observer familiar with, or at least with a vestige of understanding of, Irish history. Therefore, UK government policy tended towards a 'constructive ambiguity' in which various unpalatable activities were tolerated,[89] in the hope that these would also eventually end and were part of the transition to total disarmament.

In July 2005 the IRA finally and formally ordered an end to its armed campaign and announced that it would pursue exclusively peaceful means towards its goal, which has not changed to this day – a united Ireland.[90] The long-awaited statement was read out in the glare of the world's media by former IRA prisoner Seanna Walsh on 28 July:

> The leadership of [the IRA] has formally ordered an end to the armed campaign. This will take effect from 4 p.m. this afternoon. All IRA units have been ordered to dump arms. All volunteers have been instructed to assist the development of purely political and democratic programmes through exclusively peaceful means. Volunteers must not engage in any other activities whatsoever.[91]

Of particular note was the part in the statement that said:

> We are mindful of the sacrifices of our patriot dead … We reiterate our view that the armed struggle was entirely legitimate.

And equally:

> … There is now an alternative way to achieve our goal of a united Ireland.

But the decision had to be made, as power-sharing could only be sustained if unionists were convinced that the threat of IRA weapons was seen to be defused once and for all.

The final act of decommissioning in 2005 was announced on 26 September. It was witnessed by de Chastelain's commission colleagues Andrew Sens and Tauno Nieminen, a Roman Catholic priest, Fr Alex Reid, and a former Methodist president, Rev. Harold Good. Their statement said: 'The experience of seeing this with our own eyes, on a minute-to-minute basis, provided us with evidence so clear and of its nature so incontrovertible that at the end of the process it demonstrated to us – and would have demonstrated to anyone who might have been with us – that beyond any shadow of doubt, the arms of the IRA have now been decommissioned.'[92]

Gen. de Chastelain announced that his organisation was satisfied that 'the arms decommissioned represent the totality of the IRA's arsenal' and that all the group's arms were now beyond use. The commissioning body had handled every gun and made an inventory of the weapons.[93]

Predictably, the unionists demanded a full list of the inventory, which the IICD said consisted of a range of ammunition, rifles, machine-guns, mortars, missiles, handguns, explosives and explosive substances – much of it Libyan-supplied. The IICD based this on all estimates provided by the UK and Irish security services. But the unionists complained about the lack of photographic evidence of decommissioning and that the independent witnesses had been chosen by the IRA.

DECOMMISSIONING: THE FALL-OUT

Nevertheless, Gerry Adams said the decommissioning also presented challenges for others. 'It means that unionists who are for the Good Friday Agreement must end their ambivalence ... And it is a direct challenge to the DUP to decide if they want to put the past behind them, and make peace with the rest of the people of this island.'[94]

The IRA decommissioning meant that the demilitarisation of Northern Ireland society could proceed, and a process put in place towards finding a system of policing that would be endorsed by republicans. But continuing co-operation between such entrenched enemies as Sinn Féin and the DUP in the revived Northern Ireland government could never have been foreseen and, although it is said the honeymoon is over as of early 2008, has been amazing to behold.

One of the great achievements of decommissioning was that Gerry Adams and Martin McGuinness brought the IRA to this unprecedented new position without a major split in the organisation having taken place. Although the process of giving up arms had taken longer than its opponents had demanded, the political harm to the republicans was minimised, although many supporters would continue to regard decommissioning as a sell-out and betrayal. It would appear to them that deals were struck and the IRA sent into retirement with its aims unachieved; that a partitionist position had in fact been reinforced. The armed struggle had somehow to be justified. Gerry Adams said on the day of the final decommissioning act that the armed struggle was valid, and referred to the violence of the 1960s and 1970s as 'pogroms' against the Catholic community. He acknowledged that many people had suffered in the conflict, including republicans.[95]

In May 2006 the Stormont assembly sat for the first time since its suspension in 2002. But decommissioning did not produce a clear-cut advantage for Sinn Féin. Delaying decommissioning may have won power in the North but did not benefit Sinn Féin in the elections in the Republic in May 2007, where they lost heavily. This was a serious consequence of all the work the republicans had done over twenty-plus years to politicise their movement. The Adams–McGuinness peace process strategy, which was based on huge electoral ambitions, had not borne fruit in these elections. Sinn Féin aimed to be a significant enough electoral force in the South to go into a coalition government with what it viewed as its natural political partners, Fianna Fáil.

In order to be able to become a political force the IRA had had to abandon the armed struggle and decommission its weapons and structures. This wrought huge upheavals on the membership and its community and involved the acceptance of the heresy of consent for Irish unity and the legitimacy of the North's policing and judicial arrangements.[96] And all for what? For electoral defeat. Such was the price of peace for the IRA and Sinn Féin.

It is possible that if the IRA had made more concessions on decommissioning in 2002, David Trimble would have remained in government and power-sharing could have been well under way.[97] Sinn Féin would have appeared to the South as a fully-fledged political party and attractive in more areas than just the pro-IRA heartlands. Sinn Féin may have to wait until the 2012 Irish general election before having any opportunity to participate in the Dublin government.

The unusual development of the modern Sinn Féin makes it all the more necessary that the party succeeds electorally. Far too much has been sacrificed in the name of the republican movement for the 'normal' peaks and troughs of electoral support that other parties endure.

According to Ed Moloney, Sinn Féin 'always needed to be moving forward, ever a threat to those around it; staying still or going backwards could be fatal'.[98] And there could be no return to a military campaign as the time had passed for this to be of any relevance in the post-decommissioning world, once the party was in a power-sharing situation. It could therefore be seen to be neither here nor there.

And decommissioning, although historic, is by no means the end of the story. There were adverse responses by unionists and others in Northern Ireland. Much cynicism, mistrust and resentment continues to simmer, particularly about the permanence of the IRA's cessations. Predictably, Ian Paisley in February 2006 said that the claim that the IRA had completely disarmed was a 'blatant lie'. This was based on Independent Monitoring Commission reports that the IRA held on to some of its weapons – and that these were possibly for personal protection or area protection. Gen. de Chastelain indicated, however, that the 'quantities of arms involved were substantial'.[99]

Typical of such responses was the comment from Duncan Morrow, head of the Northern Ireland Community Relations Council, following the September 2005 act:

> No matter how many weapons are still in circulation, returning to violence would end any prospect that the word of the republican leadership could be believed again. So this is real, historic change … The vision of a shared future is more alive than it was before decommissioning, but nobody is under any illusions that we have yet arrived …
>
> People forget the IRA have enough money to restock their entire arsenal if they so desire. We have said from day one that it is more important to decommission the terrorist mindset as well as the guns.[100]

And Robin Wilson, director of Democratic Dialogue, Belfast, said:

> Gerry Adams and Martin McGuinness run the republican movement, in both its guises, with absolute authority … It is ironically for just this reason that we know the IRA's decommissioning has been, as far as anyone can know, complete. The orders have gone out and the volunteers have delivered, down to loose supplies of individual bullets.[101]

BEYOND USE?

Many of the IRA's opponents have said that the organisation remains a substantial paramilitary force that is not yet 'in retirement'. This is hardly surprising considering that the republican movement has fought a 'long war' on and off for generations – that it is far too early to assume that peace has come and is permanent. For so many, nothing short of total disbandment will do. That decommissioning has been the ultimate sacrifice for so many republicans will be of no consequence to them, considering the suffering and loss of life witnessed during the Troubles. However, it is hard to see the IRA continuing in its former state now that its weapons to all intents and purposes have been sunk beneath metres of concrete.

Gen. de Chastelain has said that it would probably take the IRA 'a hell of a long time' to amass the same weaponry again,[102] should this be desired. Many do not believe this, and even in these days of shared power in a re-established Stormont, there remain sceptical observers, not least the many unionists who believe that the IRA retains the capacity to re-arm. As has been said before, once a weapon is invented or acquired it is very hard to un-invent it; guns, explosives and other weapons can also be acquired on the black market (such as from eastern Europe); organised or small-time criminals; or can be cooked up or assembled as homemades. There are still questions surrounding the issue of licensed weapons. As of mid-2006 the number of weapons, including shotguns, held on licence in Northern Ireland was 144,554, up by a staggering 5,634 on 2001. The ratio of weapons per head of the population is currently estimated at one gun for every nine adults.[103]

It is true that any disarmament move is not irreversible. The acts of decommissioning have not removed the IRA's capacity for 'war'. Therefore, everything depends on the continued politicisation of Sinn Féin, along with the greater political environment in both the North and South of Ireland. The 'catch-up' of Catholics outnumbering Protestants in the North[104] is also seen as a way for the GFA to bear fruit eventually for the republicans – that future elections will yield the mandate for a united Ireland which the Agreement allows for should the 'majority' of voters in the North wish it. On 26 September 2005 BBC correspondent Hugh Sykes asked a loyalist, Sam Duddy, how Protestants would react if the democratic process led to a united Ireland. The response was: 'I envisage loyalists and unionists taking up arms.'[105] But as for the Irish Republican Army, as of August 2008 it appeared less likely than at any time in its entire history to be able to, or desire to resume a concerted military campaign – whatever the political outcomes. It now remains to be seen if the existing structures of the IRA, must notably the Army Council, will be disbanded; that will truly signify the end of the Armed Struggle in our time.

NOTES

1. P. Taylor, 'Disobeyed orders and a dangerous message', *Guardian*, 18 March 2008, and BBC 2 documentary, 'Secret Peacemaker', 19 March 2008 by Peter Taylor on Brendan Duddy's role.
2. 'IRA guns: The list of weapons', BBC News, 26 September 2005.
3. Personal communication, Garda former EOD operatives, February 2007.
4. 'IRA guns: The list of weapons', BBC News, 26 September 2005.
5. C. Bellamy, 'IRA has enough Semtex for 15 years', *Independent*, 19 March 1995.
6. 'IRA guns: The list of weapons', BBC News, 26 September 2005.
7. G. McGladdery, *The Provisional IRA in England: The Bombing Campaign 1973–1997* (Dublin: Irish Academic Press, 2006), p.188.
8. 'IRA guns: The list of weapons', BBC News, 26 September 2005.
9. D. Leppard, 'Rebel IRA units threaten new war', *Sunday Times*, 20 November 1994.
10. IRA statement, *Belfast Telegraph*, 8 Dec. 1995.
11. McGladdery, *The Provisional IRA in England*, p.190.
12. Anthony McIntyre cited in McGladdery, *The Provisional IRA in England*, p.191.
13. T. Harnden, *Bandit Country* (London: Coronet, 1999), Prologue.
14. IRA statement, RTÉ, 9 February 1996.
15. McGladdery, *The Provisional IRA in England*, p.191.
16. B. O'Brien, *Pocket History of the IRA* (Dublin: O'Brien Press, 2005), p.124.
17. Ibid., pp.125–7.
18. Ibid., p.129.
19. Personal communication, Ulster Intelligence Unit operative, November 2007.
20. Gerry Adams interview with Nick Stadlen QC, *Guardian*, 12 September 2007.
21. O'Brien, *Pocket History of the IRA*, p.142.
22. B. O'Brien, *The Long War: IRA and Sinn Féin* (2nd edition) (Syracuse, NY: Syracuse University Press, 1999), p.301.
23. Ibid., p.303.
24. Gerry Adams interview with Nick Stadlen QC, *Guardian*, 12 September 2007.
25. Martin McGuinness interview in O'Brien, *The Long War*, p.305.
26. O'Brien, *Pocket History of the IRA*, p.134.
27. O'Brien, *The Long War*, p.302.
28. Ibid., p.320.
29. Ibid., p.321.
30. Ibid., p.329.
31. Irish Republican Army ceasefire statement, 31 August 1994.
32. Ibid.
33. O'Brien, *Pocket History of the IRA*, p.144.
34. Ibid., p.150.
35. A. Murdoch, 'IRA gang arrested making bombs', *Independent*, 22 June 1996.
36. MIPT Terrorism & Knowledge Database, Patterns of Global Terrorism, UK 1997 overview.
37. Ibid.
38. PM statement, 21 July 1997.
39. Martin McGuinness interviewed on BBC Radio 4 *The World This Weekend*, 21 July 1997.
40. BBC News, 'On This Day', 19 July 1997.
41. MIPT Terrorism & Knowledge Database, Patterns of Global Terrorism, UK 1997 overview.
42. BBC News, 'On This Day', 19 July 1997.
43. MIPT Terrorism & Knowledge Database, Patterns of Global Terrorism, UK 1998 overview.
44. O'Brien, *Pocket History of the IRA*, p.168.
45. Martin McGuinness interviewed on Sky News, 21 July 1997.

46. 'Timeline: Road to arms inspections', BBC News, 26 June 2000,
47. 'Second De Chastelain report in full', BBC News, 11 February 2000.
48. O'Brien, *Pocket History of the IRA*, p.164.
49. 'Timeline: Road to arms inspections', BBC News, 26 June 2000.
50. Ibid.
51. '"No progress" in IRA decommissioning', *Guardian*, 2 July 2001.
52. Ibid.
53. MIPT Terrorism & Knowledge Database, Patterns of Global Terrorism, UK 2000 overview.
54. O'Brien, *Pocket History of the IRA*, p.171.
55. Ibid., p.166.
56. Ibid., p.173.
57. S. Boyne, 'Uncovering the Irish Republican Army', *Jane's Intelligence Review*, 1 August 1996. Table 4.1 also shows failed attempts at procurement.
58. A.R. Oppenheimer, 'Northern Ireland: The countdown begins', *Bulletin of the Atomic Scientists* (May/June 2002).
59. O'Brien, *Pocket History of the IRA*, p.174.
60. A. R. Oppenheimer, 'Northern Ireland: The countdown begins', *Bulletin of the Atomic Scientists*, May/June 2002.
61. Oppenheimer, 'Northern Ireland: The countdown begins'.
62. See statement by the Independent International Commission On Decommissioning (IICD), 23 October 2001, http://cain.ulst.ac.uk/events/peace/decommission/iicd231001.htm
63. O'Brien, *Pocket History of the IRA*, p.177.
64. Oppenheimer, 'Northern Ireland: The countdown begins'.
65. See *Report Of The Independent International Commission On Decommissioning* (IICD), 8 April 2002, http://cain.ulst.ac.uk/events/peace/decommission/iicd080402.htm
66. W. Hoge, 'IRA's illegal arsenal reduced in a second act of disarmament', *New York Times*, 9 April 2002.
67. Ibid.
68. IRA Green Book, pp.5–6.
69. O'Brien, *Pocket History of the IRA*, p.180.
70. R. Cowan, 'Talks on disarming suspended by IRA', *Guardian*, 31 October 2002.
71. R. Cowan, 'Secret memo on IRA sparks Trimble walkout', *Guardian*, 20 December 2002.
72. D. Bamber and A. Murray, 'Stormont spy ring is only "tip of the IRA iceberg"', *Daily Telegraph*, 6 October 2002.
73. O'Brien, *Pocket History of the IRA*, p.181.
74. Ibid., p.186.
75. M. Rose, 'Britain's "Dirty War" with the IRA', *Catholic World News*, July 2003.
76. O'Brien, *Pocket History of the IRA*, p.188.
77. A.R. Oppenheimer, 'Is the IRA laying down its arms?', *Jane's Terrorism & Security Monitor*, November 2003.
78. B. Rowan, 'Analysis: Why deal stalled', BBC News, 23 October 2003.
79. Ibid.
80. Statement by the Independent International Commission on Decommissioning (IICD), 21 October 2003, http://cain.ulst.ac.uk/events/peace/decommission/iicd211003.htm
81. Oppenheimer, 'Is the IRA laying down its arms?'
82. Adapting J. Robert Oppenheimer's postwar statement on scientists' irreversible knowledge of the making of atomic bombs.
83. Oppenheimer, 'Is the IRA laying down its arms?'
84. 'Q&A: The Colombia connection', BBC News, 16 December 2004.
85. Personal communication, Czech Republic CBRN and intelligence consultant, October 2007.
86. E. Leahy, 'FARC rebel "admits IRA trained him"', *Sunday Times*, 15 May 2005.
87. A *Private Eye* cartoon showed Gerry Adams under a headline 'IRA ends war' with a speech balloon of him saying: 'It's no longer safe for our bombers to be on the streets.'
88. M. Devenport, 'Final pieces prepared for "IRA jigsaw"', BBC News, 25 July 2005.
89. M. Brennock, 'Is the party over?' *Irish Times*, 19 February 2005.
90. 'IRA says armed campaign is over', BBC News, 28 July 2005.
91. M. Tempest, 'IRA orders end to armed campaign', *Guardian*, 28 July 2005.
92. 'IRA "has destroyed all its arms"', BBC News, 26 September 2005.
93. Ibid.

94. M. Tempest, 'IRA orders end to armed campaign'.
95. Ibid.
96. E. Moloney, 'SF leaders too slick for the party's own good', *Irish Times*, 31 May 2007.
97. Ibid.
98. Ibid.
99. 'IRA weapons claim "blatant lie"', BBC News, 4 February 2006.
100. 'Does decommissioning mean peace?' BBC News, 28 September 2005.
101. Ibid.
102. 'IRA guns: The list of weapons', BBC News, 26 September 2005.
103. Office for National Statistics and the Northern Ireland Statistics and Research Agency, cited statistics in M. St Leger, 'Call to "decommission" licensed weapons', *Irish Democrat*, 4 July 2006.
104. Which has been further complicated by the influx into the North of hundreds of Roman Catholic Poles, who may not be in any way interested in their capacity to tip the scales in favour of a Catholic majority, or involved in the future of the province as remaining British or, possibly becoming part of a reunified Irish Republic.
105. M. St Leger, 'Call to "decommission" licensed weapons'.

Eleven

Conclusion: Is This the End?

Like a nuclear deterrent in inter-state relations, the IRA's arsenal was a powerful bargaining tool in the talks, especially when the arms were not used.[1]

The responsibility lies with successive British governments, right through those decades, who turned their heads away from what was happening in the North of Ireland.

Martin McGuinness[2]

Having taken you on a journey through the most tortured period of Ireland's history – a journey soaked in blood, suffering and frustrated aims – we come back to where we began at the start of this book: in the bowels of Garda HQ in Dublin, in rooms laden with the most sophisticated improvised bombs ever made at the time of their confiscation, and enough guns to arm several battalions. Now the details of their acquisition, manufacture and use have been described and analysed in detail, you know how many of the devices worked; how they were built, and where they were deployed; how many they killed and injured; and – of prime importance – why they were necessary to wage the 'long war'.

The first object we beheld in the IRA 'reference collection' – in itself a nomenclature that obscures the enormity, extent, and consequences of the organisation's military campaign – was the Mark 15 mortar. We have seen what the mortars did – most strikingly, in the attempt to blow up John Major's Gulf War cabinet in 1991. What my Garda escorts emphasised to me was, apart from the technical capabilities of such weapons, which were variable, the PR value of many of them was uppermost. An insurgent group even as experienced as the IRA was forced to improvise at every turn, despite huge arms shipments from Libya and the US. And it was able to construct an entire makeshift missile system – the attacks on Heathrow airport in particular, although they did not hit the intended targets, sent out a message that the IRA could launch a mortar attack on a high-profile, vital aspect of Britain's infrastructure. It also showed a level of planning and patience; it took some time – a day and a half – to find the right launch spot, and under the noses of police and (so-called) security, the mortar was planted just below the grass level[3] and just outside the perimeter, not inside – making it harder to find. A photo of one of the vans holding mortars such as the Mark 10 fired at 10 Downing Street showed that the IRA had applied a special covering and paint to the roof to prevent discovery by aerial photographic surveillance.

Even failed, pre-empted attacks such as the attempt to knock out London's electricity supply with twenty-two specially constructed IEDs showed the level of capability the IRA had achieved by the early 1990s. But above all, every IED, detonator, schematic and component revealed ingenuity – that word again – of a level and scale seen only in military laboratories. The special box bombs that had been made in the Clonaslee bomb factory could be carried around as workmen's lunchboxes and had been manufactured to precise specifications and with advanced electronic components, enabling them to be detonated by remote control. Much of this skill and the details of the IRA campaign were not revealed at the time other than as republican progaganda; right up to the end, many British people showed little interest in the fate of their country's last colony, Northern Ireland, unless they were directly threatened by the IRA campaign. In the words of my Garda escorts, the men in grey suits were sent scurrying to Belfast to negotiate.

Whether or not you think the bombs and the bullets failed – and they did fail in terms of the IRA's long-term aim, a united Ireland – they succeeded in putting the republican movement on the political map beyond these shores, and their persistence enhanced the urgency to find some solution, even if only partially satisfactory for all sides, to the Northern Ireland crisis.

But the cavern of seized weapons that underpinned and fired the armed struggle for decades did not reveal what lay behind the campaign: how some of those pre-empted attacks were the result of informants working for the British and Irish authorities; how weapons came increasingly to be sabotaged by the British, often with the knowledge of the IRA; but chiefly, how many people the bombs and the guns killed, injured, bereaved and traumatised. That most of the weapons displayed were seized from the prime centre of the IRA's bomb-making operation, the Clonaslee factory in Co. Laois, was testimony to the extent of the military campaign. This, according to my Garda escorts, had been the most secret operation of all. While south Armagh was well known as a centre for the military engine, the existence of Clonaslee – which contained a bunker and an extensive engineering works – was only discovered in June 1996. This was possibly due to 'significant high-grade information' which the gardaí received from the public following the murder of an Irish police officer, Detective Jerry McCabe. The Clonaslee weapons cache, containing forty mortar tubes, Semtex, large amounts of ammonia and nitrate used in homemade explosive, along with switches, timers, detonators, guns, tail fins and other mortar parts,[4] signified a growing readiness for a renewed campaign, and its discovery was a body blow for the IRA, as were similar seizures of IEDs and IED-making equipment in London at the time.

Most historians of the IRA have concluded that the movement conducted its war as long as it did because it could always justify it. The IRA Green Book says: 'The Irish Republican Army as the legal representatives of the Irish people are morally justified in carrying out a campaign of resistance against foreign occupation forces and domestic collaborators. All volunteers are and must feel morally justified in carrying out the dictates of the legal government. They as the Army are the legal and lawful Army of the Irish Republic which has been forced underground by overwhelming forces.'[5] But by the mid-1990s that moral justification had been overtaken by changes, and the old world of certainties had been replaced by increasing pragmatism. This meant a quantum leap into a very uncertain world of negotiating with others. Much of this had resulted from necessity: the IRA had been undermined by informants, infiltrators and the 'dirty war' of the 1980s, while at the same time had grown in military maturity and capability.

But the latter was now only serving to prove that the Provisionals could carry on the war indefinitely, and much of this was to put on a show for their own supporters. There was also growing discord between the prime military proponents within the IRA and the politicisers. The southern-based engineering network that was busy making bombs did so at a pace that was becoming discomforting to the political strategists of Sinn Féin.[6] This explains much of why the decommissioning came when it did, and that while the republicans had not achieved the unity of Ireland, a degree of greater equality had arrived for the northern Catholics. The role of the IRA as defenders of that community was less relevant, despite ongoing intimidation and shows of supremacy from unionists.

Also, the IRA thought the war would be over by the end of the 1970s. They probably also assumed more support from the South (rather than the turning of its back of successive Irish governments) and that funding and weapons from the Americans would not run out. They didn't bargain for 9/11 – Sinn Féin actually lost a fundholder in the 9/11 attacks[7] – and the growing hardline stance of twenty-first-century US administrations. Nevertheless, the process of politicisation (albeit backed by the armed campaign, the tighter cell structure and more ruthless leadership) had set in quite a while before these changes. But the changes were gradual, and many more lives would be lost before they took root; the peace process took its stumbling first steps, and the ceasefires were called.

That tortuous process was littered with obstacles. Breakdowns in the negotiations were more common than breakthroughs. The IRA would crash through the deadlocks with more bombings. As a result, they were criticised for losing whatever moral ground and peace credentials they were trying to attain, most notably with the rescinding of the ceasefire ('back to porridge') – and the subsequent Canary Wharf and Manchester bombings, as well as the destruction wreaked by bombs in several Northern Irish town centres.

Otherwise, and this is my view also, the Canary Wharf bombing – while viewed as a 'moral disaster' for the IRA – made all-party negotiations possible: within three weeks of the attack, in February 1996, the prime ministers of the UK and Ireland had set the date for the negotiations to take place in June.[8]

There can be no doubt that the result of these talks – the Good Friday Agreement – signalled a new era of peace – but at a great price for the Irish republican movement. While it was intended to usher in a period of greater equality and cross-cultural identity for the northern nationalists (with no small degree of compromise required on the part of the unionists, whose position had been the very essence of intransigence), for many republicans the agreement would be a compromise too far, and made from a position of weakness rather than strength.

This to me will remain the eternal puzzle. As we have seen, by the mid-1990s the IRA still had the weapons – half the cache acquired from Libya[9] – and the expertise to continue waging a sustained campaign on the UK mainland. The level of weapons expertise discovered at Clonaslee was evidence of continued intent as well as capability. So why did they give it up when they did, with so little of their original aims gained?

The reason given by many commentators (and I have heard it said also by former IRA men) is that by the mid-1990s there was a war-weariness and a jail-weariness and a basic feeling that the ability to conduct such a sustained (and this would be essential to maintain a serious military challenge) campaign was faltering and was draining resources.

Many bomb attacks were small and sporadic (although still deadly and disruptive). This was the period when the IRA tried to bomb the London electricity supply network and failed, and when a young IRA volunteer, Edward O'Brien, lost his life on 18 February when the bomb he was carrying exploded prematurely on a bus in London, injuring nine and destroying the bus. A bomb attack on Hammersmith Bridge planned for 24 April 1996 and involving 14 kg of Semtex, in the IRA's biggest commercial explosives device planted to date, failed because the explosives had been compromised. Despite these setbacks the IRA still maintained a high level of capability. Between the 1990s ceasefires they continued to arm and train; contacts were made with US and South African suppliers of weapons that were untraceable[10] – particularly for robberies and other forms of criminal activity that would be one of the final, major obstacles on the road to power-sharing.

But there was also the growing feeling that it wasn't worth fighting for what was no longer the ultimate aim – a united Ireland – but merely a better negotiating position in the peace process. In the words of the former IRA commander Anthony McIntyre, the IRA had 'little purpose other than to further the aims of the Sinn Féin leadership' and had been reduced to 'functioning as a defence against any possible loyalist backlash, or additionally acting as a guarantor against any attempt by the Brits or unionists to renege on the Stormont agreement thus denying it any offensive role against the Brits'. Above all, the IRA was 'deprived of any of its traditional revolutionary vestige'.[11]

The ending of the ceasefire was also costly to the IRA: many valuable, skilled volunteers were being lost or betrayed. And there were serious PR implications for Sinn Féin after every attack. That is not to say that the military campaign had no purpose, or no successes. It has been said that, among the northern nationalist community, Sinn Féin was increasingly seen as the toughest negotiator for change, not the moderate SDLP[12] – having the guns and the bombs mattered; the SDLP didn't have any.

On the political side movements of seismic proportions had brought in new thinking and new attitudes, borne out of changing times, a hunger for peace and further contact between all sides through negotiation. The first cessation of the armed campaign had brought much of this about. There had also been gradual changes in the attitudes of the British political establishment; the 1997 Labour government was actually continuing what had been a gradual realisation on the part of its predecessors that the situation could not go on indefinitely. But more than these previous administrations, the Blair government was prepared to consider the demands of

Sinn Féin. It was just a question of when and how (not if) the war would end.

And Sinn Féin was not only setting its sights on political power-sharing, but its statesman leader Gerry Adams wanted to go down in history as a Nelson Mandela, not a Yasser Arafat.[13] In the face of US pressure – which would have terminated Sinn Féin fundraising, and had already resulted in the withdrawal of his visa – he issued a directive to the IRA to decommission, and three months later they did.

But this was the culmination of a long and painful process which Adams and his supporters had helped to propel in the 1980s from behind the wire of Long Kesh prison. In the words of Martin McGuinness: 'Republicans want peace. We want an honourable peace, no papering over the cracks or brushing under the carpet the humiliations, degradation and injustices inflicted on us by a foreign power ... It is time for that circle of violence to be broken. We are prepared to help break it.' It is worth noting that the mortar attack on Downing Street occurred in the same month as this statement, underlining the republicans' continuing reliance on the military campaign to drive home their message.[14]

But how could they have ever won? How can any insurgency group win against such overwhelming superiority, and against people in their land that didn't want to be part of their land? Insurgent conflicts compared to full-out warfare can be likened to a controlled nuclear reaction in a civilian reactor as opposed to the all-out explosion of a nuclear blast: sustained, sporadic attacks and brutality rather than all-out invasion and mass destruction; no overall or outright victory and no complete defeat; constant hiding, running, concealing, improvising, adapting, mutating, killing, blasting, shooting, maiming, stealing, ambushing, stopping and starting up again; your families torn apart, imprisoned, shot, starved, and still – after generations – only compromise, concession, and a distant hope that Your Day Will Come, but not in your lifetime.

POSTSCRIPT

When I returned home after my visit to the IRA inventory in Dublin, before writing the last part of this book I decided to watch two films about the Irish struggle that have meant most to me over the years. The first, an odd, darkly haunting, surreal Greek tragedy made in 1947 – *Odd Man Out* – is about a conscience-stricken IRA gunman who is shot during a robbery to raise funds for 'the organisation' and endures a mix of treachery and betrayal in the painful path towards his eventual demise. The wounded gunman, Johnny, becomes the object of an intense police manhunt and must scramble desperately about Belfast in an attempt to escape. The young IRA woman who loves him is determined to find and save him. She knows he's terribly hurt and that he'll be hanged if caught. She won't let that happen. Despite her Catholic faith and the sympathetic counsel of her elderly priest, she'll shoot Johnny and then herself if she must. At the end, she fires at the police surrounding the fugitive couple and their return fire kills them both.

So I watched this film in a post-Good Friday Agreement world where the republican struggle is now all but consigned to history, and considered all the suffering and failed aims in the sixty-plus years since it was made in 1945 – when the IRA was deemed a spent force.

The other film I watched was *The Wind That Shakes the Barley*. I found it an emotional film in many ways – not just at the end, but also from seeing the treatment meted out by the murderous Black and Tans, and from seeing and feeling the futility and fratricidal despair that was Ireland's eternal fission depicted in the tearing apart of the two brothers by the continuing guerrilla war against the British in the early 1920s, and more tragically, the agony of the ensuing Civil War. And not just from seeing how the British behaved, but about how the Irish learned some of their behaviour in government from their former imperial occupiers.

We may now live in a world where the Irish Republic is a peaceful, prosperous EU country (despite possible oncoming recession) where the story depicted in the Ken Loach film about Ireland's bloodiest period may be viewed 'only' as history. But many years will go by before the bitterness and the regrets will fade. There is no room any more (nor has there been for some time) for starry-eyed republicanism. It is hard to imagine the world's oldest insurgency organisation giving up all its weapons. Indeed, after the final act of decommissioning, the IRA floated the idea of maintaining some guns, and Dublin refused.[15] It is, nevertheless, almost impossible to think that the IRA would be eventually stood down to become the 'cherished antique'[16] it has been seen as for decades in the South.

Indeed, we may now be filled with hope for the future. That to all intents and purposes the war is over; that somewhere along the line Ireland will become one, but without exploding bombs and firing bullets. That the weapons I saw in Dublin will remain museum pieces forever, for historical interest to those who wish to learn more about how the Irish Republican Army waged its eternal struggle. That they will be seen as the eternal evidence of a fight that many believe came to nothing (as partition continues) – a war that could be summed up by one of the characters in *The Wind That Shakes the Barley*, Finbar, who says after gunning down a Black and Tan gang: 'We've just sent a message to the British cabinet that will echo and reverberate around the world! If they bring their savagery over here, we will meet it with a savagery of our own!'

The weapons may become museum pieces. But the message in these words will never be forgotten.

NOTES

1. In L. Clarke and K. Johnston, *Martin McGuinness: From Guns to Government* (Edinburgh: Mainstream Publishing, 2006), p.267.
2. McGuinness's answer to a Protestant Church leader at a Stormont lunch who suggested to him: 'Martin, this situation would move along an awful lot easier if you would say you were sorry for the events of the last thirty years.'
3. Personal communication, Garda ex-EOD operative, February 2008.
4. Much of which I viewed in Dublin. A. Murdoch, 'IRA cache find raises fears of bomb campaign', *Independent*, 24 June 1996.
5. Cited in B. O'Brien, *The Long War: IRA and Sinn Féin* (2nd edition) (Syracuse, NY: Syracuse University Press, 1999), p.344.
6. Ibid., p.366.
7. Gerry Adams in 'The Price of Peace', presented by John Ware, BBC Radio 4, 2 March 2008.
8. O'Brien, *The Long War*, p.356.
9. Ibid., p.363.
10. Clarke and Johnston, *Martin McGuinness*, p.249.
11. Ibid., p.256.
12. 'The Price of Peace'.
13. Ibid.
14. Statement by Martin McGuinness, February 1991, in Clarke and Johnston, *Martin McGuinness*, p.209.
15. 'The Price of Peace'.
16. Clarke and Johnston, *Martin McGuinness*, p.275.

Appendix 1

BOMBS AND EXPLOSIVES – HOW THEY ARE MADE,
HOW THEY WORK AND WHAT THEY DO

I have confined these definitions to conventional [non-nuclear] devices.

Explosives
An explosive is defined as a material (chemical or nuclear) that can be initiated to undergo very rapid, self-propagating decomposition that results in the formation of more stable material, the liberation of heat, or the development of a sudden pressure effect through the action of heat on produced or adjacent gases. All of these outcomes produce energy; a weapon's effectiveness is measured by the quantity of energy – or damage potential – it delivers to the target.

An explosion is the process of the substance transforming into the gaseous state. Through chemical reaction, the substance rapidly and violently changes to gas, accompanied by high temperatures, extreme shock and a very loud noise, even in small devices. The noise often denotes the type of explosive used.

When a conventional explosive such as TNT is detonated, the relatively unstable chemical bonds are converted into bonds that are more stable, producing kinetic energy in the form of blast and thermal energies.

The term 'detonation' indicates that the reaction is moving through the explosive faster than the speed of sound in the unreacted explosive, whereas 'deflagration' indicates a slower reaction (rapid burning). A high explosive will detonate; a low explosive will deflagrate.

High explosives
Explosives are classified as low or high according to the detonating velocity or speed at which this change takes place and other pertinent characteristics such as their shattering effect. An arbitrary figure of 1,000 m/sec is used to distinguish between burning/ deflagration (low explosive) and detonation (high explosive).

The term 'high explosive' (HE) means these substances decompose at very high rates. HE is a compound or mixture which, when initiated, is capable of sustaining a detonation shockwave to produce a powerful blast effect. A detonation is the powerful explosive effect caused by the propagation of a high-speed shockwave through a high-explosive compound or mixture. During the process of detonation, the high explosive is largely decomposed into hot, rapidly expanding gas.

Another prime property is brisance – the fast rise of pressure and rapid projection of mass equivalent to the creation of a strong shock front. They are relatively insensitive to heat and flame, but respond to shock and friction. For this reason, they must be exploded by detonators.

Most modern military or commercial explosives are reasonably stable and require percussive shock or other triggering devices for detonation. Some homemade explosives are also stable, most notably ammonium nitrate, but others are highly unstable, such as the hydrogen-peroxide-based HMEs. Therefore they can detonate without a detonator – and often when not intended.

Low explosives

Low explosives are said to burn or deflagrate rather than to detonate or explode. The burning gives off a gas which, when properly confined, will cause an explosion. Most low explosives are mechanical mixtures or a mechanical blending of the individual ingredients making up the low explosives.

Low-order explosives (LE) create a subsonic explosion [below 1,100 m/sec] and lack high explosives' over-pressurisation wave. Examples include pipe bombs, gunpowder, and most pure petroleum-based bombs such as Molotov cocktails or aircraft improvised as guided missiles.

Explosive and incendiary (fire) bombs are characterised as 'manufactured', implying standard military-issued, mass-produced, and quality-tested weapons. Manufactured (military) explosive weapons are exclusively HE-based.

'Improvised' describes weapons produced in small quantities, or the use of a device outside its intended purpose, or for an illegal purpose, such as converting a commercial aircraft into a guided missile or icing sugar and nail varnish into a homemade bomb. While much has been said and written about the decommissioning of weapons and acquired explosives, decommissioning the ability to make compounds made from everyday substances has presented a great challenge.[1]

Terrorists will use whatever is available – illegally obtained manufactured weapons or improvised explosive devices (IEDs) that may be composed of HE, LE or both.

Detonators

Detonators are used to trigger the explosive charge in the bomb. Because high explosives must generally be initiated by a shock wave of considerable force, this is usually provided by a detonator or blasting cap. The detonator is the source of heat that will start the combustion (or chain reaction in case of nuclear bombs). The detonator *is itself an explosive*, and has a lower ignition point than the main explosive charge.

Detonation can be defined as instantaneous combustion, although there is actually a time interval where combustion passes from one particle of explosive compound to the next. When an explosive is detonated, the block or stick of chemical explosive material is instantaneously converted from a solid into a rapidly expanding mass of gases.

Detonators are chemically, mechanically or electrically initiated. There are many types used for military and commercial (and terrorist) applications. For the purposes of this book the last two are the most relevant. Among electrical detonators, three types are used: instantaneous electrical detonators (IED), short period delay detonators (SPD) and long period delay detonators (LPD). SPDs are measured in milliseconds and LPDs are measured in seconds.

Timers

Bomb timers are used to time precisely the moment of detonation. They can be set to any time between a few minutes and several weeks, or even months. The IRA were the pioneers of most types of bomb timers. The original timer was the alarm clock, progressing to parking meter timers and video recorders, while computer laptops have also been used in IEDs.

Fuses/fuzes

A fuse (or fuze) is a mechanical or an electrical device which causes the detonation of an explosive charge at the proper time after certain conditions are met. The cartoon depiction of an explosion always showed someone lighting a fuse which would burn down to a spherical [usually black] bomb [labelled 'bomb']. In the real world it is basically a safety device to provide a time-delay before ignition. The fuse usually initiates the detonator which starts the explosive chain reaction in the larger explosive charge.

The term can be confusing. *Fuse* describes a simple pyrotechnic detonating device, like the cord on a firecracker, whereas *fuze* is used to describe a more complicated ignition device incorporating mechanical and/or electronic components in military-use bombs such as mines and artillery shells. However, the Americans always use the 'fuze' spelling. Fuses are usually black whereas detonators come in pretty bright colours.

Sources: own library references; US and British army EOD training manuals; J.A. Slotnick, PSP, regional director for NWTC Inc. and lead instructor for hazardous devices; recognition and avoidance for the corporate security community.

Appendix 2

EFFECTS OF EXPLOSIVES

The most powerful of all explosive effects is the blast pressure effect. When the explosion occurs, very hot (between 1,648 degrees C and 3,870 degrees C) expanding gases are formed in a period of approximately 1/10,000 of a second. These gases exert pressures of about 700 tonnes per square inch on the atmosphere surrounding the point of detonation at velocities of up to 29,200 km per hour. The expanding gas rolls out from the point of detonation like a ripple in the water and is known as the 'blast pressure wave'. Bombs and explosions can cause unique patterns of injury seldom seen outside combat.

Manufactured and improvised bombs cause markedly different injuries. The blast wave is the intense over-pressurisation impulse created by a detonated HE which impacts the surface of the body. The following three points, based on the experience of Lt Col George Styles, sum up the terrible effects of a bomb blast.[2]

- If a wave of energy increases that pressure by up to 4 kg, the eardrums perforate.
- If the pressure wave is between 4.5 kg and 6.5 kg, the lungs collapse, killing the victim.
- Waves created by the explosion enter the mouth and tear off the head, limbs and flesh, leaving only spinal remnants, body fragments and pieces of clothing.

The injury patterns following such events are a product of the composition and amount of the materials involved, the surrounding environment, delivery method (if a bomb), the distance between the victim and the blast, and any intervening protective barriers or environmental hazards.[3]

Blast lung is the most common fatal injury among initial survivors. Explosions in confined spaces (mines, buildings or large vehicles) and/or structural collapse kill more people. It is characterised by apnoea (cessation of breathing), bradycardia (low heartbeat) and hypotension (low blood pressure). Pulmonary injuries vary from scattered petechiae (small haemorrhages) to confluent haemorrhages.[4]

Ear injury is dependent on the orientation of the ear to the blast. Tympanic membrane (TM) perforation is the most common injury to the middle ear. Signs of ear injury are hearing loss, tinnitus, otalgia, vertigo, bleeding from the external canal, TM rupture, or mucopurulent otorhea.[5]

Abdominal injury is common as gas-containing sections of the gastrointestinal (GI) tract are most vulnerable to primary blast effect. This can cause immediate bowel perforation, haemorrhage (ranging from small petechiae to large haematomas), mesenteric shear injuries, solid organ lacerations, and testicular rupture. Blast abdominal injury should be suspected in anyone exposed to an explosion with abdominal pain, nausea, vomiting, haematemesis, rectal pain, tenesmus, testicular pain, unexplained hypovolaemia, or any findings suggestive of an acute abdomen.

TABLE A: MECHANISMS OF BLAST INJURY[6]

Category	Characteristics	Body Part Affected	Types of Injuries
Primary	Unique to HE, results from the impact of the over-pressurisation wave with body surfaces.	Gas-filled structures are are most susceptible – lungs, GI tract, and middle ear.	Blast lung (pulmonary barotrauma);TM rupture; middle ear damage. Abdominal haemorrhage and perforation, globe (eye) rupture, concussion (TBI without physical signs of head injury).
Secondary	Results from flying debris and bomb fragments.	Any body part may be affected.	Penetrating ballistic (fragmentation) or blunt injuries; eye penetration (can be occult).
Tertiary	Results from individuals being thrown by the force this explosion	Any body part may be affected.	Fracture and traumatic amputation; closed and open brain injury.
Quaternary	All explosion-related injuries, illnesses or diseases not due to primary, secondary, or tertiary mechanisms. Includes exacerbation or complications of existing conditions.	Any body part may be affected.	Burns (flash, partial, and full thickness); crush injuries; closed and open brain injury; breathing problems from dust, smoke, or toxic fumes; angina; hyperglycaemia; hypertension.

LE are classified differently because they lack the self-defining HE over-pressurisation wave. LEs' mechanisms of injuries are characterised as due from ballistics (fragmentation), blast wind (not blast wave) and thermal. There is some overlap between LE descriptive mechanisms and HEs' secondary, tertiary and quaternary mechanisms.

TABLE B: OVERVIEW OF EXPLOSIVE-RELATED INJURIES[7]

System	Injury or Condition
Auditory	TM rupture, ossicular disruption, cochlear damage, foreign body
Eye, Orbit, Face	Perforated globe, foreign body, air embolism, fractures
Respiratory	Blast lung, haemothorax, pneumothorax, pulmonary contusion and haemorrhage, A-V fistulas (source of air embolism), airway epithelial damage, aspiration pneumonitis, sepsis
Digestive	Bowel perforation, haemorrhage, ruptured liver or spleen, sepsis, mesenteric ischaemia from air embolism
Circulatory	Cardiac contusion, myocardial infarction from air embolism, shock, vasovagal hypotension, peripheral vascular injury, air embolism-induced injury
CNS Injury	Concussion, closed and open brain injury, stroke, spinal cord injury, air embolism-induced injury
Renal Injury	Renal contusion, laceration, acute renal failure due to rhabdomyolysis, hypotension, and hypovolaemia
Extremity Injury	Traumatic amputation, fractures, crush injuries, compartment syndrome, burns, cuts, lacerations, acute arterial occlusion, air embolism-induced injury

ELEMENTS OF AN EXPLOSION

Blast

Air being propelled at tremendous force and speed creates an over-pressure travelling outward in all directions away from the source for great distances.

Augmented Pressure

The pressure wave, reflected and channelled by the design of buildings and layout of streets. This causes the pressure effect to last longer and can increase structural damage.

Fragmentation

Any item that is part of or near to the bomb when it explodes becomes a projectile. The larger the explosive charge, the farther the fragments will travel. Fragments normally travel in a straight line but, like a bullet, can also be deflected.

Secondary Fragmentation
This occurs as the blast over-pressure hits and breaks structures, e.g. windows, doors, collapse of false ceilings, office equipment, etc.
Partial Vacuum
Return to normal pressure. At this stage, windows not destroyed by the initial blast may be sucked out.
Ground Shock
The transmission through the ground of the blast wave pressure. This causes problems with gas, water, electricity, sewers, telecommunications, etc. and may also cause structural damage to the foundations of buildings and subway systems.

NOTES

1.   A.R. Oppenheimer, 'The Challenge of Detecting Explosives', *RUSI Homeland and Security Resilience Monitor*, 5, 9 (November 2006).
2.   G. Styles, *Bombs Have No Pity* (London: William Luscombe, 1975), p.170.
3.   D. Leibovici, et al, 'Blast injuries: bus versus open-air bombings – a comparative study of injuries in survivors of open-air versus confined-space explosions', *J Trauma*, 41, 6 (December 1996), pp.1030–5.
4.   Y. Phillips, 'Primary blast injuries', *Annals of Emergency Medicine*, 106, 15 (December 1986), pp.1446–50.
5.   J. Wightman and S. Gladish, 'Explosions and blast injuries', *Annals of Emergency Medicine*, 37, 6 (June 2001), pp.664–78.
6.   From http://www.globalsecurity.org
7.   Ibid.

Bibliography

BOOKS

Adams, Gerry, *Peace in Ireland: A Broad Analysis of the Present Situation* (Long Kesh: Provisional Sinn Féin, 1976).

Adams, Gerry, *The Politics of Irish Freedom* (Dingle: Brandon, 1986).

Adams, Gerry, *Who Fears to Speak …?: The Story of Belfast and the 1916 Rising* (Belfast: Beyond the Pale, 2001 [1991]).

Akhavan, J. *The Chemistry of Explosives* (London: The Royal Society of Chemistry, 1998).

Alexander, Y. and O'Day, A. (eds), *Terrorism in Ireland* (London: Croom Helm, 1984).

Arendt, Hannah, *Eichmann in Jerusalem: A Report on the Banality of Evil* (revised edition) (Gloucester, MA: Smith, 1994).

Asimov, Isaac, *Asimov's Chronology of Science & Discovery* (New York: Harper and Row Publishers Inc., 1989).

Bebie, J. *Manual of Explosives, Military Pyrotechnics and Chemical Warfare Agents* (Boulder, CO: Paladin Press, 1942).

Behan, Brendan, *Borstal Boy* (London: Arrow Books, 1990 [1958]).

Bishop, Patrick, and Mallie, Éamonn, *The Provisional IRA* (London: Corgi, 1987).

Brunswig, H. (C.E. Munroe and A.L. Kibler, transl.), *Explosives* (New York: John Wiley & Sons, 1912).

Campbell, Christy, *Fenian Fire: The British Government Plot to Assassinate Queen Victoria* (London: HarperCollins, 2002).

Clarke, Liam and Johnston, Kathryn, *Martin McGuinness: From Guns to Government* (Edinburgh: Mainstream Publishing, 2006).

Coaffee, Jon, *Terrorism, Risk and the City: The Making of a Contemporary Urban Landscape* (Burlington, VT: Ashgate, 2003).

Coogan, Tim Pat, *Michael Collins: The Man Who Made Ireland* (Niwot, CO: Roberts Rinehart Publishers, 1996).

Coogan, Tim Pat, *The IRA* (revised edition) (London: HarperCollins, 1995).

Davis, Mike, *Buda's Wagon: A Brief History of the Car Bomb* (London: Verso, 2007).

De Rosa, Peter, *Rebels: The Irish Uprising of 1916* (New York: Ballantine Books, 1992).

Dunne, T. *Wolfe Tone: An Analysis of his Political Philosophy* (Cork: Tower, 1982).

Durney, James, *The Volunteer: Uniforms, Weapons and History of the Irish Republican Army 1913–1997* (Dublin: Gaul House, 2004).

Edwards, R. Dudley, *Patrick Pearse* (London: Victor Gollancz, 1977).

English, Richard, *Armed Struggle: The History of the IRA* (London: Macmillan, 2003).

Garrison, Arthur (ed.), *Terrorism: Past, Present and Future – A Training Course* (Wilmington, DE: Delaware Criminal Justice Council, 2002).

Geraghty, Tony, *The Irish War* (London: Harper Collins, 1998).

Gurney, Peter, *Braver Men Walk Away* (London: HarperCollins, 1993).

Harnden, Toby, *Bandit Country: The IRA & South Armagh* (London: Hodder & Stoughton Ltd, 1999).

Hart, Peter, *The IRA at War 1916–1923* (Oxford: Oxford University Press, 2003).

Holland, Jack, *The American Connection: US Guns, Money and Influence in Northern Ireland* (Boulder, CO: Roberts Rinehart Publishers, 1999).

Hopkinson, Michael, *Green Against Green* (Dublin: Gill & Macmillan, 1988).

Houen, Alex, *Terrorism and Modern Literature from Joseph Conrad to Ciaran Carson* (Oxford: Oxford University Press, 2002).

Leather, Stephen, *The Bombmaker* (London: Coronet, 1999).

Lifton, Robert J. and Markusen, Eric, *The Genocidal Mentality: Nazi Holocaust and Nuclear Threat* (New York: Basic Books, 1991).

Lynch, Robert, *The Northern IRA and the Early Years of Partition* (Dublin: Irish Academic Press, 2006).

Lyons, F.S.L. *Ireland Since the Famine* (London: Weidenfeld & Nicolson, 1971).

Magee, Patrick, *Gangsters or Guerrillas? Representations of Irish Republicans in 'Troubles Fiction'* (Belfast: Beyond the Pale, 2001).

Mallie, Éamonn and McKittrick, David, *Endgame in Ireland* (London: Coronet, 2002).

McGladdery, Gary, *The Provisional IRA in England, The Bombing Campaign 1973–1997* (Dublin: Irish Academic Press, 2006).

McGuire, Éamon, *Enemy of the Empire: Life as an International Undercover IRA Activist* (O'Brien Press, 2006).

McKittrick, David, Kelters, Séamus, Feeney, Brian, Thornton, Chris and McVea, David, *Lost Lives* (London: Mainstream Publishing, 2007).

McKittrick, David, *Making Sense of the Troubles* (London: Penguin, 2001).

McPherson, Jack, *Terrorist Explosives Handbook, Volume 1: The Irish Republican Army*, Intelligence Report from Northern Ireland (reprinted by Arizona: Lancer Militaria, 1979).

Mac Stíofáin, Seán, *Memoirs of a Revolutionary* (Edinburgh: Gordon Cremonesi, 1975).

Milgram, Stanley, *Obedience to Authority* (London: Tavistock Publications, 1974).

Moloney, Ed, *A Secret History of the IRA* (London: W.W. Norton & Co, 2002).

Most, Johann, *The Science of Revolutionary Warfare: A Handbook of Instruction Regarding the Use and Manufacture of Nitroglycerine, Dynamite, Gun-Cotton, Fulminating Mercury, Bombs, Arson, Poisons, etc.* (Publisher unknown, 1881).

O'Brien, Brendan, *Pocket History of the IRA* (Dublin: O'Brien Press, 2005).

O'Brien, Brendan, *The Long War: IRA and Sinn Féin* (2nd edition) (Syracuse, NY: Syracuse University Press, 1999).

O'Doherty, Shane Paul, *The Volunteer: A Former IRA Man's True Story* (London: HarperCollins, 1993).

O'Donoghue, Florence, *No Other Law: The Story of Liam Lynch and the Irish Republican Army, 1916–1923* (Dublin: Irish Press Ltd., 1954).

Pearse, Patrick, *Ghosts* (Dublin: Whelan & Son, 1916).

Pickett, Mike, *Explosives Identification Guide* (Albany, NY: Delmar Publishers / ITP, 1999).

Ryder, Chris, *A Special Kind of Courage: 321 Squadron – Battling the Bombers* (London: Methuen, 2006).

Sharrock, David and Devenport, Mark, *Man of War, Man of Peace? The Unauthorised Biography of Gerry Adams* (London: Macmillan, 1997).

Short, K.R.M. *The Dynamite War: Irish-American Bombers in Victorian Britain* (Dublin: Gill & Macmillan, 1979).

Smith, M.L.R. *Fighting for Ireland? The Military Strategy of the Irish Republican Movement* (London: Routledge, 1997).

Stephan, Enno, *Spies in Ireland* (London: Macdonald & Co., 1963).

Styles, Lt Col George, GC, *Bombs Have No Pity* (London: William Luscombe, 1975).

Sutton, Malcolm, *An Index of Deaths from the Conflict in Ireland 1969–1993* (Belfast: Beyond the Pale Publications, 1994).

Taylor, Maxwell, *The Terrorist* (London: Brassey's, 1988).

Taylor, Peter, *Loyalists* (London: Bloomsbury, 1999).

Taylor, Peter, *The IRA and Sinn Féin* (London: Bloomsbury, 1997).
Toolis, Kevin, *Rebel Hearts: Journeys Within the IRA's Soul* (New York: St Martin's Press, 1995).
Townshend, Charles, *The British Campaign in Ireland 1919–21* (Oxford: Oxford University Press, 1975).
Urban, Mark, *Big Boys' Rules* (London: Faber & Faber, 1993).
Woodham-Smith, Cecil, *The Great Hunger* (London: Hamish Hamilton, 1962).
Yeats, W.B. *The Collected Works of W.B. Yeats* (London: Macmillan, 1989).

OFFICIAL RECORDS

Northern Ireland Annual Abstract of Statistics, 2002.

FILMS, TELEVISION AND RADIO PROGRAMMES

'Behind the Mask: The IRA and Sinn Féin' (Peter Taylor, PBS (Public Broadcasting Service) Frontline, 21 October 1997). http://www.pbs.org/wgbh/pages/frontline/shows/ira/
'Bomb Squad', Nova television documentary, US Public Broadcasting Service, PBS (Public Broadcasting Service) Airdate: 21 October 1997.
'The Brighton Bomb' and 'The Hunt for the Bomber', BBC television, 13 September 2004.
'Car Bomb', Channel 4, July 2008.
'File on Four', BBC Radio 4, May 2007.
'Death on the Rock', Thames Television, 28 April 1988.
'Inside Out in the North West', BBC Regional television, interview with Prof. Richard English, 27 February 2006.
Irish Republican Media, IRA web video archive on YouTube http://www.youtube.com/profile?user=IrishRepublicanMedia
YouTube, http://www.youtube.com/watch?v=9uezlu_LiBQ
'The IRA Conflict', PBS/WGBH Frontline television documentary transcript, 1998.
Michael Collins (dir. Neil Jordan, 1996).
Minutes of Evidence, Select Committee on Northern Ireland Affairs, memorandum submitted by Forensic Science Northern Ireland and The Northern Ireland Office, House of Commons, March 2002.
Odd Man Out (dir. Carol Reed, 1947).
'The Price of Peace', John Ware, BBC Radio 4, four-part series, March 2008.

'Provos', BBC television documentary by Peter Taylor, 1997.
'Secret History: Brighton Bomb', Channel 4 television, 15 May 2003.
'Secret History of the IRA, 1956–62', History Channel, summer 2007.
The Wind That Shakes the Barley (dir. Ken Loach, 2006).

NEWSPAPERS, PERIODICALS, JOURNALS AND PRESS AGENCIES

Agence France Presse
The American Historical Review
An Phoblacht/Republican News
Asian Military Review
Belfast News Letter
Belfast Telegraph
The Blanket
Boston Globe
Bulletin of the Atomic Scientists
Camden New Journal
Catholic World News
Chicago Tribune
Criminal Justice Studies
Daily Ireland
Financial Times
Guardian
Independent
Independent on Sunday
Intersec
Ireland's Own
Iris
Irish Democrat
Irish Independent
Irish News
Irish Times
Jane's Armour & Artillery
Jane's Explosives and Ordnance Disposal
Jane's Intelligence Review
Jane's Land-based Air Defence
Jane's Sentinel Security Assessments, Ireland
Jane's Terrorism & Security Monitor

Jane's Terrorism & Insurgency
Jane's Unconventional Weapons
Jane's World Insurgency & Terrorism
Maclean's Magazine
NBC International
New York Jewish Times
New York Times
Observer
Press Association
Psychology Today
Risk Management
Spectator
Sunday Telegraph
Sunday Times
Sunday Tribune
Terrorism and Political Violence
Time
Village

OFFICIAL REPORTS, PUBLICATIONS AND PAPERS

Aptitude for Destruction, Volume 2: Case Studies of Organizational Learning in Five Terrorist Groups, Chapter Five, Provisional Irish Republican Army, Brian A. Jackson et al., (Rand Corporation, 2005).

Business as Usual: Maximising Business Resilience to Terrorist Bombings, Case Study Bishopsgate, Home Office pamphlet.

The City of London IRA bombings of 1992 and 1993: Observations in relation to the World Trade Center attack, Jonathan Liebenau (London School of Economics Department of Information Systems and Columbia Institute for Tele-Information, Information and Communications Disaster Recovery).

Deaths Directly Linked to the Political Conflict in Ireland, July 1969 through 31 December 1993, based upon the revised figures of the Belfast Independent Research Group.

Developing the Proximity Fuze, and Its Legacy, Dr William T. Moye (US Army Material Command Historical Office, 19 February 2003).

Force Structure for High- and Low-Intensity Warfare: The Anglo-American Experience and Lessons for the Future, D. Marston, Discussion Paper (Royal Military Academy Sandhurst, May 2004).

Handbook for Volunteers of the Irish Republican Army: Notes on Guerrilla Warfare 1956 (Boulder, CO: Paladin Press, 1985).

A History of IRA Activity in England, Special Branch Report to the Home Office, 5 December 1939, PRO HO 144/21358.

IRA Green Book (IRA training manual), 1956, 1977.

IRA Army Council to the People of Ireland, Oct 1938 (Files of the Department of the Taoiseach, NAD S11564A).

Mass-Casualty Terrorist Bombings: Epidemiological Outcomes, Resource Utilization, and Time Course of Emergency Needs (Part I), J.L. Arnold, MD et al., Yale New Haven Center for Emergency and Terrorism Preparedness, New Haven, Connecticut.

Operation Banner: An Analysis of Military Operations in Northern Ireland (Army Code 71842, prepared under the direction of the Chief of the General Staff, 6 July 2007).

Perspectives on Pentaerythritol Tetranitrate (PETN) Decomposition, D.M. Chambers, (Lawrence Livermore National Laboratory, US Department of Energy, Claudia L. Brackett and O. David Sparkman, University of the Pacific, 1 July 2002).

The Proliferation of Illegal Small Arms and Light Weapons in and Around the European Union: SALW among Terrorist Groups in Europe, Dr Domitilla Sagramoso, Centre for Defence Studies, King's College, University of London, July 2001.

Protecting Buildings from Bomb Damage: Transfer of Blast-Effects Mitigation Technologies from Military to Civilian Applications, Commission on Engineering and Technical Systems (Washington, DC: National Academies Press, Div. On Engineering and Physical Sciences, 1995).

Reports of the International Independent Commission on Decommissioning, 11 February 2000, 21 October 2003, 26 September 2005.

Responding to Terrorism across the Technological Spectrum (US Strategic Studies Institute, 15 July 1994, US Army War College Fifth Annual Strategy Conference, 26–28 April 1994).

Russia Reform Monitor No. 137, J. Michael Waller, American Foreign Policy Council, 15 May 1996.

Sinn Féin Policy Document, Dublin, Provisional Sinn Fein, 1987.

The Terrorist Arsenal, British Weapons Intelligence Unit, 1993 edition.

US Government's Response to Defendant Brannigan's Motion in Limine Regarding Recovery Of Detonators Overseas, United States District Court, District of Arizona, No. CR 92-587-TUC-JMR.

Violence and Civil Disturbance in Northern Ireland, Report of Tribunal of Inquiry (Cmd. 566, vol. 2, Belfast: HMSO, April 1972).

WEBSITES

BBC News Online (various URLs)

BBC History Wars & Conflict: The Easter Rising
    http://www.bbc.co.uk/history/british/easterrising/insurrection/in05.shtml

Belfast Independent Research Group
    http://www.inac.org/irishhistory/deaths

Bloody Sunday Enquiry
    http://www.bloody-sunday-inquiry.org.uk/index2.asp?p=1

CAIN Web Service (Conflict Archive on the Internet)
    http://www. cain.ulst.ac.uk/index.html

CAIN Web Service: A Chronology of the Conflict, 1972
    http:// cain.ulst.ac.uk/othelem/chron/ch72.htm

CAIN Web Service, Membership and Arsenals of Paramilitary Groups,
    Estimates of the Strength of Paramilitary Groups, the IRA

Explosia (Semtex manufacturer) website
    http://www.explosia.cz/en/?show=semtex

Families Acting for Innocent Relatives (FAIR) petition against the
    Libyan Government, 26 May 2005
    http://www.victims.org.uk/petition.html

Federation of American Scientists
    http://www.fas.org/

Greater Manchester Police website, Manchester Bomb Investigation
    http://www.gmp.police.uk/mainsite/pages/manchesterbombing.htm

MIPT (Memorial Institute for the Prevention of Terrorism) Terrorism
    Knowledge Base http://www.tkb.org/

Index

IRA Internments and the Irish Government
Subversives and the State, 1939–1962

John Maguire
Foreword by Ruán O'Donnell

Examines a neglected period in the history of the IRA and looks at the acceptability and success of internment as an expedient in the Irish government's ongoing struggle with republican subversive organisations during both the Second World War and the border campaign. The book looks at the reasons for the subsequent drift away from the use of this measure, despite its previous successes in containing the IRA threat to the Irish State. It draws extensively on previously unavailable primary source material in various archives in both Ireland and Britain.

The oral testimony of many surviving contemporaries is supplemented by an in-depth examination of the files of the Irish government, thereby presenting a detailed political assessment of the events under consideration. In addition, the voluminous records relating to the Lawless Case held in the Attorney General's Office have been particularly valuable in documenting, for the first time, the unprecedented domestic legal proceedings in this landmark action. The book considers the overall impact of the Lawless Case in influencing the future direction of Irish counter-insurgency policy and the subsequent drift away from the use of internment as an acceptable expedient in the State's ongoing struggle with subversives.

2008   288 pages
978 0 7165 2943 9   cloth   €65.00/£45.00/$79.95
978 0 7165 2944 6   paper   €24.95/£19.95/$34.95

THE PROVISIONAL IRA IN ENGLAND
The Bombing Campaign 1973–1997
Gary McGladdery
Foreword by Richard English

In this revealing and fascinating account, the impact of the Provisional IRA's bombing campaign in Britain on both British government policy towards Northern Ireland and the internal politics of the republican movement, are examined in detail. The book highlights the early thinking of the British government and draws on recently released public records from 1939, 1973 and 1974. It makes extensive use of television documentary footage to offer a broader analysis. The book also examines republican rationale behind the campaign, the reasoning behind the use of particular tactics and the thinking behind atrocities such as the Birmingham bombings.

Using a range of new evidence, the book highlights the bankruptcy of republican strategic thinking and challenges the notion that successive British governments appeased republicans because of the threat of bombs in London. The analysis of the campaign is placed within the wider context of the ongoing violence in Northern Ireland as well as the history of republican violence in England dating back to the nineteenth century.

2006   288 pages
978 0 7165 3373 3   cloth   €65.00/£45.00/$75.00
978 0 7165 3374 0   paper   €29.95/£19.95/$35.00

THE NORTHERN IRA AND THE EARLY YEARS OF PARTITION 1920–1922

Robert Lynch

The years 1920–22 constituted a period of unprecedented conflict and political change in Ireland. It began with the onset of the most brutal phase of the War of Independence and culminated in the effective military defeat of the Republican IRA in the Civil War. Occurring alongside these dramatic changes in the south and west of Ireland was a far more fundamental conflict in the north-east, a period of brutal sectarian violence which marked the early years of partition and the establishment of Northern Ireland. Almost uniquely the IRA in the six counties were involved in every one of these conflicts and yet, it can be argued, was on the fringe of all of them. The period 1920–22 saw the evolution of the organisation from peripheral curiosity during the War of Independence to an idealistic symbol for those wishing to resolve the fundamental divisions within the Sinn Fein movement, which developed in the first six months of 1922. The story of the Northern IRA's collapse in the autumn of that year demonstrated dramatically the true nature of the organisation and how it was their relationship to the various protagonists in these conflicts, rather than their unceasing but fruitless war against partition, that defined its contribution to the Irish revolution.

2006   264 pages
978 0 7165 3377 1   cloth   €65.00/£50.00/$75.00
978 0 7165 3378 8   paper   €27.50/£19.95/$32.00

The Evolution of the Troubles, 1970–72

Thomas Hennessey

This book explores the evolution of the Northern Ireland Troubles from an ethno-national conflict into an insurgency against the British state in Northern Ireland in the crucial years of 1970 to 1972. The book combines the decisions of 'high politics' with the experiences of those on the ground, for whom these decisions made the greatest impact. It tells the story of ordinary people caught up in extraordinary events covering the evolving Provisional IRA insurgency and the British Army's counter-insurgency. Key areas covered include: the Falls Road Curfew; Anglo-Irish relations; North-South relations on the island of Ireland; the fall of the Chichester-Clark Government; the premiership of Brian Faulkner; internment; Bloody Sunday; and the suspension of Stormont.

2007   384 pages

978 0 7165 2884 5   cloth   €55.00/£45.00/$75.00

978 0 7165 2885 2   paper   €24.95/£18.95/$35.00

Transforming the Peace Process in Northern Ireland

From Terrorism to Democratic Politics

Aaron Edwards, and Stephen Bloomer (Eds)

Foreword by Richard English

This book focuses on the decade since the signing of the Belfast/Good Friday Agreement in 1998, as political and paramilitary actors attempt to adjust to the rigors of democratic participation. It delineates the key stumbling blocks in the current peace and political processes and examines in detail just how the conversion from terrorism to democratic politics is being managed in post-conflict Northern Ireland. It aims to fill a gap in the literature by juxtaposing 'top-level' political party and inter-governmental politics alongside 'middle-range' civil society interventions and 'grass-roots' community level politics. Moreover, it provides an empirically informed examination of the central political ideologies, parties and identities at play, as well as the methodologies by which paramilitary groupings are attempting to deal with the legacies of the past conflict. The book draws its contributors from across the disciplinary boundaries of political science, history, anthropology, sociology and political sociology and is situated within a broad analytical and theoretical framework.

Contributors: James W McAuley, Christopher Farrington, Catherine O'Donnell, Jonathan Tonge, Lyndsey Harris, Stephen Bloomer, Anthony McIntyre, Neil Jarman, Claire Mitchell, Kevin Bean, Paul Dixon, Aaron Edwards, Michael Kerr and Eamonn O'Kane.

2008   272 pages
978 0 7165 2955 2   cloth   €65.00/£45.00/$79.95
978 0 7165 2956 9   paper   €26.95/£19.95/$32.95